WITHDRAWN

D1066260

LORD'S
1946–1970

796.358
K 41l

LORD'S
1946–1970

Diana Rait Kerr
Ian Peebles

GEORGE G. HARRAP & CO. LTD
London   Toronto   Wellington   Sydney

BETHEL COLLEGE LIBRARY

First published in Great Britain 1971
by GEORGE G. HARRAP & CO. LTD
182–184 High Holborn, London WC1V 7AX

© *Diana Rait Kerr, Dennis Edward Ryland, and Hans Siegel* 1971
All rights reserved. No part of
this publication may be reproduced
in any form or by any means
without the prior permission of
George G. Harrap & Co. Ltd

ISBN 0 245 59887 1

Composed in 11 *on* 12 *Baskerville type and printed by*
Cox & Wyman Ltd, London, Fakenham and Reading
Made in Great Britain

Preface

SIR PELHAM WARNER's history of Lord's, published as the ground returned to normal after its war-time occupation, was a chronicle of 158 years, in which M.C.C. grew from a select association of aristocratic gentlemen into a rich and powerful legislative body. By contrast, the twenty-five years covered in the present volume are but the twinkling of an eye. Nevertheless, in this brief spell changes have occurred whose consequences challenge the import of years gone by.

For M.C.C. 1970 was the end of an era; a year as historic as the year of its formation, for it was the year in which the Committee delegated its administrative powers and responsibilities as the governing body of cricket in the United Kingdom to a more broadly based national body. From then on much of M.C.C.'s former power would be vested in the Cricket Council.

Messrs Harrap have decided that this is an appropriate occasion to bring Sir Pelham Warner's history up to date, but, because the sequel covers such a short spell by comparison with his book, the balance is necessarily different and the story has been chronicled on a broader scale, embracing world-wide events which have involved M.C.C. and Lord's. In our collaboration we have tried to stick to our individual lasts—Ian Peebles as chronicler of the matches and the players and Diana Rait Kerr as recorder of the broader canvas of events and administration. Inevitably there has been some overlapping of subjects which relate to both our stories, but we make no apology for failing to keep our respective briefs in watertight compartments or presenting the same events from different viewpoints.

We are both indebted to many people for help and co-operation. We want to thank particularly the Committee of M.C.C. for granting access to minutes and other documents at Lord's. We are also deeply grateful to the Secretary and numerous members of the staff at Lord's for constant help in seeking out information and particularly to Stephen Green for hospitality in the Library. Mr Ronald Aird has read the manuscript and given much valued guidance and encouragement, and Miss Netta Rheinberg has given invaluable help with research and welcome constructive advice. We have also drawn heavily on the contents of *Wisden*, *The Cricketer*, and the National Press, particularly *The Times* and *The Daily Telegraph*, to whose editors we extend grateful acknowledgment. For the photograph on the jacket we are indebted to Mr Patrick Eagar. The photograph showing defensive illumination at Lord's was supplied by Messrs Topix, the remainder by Messrs Sport and General. Lastly, we should like to express our appreciation to Mr Bill Frindall for his admirable statistical appendix, which updates the figures given in the former volume.

DIANA RAIT KERR
IAN PEEBLES

Contents

Illustrations

I

Promise and Performance 1945-1948

THE bells of St Paul's had rung in the New Year of 1945, bringing
to Londoners the welcome assurance of freedom from the fear of
invasion and the promise of peace before the dawn of another year.
When the M.C.C. Annual General Meeting was held at Lord's in
May, the Pavilion and other main buildings, occupied for so long
by the R.A.F., had already been derequisitioned, and the Long
Room, though shabby, had assumed an air of peace-time normality,
with the Ashes restored to their glass case and the pictures rehung
after their sojourn in a country rectory.

Sir Pelham Warner, in his unique position of writer and master-
mind behind so many war-time matches, has described the
cricket *in excelsis* which was played in that season: the Victory
Tests, celebrating V.E., and the superb match between England
and the Dominions, with Walter Hammond and Learie Constantine captains in a game whose brilliance and excitement, remembered a generation later, seem as bright in retrospect as on those
August days of 1945. This was cricket as it should be played—a
splendid augury for post-War cricket and a symbol of a return to
normality and freedom from the horror and anxieties of war.

The 1918 armistice had seemed to catch the cricket world
unawares; the result had been the unsatisfactory makeshift programme of two-day matches which nobody had liked or approved.
M.C.C. and the Advisory County Cricket Committee had learnt
the lesson well, and this time careful preparations were made in
advance for the resumption of normal peace-time cricket. As early
as 1943 a Select Committee had been appointed to consider and
advise how the game could be restarted quickly and effectively.
This Committee, chaired by Sir Stanley Jackson, was representative of every department of the game and had authority to seek
additional advice from leading county representatives, cricketers,
and umpires. Their report, issued in January 1944, considered in
detail the whole structure of county cricket in the anticipated
framework of post-War conditions and offered plans for a return to

normality as smoothly as possible in the shortest possible time. Thus, when peace came in the late summer of 1945, a rationalized plan for resuming the Championship in 1946 had already been approved by the A.C.C.C. and, thanks to the far-sightedness and wisdom of Sir Stanley Jackson's Committee, the season got under way without a hitch. Even one of the wettest summers on record failed to quench the enthusiasm of players and spectators, together determined to offer and receive the maximum in enjoyment.

At Lord's the demobilization of Colonel Rait Kerr and Mr Aird in the autumn of 1945 had released the acting Secretary and Assistant Secretary (Sir Pelham Warner and Colonel Hugh Henson) from the duties they had carried out with such devoted enthusiasm. Sir Pelham now found time to write his history of Lord's, and Colonel Henson returned to manage the affairs of Gloucestershire. Other members of the M.C.C. staff returned; new staff were engaged—including a full-time Curator of the M.C.C. Collection—and Committees and Sub-committees laboured in top gear to put the machinery back in motion.

The rationalized scheme for the Championship reduced each county's programme to twenty-six matches—eliminating the need for percentages in the scoring system. The curtailment had been devised to facilitate arrangements for touring-team and trial-match programmes—after an interruption of six years a need was foreseen for additional opportunities to assess the potential of England players—to relieve the strain on players, and to provide an opportunity for introducing a knock-out competition. When the report was published the suggestion of a knock-out competition stole the thunder from the Select Committee's more concrete proposals. Such headlines as "Cup for County Cricket" captured the public's imagination and gave the impression that what was intended as a tentative suggestion was already a *fait accompli*. The practicability of such a competition, for which three-day matches were envisaged, had still to be worked out and many imponderables solved, not least the incidence of drawn games. The A.C.C.C. wisely decided not to add the immediate problems of a new competition to the existing difficulties and uncertainties of the first post-War season, but to ask the Secretary of M.C.C. to head a Committee to consider whether or not a practicable scheme could be arrived at. By 1947, with the Control of Engagement Order imposing limitations on the recruitment of players and a ban on mid-week sport threatening to curtail existing programmes, the scheme was laid upon the table to await more propitious times.

All-India had accepted an invitation to tour England in 1946, and were due to arrive, under the Nawab of Pataudi, *père*, in April. Arrangements for their itinerary were complicated by a lack of hotel accommodation and transport difficulties. They were the first Test team to arrive by air—travelling in small groups at a time when air travel by whole teams was not yet accepted. In June they made history when they travelled as a team from Cardiff to Portsmouth by Dakota, turning a train journey of five hours into an air flight of forty minutes—the first instance of a complete team flying in Great Britain. These were days of shortages and coupons. As late as 1949 the M.C.C. Committee, unable to buy towels for the Pavilion, considered asking members to contribute clothing coupons, and county committees appealed to their members for coupons to equip their players with boots and flannels. There was such difficulty in fitting out the Indians that they were faced with having to play their opening matches in grey flannels. The purchase of cricket equipment was controlled by buying certificates; new cricket balls had to be rationed, and there was a waiting list for re-blading bats. On the grounds, controls and uncertainties affected building and stand maintenance, which could only be done under licence; in 1948 there was a near crisis at Lord's when it seemed likely that part of the Mound Stand might not be available for the Australian Test. Until 1961 National Service continued to claim young men at eighteen, so that counties lost their most promising young cricketers at the moment when budding talent was beginning to bloom. Shortages of food, which was rationed until 1952, were suggested as a possible contributory factor in the slow recovery of English cricket after the War. The 1948 Australians, conscious of their own plenty, refused the temptation to supplement their English rations, deciding that to do so would be to take an unfair advantage over their opponents. Instead they brought with them 200 cases of canned meat, which were handed over ceremonially to the Minister of Food for distribution among the people of Britain to compensate for the food the team would eat while they were here. Today this sounds a little naïve, but at a time when the receipt of a food parcel from overseas made a red-letter day in most British households the gift was rightly valued as a warm-hearted gesture typical of the donors, and accepted with gratitude and appreciation.

This was the background against which English cricket got into its stride in 1946, making light of difficulties which in more affluent days might seem insurmountable. Father Time, swept aside by the cable of one of the Lord's anti-aircraft barrage balloons, was erect once more in his place on the Grand Stand, waiting severely to remove the bails when Middlesex, playing a one-day pipe-opener on May Day, decisively beat a M.C.C. side whose strong contingent of England players included the present Treasurer and Secretary of M.C.C. as well as the co-author of this book. When Robertson and Brown opened for Middlesex they emerged for the first time through the centre door of the Pavilion, the M.C.C. Committee having decided during the previous winter to discontinue the practice of the professionals using a separate dressing-room and coming out on to the ground through the small wicket gate between the bowlers' room and the old "A" Enclosure. Another move towards democracy was seen on the score-cards, where every player had his initials printed before his surname—no longer was a Gentleman to be referred to as Mr Brown and a Player as plain Smith. But, following a popular demand to differentiate between amateurs and professionals out of interest rather than snobbery, a compromise was later reached by the placing of the pros' initials after their surnames.

Behind the Pavilion windows M.C.C. held their 159th Annual General Meeting. Sadly, Mr Stanley Christopherson, President since 1939, was not well enough to hand over in person the office of President to his nominated successor, General Sir Ronald Adam. "Stanley Chris" had been a splendid war-time President, whose activity and enthusiasm in partnership with "Plum" Warner were the inspiration behind the war-time matches at Lord's, which gave such immeasurable pleasure and raised over £23,000 for charity. His seven years' tenure of an office which normally is held for one year is a record approached only by that of Lord Hawke, President during the First World War. In appreciation of Sir Pelham Warner's great services to M.C.C. and cricket in general, his portrait had been commissioned of Mr A. R. Thompson and hung in the Long Room. Sir Pelham had much enjoyed the sittings, but unhappily the Committee and members later expressed a wish for a photographic likeness of him as a cricketer rather than as an "elder statesman". Mr Thompson's picture has for some years been on loan to the Warner family, but it is my personal hope that it may some day be restored to Lord's. As a thanksgiving for victory the Club honoured with Life Membership Sir Winston Churchill, General Eisenhower, and nine of our own Service leaders.

The county programme opened at Lord's on May 8 with a match between Middlesex and Leicestershire which set a pattern for the positive spirit which characterized the first post-War Championship. The first day was lost through rain, but, thanks to determined batting by the old firm of Robertson, Brown, Edrich, and Compton, under the dynamic captaincy of Walter Robins, Middlesex were able to declare twice and force a decisive victory with twenty minutes to spare. Compton was in particularly brilliant form, and Robertson and Brown hit 71 in 43 minutes. That the vigour of the Middlesex captain was not unique is borne out by a letter printed in *The Times* a week later over the signature of four of the Worcestershire Fosters, who wrote of their intense pleasure, congratulating the county captains concerned, at the sporting results of the early county matches. But by mid-season it was becoming clear that some captains were overstepping the legitimate limits of sporting cricket and conspiring to produce contrived finishes. In July M.C.C. announced that they had been forced to remind the county clubs of a communication issued in April 1932, stating that freak declarations were not in the interests of the game or of the County Championship. They pointed out that if collaboration was held to be justifiable in May or June it would be equally justifiable in August, when the immediate result of the Championship was of great public interest, and that as long as M.C.C. were required to decide the Championship they would be reluctant to exclude points because they proved to have had an important bearing on the Championship. Towards the end of the 1946 season Middlesex were running neck and neck with Lancashire before finishing second to Yorkshire in the Championship.

India were not the only overseas team to visit Lord's in 1946: the Dutch Flamingos were particularly welcome visitors, and celebrated the first of many post-War visits by beating M.C.C. by five wickets. During the War the Dutch had collected all their cricket gear and dispatched it to P.O.W. camps in Germany; so early in 1946 a "Save Dutch Cricket" fund had been launched to make up the resulting shortage and put Dutch cricket on its feet again.

On January 15, 1946, the Imperial Cricket Conference had met again at Lord's after a lapse of seven years. Representatives of England, Australia, South Africa, New Zealand, West Indies, and India now agreed a seven-year programme of international tours, including, for the first time, matches between West Indies and India and India and Australia. In the previous year Australia's Minister for External Affairs, Dr Evatt, on a visit to England, had made a moving plea for an early English tour of Australia, which M.C.C. had accepted, not without some misgivings, for 1946-47.

The 1920–21 tour, undertaken before English cricket was on its feet again after the First War, was a warning against asking too much of our cricketers too soon, but it was hard to turn a deaf ear to Dr Evatt's insistence and the pressing invitation of the Australian Cricket Board of Control without appearing to show deep ingratitude to a nation who had fought by our side in the War and whose cricketers had recently given such tremendous pleasure by their performances in England. At the suggestion of the Australians it was agreed by the I.C.C. that, as an experiment for the 1946–47 series in Australia and the 1948 series in England, Tests between England and Australia should be limited to thirty playing hours (six days in Australia and five days in England), but that this limit should be without prejudice to the final Test being played to a finish if the margin of advantage was no more than one match.

So the first post-War season culminated with the pinnacle of excitement and anticipation which always attends the selection and departure of an English team for Australia. On August 31 the M.C.C. team sailed from Southampton in the *Stirling Castle* to do peaceful battle against the most senior of our major cricketing enemies, with Walter Hammond at the head of a band of star batsmen: Len Hutton, Denis Compton, Cyril Washbrook, Joe Hardstaff, Bill Edrich . . . England's team appeared promising at least, even in face of the Australians we had seen in England in their Services' sides. But our bowling was an uncertain quantity, with Farnes and Verity lost in war and no-one yet to match the speed of the one and the guile of the other. Lack of penetration in bowling and poor catching were, indeed, the principal factors in England's defeat by three matches to none (two drawn). Alec Bedser and Douglas Wright were bowled almost into the ground; nevertheless both showed quality which, allied with Godfrey Evans's agility behind the stumps, heralded a brighter future. Hammond, seemingly weighed down by the cares of captaincy and ill-health, was seldom at his best, though at Adelaide in January he played a great innings of 188 against South Australia, bringing his total aggregate past the 50,000 mark. He was unable to play in the final Test against Australia, when the captaincy devolved upon Norman Yardley, and at the end of the tour he announced his retirement from international cricket. The closing hours of every Test were broadcast live from Australia, and enthusiasts abed in England roused themselves before the crack of dawn to follow every ball. I can even remember one fanatic boasting that, to create the proper aura, he donned his flannels! We

THE 1948 AUSTRALIAN TEAM IN ENGLAND

Left to right—*Back row*: R. N. Harvey, S. G. Barnes, R. R. Lindwall, R. Saggers, D. Ring, W. A. Johnston, E. R. H. Toshack, K. R. Miller, D. Tallon, S. Loxton. *Front row*: K. O. E. Johnson (Manager), R. Hamence, I. W. Johnson, A. L. Hassett (Vice-Captain), D. G. Bradman (Captain), W. A. Brown, A. R. Morris, C. L. McCool, W. Ferguson (Scorer).

N. W. D. YARDLEY AND D. G. BRADMAN
Opposing captains in the 1948 Test.

W. WATSON AND T. E. BAILEY
Heroes of the 1953 Test.

were kept on tenterhooks as Compton completed his second hundred in the fourth Test, with Evans, uncharacteristically quiescent, keeping intact the opposite wicket as he remained for ninety-five minutes before he scored his first run. The final match of the tour, against New Zealand at Auckland, was watched ball by ball by the oldest living Test player, Samuel Jones. He had played twelve times against England in the eighties, and was sole survivor of the Australian team who first won the Ashes at the Oval in 1882; 1,297,876 Australians had paid £A135,800 to watch the team, beating the previous record by £29,277.

At home the close season was used to make plans for consolidating the remarkable spirit of revival of the previous season. The A.C.C.C., meeting at Lord's in November, issued an instruction to umpires to report to M.C.C. any suspected agreement between captains regarding declarations aimed at securing contrived finishes. In January the M.C.C. Committee approved the final draft of the new Code of the Laws of Cricket for submission to members at a special general meeting following the A.G.M. in May. The revision had involved three years of careful preparation, examination of the old Code and its interpretations, and consultation with cricketing bodies on every level at home and overseas. At a well-attended meeting the new Code was warmly received by the members, but to allow time for printing and distribution it did not become effective until the English season of 1948. The M.C.C. Cricket Sub-committee, anxious to improve the standard of M.C.C. teams at Lord's, initiated a new scheme aimed at widening the field of professionals who might be available by the inclusion of any professionals who had played in a M.C.C. touring team, and offering engagements to a limited number of leading county players likely to be disengaged at the time of the more important M.C.C. matches. As a result twenty-eight names were submitted by the counties, and sixteen were offered agreements for a year.

1947 was a year of splendour. Nearly three million people paid to watch cricket, showing an interest seldom equalled in the history of the game. The season started grimly enough with the M.C.C. team returning beaten from Australia, with a ban on mid-week sport threatening the cancellation of the South African tour (until the Government decided that cricket was not a threat to industry), and with the arrival of the South Africans in inhospitably bitter April weather. Some of the players brought their wives, and, despite a mantle of protest donned by their Manager, Algie Frames, they brought much gaiety and pleasure to their

B

English hosts. They were entertained to lunch at Lord's on an Arctic day shortly after their arrival; within a couple of weeks the cold had turned to a blazing heat, which continued throughout the summer, allowing "the Middlesex twins", Compton and Edrich, in their joint *annus mirabilis*, to pile on the runs, setting new records which seem unlikely to be broken and striking despair into the hearts of the South African bowlers. Never before had cricket known such a boom. The post-War euphoria, dampened by the rain of 1946, was uninhibited. The tourists were tremendously popular, day after day was gloriously fine, and grounds everywhere were packed with people come to enjoy the cricket and the sun. At Bank holiday and on almost any Saturday long queues circumnavigated the wall of Lord's long before the gates were open, and from lunch-time onwards boards at strategically situated Tube stations warned intending passengers that the ground was closed. No "box" tempted people to stay at home to enjoy the cricket from an armchair and switch off if they were bored—and it was seldom boring!—and petrol-rationing prevented joy-riding by car. At the end of the season the public enthusiasm was reflected in the Middlesex exchequer, which, on an entrance charge of 1s. 6d., from which entertainment duty was deducted, showed a profit of £5203 on the season. Middlesex had won the Championship, bringing it South for the first time since they themselves won it in 1921—a triumph for their captain, Walter Robins, who, like Sir Pelham Warner before him, had led his side to victory in the season of his retirement. The Lord's Test, described elsewhere in these pages by Ian Peebles, was unique as a royal occasion, for their Majesties King George VI and Queen Elizabeth with the two Princesses, lately returned from a State visit to South Africa, were present *en famille* on the third day to meet the team and watch the game from the Committee Room. The South Africans, like Middlesex, filled their coffers, taking home a handsome profit of £10,000 after donating half their gates against Surrey and Lancashire towards rebuilding the war-damaged grounds at the Oval and Old Trafford.

Within a few weeks of the Test the engagement was announced of H.R.H. Princess Elizabeth to Lieutenant Philip Mountbatten. The Eton *v.* Harrow match, not yet fallen into decline as one of the major events of the London social season, was made even more glamorous than usual by the presence of the newly engaged couple with the King and Queen and Princess Margaret in one of the Clock Tower boxes. The ground was crowded with elegant and lovely debs profiting by the luncheon interval to parade the New Look, with which high fashion had ousted the semi-mini utility styles of war, and escorted by young men who would have had short shrift had they failed to appear in the regulation top-hat and tails. The Varsity Match too attracted a crowd, vast by comparison with the sorry few who support it today. More conscious of the cricket than the "spectators" of the Eton *v.* Harrow, they nevertheless preserved something of its garden-party elegance. The Cambridge opening pair brought down on their heads much disapprobation from the old alumni of their university by appearing improperly dressed, respectively in a Quidnunc and a Crusader cap, rather than the Varsity blue. Clothes-rationing was offered and condemned as a feeble excuse—for could they not, asked Rockley Wilson, have *borrowed* blue caps?

M.C.C. is still, as its founders intended it to be, a private members' club. Its "out" matches in the realm of club cricket are not much advertised, nor do the public in general realize what efforts are made to help and encourage schools and clubs wanting fixtures. In 1946 the programme was inevitably modest, but in 1947 the Cricket Sub-committee were able to bring the list up from 50 to 100, giving priority, with the encouragement of young cricketers always in mind, to schools. The B.A.O.R. tour, started in 1946 under the captaincy of Lt.-Colonel R. T. Stanyforth, was repeated. These tours to British Forces in Germany were repeated annually for several years, with the tourists often faced by future Test and county players on National Service.

The luxurious sunshine and hard wickets of 1947 flattered cricket; batsmen particularly responded to the warmth on their backs with a generous spate of runs. It was tempting to imagine that English cricket had suddenly rid itself of war-time fatigue and recovered its peace-time form overnight. The decisive defeat of South Africa in the Tests was a sweet solace after our failure in Australia, but discerning critics were not slow to point out that but for the dominance of Compton and Edrich the result might have been very different. Mr Harry Altham, writing in *The Daily Telegraph* had no illusions; this is what he said:

> It has been my fortune recently to talk with some of the most experienced and distinguished figures in the game, and they are unanimous that the out-cricket in much that passes for first-class cricket is little short of lamentable and that this is at least reflected at the highest level.

It would seem that with the exception of Wright, no English

bowler of the past season would have been considered as such for our
Test eleven of, to take a convenient date, 1907, the year in which
the South Africans showed us what the perfected googly meant. We
have no bowler of real pace at all; our two best exponents of length
and flight are Goddard and J. C. Clay, respectively 46 and 49 years
old.

Fine cricketer though he is, Howorth cannot be compared as a left-
hand bowler with either Rhodes or Dennett, neither of whom could
get a place in the 1907 team because an even greater artist, Blythe,
was there—to take 15 wickets in the Lord's Test and save the rubber
for us.

Above all, the fetish of the in-swing and the defensive short-of-a-
length bowling even with the new ball persists and flourishes, and
until this bogey is exorcised our attack cannot recapture the true test
match standard. I remember Jack Hobbs telling me years ago that
the ball he feared above all others was the one that "left him" late in
flight. On the day he sailed for South Africa Alan Melville told me
exactly the same thing.

The fetish of the in-swing and defensive short-of-a-length bowling still flourishes, alas, a generation later, presenting a major
obstacle to a more positive approach to the game.

There did indeed appear to be an urgent need to find some way
to encourage the bowler. A few months earlier Douglas Jardine
had asked rhetorically, "Today, does anyone go to see anyone
bowl? . . . They used to go to see Lohmann and Richardson;
Barnes; McDonald: Larwood and Verity." A year later they
would flock to see Lindwall and Miller, but currently in England
it was true that the batsman had stolen the glamour as well as the
balance of power from the bowler. Jardine's solution was to
experiment with a smaller ball, which, he urged, would help
bowlers to impart swerve and spin and reverse the pendulum
without tampering with the Laws. Although his idea was not
immediately taken up, the M.C.C. Cricket Sub-committee did
give a good deal of time and thought to the make-up of cricket
balls. They were primarily anxious to discover why post-War
cricket balls did not stand up to wear and tear, but the opportunity
was taken to ask the manufacturers if it would be possible to
specify more precisely the type of thread to be used, and if a reduction in the tolerance of size and weight would add materially to the
difficulties of manufacture. Investigation at Lord's had shown that
balls of five different manufacturers had different characteristics of
size, weight, seam, and finish, with a general tendency to be small
and light. At Whitsun 1949 the counties experimented with a ball

with an enlarged seam, but it was not until 1952 that experiments were made with a ball that was slightly reduced in diameter, as well as having a slightly thicker seam. A final trial in twenty-five non-competition matches in 1955 failed to produce the hoped-for results, and with an almost total lack of enthusiasm from the players, and the original need to help bowlers no longer apparent, the A.C.C.C. decided to shelve the matter.

In preparation for the arrival of the Australians in 1948, great efforts were made to improve the ground. Conferences were held with the head groundsman, Austin Martin, who had instructions to do everything possible to speed up the pitch. Attention was also paid to the practice wickets on the Nursery ground, and the area which had been given up for allotments during the War was reclaimed. M.C.C. were already looking ahead towards their great endeavour to train young cricketers, which was to be the result of the Cricket Enquiry; at a time when there was a move towards the provision of artificial pitches, where good grass pitches were not available, a concrete pitch was for the first time laid down at Lord's. Another innovation, in preparation for the Australians, was the installation of what is euphemistically referred to as a "Public Address System"—loudspeakers at Lord's.

Immediately after Christmas a M.C.C. team sailed for the West Indies, with G. O. Allen as captain. Very few of the star players felt able to undertake this tour after three consecutive seasons of continuous cricket, at home and abroad, and it had not been easy to collect a team which was in any way representative of England. There was great interest over the release of the promising young Yorkshire batsman G. A. Smithson, a "Bevin Boy", due to leave the mines within a matter of days of the departure of the team. Eventually the Minister of Labour agreed to release him on leave on the understanding that he would return to Askern Colliery after the tour. From the start the team were dogged by injury, and they returned to England with the depressing experience of having failed to win a single game, though of the eleven played only two were lost. West Indies were already approaching the tremendous peak of form they were to show in England in 1950, and it was clear that any country that hoped to beat them must field its strongest side. Against a country lacking its star players and not fully recovered from the strains of war the fresh, vigorous approach of such exceptionally fine young players as "the three Ws" was invincible.

As a prelude to the visit of the Australians, the West Indies experience was about as discouraging as it could be, more so when it became apparent that Don Bradman had the good fortune to crown his international career by leading one of the strongest— perhaps the strongest—all-round sides that even Australia had ever sent abroad. Not only was there tremendous strength in batting— in depth, almost down to No. 11—but we saw once more in Lind- wall and Miller a great fast-bowling partnership, able to strike dis- may into the hearts of batsmen who had grown up since the days of Larwood and Voce. And in Keith Miller the Australians had, surely, one of the most spectacular players and greatest all- rounders of our own or perhaps of any other age. No game ever went to sleep as Miller tossed his mane—which would not now be considered exceptionally long—and ran up to bowl; as he moved his feet to drive the ball high up into the Pavilion, or fielded close to the wicket, taking impossible catches or menacing the batsman whose feet strayed from the crease.

During the Lord's Test there was a charming ceremony when Air Commodore Ewart, Air Officer Commanding the R.A.A.F. Overseas H.Q., London, supported by the Manager of the Austra- lian team, Keith Johnson, Lindsay Hassett, and Keith Miller (all ex-R.A.A.F.), handed over to the President of M.C.C., Lord Gowrie, a plaque with the R.A.A.F. crest illuminated on vellum and an inscription in appreciation of all M.C.C. had done for Australian Service cricketers during the War. On the Sunday there was another delightful occasion when the whole team were Lord Gowrie's guests at Windsor Castle, where he was Lieutenant Governor. In the afternoon the party were received by H.M. Queen Mary at Frogmore. On a beautiful afternoon the Queen stood in the sunshine outside the door of the house, alone except for a lady-in-waiting, posing with enormous patience with Brad- man and other members of the team while innumerable cameras clicked. At tea, back in Lord Gowrie's house, there was a moment of great hilarity when ex-A/C Miller slipped a 6d. tip to Marshal of the R.A.F. Lord Tedder as he handed him a cup of tea.

By a happy coincidence Don Bradman's farewell appearance at Lord's coincided with his fortieth birthday, which he celebrated appropriately and typically with an innings of 150 at the expense of the Gentlemen of England. To mark the occasion George Portman, on the point of retiring after fifty years in charge of the Lord's catering, created a tremendous birthday cake. Mr Portman was one of the great Lord's characters. Engaged as a mere boy by Sir Francis Lacey when the catering under independent manage- ment had fallen to its nadir, he built it into a prosperous business highly profitable to M.C.C. Whether or not he was born within earshot of Bow Bells, he had the ebullience and humour of a true cockney, who would not have looked out of place alongside Bud Flanagan and the Crazy Gang.

The Australians departed unbeaten, leaving England with a sense of inferiority. But, in a letter to the Secretary of M.C.C. after he had received his knighthood in the New Year Honours, the Don wrote:

> I felt that our last tour was a great success from your point of view as well as ours. We may eliminate playing results because I am convinced we had a particularly strong side, but there is no doubt a splendid feeling existed, and I shall certainly continue to work for this spirit of goodwill between our two countries.

As a prelude to the Australian tour the county secretaries had asked the Secretary of M.C.C. to negotiate a co-ordinated agreement with the B.B.C. for broadcasting the five Tests—previously each county had negotiated separately. A fee of 250 guineas per match was suggested, exclusive of Australian Broadcasting Corporation rights to broadcast to Australia. Television was not included in the proposed agreement, because it was still comparatively limited and only concerned Lord's and the Oval in the London area. The broadcasts were heard by millions, and in New Zealand people sitting up to listen in "uncharted hours" caused such a heavy rise in electricity consumption that there was a power failure.

The demand for Test tickets was tremendous. At Lord's, during the first week in March, the entire Pavilion staff were involved for a whole week opening the mail, and many thousands of applications had to be returned. The receipts of £43,000 with gross attendances of 132,000 set a new English record, which, however, was beaten a fortnight later when 133,740 attended the third Test at Old Trafford.

In mid-July a handsome laurel wreath embellished the W. G. Grace Gates for the centenary of the Great Cricketer, and the Gentlemen *v.* Players match, which he had made so peculiarly his own over so many years, coincided nearly enough with his birthday on July 18 for the match to be turned into a celebration in his honour. It would have been appropriate if the Gentlemen could have beaten the Players, but a fair chance that they might have done so was scotched when Hutton turned the tables with a masterly 132. Middlesex could not sustain their high success of 1947; the calls of five five-day Tests had robbed them of the services not only of Compton and Edrich but also of their left-arm spin bowler, Jack Young. Their fast bowler, Laurie Gray, took his Benefit and realized £6000, which was then a Middlesex record.

At the request of the county clubs the M.C.C. Committee had organized a nation-wide testimonial for Frank Chester, the celebrated umpire. When war broke out in 1914 Chester was only eighteen but showing already a promise of becoming a great player, which was destroyed by the loss of his right hand. At the exceptionally early age of twenty-six he became a first-class umpire, bringing to that career a shrewd judgment and a professional expertise which set a new standard of international umpiring. When he eventually retired in 1955 he had completed thirty-four years on the first-class list and stood in forty-eight Tests. At the end of 1948 the fund had reached £2350, and it was decided to keep it open for another year.

On June 21, in the match between M.C.C. and Cambridge University, Captain J. H. G. Deighton had the very rewarding experience for an amateur of doing the hat-trick at Lord's for the second year running: in 1947 he had done it for the Army against the Navy.

2

The Games and the Players 1946

IF the facade of English cricket was fully restored in 1946 it was hardly to be expected that the fabric was complete. War-time casualties and age had taken a heavy toll, and the younger generation, trained in the difficulties and shortages of their youth, had not yet had time to assert themselves. In the circumstances it was remarkable how many familiar names reappeared and how successfully the veterans acquitted themselves. Wally Hammond would be forty-three in June of this season, but batted in the same glorious way, if with an added air of restraint. Bill Bowes emerged from prolonged captivity to bowl with a perpendicular arm and a good measure of remaining pace and life. They were typical of many of their contemporaries. It was fortunate that the splendid batting side which England had assembled just before the War had been, for the most part, so extremely youthful. Hutton, Compton, and Edrich returned to the game fully seasoned in the craft, but still young in years and spirit. Washbrook had not advanced so far as this trio, but had played for England and had many years before him. Douglas Wright was the only bowler who could look to a reasonable continuance of his Test Match career. As the season progressed the most encouraging development in this field was the emergence of Alec Bedser as a bowler of high international quality. He was fortunate in immediately finding in T. G. Evans a wicket-keeper of the topmost class.

The cricket seen at Lord's in this season was certainly as entertaining as any to be found throughout England. The Middlesex captain, Walter Robins, was still a useful man with the bat and a magnificent fielder; the majority of the players who had served under him in 1938 were available, and he led them once again with stimulating enterprise and enthusiasm. The greatest loss was Jim Smith, but this was to some extent compensated by the advance of Jack Young to become the best slow left-hander in the country. With Compton, Edrich, and Robertson to lead the batting, Middlesex were a side worth watching. They won six of their matches at Lord's, but many were spoiled by the indifferent weather. Compton made 147 not out against Northants, 122 against Warwickshire, and 235 against Surrey, adding 296 for the second wicket with Edrich. He also added to the general entertainment and excitement with some highly original running between the wickets which resulted in his being run out thrice on his home ground and a general tautening of his partners' nerves.

On June 22, 24, and 25 Lord's had its first official Test Match since 1939. In his first appearance for England Alec Bedser took seven wickets for 49, and India were all out for 200 on the first day. Hutton and Compton fell to Amarnath when the score was 16, and Washbrook and Hammond had followed by the time the score had reached 70, but Hardstaff joined in several good stands and had made 205 not out when the innings closed at 428. Bedser took four for 96 in India's second innings of 275, and Hutton, with Washbrook, knocked off the runs, to bring England home by ten wickets.

The University Match which followed in July was a rather patchy affair, which Oxford won by six wickets. Cambridge made 201, and Oxford topped this by 60 runs in the first innings. The credit for this went almost entirely to Donnelly, who went in at the fall of the second wicket and made 142 out of 194 runs scored, in just under three hours. This was a beautiful innings, characteristic of Donnelly at his best and, not unexpectedly, outclassed all else. The Cambridge batting blew up in their second innings, and Oxford had only to get 68 on the last day. One heartening feature was the attendance, which was 12,000 on the Saturday and 8000 on the Monday. Those who were led to believe that the match was to be restored to its old-time glories were, however, due to be sadly disappointed over the ensuing years. This promising revival was doubtless largely due to the prevailing mood of nostalgia which brought such a boom to cricket as a whole. I myself felt that I had some personal stake, for in the dearth of all articles of clothing cricket blazers were unobtainable, and an appeal was made to old Blues to lend what they could to help. Thus sixteen years after its original appearance my Dark Blue Blazer reappeared on the person of Ron Maudsley without, regrettably, bringing him any great luck.

The Gentlemen v. Players match turned out to be a one-sided and disappointing affair. The Gentlemen were led by Walter Hammond and included Donnelly, Yardley, and Valentine, but were woefully short of bowling of the required standard. The weather was fitful, and showers several times interrupted the play. Washbrook made a century at No. 1, and Fishlock, Ikin, and Compton all got into the eighties. The Players declared at 399 for five and, despite a majestic 70 from Hammond, the Gentlemen made only 144 all told. When he was out for 0 in the follow-on the batting again disintegrated, and the side went for 115. Pollard, of Lancashire, demonstrated that he had preserved, and possibly improved, his ability to move the ball sharply from leg to off by taking nine wickets for 53 in the match.

One happy memory of this game was the complicated state of a radio commentator trying to cope with the eminently spoonerable names of Fishlock, Washbrook, and Hardstaff. He achieved almost every possible permutation of the component syllables, notably "Washlock" and "Fishstaff", but later denied that he had actually referred to one of the trio as "Fishcake".

During 1946 a number of cricketers who had been variously connected with Lord's died. It is doubtful if many of the younger generations knew what a very good cricketer Sir Francis Lacey had been in his earlier days before becoming Secretary of the M.C.C. He had played several very successful seasons for Hampshire and, in 1887, had created a record for county matches by making 323 not out against Norfolk at Southampton. In 1898 he succeeded Henry Perkins, and remained in office for twenty-eight years, a most admirable administrator, if rather more austere than his ebullient predecessor.

On the other side of the world, at Hobart, Tasmania, Joe Darling died a prosperous farmer and a member of the Legislature. In four visits to England he had played a number of matches at Lord's, including four Test Matches. So far as these went it was not his luckiest ground, for his best score was 41 in his last Test appearance there, as captain in 1905.

Midway between those widely divided points Ernie Vogler died in his native South Africa. There were those good judges, G. A. Faulkner amongst them, who thought that Vogler at his best was second only to Barnes, but he failed to sustain his enormous talents and had a brief career in the highest class of cricket. In 1905 he decided to turn professional and started to qualify for Middlesex, but returned to South Africa before he completed the required three years. His decision may have been influenced by the fact that there was a certain amount of criticism at Middlesex recruiting a further overseas player in addition to the two Australians, Trott and Tarrant, already in residence. In 1907 Vogler returned to

Lord's, where, in the only Test Match he played there, he took seven wickets in England's one innings.

At home J. H. King, of Leicester, died at seventy-five. His only Test Match had been at Lord's against Australia in 1909, and many people felt that he was an unlucky man not to have played more often. At least Lord's brought him one good stroke of fortune. Just before the Gentlemen and Players match of 1904 Johnny Tyldesley was injured, and it was necessary to have an immediate substitute. King, being present as a member of the M.C.C. staff, was pressed into service and made a century in each innings, a record which will remain unique unless the system of professionalism is sometime revived.

In late July those scanning the scene for future talent had an encouraging couple of days. The youngest player ever to appear in an official match at Lord's, thirteen-year-old M. C. Cowdrey, batted beautifully to make 75 for Tonbridge against Clifton on a difficult wicket, just over half his side's score from the bat. In his second innings he made 44 and, taking eight wickets with his leg-spinners, saw his team win by two runs.

3

The Games and the Players 1947

THE great post-War enthusiasm amongst the public was fully rewarded by the season of 1947. Climatically it was an immediate and lasting improvement on its predecessor, for three very good months were followed by an exceptionally warm and sunny August. Despite the lack of success in the winter's tour of Australia (which had been anticipated), English cricket was beginning to find its feet again, although shortages of diet and equipment were still acute.

There was plenty of fine play in all parts of the country, but as, in the nature of things, a bowler's expectation of useful life as such is less than that of a batsman, there had been greater wastage to make good. So, with good, hard wickets aplenty, it was a year in which the major part of the entertainment lay in high and rapid scoring. There was, at the same time, some good bowling, with two veteran off-spinners, J. C. Clay and Tom Goddard, at the top of the averages, followed by Young, Bowes, Howorth. Laker was the only new name in the first six.

Ten batsmen averaged over 60, Compton scoring 3816 runs and Edrich 3539. Thus, with Middlesex winning the Championship, Lord's again had full share of the pleasures of this bumper season. It opened with the customary M.C.C. fixture against Yorkshire, which was chiefly notable for the early form of Compton and Robertson. The first Middlesex match was against Somerset, and was as good a battle of nerves as anyone could wish for by way of a start. After much fluctuation of fortune the teams emerged after lunch on the third day with Somerset 16 runs short with one wicket in hand. Largely owing to the calm judgment of Tremlett, who had already taken eight wickets in his first county match, Somerset succeeded. It was the only match Middlesex lost at Lord's until mid-August.

Directed by Robins with constant and energetic vigilance, the leading Middlesex batting quartet chased along at great pace. On August Bank holiday Edrich and Compton both made hundreds, and George Mann, ever ready to attack or sacrifice his wicket as his side required, hit gloriously for an hour. In June Robertson and Brown made 310 for the first wicket in three hours against Notts and, in the next match, 222 against Yorkshire. Jack Young proved himself to be a really effective slow left-hander on hard wickets, and the fielding was keen and unrelaxing. It was all joyous stuff, and cricket seemed to have surmounted its perennial problems.

The South Africans came thrice to Lord's, to be beaten by M.C.C. and England, draw with Middlesex, and be scourged on each occasion by one or both of the "Middlesex twins". This was especially so in the Test Match, which England won by ten wickets. Taking the field with a rather tender bowling side, the South Africans got rid of Hutton and Washbrook for 96. This brought Compton and Edrich together, and 370 runs were added for the third wicket. Edrich kept pace in a sustained flow of scoring strokes, and was in every way a perfect foil; but Compton was the dominating figure. Not since Bradman in the thirties had any batsman had such an array of scoring strokes or so many which were patently individual. Although very different in temperament and approach they shared an extraordinary stamina in unrelenting pursuit. The chief difference lay in the fact that Bradman always applied himself with a cool, unwavering concentration, while Compton seemed to be borne along by a carefree joy. This difference was best illustrated in their running between the wickets. Bradman was fast, decisive, and an unfailing judge of speed and distance; Compton was so joyously haphazard that John Warr remarked that his call was merely an opening bid.

This combined effort enabled England to declare at 554 for eight wickets, and, despite a characteristically graceful century from Alan Melville, South Africa were 227 behind at the follow-on. They did just well enough to make England bat again for 26 runs.

Two very useful University sides came to Lord's in early July to play a draw. Oxford, captained by Donnelly, with Pawson and Kardar, and three very good seam bowlers, were the stronger side but, when Cambridge followed on 256 behind, Bailey, portending many things to come, defended stubbornly and soon put his side beyond danger.

The Gentlemen and Players was one of the less fortunate matches in this season of fine weather, and also ended in a draw. Donnelly made 162 not out and Edrich 79, which accounted for the major part of the Gentlemen's 302. The Players, with 101 by Washbrook, led by 32 runs before declaring. They looked very much like winning when five wickets went down before the innings defeat was saved. Thereafter the remaining Gentlemen all got a few, and the score reached 209, leaving the Players a few overs before bad light ended the match.

Lord's had now enjoyed two great innings from Donnelly, who vied with Arthur Morris as the leading left-handed batsman of the decade. Essentially an orthodox player, he picked the bat up in an easy, rather long-armed sweep which lent power to his many strokes and an easy grace to their execution. Looking back twenty years, it is difficult to think that he has been excelled by any left-handed rival in his command of all and every circumstance.

In August the Combined Services easily defeated the Public Schools. Facing a total of 305, the Schools lost four wickets for a score of runs, but a seventeen-year-old, Peter May, hit 146 out of his side's first innings of 239. Two years previously his coach, George Geary, had taken a friend to see him bat with the confident assertion that they were about to watch a future England batsman. The discerning onlookers at Lord's must have endorsed this far-seeing view.

In March Sir Stanley Jackson died. Stout-hearted and a York-shireman in every fibre of his being, he was also very much a man of Lord's. There he had played for Harrow, Cambridge, M.C.C., the Gentlemen, and England. In five Test Matches he had never failed his country, for, if his last innings read "b. Armstrong 0", he topped the bowlers. In 1902 he had the strange experience of taking guard when England had lost two wickets for no runs, a situation which he and MacLaren had rectified, adding 102 undefeated, when rain finally washed the match out.

In July his old and formidable opponent Warwick Windridge Armstrong died in Australia. Lord's had seen him many times, growing from the slim young man of 1902 to become the massive, twenty-two-stone giant of 1921. In his last Test Match at Lord's he inflicted one of the greatest defeats England has ever suffered there. In his ascendancy he was respected, if not always beloved, at Head-quarters, being a determined and somewhat dictatorial man. His battles over, the writer recalls him in bowler hat and city suit, dominating the Long Room, a benign and charming guest.

When he died in July, aged fifty-nine, George Challenor was still a legendary name in the West Indies, where it was thought that he could take his place with the greatest batsmen of any day. Many unbiased judges felt that this was a fair judgment. It was a pity that when he played in the first Test Match ever between England

and West Indies in this country he was about at the end of his career. At Lord's he was caught at the wicket off Larwood for 29 and bowled by Maurice Tate for 0. A decade earlier this would have been a three-handed contest worth travelling far to see.

"Old" Joe Hardstaff, who died in April, had long been attached to the Lord's ground staff. Strong, stocky, and bold, he was one of a great school of Nottingham batsmen. He was a great success in Australia, but never played for his country at home.

MacKinnon of MacKinnon died in February within a few weeks of his ninety-ninth birthday, the greatest age ever reached by a first-class cricketer. At Lord's, seventy-six years before, he had played in "Cobden's Match".

THE MONARCH AT LORD'S, 1950
A great West Indies team presented to H.M. King George VI.

THE MONARCH AT LORD'S, 1967
A greeting for Pakistan from H.M. Queen Elizabeth II.

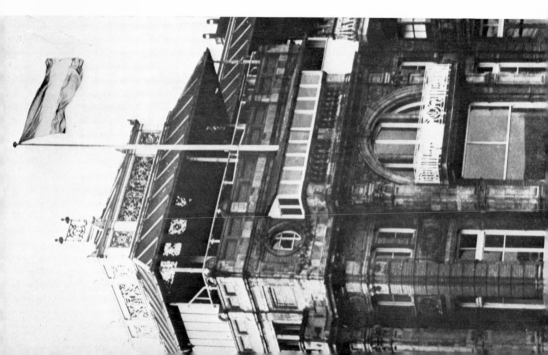

Left: ENGLAND WIN THE ASHES, 1954–55
Flag hoisted at Lord's to proclaim the news.

Right: SIR PELHAM WARNER 80 NOT OUT
The scoreboard illuminated on the night of his celebration dinner.

4

Building for the Future

1948 was the year on which the post-War planners had set their sights as a target for the recovery of English cricket to something like normality. But now that 1948 had come, bringing with it a triple defeat, twice now at the hands of Australia and once by West Indies, it seemed that the hoped-for recovery had got no further than the end of the beginning. It was to be a year of deep heart-searching and intensive committee-room activity: was there something fundamentally wrong with the structure of English cricket? Was there talent trapped unnoticed in the lower grades of cricket, unable to rise to the top because of a pattern of life and economic pressures which militated against recruitment of players for six-days-a-week cricket? Jack Fingleton, writing for *The Sunday Times* and *The Cricketer*, was convinced this was so. Whereas in Australia, where first-class cricket was played at week-ends on a part-time basis, any player could rise through grade cricket to play for his state and catch the eye of the national selectors, there was no provision in England for the ordinary cricketer who did not wish to play as a professional and could not afford to play as a full-time amateur ever to reach the top. The Board of Control came in for much criticism, especially over the dropping of Hutton after his unconvincing performance against the fast bowlers at Lord's; the final humiliation in the Oval Test led to a Press campaign for the reconstruction of English cricket. We were still relying on the small nucleus of brilliant batsmen who had risen so rapidly just before the War. Having achieved stardom in their teens, they were still far from being over the top, but there seemed to be little or no sign of young talent of the same class growing up to support them. Worst of all, no bowler had appeared faster than medium pace. The main burden of opening the bowling fell on Bedser, who was overworked; as his partner we relied on a batsman—Edrich. The lack of fast bowlers brought the inevitable side-effect of a batting problem, for the only batsmen who had any experience of standing up to fast bowling were the handful who had already played

c

against the Australians. The rest were swept aside, for lack of practice, by the onslaught of Lindwall and Miller.

Already in early summer, with the report of the captain of the M.C.C. side in West Indies fresh on the table, the M.C.C. Selection and Planning Sub-committee had considered in depth the whole position regarding the future of international cricket. Our failure to raise a team which could be regarded as fully representative of England, the dearth of adequate reserves to take the place of the stars when they were not available, and the vulnerability of the players to injury, all indicated that too much was being asked of English cricket too soon. Even before the War the 1937 Findlay Commission had advised that the stamina of English professionals was being sorely taxed by a plethora of cricket, and it had been agreed to reduce the number of M.C.C. overseas tours arranged for the years between 1941 and 1946. But peace brought with it a wholly natural and pressing urge to make up for the years which the locust had eaten, with a schedule of continuous tours crowding one on top of another in unbroken sequence. It was logical to conclude that there was an urgent need for relief from the pressure of continuous overseas tours. It was with deep regret, knowing the disappointment which would result in India, and in face of Ministerial pressure to think again, that the M.C.C. Committee adhered to a decision, taken with great reluctance, that they must accept the recommendation of their Sub-committee to cancel the forthcoming tour of India, scheduled for 1949–50. The Selection and Planning Sub-committee's full report on the future of international cricket was laid before the Imperial Cricket Conference in July.

Starting with a reminder of the Findlay Commission's recommendation, the report went on to examine reasons for the slow recovery of English cricket: the continuation of National Service and the recent Control of Engagement Order; the competition of full employment at high wages tempting players away from cricket as a career; intensification of post-War reaction, causing uncertainty in the players' outlook towards the game—all militating against the recruitment and development of fresh talent. Considerations directly affecting overseas tours were cited: the very high accident rate instanced by the M.C.C. tour in West Indies, and due perhaps to the age and strain on the players in conjunction with diet deficiency; opportunities for full winter employment for high wages deterring players from accepting invitations which broke into such employment; uncertainties in arranging

sea passages. M.C.C. were forced to the conclusion that the
situation warranted a curtailment of tours in the immediate future.
No important problem was presented by teams visiting England,
but relief in respect of M.C.C. overseas tours was urgent and
essential. Winters in which it seemed improbable that the leading
English players could accept invitations should be left blank—
the winter immediately before a M.C.C. Australian tour was
particularly unsuitable, as both county committees and Selectors
might well think that leading players should rest. Only in exceptional circumstances should two M.C.C. tours take place in
successive years. M.C.C. stressed that they felt bound to give
priority to their older traditional foes, the co-founders of the I.C.C.,
Australia and South Africa. However, to meet the requirements
for tours to other countries, it was proposed, without upsetting the
traditional arrangements by which visits between England and
Australia were exchanged every four years, to stagger Australia's
visits to England alternately at five- and three-year intervals. As
for South Africa, the aim was to retain their visits at not less than
five-year intervals and M.C.C. tours to South Africa at not less
than six-year intervals—though in the event only three tours to
South Africa have taken place since the War.

M.C.C. pointed out that these arguments were of equal importance to English cricket and overseas bodies, for it was no
longer possible, as in earlier days, to send adequate teams to
South Africa, New Zealand, West Indies, and India without calling on all the leading English players. Whereas the field of selection in England had narrowed, the standard of cricket in these
countries had risen to such a high level that it was clear that to
satisfy the hosts and maintain the prestige of English cricket the
strongest teams must be selected for all tours.

The report appealed to overseas boards to compensate for the
future reduction in M.C.C. tours by visiting each other. And
English county committees were asked to support the tours wholeheartedly, recognizing that visits of overseas teams to England
depended on a reasonable number of return visits being made.
M.C.C. undertook that, while they were unable to give any guarantee as to the composition of a team, they would always endeavour
to produce the best possible team for all tours. However, if it were
clearly impossible to collect a fully representative team, they would
reserve the right to decide that it should not play official Test
Matches—leaving the hosts the option of cancelling the tour or not.

Financially M.C.C. still did not aim to make any profit from tours to South Africa, West Indies, and India, but they stipulated that the hosts must undertake to cover expenses. In the ten years before the War the cost falling directly on M.C.C. in connection with tours to South Africa, West Indies, India, and New Zealand amounted to considerably more than £4000—and the recent tour of West Indies had created a minimum liability of £1100.

The report was circulated to county committees in July, and when their representatives met at Lord's at the A.C.C.C. in November it received their unanimous approval. The cancellation of the Indian tour left a blank winter preceding the 1950–51 tour to Australia and New Zealand. The tour to India followed in 1951–52, and the Australians accommodated India by deferring until 1953 their next visit to England, leaving 1952 free for an Indian tour. The counties agreed that in future there should be no tour to this country by an overseas side in the year following an Australian visit. However, by 1954 Pakistan had entered the Test arena, and so this dictum never became effective. In his annual speech to the county secretaries in December, Colonel Rait Kerr referred to the report again, pointing out the heavy load which was falling on a very few great players and on the limited number of players who qualified for the selection field, many of whom had perfectly good private reasons for hesitating to accept invitations to tour every winter.

The Cricket Sub-committee, meeting in October, discussed at length the current standard of English cricket in general, with the outcome that the M.C.C. Committee agreed to their recommendation to institute an enquiry into the future welfare of English cricket. In commending the idea to the counties at the A.C.C.C. in November the Treasurer of M.C.C., Lord Cobham, explained that the proposed enquiry referred particularly to the possibility of providing the youth of the country with more and better facilities for cricket. There were two million elementary and secondary schoolboys who had little or no opportunity to learn to play properly. Because of lack of facilities for good cricket a large proportion of the youth of the country was being lost to the game, and facilities in the shape of grounds, coaches, and cricket gear should be brought within their reach or the standard of the game would drop, with consequent loss of public interest.

Mr G. O. Allen, from whose fertile brain the idea of the Enquiry was born and who, as Chairman of the Standing Sub-committee on Coaching, was to play an active part in putting its recommendations into practice, itemized their terms of reference: to recommend how to bring into practice organized coaching schemes; instruction for coaches; instructional films; indoor cricket schools; teaching of the history and tradition of the game, and how to organize cricket for boys between school-leaving and National Service. The Enquiry was not to be concerned with international or county cricket, but only with lower-grade cricket, especially boys' cricket at primary and secondary schools. The counties were wholeheartedly in support. In February 1949 it was announced that a Steering Committee had been appointed whose brief was to recommend the machinery by which the Enquiry was to be conducted. They were exceptionally fortunate in having as Chairman Mr H. S. Altham, whose unbounded enthusiasm was the mainspring of the work of the Enquiry, whose report, published in 1950, led to the setting up of the M.C.C. Youth Cricket Association. By setting this enquiry afoot, and subsequently creating the Y.C.A. with Mr Altham as its Chairman, M.C.C. took a step which may well prove to have been their most far-reaching and important act of the last twenty-five years.

It had become evident that the complexity of domestic and international cricket administration, involving ever broader responsibilities for M.C.C., was straining to breaking-point the resources of the administration at Lord's, geared as it still was almost to pre-First World War conditions. A special sub-committee appointed to consider the question of the M.C.C. secretarial organization now recommended that there was a need for a second Assistant Secretary to relieve the Secretary of much of the direct handling of the Club's affairs, leaving him free to deal with major policy problems and external relations. As a result Mr J. G. Dunbar was appointed as Assistant Secretary in charge of administration— an appointment he took up on February 28, 1949. The principle of decentralization was extended to Committee work, with Sub-committees laying down policies on which the Secretariat could act, thus relieving Committees of unessential work and leaving them more time for really important matters.

So before the opening of the 1949 season momentous decisions had been taken affecting cricket's future. By contrast a proposal was made at the M.C.C. Committee in October 1948 which had more bearing on the past: it was proposed that Honorary Cricket Membership might be accorded to really distinguished professional cricketers who had retired from active play. The proposal was approved by a Special General Meeting of members at Lord's on July 14, 1949, and a fortnight later twenty-six England players of the past were duly elected. They were, S. F. Barnes, C. J. Barnett, W. E. Bowes, L. C. Braund, G. Duckworth, A. P. Freeman, G. Geary, G. Gunn, J. W. Hearne, E. Hendren, G. H. Hirst, J. B. Hobbs, H. Larwood, M. Leyland, C. P. Mead, E. Paynter, W. Rhodes, A. C. Russell, A. Sandham, E. J. Smith, H. Strudwick, H. Sutcliffe, M. W. Tate, E. Tyldesley, W. Voce, F. E. Woolley.

1948 ended on a much more optimistic note, with a M.C.C. team in South Africa putting England one up after winning the first Test at Durban. The match had been packed with thrills from the moment on the first day when Allan Watkins dismissed Dudley Nourse with an amazing diving catch, to Alec Bedser's single run which brought the scores level off the sixth ball of the final over. In the spring of 1949 they were to return to England unbeaten, with the rubber won by two matches to none (three drawn)—a success which was in great measure due to the inspiring leadership of George Mann. His not-out century in the final Test initiated a batting recovery after a remarkably poor start which brought England the respectable total of 395, and, faced with Nourse's challenge to make 172 in 95 minutes, he rejected the temptation to retain the rubber with a tame draw and, by electing to go for the runs, offered the spectators a day of high drama and secured for England a breath-taking victory. Above all, largely by his own example, he confounded the critics of England's out cricket by welding the team into a first-class fielding side.

The visitors for 1949 were Walter Hadlee's New Zealanders, a delightful and popular side who were in the exceptionally happy position of having two left-handed batsmen of world class. Martin Donnelly was famous already; the memory of his splendid century for the Dominions was alive. Demobilized, he had got an automatic Blue for Oxford, played once for Middlesex, against the Indians, but then joined Warwickshire. In 1949 he equalled Percy Chapman's feat of making centuries at Lord's in the VarsityMatch, Gentlemen v. Players, and a Test. Bert Sutcliffe, six years younger and as yet a stranger to England, with nine years of international cricket ahead of him, produced if anything a more splendid array of strokes than his more experienced partner. As if to gild the lily, the summer was, on the whole, gloriously fine, with hard wickets favouring the batsman. The New Zealanders played four three-day Tests, all drawn. The incidence of drawn matches led to a reassessment of the duration of Tests, in the light of the levelling out of standards in all the Test-playing countries, and to the eventual adoption of the standard thirty hours, played over five or six days, according to the playing hours prevailing at home or overseas. Receipts for the Lord's Test topped £21,000, and the New Zealanders returned home with a handsome profit on the tour of £15,000. In this season there appeared in the England side two new faces, both all-rounders, who in different ways were to contribute to English cricket in future years. Brian Close, selected for the third Test at the age of eighteen, was the youngest player ever to appear for England. In 1950–51 on an early tour in Australia, for which he received deferment from National Service, he failed to achieve the success which had been hoped for, and it was not until 1963 that he made more than an occasional appearance for England, and established himself as a courageous and aggressive all-rounder who was eventually entrusted with the captaincy. Trevor Bailey, by contrast, had an immediate success. He played in all four Tests against New Zealand, not only taking more wickets than any other bowler and giving the ball a lift off the pitch which had seldom been seen in England since the War, but achieving a batting average of 73, only a little behind Len Hutton and well ahead of Edrich and Compton. In the third Test Freddie Brown renewed his personal battle with New Zealand after a break of twelve years, bringing to the captaincy a robust urgency which was to serve England well when he led the next M.C.C. team to Australia.

The England captain, F. G. Mann, had four Middlesex men besides himself in the England team for Lord's. Robertson, deputizing as opener for the injured Washbrook, made a century and was unlucky not to be played again. He dropped a powerful hint to the selectors by making 331—the highest individual score in England since 1938—for Middlesex at Worcester on the opening day of the third Test. Following current Middlesex tactics of declaring on the first evening in the hope of a quick wicket before the close, Mann caused quite a furore by closing England's innings at 313 at 6 P.M. on the first day, on the false supposition that the experimental rule which permitted this in county cricket applied also to the Tests. Fortunately the New Zealanders kept their wickets intact during the quarter of an hour or so they had to bat, so no great harm was done.

When Middlesex climbed to the top of the Championship again, sharing the honours with Yorkshire after a tight struggle, George Mann, in his last year as captain, had the satisfaction of following in his father's footsteps. The Championship had not been shared since 1889, and Middlesex have not won it since. This was Denis

Compton's Benefit year. He took his Benefit match in the traditional Whitsuntide fixture against Sussex, and in a dry season was
exceptionally unlucky in having the Saturday morning rained off.
Nevertheless, 35,000 people watched the match, and on Monday,
when Compton made one of the most splendid centuries of even his
career, the gates were closed before lunch. His Benefit fund eventually reached £12,000, a total only bettered by three other
cricketers and never by a Middlesex cricketer. Few other Middlesex men have given the public quite such intense and carefree
pleasure and none in the post-War era.

At the M.C.C. A.G.M. on May 4 the retiring President, Lord
Gowrie, had nominated the Duke of Edinburgh as his successor.
Since the First Gentleman had supported M.C.C. in its earliest
years the Club had been honoured by a long line of royal patrons,
but Prince Philip was the first royal President; he was also one of
the youngest. His year in office brought a continuation of the
back-room activity of the previous year. His active interest in youth
commended to him the work which the Cricket Enquiry were seeking to do for young cricketers and, in his joint capacity as President
both of M.C.C. and of the National Playing Fields Association, he
personally initiated the joint committee of those two bodies, whose
efforts produced a specification for a technically satisfactory and
economically practicable artificial pitch.

The M.C.C. Cricket Sub-committee concerned itself early in the
year with the status of amateurs. From the time when serious international cricket began and the Grace family heralded the Golden
Age of the English amateur, English cricket had drawn strength
from the spirit of adventure with which the true amateur complemented the staider approach of the professional. Every county had
its quota of amateurs, and a generous proportion were good enough
to play for England. The oft misquoted prayer of Lord Hawke
(who so successfully welded a collection of brilliant individualists
into the most consistently powerful team in England) that the time
would never come when an amateur could not be found to captain
England reflected the fact that in his day there always were amateurs available with a flair for leadership married to cricketing
skill. England was the only country where first-class cricket involved six-days-a-week "daily breading" from April till September,
and in 1949 the economic pattern of life, with the need for full
employment, was decimating the amateur ranks and taking away
from the game gifted players whom it could ill afford to lose. Plenty
of great cricketers, from Lord Frederick Beauclerk to W. G. Grace,

might reasonably have been labelled "shamateurs", but the time was not yet ripe to take the realistic step of abolishing the distinction between amateur and professional. Meanwhile more and more amateurs who were not in the happy position of having cricket enthusiasts for employers were compelled to accept emoluments; fewer and fewer could afford to play just for the fun of the game. Not only were the amateurs dwindling numerically; in a professional milieu the few who remained tended to acquire a professional approach to the game, substituting an attitude of safety first for the old spirit of free adventure. Already the shortage of amateurs and this change of approach were reflected in the quality of captaincy, with insufficient talent coming on to replace the pre-War leaders and some counties putting young tyros in charge. Only Warwickshire (and Sussex as an emergency measure) took the forward-looking step of appointing a professional captain, H. E. Dollery—who led his county with distinction.

At this point in history the M.C.C. Cricket Sub-committee were convinced that action must be taken urgently to encourage the amateur to remain in the game. An attempt to get the counties to agree on a standard policy for allowances failed because of wide differences in interpretation. A sub-committee appointed to consider expenses recommended that allowances should be made for travelling, hotel expenses, gratuities, renewal of equipment, and reasonable entertainment allowances for captains, but they did not feel able to recommend payment for broken time. When the next M.C.C. team went to Australia in 1950–51 the allowance was £300, with an extra £50 for the captain.

1949 saw the passing of several distinguished ex-Presidents of M.C.C.: Lord Ullswater (President in 1923), who was much interested in the Club's pictures, Lord Lucan (1928), Lord Cobham (1935), the reigning Treasurer, and Mr Stanley Christopherson (1939–46). At a time of financial anxieties the honourable office of Treasurer was bestowed upon Mr H. S. Altham, adding the heaviest burden of all to the innumerable labours of love he was to perform for cricket in a very full life of retirement from active schoolmastering.

On April 20 Jimmy Cannon died. He had come to Lord's as a ball boy in the tennis court in 1879, advanced soon to the status of holding the horses' heads for the members. After sixty-five years' service under four Secretaries he had attained the rank of Chief Clerk and the inarguable status of a Lord's character of the best vintage. He would point with pride to himself, a manikin among

the members in a large composite photograph of Lord's taken in
1881. As an octogenarian in retirement he preserved the trim,
perky figure of his youth, always dapper in pin-stripe suit, with the
inevitable buttonhole and a straw boater. The twinkling eyes were
as lively as ever, but had a tendency to water as he recited a fund of
stories about Lord's as he knew it under Mr Perkins and Mr
Lacey—Sir Francis.

The new Treasurer was faced with a deficit in the Club's
accounts for the first time since the War. In 1948 there had been a
nominal surplus of £12,000, but since this included non-recurring
items exceeding that amount, the Committee had warned the
members that it was likely that they would have to implement the
authority they received in 1946 to raise the subscriptions of members elected before 1946 from £3 to £4. Clearly the time had come
to review the whole structure of the Club's finances, and an
appreciation of the situation prepared by the Secretary was considered by the Finance and General Purposes Sub-committee.
Revenue increases since 1945 had been absorbed by rising prices,
so that, while, compared with the pre-War era, M.C.C.'s income
had increased by approximately 70 per cent, expenses had risen by
105 per cent. The capital reserves, at £191,186, were well behind
the estimated cost of projects currently under consideration, and in
their report on the situation the Finance and General Purposes
Sub-committee advised the Committee that the Club was in no
position to undertake any new expenditure unless it was either
unavoidable in the interest of cricket or likely to be profitable. An
exception was made for the rebuilding of No. 6 Elm Tree Road,
which was required urgently as a residence for Mr Dunbar, and
for the new bakery under the Mound Stand, which replaced the
old stone ovens in the Tavern basement in which, under Mr
Portman's supervision, loaves were baked which had a well-
deserved reputation for being the best in London.

It was fortunate perhaps for Mr Altham's peace of mind that the
financial implications of the Cricket Enquiry Committee's report
were considered before he was called upon to add the office of
Treasurer of M.C.C. to his role of Chairman of the Cricket
Enquiry Committee. So he was spared the embarrassment of seeking financial provision for objects on which he had set his heart
from resources it was his duty to conserve. The Finance and
General Purposes Sub-committee's advice was that, from existing
resources, M.C.C. were not in a position to incur any liability
beyond a reasonable contribution by way of a capital grant to the

Trust which it was proposed to set up, and they recommended that approaches should be made to the Ministry of Education and to King George's Jubilee Trust and other charitable bodies for support. Members were therefore asked to make a once-for-all capital grant of £15,000 to enable the central organization of the Youth Cricket Association to be set up and financed for a limited period, on the understanding that a majority of the counties would undertake to set up, finance, and administer Area Youth Cricket Councils. At the same time it was agreed to sponsor the first of a series of books published under the guidance of the Y.C.A., in support of its objects—a boy's annual (the first of three) called *The M.C.C. Book for the Young Cricketer*. To the Technique Sub-committee was commended the preparation of a standard manual on coaching, which was achieved as *The M.C.C. Cricket Coaching Book* in 1952.

5

The Games and the Players 1948

ONE event above all others was calculated to lift the cricket-lover's heart in the age of austerity which still prevailed almost three years after the cessation of the War. In 1948, for the first time in ten years, an Australian Test Match series would be played in England. The interval was the longest in the history of these events, and the changes in that time in the life of the world in general, and Britain in particular, were greater than in any other decade.

To the older generation the series was, apart from its actual attractions, an assurance that something of the joys and grandeurs of the world they had known in early youth had survived. To a generation that could not remember the days of Hammond and Bradman, but had been inspired by a love of cricket, and many a legend lovingly retold by those who had instructed them in the face of much difficulty, it was an experience and a fulfilment. Beyond the more active devotees was a vast public, bred largely of radio, who, less interested in technicalities, were absorbed in the fierce but friendly competition between England and her old Dominion. Cricket, one of the more complicated and lengthy games, had immediately proved a most successful subject for broadcasting, a happy paradox for which the early commentators must be accorded a fair share of credit.

The composition of the Australian team was itself of unusual interest. The key to the situation was the triumphant return to cricket of Bradman. After a long period of inactivity and a severe illness there was considerable doubt as to whether he would attempt to resume a serious career, but his decision to do so was triumphantly vindicated by his success against Hammond's team in 1946–47, and underlined by his domination of the Indian bowling in the following season. It was hardly to be expected that he would regain the phenomenal standards of batsmanship he had set in the thirties, but, judged by any standards, he was still the master batsman. As importantly his presence lent immense morale to the team, and his captaincy was unexcelled in its judgment, discipline, and ever alert knowledge.

There were three other "veterans". Hassett, Brown, and Barnes had toured in 1938, and Hassett had been a prominent figure in War-time Services cricket in England. Miller was likewise already an established personality in this country, but the newcomers were otherwise only recognizable by reputation.

The Australians came four times to Lord's. In May M.C.C. fielded a strong batting side in which Hutton, Robertson, Compton, Edrich, and Yardley were aided by Donnelly, but were crushed by an innings. Bradman made 98 and Miller 163 in an innings of 552, and the home batsmen were undone by the superb Lindwall-and-Miller combination, which opened the way for Toshack and Johnston.

In five June days, from the 24th to the 29th, the Test Match was lost by 409 runs after an Australian declaration. From an English point of view it was full of rather melancholy interest. On the first day England did well in getting seven of this powerful Australian batting side out for 258, largely due to some good bowling, led by Bedser, but next morning the last three wickets added 92. This should not have been, for Toshack and Johnston made 49 of them.

When England batted Miller was injured and unable to bowl, but this merely gave opportunity to Johnston, a superb and most versatile quickish left-hander. But it was Lindwall who dominated the scene, then in the eye and now in the memory of the observer. He may at a later stage have been an even more skilful bowler, but this was his most effective age. Seen at the Pavilion end, his beautiful rhythmical run, the gathering momentum, the expansion into the last, upstepping, ranging stride, and the long, co-ordinated sling of arm and shoulders were, in the words of the poet Gray, "a fearful joy". No such action had been seen since the Larwood of fifteen years earlier. Indeed, there existed a great similarity from the final poise and through the delivery between these two perfect actions, the difference being that Larwood's arm swung in an absolutely perpendicular plane, whilst Lindwall's was perceptibly flatter. Whatever the view of the purist, it is arguable that this was in some respects an advantage, and certainly did not affect the accuracy of the aim in length or line.

Only 17 runs had been scored when he had Washbrook caught behind, and Johnston bowled Hutton at 32. The light was now none too good, and Lindwall bowled Edrich at 46. The next man

in was Dollery, and few batsmen have faced a more daunting prospect in a first Test Match. The first ball was lightning-fast, well up,
and Dollery in a convulsive, hurried stroke got the bottom of the
bat to it. The second was, if anything, quicker and, out of the dark
background, must have been almost impossible to an incoming
batsman. It wrecked Dollery's stumps, seemingly before he con-
templated any reply. Compton and Yardley batted heroically
awhile, and the tail did better than the head, but England were
out for 215.

Barnes, Morris, and Bradman laid the foundation of a big second
innings, and Miller, in company with Lindwall, enjoyed himself,
so that England were set 596 to win. When Hutton was harassed
out by Lindwall, and Edrich failed for the second time, the way
was open for Toshack with his medium left-handed cutters, and
England failed by 409 runs. One pleasing feature was that Dollery
played a very good innings of 37, so was equal-top scorer with
Washbrook.

Returning from the Old Trafford Test Match in July, in which
they had rather the worse of a draw, the Australians beat Middlesex in a set-piece encounter by ten wickets. The match produced
some interesting individual performances but not remarkable
scoring, despite centuries from Morris and Loxton. Sims bowled
remarkably well to take six wickets for 65, and Compton made 62
out of the Middlesex first innings of 203. In the second innings
John Dewes made 51 out of 135, which led to his selection for the
last Test at the Oval. There the position of an England opener
against the full blast of Lindwall and Miller, not unnaturally,
proved a different and overwhelming proposition.

At the end of August, the series won and Festival cricket just at
hand, the Australians made their last appearance at Lord's. The
Gentlemen lost the toss on a good wicket and were thrashed for a
day and a half until, when Hassett had reached 200 not out,
Bradman declared at 610 for five wickets. The Gentlemen batted
adequately, Edrich getting 128 in the second innings, but still lost
by an innings and 81 runs.

Perhaps the most notable point of the whole occasion was that it
was Bradman's last at Lord's. That he made 150 (then giving his
wicket away) was less notable, in view of his habit of making
centuries and the extremely benevolent circumstances.

On a personal note I had vivid memories of his first innings at
Lord's, having played for M.C.C. in the 1930 match. He arrived,
having made 556 runs for three times out, and came in when the

unfortunate Archie Jackson was out for nought. From the first glimpse there could be no doubt of the altogether exceptional quality of this new phenomenon. It could be seen epitomized in his immediate reactions on the arrival of the slower bowlers. He would wait till the ball was late in its flight, then dart down the wicket right to the pitch, which he had accurately determined before making a move. There was a galvanic quality about the speed and decision of this move beyond any batsman I had ever previously seen. There were wiseacres who could with relish point to the gap between bat and pad, and various other academic unorthodoxies bound to bring disaster. They could have done so eighteen years later, but their relish had by then given way to disillusion. He made 66 and at least one mistake. He edged Gubby Allen breast-high to Greville Stevens in the slips, to see the catch go down. By way of apology the fielder, a man of engaging and matchless effrontery, asked the bowler why he didn't bowl at the wicket.

As he left the middle for the last time Don Bradman must have felt very much a man of Lord's. He had always felt that his 254 in the Test Match of 1930 was his greatest of all innings, and in 1934 he had terminated a rare spell of bad form and ill-fortune with a hundred in under the hour against Middlesex. This latter event was prompted by advice from Pat Hendren "to have a go" when an uncertain start seemed to presage further failure.

The side he led off must rank as the most successful Australian side to visit this country and one of the greatest. Had O'Reilly operated on the field instead of in the Press box it would have had claims to be *the* greatest, but when one introduces such trans-positional "ifs" it opens a very wide and speculative field.

The Gentlemen and Players match was given additional distinction in being played as a Celebration Match for W. G. Grace. There was some spirited play worthy of the occasion, and the Players, set 233 to win in 145 minutes, did so by seven wickets. The prospect was a distant one when the first hour brought only 70 runs, but, aided by Compton and Crapp, Hutton routed the amateur bowling, to finish 132 not out. Here, surely, is another matter for limitless speculation. Temperament, background, and circumstances combined to mould Hutton so that he is remembered as a player of superb and precise defence, watchful and enduring, accumulating runs from every mistake the attack might make, but seldom dominating and disrupting. But those who have had a glimpse of the dazzling series of strokes he could produce when impelled to do so can only wonder what his career might have been had he played for Sussex as an amateur.

Middlesex descended to third place in the Championship, but gave the Lord's crowds plenty of fine, spirited cricket. F. G. Mann had succeeded Robins and proved an ideal captain. Less dynamic than his predecessor, he was a leader who automatically gained the affection of his side by his warmth and consideration, and their utmost respect by his fibre and quiet strength. Like his father, who was now President, he was the most selfless captain, without thought of anything but the interests of his side and its individual members. Under his leadership Middlesex once again set a wonderfully gay and entertaining standard of cricket. Compton, Edrich, and Robertson all averaged over fifty runs an innings, but more notable was the spirited way in which they invariably obtained them. Robins, relieved of the responsibilities of office, played a dozen matches with great success, making a hundred against Kent at Dover. Young, Gray, and Sims bowled well, although no one succeeded in topping the 100 wickets. In May Edrich (168) and Compton (252) had an unbroken stand of 424 for the third wicket against Somerset at Lord's, an English record created with such expedition that Mann was able to declare with fifty minutes left for play on the first day.

Oxford were a well-balanced team this season, and won the University Match by an innings and 8 runs. The Cambridge batting was destroyed in the first instance by some good seam bowling by Whitcombe, who took seven for 51 in an innings of 209, and came apart on the last day against the googlies of Van Ryneveld, whose seven wickets cost 57. Webb, twelfth man the previous year, made 145, batting at No. 6, and Mallett hit freely at No. 9 to make 57, and Oxford declared at 361 for nine wickets.

Two prominent figures who had close associations with Lord's died in 1948. Sir Timothy O'Brien and Sir C. Aubrey Smith had originally met when they played against each other in the University Match of 1884. From there both had proceeded to distinguished careers in the wider fields of cricket, and were notable personalities in their differing ways. Sir Timothy was a dashing, fiery Irishman who left a series of diverting legends about his robust and outspoken altercations with various worthy opponents, including the brothers Grace themselves. The Surrey authorities, doubtless in self-defence, sought to bar him from the Oval after a Bank holiday scene, but this ban he immediately circumvented by entering the Pavilion under the sponsorship of a Surrey member who happened to be his butler. When his great active days with England and Middlesex were done he remained a stout supporter of Middlesex and a benevolent and frequent visitor to Lord's.

C. Aubrey Smith had a remarkable career as a cricketer but an even more remarkable success in his profession. He bowled his off-breaks from an oblique carving run-up from the region of mid-off, an idiosyncrasy which earned him the nickname of "Round-the-corner" Smith. He had much success for Sussex, and led Shrewsbury's team in Australia in 1887 and captained England against South Africa in 1888–89. He was a handsome, upstanding man and a matinée idol, but by his mid-sixties his cricket and stage successes were at an end, his future seemingly precarious. The legend runs that a fellow-actor suggested that he might try this "bioscope" (although the narrator may have used the word to give colour to his tale). Smith was said to have demurred, saying he had done so before without conspicuous success. "Well," rejoined his adviser, "at least you have nothing to lose."

The sequel is well known to cricketers and cinemagoers alike. Smith was an immediate success in Hollywood, where, constantly employed, he embarked on a second and wholly triumphant career. When he returned to England in 1938 he was rich, renowned, and doyen of the English colony in Hollywood. There he played and fostered the game he loved, and when Gubby Allen stayed with him caught a blinding slip catch off his guest's bowling at the age of seventy-four.

Such was his importance as a film star that he was able to stipulate in his English contract that he should be released from duty each time the Australians played at Lord's. Which leads to another tale, the moral of which is that cricket is the truest democracy and most effective leveller of human beings. His presence on top of the Lord's Pavilion was born in on two mature members when he made some telling comments on the play. Presently one turned to the other. "Who's this fella with the loud voice?" he enquired. His companion scrutinized this world-famous figure for some moments. "Hm," he said. "Fella named Smith— used to play for Sussex."

D

6

The Games and the Players 1949

WITH the approach of the fifties the number of cricketing nations accorded Test Match status had increased to six. Whilst the increasing popularity of the game in the Commonwealth was in every way an admirable development it posed certain problems for the English cricket authorities, as representing the origin and centre of the international organization. Until the War there had been ample resources to deal with the demands of visiting sides to this country and provide teams for the return tours overseas. Australia and, to a lesser extent, South Africa had been the two major powers, calling for the full available strength whether at home or overseas. West Indies, New Zealand, and India had been doughty opponents, especially on their own pitches, but in these cases England could put adequate sides into the field, without calling on all their top players. Thus Test Match players were fairly fully employed without being overworked.

The lesser powers played three Test Matches, and, as these were limited to three days apiece, there was comparatively little disturbance to the domestic programme. But the New Zealand team was scheduled to play four Test Matches in 1949. These were still limited to three days, but it was agreed that West Indies would play four of four days in 1950, as would India in 1952.

It was said that the New Zealanders, disappointed that they had not been given four-day Test Matches, were determined to demonstrate that they could not be beaten in three days. Whether this was so or not, the series turned out to be a rather dull, defensive affair of four draws. An attempt was made during the season to extend the last two matches by a day, but, with the programme already agreed, the New Zealand authorities felt they were unable to make the extensive alterations necessary to achieve this.

The New Zealanders' match against M.C.C. in May attracted 28,000 spectators on the first day, but the play foreshadowed that of the Test Matches. The tourists bowled accurately to a deep-set and very efficient field, and the home side were always in check in making 379. Burtt, a precise slow-medium left-hander, governed the scoring rate by bowling just on sixty overs for 98 runs and six wickets. When the New Zealanders had made 313 at roughly the same pace only three and a half hours' play was left, and rain came to reduce this to one hour.

The second Test Match was played in June at Lord's on a perfect wicket, which, after a fairly lively start, seemed to grow more placid as the game proceeded. Neither side had any very penetrative bowling in the circumstances, and England, winning the toss, batted twice, to declare at 313 for nine and 306 for five. New Zealand made 484 in their one innings. From these figures it may be judged that there was little excitement concerning the outcome, but at least the large crowds were rewarded by some attractive batting on each of the three days.

In England's first innings Compton made 116. He took a little under four hours, which was very leisurely going for him, but no innings he ever played could be described as dull. When he had done Sutcliffe gave the New Zealanders a brisk start by making 57 in an hour and a half, after which Donnelly dominated the scene to score 206. Like Compton, he was slightly out of character in playing a solid and watchful innings, rather than giving rein to his natural bent for stroke play. In his case this was a matter of policy. His fellow left-hander, Sutcliffe, was in sparkling but variable form in this season, and Donnelly willingly assumed the role of the solid key-stone around which the batting was built. If it was an enforced and alien mood he did not complain, and demonstrated what a fine, solid defence complemented his power of stroke. On the final day Jack Robertson completed the entertainment with 121 played at almost exactly the same tempo as that of the other two centurions.

Unlike the Test Match, the Gentlemen v. Players match not only achieved a result, but was enlivened by violent fluctuations which kept the outcome in doubt until the last half-hour's play. The Gentlemen had a batting order so evenly graded on paper that S. C. Griffith batted at No. 11. Against some good bowling by Hollies, Perks, Jackson, and Close, most ably manœuvred by Denis Compton, the Gentlemen certainly batted evenly, but with a general indifference which mustered no more than 105 all told. To this the Players replied with 234, to which Close contributed 65. The Gentlemen were still 44 runs behind when their fifth second-innings wicket fell, and it seemed that they might well go down by an innings. But Van Ryneveld, Mann, and Bailey batted with such spirit that the total reached 267. Set a gentle exercise of 139 runs on a wicket unmarred by a few showers of rain, the Players lost their six leading batsmen for 69. It was left to Jenkins and Evans to rescue their fortunes, which they did with an admirable unbroken stand of 70 in 40 minutes. It was largely Evans's match, for he let only eight byes in taking five catches and making two stumpings.

Cambridge won the University Match by the comfortable margin of seven wickets. They batted consistently until early Monday morning to make 359, after which Warr and Wait were soon amongst the Oxford batsmen. Van Ryneveld as captain and mainstay of his side was run out at this critical moment, and Oxford followed on 190 behind. At the second attempt they batted very respectably, but the lead of 133 which they finally established was not sufficient to enable their bowlers to make a real fight of it.

Middlesex again gave their supporters at Lord's a fine season's cricket, to emerge joint Champions with Yorkshire. In the early spell, when, as usual, they played uninterruptedly at Lord's, apart from a visit to Oxford, they had the high proportion of six draws out of nine matches. This was due chiefly to high scoring on both sides, although rain did interfere with several matches. Compton celebrated the occasion of his Benefit match with 182 against Sussex, which *Wisden* described as "one of the best innings of his distinguished career". When he had done his brother Leslie lent a fraternal hand with a hard-hit 59 not out. The veteran John Langridge then made 139 in the second Sussex innings, which ensured that this match was amongst the draws.

Returning to Lord's, Middlesex were beaten by Surrey in late August, but won the other three matches, the last win, against Derby, establishing them at the top with Yorkshire. There was a mild sensation in the Lord's Pavilion and the Press-box during this final game. Gladwin, of Derby, returning to the dressing-room after being run out, cast his bat away in a moment of irritation. Great was his embarrassment when, with a sharp crash of broken glass, it disappeared through the nearest window.

In 1949 Lord's lost a number of loyal servants and adherents. Lord Cobham was, as all Lytteltons, a cricketer in every sense of the term. He was an ex-President and, at the time of his death, Treasurer of M.C.C. He had played cricket wholeheartedly, if with less success than some of his relations, and he had been as keen and untiring a President of Worcestershire as he was of M.C.C.

Mr Stanley Christopherson had been a fast bowler of lively pace in the eighties. He met with much success for Kent, played for the Gentlemen, and his one Test Match was against Australia at Lord's in 1884. With the years he became a considerable figure in the City, and was eventually a War-time Chairman of the Midland Bank. From 1939 to 1946 he was President of the M.C.C., which is the longest span in the history of the Club. With Sir Pelham Warner he worked indefatigably to keep cricket going in the face of every sort of difficulty, through all the dangers, shortages, and problems of that time. As he was then entering his eighties and Sir Pelham was not far behind their energy and efficiency were testimony to their devotion to the game and the Club.

Arthur Fielder, of Kent and England, died in St Thomas's Hospital. Perhaps amongst his parting memories was a day in July of 1906 when he took all ten wickets in the Gentlemen and Players match at Lord's. His record stands alone to this day and, considering that Jessop batted at No. 8, was created against some worthy opposition. Not the least remarkable feature was that his side lost the match. In this misfortune he may have felt some bond of sympathy with his second victim of the innings, P. A. Perrin, who two years previously had made 343 not out against Derbyshire and also managed to finish on the losing side.

7

Welcoming New Heroes and Commemorating the Fallen

1950 was the summer of the West Indians. Seldom has a new decade been ushered in by the visit of a team who individually and collectively so wholly captivated the public's imagination. It was not just their skill—and they were superlatively skilful—which impressed; it was even more their refreshingly uninhibited approach to the game. For them every match seemed a delight, to be entered into with zest. A famous cricketer of earlier years, having watched Worrell and Weekes batting in the Lord's Test, declared delightedly, "It took me back to 1912; that's how the great players batted then." And when, at Lord's, they had their first Test victory in England their supporters invaded the ground with unrestrained joy, celebrating such a great happening with an impromptu steel band; so the calypso *Cricket, Lovely Cricket* was born. By repute their strength lay in batting—"the three Ws" were already famous—but it was the wholly unpredicted dominance of two hitherto unknown but henceforth famous spin bowlers, "my little pals" Ramadhin and Valentine, which overwhelmed their opponents.

West Indies were the first non-Australian visiting team to play five-day Tests in England, but the matches continued to start on a Saturday. So when His Majesty the King was present at Lord's on Saturday, June 24, he saw the opening day. The receipts at that match amounted to £35,293, and the team took home a handsome profit of £30,000.

Appropriately, Prince Philip nominated as his successor to the Presidency Sir Pelham Warner, Trinidad-born and brother of the captain of the first West Indies team in England. No greater friend and admirer of the cricketers of the Caribbean could have been chosen. His enjoyment of the way they played their cricket was barely tempered by their decimation of England's cricketers.

When the Imperial Cricket Conference met at Lord's during the

Test the principal business concerned the status of India. Since Partition she had remained in the Conference as a provisional member pending a decision regarding her position in the British Commonwealth. Now that she had elected to remain in the Commonwealth, and since it was clear that separation had not materially affected the standard of play of representative teams selected by her Board—membership depending on this criterion—there was no longer any reason for witholding the privilege of full membership. The Indian representative, Mr de Mello, announced that Pakistan had made it quite clear that it would not be possible for her to join with India in a strong All-India subcontinental Test unit. The newly formed Board of Control for Cricket in Pakistan had been given full information about the rules of entry to the I.C.C., but they took the view that, as a former part of a member nation, her entry should be automatic. That the other nations decided that she must wait until her cricketing status was clarified and the rules complied with caused bitter disappointment in Pakistan. Seeing that this had become a political issue, the members felt it necessary, in redrafting the rules, to stress the original object of the Conference: the establishment of a purely cricket body of which the primary function had been and would be to determine the Test Match status of cricket-playing countries in the British Commonwealth on the simple basis of cricket skill, and that it should not be concerned with any matter outside the actual conduct of international cricket.

Middlesex in 1950 had a lean season and dropped to fourteenth place in the Championship. Returning to lead the side through a transitional period, Walter Robins predicted before the season started that they would not have enough talent to do well. The well-tried opening pair of Robertson and Brown wavered, with Brown descending in the batting order. Both Compton and Edrich were absent for long periods, Compton for two months between May and July for a third operation on his right knee, and Edrich for a month in July with a strained back. But among the twenty-four players who appeared at one time or another were three colts of whom more was to be heard. Alan Moss played only once, and his four wickets cost him 307 runs, but here was the fast bowler Middlesex needed to take the place of Laurie Gray. Don Bennett at sixteen showed promise of quality and all-round ability which was to make him an invaluable county player without ever achieving his potential in wider fields. The third was the seventeen-year-old Fred Titmus, who, as an off-break bowler and middle-

order batsman, would become an automatic choice for England
and join J. T. Hearne, the only other Middlesex man in the distinguished company of those who have captured 2000 wickets. In
the absence of Robins from eighteen matches, as many as six
players deputized as skipper, from whom Edrich and Compton
were appointed joint captains for the following season.

Once more, with a M.C.C. tour in prospect, interest focused on
an Australian summer, and newspapers headlined doubts about
the England captaincy and the state of Denis Compton's knee.
Both Norman Yardley, the reigning captain, and George Mann
were unable to tour, but an obvious alternative candidate, whose
forthright leadership of Northamptonshire singled him out as far
more worthy than mere third choice, was at hand in the person of
F. R. Brown. His captaincy in Australia, as in Northants, was outstanding, and though they could not bring home the Ashes, the
team's record, culminating in a decisive victory in the final Test,
demonstrated at last a real resurgence of English cricket. For the
first time a professional, Denis Compton, was appointed vice-
captain of a M.C.C. touring team. The surgeons had given him a
clean bill after his operation in June, but continued pain caused
much anxiety, not least when, on arrival in Australia, the knee was
found to be swollen. The anxiety was partially allayed by a
masterly century at Perth, but he had to stand down from the
second Test and, though he made runs in lesser matches, his Test
record was miserable. So the main burden of run-making fell again
on Hutton. In the early Tests he moved down the batting order to
strengthen the middle of the innings, leaving R. T. Simpson to
open with Washbrook. The most disappointing aspect of the tour
was the comparative failure of the younger batsmen. This team was
physically no less fragile than its predecessors, and in January
reinforcements, in the persons of Roy Tattersall and Brian Statham,
were flown out from Lancashire. In New Zealand the twenty-
year-old Statham, embarking on a career of seventy Tests, made
Bert Sutcliffe the first of his 252 victims. It was Bedser, with thirty
Tests wickets in Australia and thirteen more in New Zealand, who
dominated the bowling, ably supported by Bailey and the skipper,
whose reversion to medium-paced swing bowling from his normal
leg breaks earned him eighteen Australian wickets.

When the Australian leg of the tour was completed the President,
Sir Pelham Warner, issued this message:

I should like to congratulate Australia on retaining the Ashes. As
they have so generously acknowledged, good fortune has not been

with us. I think everyone would like to pay a tribute to Brown's inspiring leadership and to his success on the field. Though beaten he may well claim that he and his men surrendered with all the honours of war.

During the summer of 1950 I had the privilege of arranging for the National Book League in the beautiful house in Albemarle Street which is their headquarters an exhibition of cricket books and manuscripts, supplemented by pictorial records of the game. Never before had so representative a collection of rare and interesting items been exhibited to the public, and His Majesty King George VI headed a list of distinguished collectors, authors, and publishers who generously contributed loan exhibits. The exhibit from the Royal Collection was a charming eighteenth-century *gouache* painting by Louis Bélanger, which was once on long-term loan to M.C.C. The Mayor and Corporation of Guildford contributed their *Book of Court*, containing the evidence of John Derrick that he played cricket near the Grammar School around 1550, and documents of the seventeenth century testified to the lawlessness, not to say violence, of cricketers who desecrated the Sabbath or defaulted in paying their wagers. The very large contribution from the M.C.C. Library included the earliest surviving minute book of the Committee, begun in the hand of Benjamin Aislabie after the great fire of 1825. The exhibition was opened by the President, Sir Pelham Warner, who, ever a jealous guardian of traditional courtesy, profited by the occasion and the presence of Mr Arlott (in his literary hat) to take issue with radio commentators for encouraging what he took to be the deplorable modern usage of Christian names—a protest which drew a persuasive defence from John Arlott, cricket commentator. Sir Pelham was probably the last man to appear "properly dressed" in tails and top-hat at the Varsity Match. He eventually conceded defeat on that score, but I doubt very much that his old-world dignity would ever have permitted him to fall in with today's universal familiarity of Tom, Dick, or Harry.

When the end of the War was in sight the M.C.C. Committee had decided that, as a memorial to the cricketers of every land who had given their lives in the two world wars, a gallery should be built in which cricket's heritage as represented by historic pictures and relics of every kind should be exhibited to the public and preserved for posterity. Overseas cricket boards were enthusiastic, and by 1951 promises were high that work might commence on Mr John Markham's designs for a conversion of the disused

Rackets Court. But hopes were dashed when it was found that in the interval of waiting for a building licence the cost of the plan had rocketed so far above the estimates that it was feared the whole project might have to be abandoned. The National Book League Exhibition had drawn attention to the importance of the Library and the pressing need to accommodate it. The original intention had been that a library should form an integral part of the Memorial, but since it now seemed almost certain that this part of the scheme would have to be dropped, the Committee agreed that the old general office, where Jimmy Cannon had once reigned, should be decorated and furnished with bookcases. The cultural side of the Club's activities was further in evidence in the summer of 1951, when the Festival of Britain was celebrated throughout the land to mark the centenary of the Great Exhibition. M.C.C. contributed with advice and loans to the displays illustrating cricket and tennis, both "real" and lawn, at the great exhibition on the South Bank and to the exhibition of books at the Victoria and Albert Museum. Cricketwise the occasion was celebrated at Lord's by a Gentlemen *v.* Players match, to which *Wisden*, praising centuries by Compton and May, and Compton's final catch in extra time to secure victory for the Players, accorded the *cachet* of "worthy of its great traditions". Fortuitously, in a summer dedicated to parading British tradition, M.C.C. honoured the founder of their ground by the renewal of the leger stone which marks his grave in West Meon churchyard in Hampshire.

The year had opened with weighty considerations of administration. Following the staff reorganization of 1950, a special sub-committee appointed to review the higher organization of M.C.C. now presented a report which led to a rationalization and re-organization of the Committee and its sub-committees, with a reduction in the period of consecutive service of Committee members from four years to three, a reduction in the number of Trustees, and the end of honorary auditors. Perhaps most important was a modification in the procedure for the appointment of the President so that, instead of being required to take the chair at the moment of his nomination at the Annual General Meeting, he would have five months as President-elect before taking office on October 1. The reigning President was Mr William Findlay, a former Secretary, who thus held office a little longer than the allotted span before handing over to his chosen successor, the Duke of Beaufort. In an organization where the Presidential nomination is a close secret, by long tradition locked in the breast of his predecessor, the new procedure was a practical modification which has been of great benefit, particularly if the new President has not previously served on the Committee.

The pruning of capital expenditure in 1949 and the subsequent increase in members' subscriptions had not removed the Committee's financial anxieties; the 1950 accounts showed a deficit of £2637. Cricket, like the housewife, was feeling the effects of the spiral in the cost of living, which at Lord's, even with the utmost economy, had risen by 25 per cent since 1947 and promised an even sharper increase to more than double that amount in the foreseeable future. In simple terms the Committee had to find means to bridge an estimated future annual deficit of £13,500. They rejected the superficially easy solution of raising the subscriptions to £6 because, coming so soon after the previous increase, they felt a fresh rise would cause resignations and bear hard on the younger members and on those who used the Club least. However, at the A.G.M. approval was obtained for an increase in the number of members, bringing the quota up to a ceiling of 8000, to be reached gradually over a period of five years. Middlesex too were allowed an increase from 1500 to 2000 members on the understanding that the capitation fee on all their members should be raised from 10s. to 15s. and that they should be prepared to review the terms of their agreement at any time at the request of M.C.C.

The most far-reaching outcome of the financial review was that, in line with the times, the Committee decided to seek the approval of the members to break the restrictions which compelled the Trustees to hold the Club's funds in gilt-edged securities. At a Special General Meeting in November the members gave the Committee the power to employ a firm of financial advisers and, by adopting a less conservative policy, secure elasticity in handling the Club's investments which would offer opportunities for capital appreciation. At the same meeting the members formally approved the inauguration of the M.C.C. Youth Cricket Association with a capital grant of £15,000 to be operated under the auspices of King George's Jubilee Trust.

In May the long-drawn-out case of Bolton v. Stone came to a stately conclusion in the House of Lords, with final judgment given in favour of the defendants, the Committee of the Cheetham Hill Cricket Club. This was a test case in which M.C.C. had been actively interested. Its history began on August 9, 1947, when Miss Bessie Stone, standing in the highway outside her house in Cheetham Hill, was hit by a ball struck out of the ground of the adjacent Cricket Club. The hit—100 yards over a seven-foot fence —was said to be quite exceptional, and when the case was heard at the quarter-sessions Mr Justice Oliver acquitted the defendants of Miss Stone's charge of negligence and held that the alternative charge of nuisance was not established. Miss Stone had then taken the case to the Court of Appeal, who had reversed the decision, giving judgment that a public nuisance had not been established but that the defendants, knowing that balls had been hit over the fence, owed a duty to take reasonable care to prevent injury to users of the highway and that they had failed to exercise the care which the circumstances demanded and were therefore liable for damages for negligence. The case, involving as it did the possibility that clubs playing on every village green could be held liable for compensation to any spectator or passer-by, aroused much interest. M.C.C., the National Club Cricket Association, as well as the Football Association and the Association of Municipal Associations, were all sufficiently concerned to give moral support and financial backing to the Cheetham Cricket Club when, with Sir Walter Monckton and Mr W. A. Sime acting for them, they were successful in getting their appeal upheld in the House of Lords.

The South Africans were the visiting tourists, with Dudley Nourse as captain and "Tufty" Mann bowling his left-arm spinners in his last series before he broke down on the eve of the final Test and died so tragically and so prematurely less than a year later. Mann was not the only casualty: with Athol Rowan's knee continually suspect and Nourse's thumb broken early in the tour, the side were more affected by injury than most. They did not have a great match record, but they returned well rewarded, enriched financially to the tune of £17,500 and having, in such players as McLean, Waite, McGlew, Van Ryneveld, and Endean, discovered a fund of talent which would soon create a South African cricket boom. The team had been honoured by a visit from the King during the M.C.C. match in May; at the Lord's Test Princess Elizabeth deputized for him and greeted the players during the tea interval on the second day. The system of beginning five-day Tests on a Thursday began this year, and the Lord's Test was virtually over when the South Africans were all out at lunch-time on Saturday; indeed, Alec Bedser, forgetting that England had 16 runs to make, made a premature grab for the stumps, sensing perhaps that the days of trophy-grabbing were numbered, for the tradition was discontinued after 1951. The friendly game put on to entertain the large crowd after England had made the winning hit at 2.20 P.M. was played in a holiday mood of high comedy bordering on farce. I have always held that during his innings Len Hutton chanced his arm and his wicket to play, at the Pavilion end, against whose bowling I am unable to remember, a copybook early Victorian draw stroke, straight from *Felix on the Bat.*

Middlesex, now under the joint captaincy of Edrich and Compton, rose from their lowly position to a respectable seventh in the Championship table, with Compton starting the season in high form and making a bid for the coveted thousand runs in May; Robertson batting immaculately—was there ever a better opener who played so seldom for England?—and his partner, Sid Brown, producing a truly wonderful 232 not out against Somerset at Lord's.

In June a great Anglophile and lover of cricket, Fares Sarofeem Bey, brought an Egyptian team to Lord's and lost to M.C.C. by four wickets. Sarofeem Bey commemorated the occasion by presenting a showcase for the Long Room, to be transferred later to the Memorial Gallery. In August M.C.C. beat the Flamingos by nine wickets, but they had rather the worse of a washed-out draw against the Gentlemen of Ireland, for whom E. D. Shearer made 101 not out. R. Aird, in his silver jubilee year as Assistant Secretary at Lord's, opened the batting for the Club.

In August R. W. V. Robins led a M.C.C. team of fourteen amateurs on a three weeks' tour of Canada—the first since 1937. The team brought enormous pleasure and encouragement to Canadian cricketers, and they delighted their hosts by their aggressive play. M.C.C. were easy victors in the two representative matches, played at Vancouver, on the beautiful Brockton Point ground, and at Toronto.

The winter season of 1951–52 brought the postponed visit to India, Pakistan, and Ceylon, but, as for the West Indies tour of 1947–48, it was impossible to collect an English team that was at full strength; the Lancashire captain, Nigel Howard, led a side which lacked some of the top stars, notably Hutton, Compton, and Bedser. India made history for herself by winning the final Test, comprehensively, by an innings, with England discomfited by the bowling of Mankad, who took eight for 55 in the first innings, and India, with centuries from Roy and Umrigar, amassing a great score. With England winning the fourth Test at Kanpur and the other three matches drawn, honours were even. Pakistan derived much joy and elation by their defeat of M.C.C. in the unofficial 'Test' at Lahore; this was a personal triumph for Fazal Mahmood,

whose break-backs and leg cutters on the matting wicket confounded the English batsmen; also for the sixteen-year-old Hanif,
whose imperturbable batting against Shackleton, Statham, and
Tattersall on the fiery wicket ensured his team's victory. At
Colombo, in the final match of the tour, M.C.C. were completely
outclassed by a Commonwealth eleven in which the cricketers of
India, Pakistan, and Ceylon were reinforced by Neil Harvey,
Keith Miller, and Graeme Hole. The result was defeat by an
innings and 259 runs!

Two members who died in 1951 must surely rank as "characters"—great in different ways. Lionel Lord Tennyson is a famous
cricket personality, and my friend Ian Peebles has written about
him. Less famous but as great a personality was the nonagenarian
Billy Williams. Not only was he one of the most versatile players
who ever stepped on to a cricket field, but for the longevity of his
career he might have laid claim to Tom Walker's nickname, "Old
Everlasting". His association with Lord's began as a Middlesex
wicket-keeper in 1885-86. Then, after an absence of fourteen
years, he reappeared as a leg-break bowler, having in the interval
toured the West Indies with Sir Arthur Priestley's team. In 1934,
now seventy-four years old, he played for M.C.C. against Lords
and Commons at Lord's and took the wickets of Lord Dalkeith,
Lord Tennyson, and Major Lloyd George for 16 runs, and then
retired, having, reputedly at least, taken 100 wickets in every one
of the last fifty-five seasons of his long career. The ball with which
he secured his three parliamentary scalps, suitably mounted with a
silver shield, is now in a glass case at Lord's.

At the end of the year my father told the Committee that he
wished to retire before the end of 1952. He was now past his sixtieth
birthday, and his health had suffered from the strain which the
burden and anxieties of the ever more complex pattern of cricket
administration now imposed. He had been determined to see
through the administrative reorganization of the last few years and
had wanted to see the recommendations of the Cricket Enquiry
put into effect by the formation of the Youth Cricket Association.
These objectives having been achieved, he felt the time had come
to hand over to a younger man. He had come to Lord's in July
1936, appropriately, as an ex-Sapper, taking over the reins from
Mr Findlay on the day of the Gunner v. Sapper match, in which he
had often played. During his sixteen years' tenure of office it was
perhaps his most important task to prepare the draft of the new
Code of the Laws, which became effective in 1948, and its prepara-

tion led him to make a deep study of their history. For me as his daughter to assess his stature as Secretary is not possible. Sir Pelham Warner wrote in typically graceful and generous terms of his administrative ability and his industry. I believe Sir Pelham was mistaken on one point—a hint that he found it hard to delegate. It is my judgment that, while he always kept a firm hand on the tiller, he did in fact delegate a good deal to those under him, expecting from them the same high standard he demanded of himself. Provided the goods were delivered, he did not interfere; failure demanded an explanation, which, if reasonable, was accepted. In return for the loyalty that was demanded of them the staff always knew that they could rely on his complete loyalty to them.

For his farewell speech to the county secretaries in December 1951 he took as his subject the growing incidence of drawn matches, which, in his judgment, transcended all the ills which currently beset county cricket. By means of a graph he demonstrated the parallel between finished matches and attendances which, since 1947, had moved up and down the chart in almost exact partnership to a record "low" in 1951, when the percentage of drawn games reached 50 per cent, as compared with 25 per cent in 1947. The speech culminated with a plea to county committees to encourage their captains and players to heed a dictum of A. G. Steel, in 1900, that cricket must be eager, quick, and full of action.

The choice of Ronny Aird as the new Secretary was a foregone conclusion and a highly popular appointment. Appointed Assistant Secretary under Mr Findlay in 1926, soon after he came down from Cambridge, he had served an apprenticeship of almost twenty-six years, endearing himself to members and staff alike. Because of his charm and delightfully easy manner he was often thought to be easygoing, but while the charm was of the genuinely deep-rooted and rare kind that never cracks, it none the less masked experienced judgment and firmness in principles which really mattered. To complete the new team and fill the vacancy for an Assistant Secretary in charge of cricket, the present Secretary, Mr S. C. Griffith, was appointed early in 1952 to join the staff in October.

8

The Games and the Players 1950

AFTER the benevolence of the warm, dry summer of 1949 the cricket season of 1950 was, by way of contrast, one of rain and cloud. This was unfortunate because a visiting side as fascinating as Bradman's Australian side toured the country. Although they had been successful in their own country West Indies had as yet to win a Test Match in England. Three tours had been undertaken, in 1928, 1933, and 1939, on each of which the team had proved enormously popular, bringing to the game an unaffected joy and volatility which delighted the sober English crowds. Great individual players had emerged, but until the War the team had never seemed collectively to be geared to the top Test Match standards —again outside their home grounds. When M.C.C. toured in 1947-48 they found the opposition extremely strong, and lost decisively to a side which, given a little more bowling strength, had the makings of greatness. The strongest hopes were Weekes, Worrell, and Walcott, three exceptional batsmen.

When West Indies came to Lord's on May 20 they had already beaten Yorkshire, and Weekes, in his last two innings, had made 232 at the Oval and 304 not out at Cambridge. The Lord's pitch being on the soft side, Goddard put M.C.C. in to bat, and, against some fine left-hand spin from Valentine, the total reached only 188, of which Edrich made 64. West Indies did no better, and were 18 behind on first innings. The home side did fairly well in their second innings, and, set 266 to win, West Indies collapsed against Sims and were beaten by 118 runs. At this point the prospect of winning their first series in England seemed remote.

The prospect was even further removed when, on a strange, dusty pitch at Old Trafford in early June, England won the first Test Match by 202 runs. Valentine always looked dangerous, taking ten wickets in the match, but Ramadhin, who was attracting increasing attention, had to be content with four rather expensive wickets, his bag in the first innings being Nos. 10 and 11 for 90 runs.

TOURIST TRAVEL OLD STYLE
The 1954–55 M.C.C. team on board the *Orsova*. They brought back the
Ashes from Australia.

**TOURIST TRAVEL
NEW STYLE**
The 1967 M.C.C.
team leave for the
West Indies. They
recovered the
Wisden Trophy.

R. W. V. ROBINS
A great Middlesex captain.

THREE MUSKETEERS
J. D. Robertson, W. J. Edrich, D. C. S. Compton.

Thus it was in confident mood that England took the field on June 24 at Lord's for the second Test Match. By early Monday morning they had dispatched the opposition for 326, and Hutton and Washbrook had little difficulty with the modest new-ball attack. When the slow bowlers came on there were no immediate signs of danger, but at 62 Hutton went down the wicket to Valentine and was stumped. The next hour's cricket was one of the most revealing ever seen at Lord's.

Edrich was at once in difficulty with Ramadhin, and as the batsmen's confidence ebbed, so did the bowler's increase. In the course of the next few overs his status advanced from unproven possibility to major problem. He bowled a beautiful flight and length, and it was soon apparent that neither batsman could pick the direction of his spin. Washbrook, ostensibly well set, played at three balls in succession and failed to touch one. Obviously baffled, he walked out and gave the pitch a thoughtful prod, to be informed by a deep Caribbean bass voice that this was not the cause of his troubles—it was "de bolah"—a concise appreciation.

The overs dragged along, a dozen runs came in more than an hour, then uninterrupted disaster. At 74 Washbrook was stumped. Doggart, playing in his first Test Match, could hardly have chosen a worse moment. He made his entry, having sat for an hour watching two of England's leading batsmen reduced to impotence by a type of bowling which he himself did not particularly favour. Before he had scored he was deceived into an attempted sweep, and lbw to Ramadhin. Parkhouse was bowled for nought by Valentine, and Edrich's trying 60 minutes was ended by a catch off Ramadhin. Nine wickets were down for 122, and it was left to Wardle to swing the bat and raise the score to 151, he being undefeated with 33.

Given a lead by Weekes and Worrell, who made 63 and 45, the West Indian batsmen then showed their true form, and the match was soon beyond England's grasp. When Walcott was dropped at 9 it was the last stage at which there might have been a battle, but, as he went on to make 168 not out and, with Gerry Gomez, set a new sixth-wicket record of 211, England were left to get 600. To this end they batted very much better than at the first attempt, and with one day left had six wickets in hand. Washbrook had made a splendid 114 not out, but, after 20 unproductive minutes on the following morning, was bowled by Ramadhin. The later batsmen were once more unequal to the West Indian spin, and

E

the innings ended at 274. Wardle again hit bravely, but the margin of defeat was 326.

West Indies had won their first Test Match in England, and there were tumultuous scenes as the last English wicket fell. Their numerous supporters rushed on to the ground and towards the Pavilion, where a line of policemen suddenly, and rather unnecessarily, appeared. The guitarists and calypso-singers burst into song—as well they might, with such a glorious concatenation as Ramadhin and Valentine to aid their lyrics.

When West Indies returned to Lord's in late August to play Middlesex they had trounced England in three Test Matches out of four, and established themselves as a leading cricket power. Their batting was comparable to the full strength of the Australians and, if they lacked anything as forceful as the Australian fast bowlers, the spin attack was the best combination of its kind in the world. The county gave them a very good run in a drawn game. Robertson made 105 out of a first innings of 311 and, although Ramadhin was rested, he had to cope with Valentine, who took five wickets. Christiani made a fine 131 not out in reply, which enabled his side to lead by 32 runs. Middlesex did well on a good, lasting pitch to declare at 209 for four. West Indies then lost three quick wickets, but Christiani, promoted to No. 1, immediately resumed his best form, so that when time was called at 148 for three he had made 100 not out. He reached his second hundred by hitting the last over of the match for 13, to become the second West Indian to make two centuries in a match at Lord's, George Headley having done so against England in 1939.

Once again the Gentlemen and Players had an exciting finish to an interesting game. When the Gentlemen's batting faltered F. R. Brown, their captain, came in at No. 8 to thrash the bowling for 110 minutes and make 122 out of the 131 runs scored in that time. Dollery, the opposing captain, made just one more in rather less impetuous style for the Players, who declared at 308 for nine, 17 behind the Gentlemen. The Gentlemen batted very briskly to declare at 235 for four, which gave the Players a very fair chance of getting 253 in two and a half hours to win.

The Players had got to 217 for three, and there were twenty minutes in hand, when an almost unaccountable collapse took place—precipitated by a hat-trick by Knott. In seventeen minutes six wickets fell, and Hollies, very much a No. 11, had to survive five balls. This he succeeded in doing, and the result was a draw. As 11 runs were still required it may be said, without disrespect to

Hollies or his partner Wright, that the position was rather in favour of the Gentlemen.

The University Match also ended in a draw, chiefly because of rain on the second day. With the advent of May and Sheppard, Cambridge could boast a leading quartet of batsmen, all of whom had played or would play for England, Dewes and Doggart already having done so. Apart from Sheppard, who made 93, however, they made little use of their first innings on a good wicket and were all out for 200. Oxford were only slightly beset by rain over the week-end, but batted even less effectively to make 169. When rain ceased and play was restarted late on Monday afternoon Oxford lost Van Ryneveld for a spell, owing to a cut eye, and Cambridge recovered sufficiently from a poor start to declare at 193 for seven the following day. Left 225 to win in just over two hours, Oxford had lost five wickets for 122 at the close. Carr brightened the closing hour by some fine hitting in making 55.

Middlesex's misfortune this season stemmed from a number of causes, of which the worst were the injuries to Compton's knee and Edrich's back. Sims still bowled well on occasion, but inevitably was losing some of his life and spin towards the end of a very long career. So long was his span, in fact, that he qualified for a second Benefit, which took place in June, when Yorkshire overwhelmed his side by 229 runs after declaring twice.

At least the spirit of Middlesex under Walter Robins was undimmed, and even in the prevailing adversity he maintained a lively, positive attitude whatever the state of the game. The chief complaint amongst Middlesex supporters was one of long standing. Owing to the commitments of Lord's to various long-established functions the permanent tenants were not seen there from the beginning of July to mid-August.

In March D. W. Carr, most successful of the English googly pioneers, died at the age of seventy-eight. He had reached almost half his allotted years when he first appeared in 1909 for Kent, with such dramatic success that he was picked for the Gentlemen v. Players match at Lord's. His six wickets for 71 in the first innings must have greatly enhanced his chances of playing for England in his first season, which he did in the last Test, at the Oval. His first wicket at Lord's was the great David Denton, who died just a month before he did.

Mr Charles Pilkington, who died in January, had been an actor in one of the more controversial and demonstrative scenes to take place at Lord's. He played as a freshman in the University Match of 1896. At this time the follow-on was compulsory, and, when Oxford looked like following on, Frank Mitchell, the Cambridge captain, caused 12 runs to be given away in byes in order to prevent them. There was intense feeling and some uproar at what was regarded as bordering on sharp practice. But it had sufficient effect to cause an alteration in the law. In the immediate circumstances it proved unavailing, for Oxford made 330 for 6, to win the day.

9

The Games and the Players 1951

A HAPPY event early in the year made an encouraging prelude to the English cricket season of 1951. In February at Melbourne England won a Test Match against Australia for the first time since 1938. It was the last in the series, and a very appropriate reward to F. R. Brown, who, as captain and cricketer in his own right, had surpassed all expectations in leading his side on the most arduous of all cricket tours at the age of forty. Loudest in his praise, and as delighted in his success as any, were the Australian Press and public. Australia was still King of the Castle, but Bedser had taken thirty wickets, Evans had kept to him superbly, as he had done to every other bowler, and, with a strong batting potential still developing and expanding, England had every reason for optimism.

The home season of 1951 did not, however, turn out to be particularly brilliant. In reviewing it the Editor of *Wisden* felt constrained to say that "The Summer of 1951 will go down into cricket history as one that did not set a high standard of play". Several factors may have contributed to this disappointing situation, but the combination of two attracts immediate attention. The weather, especially in the early stages, was miserable, and the South African tourists impressed the public as a solid, pedestrian batting side after the fluent pyrotechnics of "the three Ws" and the young Christiani.

Largely because of these two factors the South Africans had the rather negative record of twenty draws, five wins, and five losses in their first-class matches. In the series they got off to a good start by winning the first match at Trent Bridge, but thereafter lost three of the remaining four. There were two particularly popular figures in their midst. The team was managed by Syd Pegler, one of the great leg-break bowlers, and a very old friend and foe. And amongst the "new boys" was Geoff Chubb, who bowled fast medium with great zest and good nature, starting his Test career at the age of forty.

The South Africans were pretty weatherbeaten by the time they came to Lord's, on May 19, to meet M.C.C. Here they were greeted by a biting east wind and a damp and threatening sky. Bowled out by Tattersall for 190, they were led by 81 on the first innings. Compton made 147, being missed off Chubb four times when pressing on after his century. As Robertson made 51 and Brown 33, M.C.C.'s success to this stage had been somewhat selective, and little further was possible, as rain permitted only twenty minutes' play on the last day. At this point the South Africans were 97 for two in their second innings.

King George VI arrived just after the rain had settled down to continuous thundery torrent, and the teams were presented to him in the Committee Room. It was his last visit to Lord's.

The weather, which had lent South Africa some help towards their victory at Nottingham, had a fair hand in their downfall in the second Test Match at Lord's. On winning the toss for the only time in the series, Brown saw to it that his batsmen made the most of the amiable conditions on the first day. The South Africans, especially the left-handed Mann, bowled very accurately, but, thanks to Compton and Watson, England were all out for 311 just after six o'clock. Rain fell heavily in the night and, as in the M.C.C. match, the South Africans had to face Tattersall on a soft pitch. At first Eric Rowan played with such a fine defiance that it seemed his side might transcend this disadvantage, but at 47 he was most brilliantly caught by Ikin at short leg, and the batting from then on failed. In a total of 115 Tattersall took seven wickets for 52, a remarkably similar analysis to his eight for 51 in the M.C.C. match.

When, in the follow-on, South Africa had lost four wickets for 57 runs it was possible that the match might end on the second day. Cheetham and Fullerton then put up a good stand for the fifth wicket to play out time. When Statham bowled Cheetham next morning 94 runs had been added, but it proved to be the last serious resistance. Early in the afternoon England had made the 16 runs to win without losing a wicket. Thus the teams left Lord's all square and, apparently, with little to choose between them.

It was not until late August that the South Africans played Middlesex. The weather again affected the play, this time to the point of ruination. The South Africans batted well in the middle stages to make 297, Fullerton retrieving an indifferent start to be 89 not out. On the second day there was just over an hour and a half's play, and on the third none at all, so that, with Middlesex 136 for two, honours, as far as they extended, were even. It was a matter of much regret to all lovers of Lord's cricket ground that the newcomers should thrice have seen it in such dismal conditions.

Yet again the Gentlemen *v.* Players was a splendid cricket match. Not only was there abundance of good play, but Compton calculated his declaration with such prescience that his side won in the extra half-hour by just 21 runs. In fact, Compton had an altogether triumphant three days. He won the toss, made 150 in his very best vein in the first innings and 74 not out in the second. As the result of his efforts the Players made 361, the main supporter being Jack Robertson, with 80.

The Players had a good bowling side, led by Bedser and Statham, and two wickets had gone for 53 when May came in half an hour before lunch on the second day. He made 2 runs before the interval, but had a good look at the opposition in the process. In the afternoon he showed his true quality against the best professional bowling in making 119 not out. Here was a batsman in the finest orthodox tradition, his play founded on a straight-back lift and fine, cleaving sweep of the blade. The following week he was to go to Leeds to make a century in his first Test Match, thus amply fulfilling his coach George Geary's prophecy, made of him when he was fourteen.

The Players, leading by 60 runs, pushed on in their second innings, and Compton made his declaration at 188 for three, leaving the Gentlemen 244 to get in two and three-quarter hours, a very fair proposition. Responding to this challenge, Sheppard and Edrich put their side in a very promising way with 50 in half an hour, but Compton, who could do nothing wrong, called on Ikin. This gamble succeeded to the extent of defeating both batsmen and, with the return of Bedser, the Gentlemen were never from then on quite abreast of the situation.

Oxford were somewhat unexpected winners of the University Match. On their arrival at Lord's they had only succeeded in beating the Foresters, whilst Cambridge, with Sheppard, May, and Subba Row to bat, and Warr and Wait to bowl, looked a much likelier side. The one department in which Oxford excelled was in fielding, a talent which turned out to be a decisive factor in a low-scoring match.

Oxford batted first, but to no great purpose in making 178. Had the Cambridge batsmen produced their normal power they could easily have established an overwhelming advantage by the second day. But when May went for 30 the will seemed to go out of them, and the total reached only 168, of which 27 were extras. Boobbyer

made 80 and Carr 50 in Oxford's second innings of 208, but the
rest of the side were routed by Subba Row's "tweakers", his
analysis being an all-time best of five for 21. Cambridge should
have been equal to the task set them, but Divecha reverted to
off-spin on a wearing wicket with great success, and Oxford won
by 21 runs.

Middlesex had a better season, rising to seventh place in the
Championship. They were at their best at home, and five of their
eight victories were won at Lord's. They still laboured under
certain handicaps, the chief again being the uncertainty concerning
Compton's injured knee. Although there were several enterprising
players in the side nothing in the whole contemporary cricket
world could rival the carefree, unpredictable brilliance of a
Compton innings, where originality and enterprise were enhanced
by an ever-present streak of comedy. Robertson, always a very fine
county batsman, had a splendid season, rewarded by a satisfactory
Benefit match against Sussex during the Bank holiday.

Frank Tarrant died in his native Victoria in January 1951. He
had come to Lord's in 1903, completely unknown, to join the
ground staff, and by 1907 was described as the greatest all-round
cricketer in the country. Because of his early emigration Tarrant
never played for his country, which he would certainly have done
in other circumstances. After the First War he departed to India
and thence to Australia, but Lord's must ever be his spiritual
home.

In June Lionel Hallam Tennyson died at Bexhill. He was sixty-
one years old, and into almost every one of these he had crammed
a glorious mixture of triumph, disaster, and adventure. It was
typical of this enthralling and diverting career that its author
should be summoned to Lord's, amongst sixteen others, to provide
an England side in 1921. Selected against long odds, he batted with
a fine, *insouciant* courage, accompanied by the dash of good fortune
it deserved. From there he succeeded to the England captaincy. It
was said that amongst the onlookers was a friend who, in the
previous year, had laid him 1000 to one against receiving this
appointment. This friend was a man of strong nervous system
and survives, at the moment of writing, hale and hearty.

IO

Gloomy Predictions refuted by Coronation Victory

THE retiring Secretary's concern over the plight of county cricket was echoed by the A.C.C.C. when they met at Lord's in March 1952: Mr Altham, speaking on this occasion as representative of Hampshire, proposed that a Sub-committee be appointed to examine the state of county cricket and to recommend how best to meet the existing public demand for more attractive cricket and at the same time resolve the financial difficulties in which many county clubs found themselves. He reminded the county representatives of some words in the 1937 Findlay Report which were equally relevant in 1952 (and even more today): that, having regard to the cost involved, the appeal of the game to the public, except in a fine season, was not sufficient to make it self-supporting. The reasons for the dullness of cricket were the virtual disappearance of the amateur, the increase in the number and duration of Tests, with a resultant tempo and technique which was being copied in county and other cricket, and the preoccupation of batsmen with defence, largely dictated by bowlers. The remedies he suggested were fourfold; firstly, the paramount need for county committees and captains to convince their players that their livelihood depended on making the game attractive to the public; secondly, a re-examination of the lbw law; thirdly, reconsideration of the system of scoring points in the Championship; and, finally, a need for groundsmen to prepare faster pitches. The resolution was carried by a commanding majority, and the counties asked M.C.C. to collate and assess for further consideration suggestions submitted to them by the counties. The M.C.C. Cricket Sub-committee, equally depressed by the state of English cricket, gave wholehearted support to the A.C.C.C.'s decision to enquire how it should be improved. For themselves, serious consideration was given to possible amendments in the lbw law, in particular to Sir Donald Bradman's repeated proposals that, to encourage off-side play, the law should be extended to apply to balls pitching on the leg side. This view has never had as much support in England as the opposite suggestion to revert to the "old" law (which would limit lbw decisions to balls pitching between wicket and wicket), and the 1952 Cricket Committee were by no means convinced that it would have the effect anticipated by the Don. The cricket-ball industry had now at last arrived at a specification for an experimental ball measuring between $8\frac{11}{16}$ inches and $8\frac{13}{16}$ inches in circumference and of the same density as and therefore slightly lighter than the standard ball and with a thicker seam, and it was possible to envisage using these in Festival matches in 1953.

A forecast of the 75-yard boundary came from the counties; although M.C.C. did not then feel that a uniform boundary on every ground could be recommended, they agreed that there was no reason why individual counties should not experiment with shorter boundaries. Other points put forward by the counties were the desirability for faster pitches; discussion on the amendment of the scoring system, with the possible elimination of first-innings points; a compulsory declaration after six hours; and the introduction of regional matches to replace second matches by some counties against the tourists.

The complex considerations involved in introducing regional matches were delegated to a special sub-committee, who produced recommendations aimed at starting regional matches in 1955, with two per annum against the tourists. But the counties were divided about the possible benefits, both financially and as a spectacle. Overseas bodies were not enthusiastic, and the idea was allowed to drop.

Meanwhile, as if in answer to the Secretary's prayer and in denial of the anxieties of M.C.C. and the counties, the players in the middle brought a more positive spirit to the game. The number of matches finished rose by thirty-six over 1951, though in too many cases a finish was only arrived at after dull play in the opening innings had given place to wild declarations and village-green batting on the final day.

Middlesex got off to a great start, even though their colours were lowered by Glamorgan, who gladdened the hearts of Welshmen in Cardiff and Swansea by winning their first-ever victory at Lord's in May. Half-way through the season, with ten matches won outright and 120 points gained, Middlesex stood second in the table. But the tide turned against them; nothing went right, and, with no more than 16 points in their last fourteen matches, they were lucky not to drop below fifth place. Jack Young, most economical of left-arm bowlers and now in the twentieth year since his debut, took a well-earned Benefit in the match against Sussex at Whitsun. Unhappily, rain severely curtailed play on the Saturday and Monday.

It was Surrey, under the dynamic leadership of their new captain, Stuart Surridge, who roused the public's imagination. His enthusiastic determination to win matches resulted in twenty wins in twenty-eight matches to secure for Surrey the first of an unrivalled sequence of seven championships. It was thirty-eight years since Surrey had last won, and by a happy chance her return to the top came to crown the seventieth year of her greatest batsman, Jack Hobbs, who had dominated the batting in Surrey's Championship year of 1914. So the Championship dinner in December was a double celebration. Surrey were the first county to receive at the hands of the previous champions, Warwickshire, the Champions' pennant, which is now given annually by each retiring champion county to their successors, and flown on every ground where the reigning champions play.

India were the tourists in 1952, and they landed at London Airport on April 22 to a miserably chilly welcome in pouring rain, which washed out their opening practice at Lord's. But a week later the sun ushered in the season as if in promise of a smiling summer, and a goodly crowd flocked to Lord's to see the M.C.C. batsmen make a determined attack on Yorkshire's bowlers. May opened with a scowl, which changed again to shimmering heat, to greet the Indians on the Saturday of their match against M.C.C., when 25,000 spectators had the delectation of seeing R. T. Simpson and T. W. Graveney hit centuries with superb artistry. On the windy, cheerless Monday of the match the teams were presented to the Duke of Edinburgh.

The Lord's Test was signalized by the first visit of H.M. Queen Elizabeth II since her accession and as Patron of the Club. The play was distinguished by fine batting on both sides: great innings by Mankad and Hutton and a lightning century by Evans. Also, not least important for England's future strength, the first appearance in a Lord's Test of Freddie Trueman, who made his presence evident by following up a devastating spell of bowling at Leeds by adding eight more wickets to the seven he had taken there—a useful start to his final tally of 307 Test wickets. With Bedser, already established as one of the world's great bowlers, now supported by Statham and Trueman to contribute real pace to the attack, England's greatest problem of a few years back was resolved.

This was the first season in which the public were no longer entertained by the comedy of the players scrambling for stumps at the end of the match. India and England had agreed that the practice should cease in 1952, and at the I.C.C. all the nations decided that in future the umpires should collect the stumps and bails and hand over one set to each team to be distributed to the players by their respective captains. But a much more important innovation which set the cricket world buzzing at the time and claimed banner headlines in the popular Press was the appointment of a professional captain of England. On May 26 the Board of Control announced that Leonard Hutton would lead England in the first Test, and, having proved himself at Leeds and at Lord's, he was confirmed in his command for the rest of the series. Seen in perspective at a distance of time during which the status of the amateur became so artificial that the distinction between "Gentlemen" and "Players" was finally abolished, the choice has a quality of inevitability, but at the time it was regarded in some quarters, outside rather than inside the Committee Room at Lord's, as sensational. Len Hutton was to prove himself an able and shrewd captain, erring perhaps on the side of caution, but dedicated to the task in hand. He laid down his burden after the 1954–55 tour of Australia, having led England twenty-three times and recovered the Ashes from Australia, and on his retirement he was honoured with a knighthood.

At the I.C.C. in July Pakistan, sponsored by India, realized her ambition of becoming a member of the Conference and achieving full Test Match status. This meant, incidentally, that, with a Pakistan tour of England fixed for 1954, England had to abandon the Utopian dream of a season devoted entirely to domestic cricket.

If the quality of the cricket appeared in some degree to contradict the pessimism of those in authority, it was marred by a sore which was soon to fester into a deep wound, infecting the whole cricket world and poisoning relations between the countries. At Worcester, Cambridge University's fast bowler Cuan McCarthy was no-balled by P. Corrall for throwing, and the old Middlesex wicket-keeper W. F. Price brought the wrath of the Oval crowd upon his head by no-balling Tony Lock in the Surrey v. India match. The Selectors testified that they did not find Lock's action suspect by selecting him for the final Test; it was several years later that he himself was shocked by his own action as demonstrated on film and changed his delivery.

In the absence of the Eton boys, quarantined at Eton because of a case of polio, Eton *v.* Harrow threatened to be played to a muted accompaniment, with the vocalists of Harrow lacking competitive antiphony from the Eton benches. But there was nothing muted about the enthusiasm of Harrow supporters when Harrow, undaunted by a brilliant spell of bowling by Charles Robins, swept to victory by seven wickets at 2.30 P.M. on the second day. The early finish enabled a large crowd to throng the Long Room and see the recently discovered Eton Upper Club score-book of 1805, containing the score of the first match between the schools, with Lord Byron playing for Harrow, who on that occasion, in the poet's own words, were "most confoundedly beat".

Following the poor financial return of the 1951 season a further blow was threatened by the Conservative Chancellor of the Exchequer, Mr Butler. His proposal to increase the existing entertainment tax by 100 per cent plus a charge of $\frac{1}{2}d$. on every admission to a match would, on the basis of the 1951 admissions, have cost the counties £31,000, which for the poorer counties appeared very much like the *coup de grâce*. Pressure which was brought to bear both in and out of Parliament was effective in persuading the Chancellor to agree to a stay of execution by delaying the imposition of the new tax until mid-September, when the cricket season was ended—and to promise that he would reconsider the position before the next season. So there was time for a detailed case to be prepared by the Secretary of M.C.C. and presented by a deputation of representatives of M.C.C. and the counties. Happily the Chancellor was impressed by the arguments put forward, backed by pressure from a group of Labour M.P.s who tabled a motion calling attention to the effect of entertainment tax on county cricket and to the precarious condition of first-class cricket as a national institution and to the great apprehension that existed that the projected increase might have disastrous results for the national game. In his Budget of April 1953 the Chancellor felt able to announce that, recognizing that in this country cricket occupied a special place among sports—not only as forming a part of the English tradition, but also as a common interest helping to bind together the various countries of the Commonwealth—he had decided to exempt cricket from entertainment tax altogether.

So we come to 1953, the year of the Coronation, with the announcement on the very day of her crowning that a team of

superlatively brave subjects of the Queen had conquered Everest—
later in the summer Hillary and Sherpa Tenzing visited Lord's.
The year too in which, quite without precedent, the Coronation
Honours contained a knighthood for a retired professional cricketer, and, crowning all for English cricket followers, the year in
which, under a professional captain, England wrested from Australia the Ashes which they had clasped so firmly since 1934. And
1953 was the year in which the face of Lord's began to show the
first evident signs of the radical surgery which it was to suffer until
the completion of the new Tavern stand in 1968. During the
winter a new Coronation Garden had been laid out behind the
old "A" Enclosure. The undistinguished boundary wall was
knocked down so as to bring in part of the war-destroyed houses
in Grove End Road for the creation of a delightful bosky refuge,
providing, in contrast to the Harris Garden at the other side of
the Tennis Courts, peace and shade rather than the gaudy brilliance of bedding plants. A feature of the garden was the rare weeping
ash, soon to be provided with a circular seat around it, placed
there in memory of a former Secretary, the recently retired President, Mr William Findlay, who died on June 19, three days before
his seventy-third birthday. "Billy" Findlay was a delightful person,
but, brought up as he was in the tradition of Sir Francis Lacey,
whom he succeeded as Secretary, he was an adamant stickler for
tradition and implacable where any infringement of the rules of
the Club were in question. But he was one of the kindest men I
remember, giving to my father, when he succeeded him, wise
counsel and an endearingly warm welcome to a comparative
stranger. They became close friends, and it was a happy coincidence that he was President when the time came for my father to
retire. In 1955 Mrs Findlay presented the excellent likeness of him
which now hangs in the Committee Room.

The garden was one of the best pieces of pure embellishment
achieved by M.C.C. to counteract the disembellishment which
followed inevitably in the train of urbanization and commercializa-
tion in the Test Match era. It was an invaluable adjunct to the
otherwise stark entrance to the Imperial Cricket Memorial Gallery,
which, with a multiplicity of vicissitudes overcome, had now been
completed. The opening ceremony was performed by H.R.H. the
Duke of Edinburgh on Monday, April 27, in the presence of a
distinguished gathering who included the High Commissioners of
the countries represented at the I.C.C., great cricketers past and
present, and the Australian team, grouped hopefully around the

Ashes. Later in the season the Gallery was visited by H.M. the Queen and also by Queen Salote of Tonga and by that great devotee of Lord's the Prime Minister of Australia, the Right Hon. R. G. Menzies. The Memorial was dedicated by the Bishop of London, Dr Wand, whose chaplain in attendance was the son of the distinguished Repton and Cambridge University bowler, A. F. Morcom, hero of the Varsity Match of 1906. In his speech Prince Philip spoke of the almost universal delight in cricket throughout the Commonwealth; this had resulted in attracting a wide and devoted following, bound together by ties of affection for a wonderful game, who formed a great brotherhood of kindred spirits all over the world. The Memorial was intended to commemorate cricketers of all lands, in every walk of life, and the Prince reminded the audience that though many would be commemorated by their regiments or in their home towns, their friends would rather remember them as cricketers. The Memorial tablet reads, TO THE MEMORY OF CRICKETERS OF ALL LANDS WHO GAVE THEIR LIVES IN THE CAUSE OF FREEDOM, 1914–1918; 1939–1945. *Secure from change in their high-hearted ways.* This line, by James Russell Lowell, was chosen by the Hon. George Lyttelton, who justified his choice to the Committee in an apologia which was not the least distinguished of many memorable utterances by that very imposing representative of a highly distinguished family, remarkable not only for their skill as cricketers and the penetration of their knowledge of the game, but also for the power of their oratory. It fell to him to make the speech in honour of the visitors at the M.C.C. dinner to the Australians in 1953. The script of that speech is not preserved, but those of his speeches in reply to the toast of the M.C.C. Committee at the annual dinners in 1952 and 1954, written in his own superb hand, were deposited in the Library at Lord's.

The liner *Orcades*, held up by engine trouble, had landed the Australians at Tilbury ten days late. Yet another team had cause to wonder at the promised sweetness of an English April in the bitterness of experience. But a bleak welcome left Lindsay Hassett unabashed when, in a typically humorous speech, he admitted that rumours had reached his ears that for the first time for many years English cricketers and their followers thought they were going to win the Ashes. After the initial net practice the Australians returned to Lord's to face an inhospitable rain-soaked pitch on Saturday, May 16, having in the meantime secured an unbroken run of four victories by an innings. Helped by the state of the pitch, M.C.C. stemmed the flood of victory, holding the Australians to a draw and, with the combined speed and craft of Miller, Davidson, and Ring failing to dislodge Trevor Bailey, giving them a taste of things to come. The Lord's Test, played for once in shining weather, was, of course, Watson and Bailey's match; their stand in a game where favours seesawed from one side to the other finally secured for England a draw so thrilling that the fortunes of the pair even drew cheers from the crowd on the Centre Court at Wimbledon, who were kept informed of their progress. The gate receipts of £57,716 were the highest ever taken at any cricket match in the world—and the total receipts of £200,194 paid by 549,650 people set a new record for any series— a most welcome replenishment of the coffers of the county exchequers.

"Meteorological" was the adjective used by the cricket correspondent of *The Times* to describe the opening day of the Middlesex match against the Australians, with a freak storm compounded of lightning, thunder, and hail comparable to the phenomenon of the 1968 Test swamping the ground early in the afternoon. Fortunately the Coronation-year visit of H.M. the Queen to Lord's had been fixed for the Monday, when in the afternoon she and the Duke of Edinburgh saw the Australians launched on a mammoth innings which brought them 416 runs on the eve of the fourth Test, but disappointed the spectators on the last day, when it became clear that Hassett was less interested in winning the match than in exercising his batsmen and resting his bowlers. The pressure on all international captains to aim first and foremost at winning Tests is so great that all, or nearly all, succumb at some time to the temptation to use lesser matches as practice games, but national prestige which demands sacrificing individual matches to the all-important target of winning the rubber can be bought at too high a price for the ultimate good of cricket. It is certainly not endearing to the paying public who have looked forward with eager anticipation to seeing a touring team giving of their best. When England won the final Test and recovered the Ashes at the Oval, Middlesex supporters could console themselves in the face of a sudden total reversal of their fortunes in the Championship with the knowledge that it was their own heroes, Edrich and Compton, who finally steered the ship into harbour, with Compton making the winning shot to the boundary with one of his famous leg sweeps. But the heroes of the rubber were, after the captain, the redoubtable Bailey; Lock and Laker in the final Test; but most of all Alec

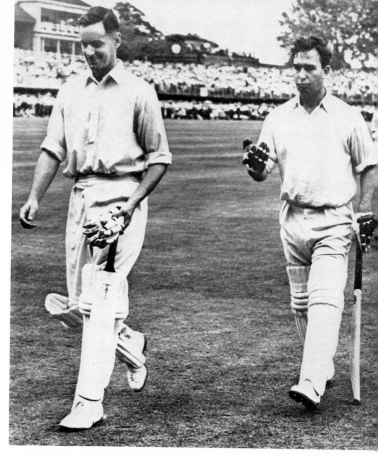

P. B. H. MAY AND
D. C. S. COMPTON
IN PARTNERSHIP,
1955
In England's second
innings against South
Africa May made 112
and Compton
completed 5000 runs
in Tests.

GREAT BOWLING BY J. B. STATHAM, 1955
He bowled throughout South Africa's second innings and took seven wickets
for 39 runs.

OLD ENGLAND PLAYERS ENTERTAINED BY ROTHMANS, 1961

Left to right—Back row: L. B. Fishlock, J. L. Hopwood, G. Geary, A. W. Wellard, E. W. Clark, W. Voce, T. J. Durston, R. Appleyard, G. Brown, T. P. B. Smith, E. J. Smith, G. Duckworth, E. Hollies. *Front row*: D. C. S. Compton, T. W. Goddard, J. W. Hitch, J. N. Crawford, F. E. Woolley, Sir J. B. Hobbs, W. Rhodes, S. F. Barnes, J. Gunn, H. Young.

Bedser, whose thirty-nine wickets in the series were a record for either country.

The meeting of the I.C.C. in July was made historic by the presence for the first time of a representative of Pakistan, Mr S. Nazeer Ali. It was now twenty-seven years since the founder members, England, Australia, and South Africa, had welcomed India, New Zealand, and West Indies to the company of Test-playing countries. The seven countries who sat round the table at Lord's in 1953 gave evidence of the regard in which they held M.C.C. as leaders of international cricket by taking up a suggestion which had been made by the New Zealand representative, Sir Arthur Sims, a year earlier, that representatives of M.C.C. would be welcome in their countries. Already it had been arranged for Mr Aird to make a goodwill visit to Australia and New Zealand during the M.C.C. tour in 1954–55; since then several Presidents of M.C.C. have been royally entertained by member countries, and since he became Secretary Mr Griffith has made several overseas visits.

Middlesex, with Edrich in sole command and the evergreen Sims retired from the side to become county coach, started their season away from Lord's with a Compton century and a tie with Northamptonshire at Peterborough. As of habit they buoyed up the hopes of their fans early in the season only to run out of wind within sight of the winning-post. On Whit Saturday Sir Pelham Warner entertained at the Sussex match the Crown Prince of Japan and Mr and Mrs Clement Attlee, who, on a beautiful day, joined a huge crowd to relish a fine innings by S. M. Brown in his Benefit match and a sparkling hundred by Denis Compton on his thirty-fifth birthday. Sid Brown had richly deserved his Benefit, for he and Jack Robertson had staked a strong claim to be regarded as the best pair of opening batsmen in any county since the War.

Spectators at Lord's were now edified and either interested or irritated by the introduction of numbered lights over the score-board to indicate the identity of fielders—a poor man's version of the Australian-style all-informative boards which make the traditional English score-cards redundant. Would-be spectators in doubtful weather had the convenience of telephoning for prospects of play on a special line on which the latest bulletin of hopes and fears was relayed by the operator. The popularity of the service was proved when, in perfect weather, more than 13,000 calls were handled during the Lord's Test alone. The extension of the G.P.O.'s cricket service to include the latest score has now reached

F

the proportions of twelve million calls a year. On June 11 it fell
to the President, the Duke of Beaufort, to unveil the new inn sign
outside the Tavern, thus proclaiming the restoration of its traditional name from the more prosaic and pretentious Lord's Hotel.
The handsome board was executed by Mr Cosmo Clark, R.A.,
who painted on one side Thomas Lord, as he appears in his portrait in the Long Room, the successful middle-aged proprietor of
the premier cricket ground, respected vestryman of the Parish of
St Marylebone, and prosperous wine merchant. On the reverse the
beloved Kentish giant Alfred Mynn stands erect, preparing for one
of his lightning round-arm deliveries. The sign has now been
moved a few hundred yards farther west, where it offers a welcome
to the new Tavern, looking particularly handsome at night when,
with the pressure of heavy traffic reduced, its bright lights beckon
from a distance along the whole length of St John's Wood Road.

Until fairly recently commuters on the line to Amersham and
Aylesbury (including your humble authors) departed from Baker
Street in a train motivated by an electric locomotive (which was
exchanged for a steam-engine at Rickmansworth) bearing the
name of some famous English worthy. In 1953 London Transport
fittingly named one of these locomotives *Thomas Lord*, and *Thomas
Lord* did yeoman service until, on the day when new locomotives
and rolling stock came into use on an all-electric line, he went into
honourable retirement. But his name-plate was removed and
presented to M.C.C., and fixed to the heavy roller to add a few
pounds to the load drawn by the 10-manpower human locomotive
which operated it.

In 1953 two of England's most famous cricketers celebrated their
eightieth birthdays: Sydney Barnes, dubbed by many who saw
him as England's greatest bowler, was eighty in April. There were
special celebrations in his native Staffordshire, where, with his
beautiful script, he still worked as an engrosser of important documents. The county club commissioned a portrait of him by Harry
Rutherford, which was presented to M.C.C. in the following year,
and has hung ever since either in the Long Room or in the
Memorial Gallery in company with W. G. Grace. Barnes was one
of the first of the select company of retired professional cricketers
who were given Honorary Cricket Membership of M.C.C., and
until his death as a nonagenarian he was to be seen, a tall, erect
figure, at the Lord's Test, often with Wilfred Rhodes on his arm
after Rhodes had lost his Yorkshire companion George Hirst and
his blindness demanded a guide and another pair of eyes to see for

him. The second octogenarian was Barnes's most ardent admirer, Sir Pelham Warner, under whom he had bowled England to victory when they brought back the Ashes from Australia in 1903–4. Sir Pelham's birthday fell in October, and, to complete the celebrations, M.C.C. held a dinner for him in the Long Room on November 24. Through the uncurtained windows the floodlit score-board in the Grand Stand illuminated Father Time presiding over the score, 80 NOT OUT. He had recently retired from the M.C.C. Cricket Sub-committee on which he had served for forty-three years, seven years as Chairman. In 1954 he celebrated his diamond jubilee as player, captain, and committee member of Middlesex and was given an inscribed silver salver by the county club in appreciation of the occasion.

The Games and the Players 1952

IN 1952 India, for the first time from her new status as an independent nation, sent a team to England. There had always been a considerable interest in this country in Indian cricket, largely founded on the brilliant play of Ranjitsinhji and his nephew, Duleepsinhji. But when the public had had some actual experience of Indian teams it became clear that the methods and attitudes of these two great players were little guide to the general outlook of their lesser compatriots. Indeed, caution and patience appeared to be the dominant characteristics of the teams and their individual members. True, there had been several enterprising and magnificent players in the thirties, but they were the exception rather than the rule.

Conditions in India accounted for much of this negative attitude. Wickets were of such extreme ease of pace that unless a batsman made a palpable mistake it was exceedingly difficult to remove him. Fast bowlers especially were at a discount. Thus, in a land notable for its lack of hustle, a batsman tended to wait for the bowler to make a mistake, and to score only from the loose ball. This was extremely bad training and preparation for the very different conditions in other countries.

The Indian side of 1952 bore out these shortcomings in a melancholy record, winning but four of the twenty-nine first-class matches they played. In the four Test Matches they were overwhelmed by Bedser and Trueman, the latter's pace causing great consternation. The onlooker had the impression that these were somehow skilful cricketers in miniature, their delicate skill ineffective against the robust English tactics.

One of their happier matches was against M.C.C. Graveney and Simpson both made centuries, but, there being three run-outs, M.C.C.'s total of 383 for eight was not too discouraging on a good wicket, Ghulam Ahmed took four wickets, and made a very good impression with his nice, flipping off-spinner's action. The Indians made a respectable reply of 255, and Bailey gave them a very

generous declaration at 83 for two. When the second innings
faltered Bailey again showed his goodwill in not pressing his
advantage, so that Umrigar and Manjrekar played out time in an
unbroken stand of 140.

Having lost the first Test Match, India were much strengthened
for Lord's by the inclusion of Mankad. It was a great pity, from
every point of view, that he was not a regular member of the side,
but a league engagement took priority and led to some disagreement. Here was exactly the man needed to set the standards so far
lacking. A magnificent all-rounder, he was tough, experienced,
and a dominating, aggressive batsman. India's good showing in
this match was largely due to his presence.

When India won the toss he led the way, and soon showed that
Trueman's pace had no terrors for him. When Jenkins bowled he
hit his fourth ball high over the screen and far into the Nursery.
When he was out for 72 Hazare batted well for 69 not out, but
again the batting crumpled, and the total was no more than 235.
England replied with 537, Hutton and Evans both making hundreds. Mankad took half the wickets for 196 runs, an effort extending to seventy-three overs.

He had bowled thirty-one of these on the Saturday, but went in
first again. As before, he played confident, aggressive cricket, and
by the close of play he and Hazare had raised the score to 137 for
two wickets. On the Monday, in the presence of the Queen, the
two batsmen took the score to 270, setting a new Indian record for
the third wicket. Mankad made 184, but when Hazare was out
immediately after, the batting again failed to exploit the advantage
offered. At least England were made to bat again, which they did
in a very leisurely way to make the required 79 runs for two
wickets.

The Gentlemen and Players once again could fairly claim to be
the "Match of the Year". This time the Players won by 2 runs. On
Hutton's winning the toss the Players made 265 in such even style
that only Nos. 10 and 11 failed to get into double figures. The
wicket was a mild example of the deplorable "sporting" pitches of
the fifties, and Bedser and Laker, given a measure of help, were too
good for most of the Gentlemen. May made 45, but when he went
five wickets fell for 27, and his side were out for 146. Although
Marlar bowled his off-breaks very well the Gentlemen lacked the
weight of artillery to take full advantage of the pitch and, on the
Players' declaring at 203 for six, set out to make 323 to win.

Against this powerful professional bowling four wickets fell for

73, but Palmer was on top from the very start of his innings. He added 105 with Insole, and then 70 with his captain, Brown. When he was seventh out at 305 there were twelve minutes left with 18 runs wanted, and the match was again poised for its seemingly annual sensational finish. The Gentlemen went boldly for victory, but with the first ball of the last over Laker bowled Marlar and, once again, the Players had won by a minute margin. Not the least remarkable feature of the day was a six by Palmer, all run off a chop in the direction of third man.

Cambridge had much the best of a drawn University Match. The position at the close, with Oxford only 43 ahead and one wicket standing, was probably a fair indication of the relative strengths of the two teams. Cambridge were a strong batting side, with Sheppard, May, and Subba Row pre-eminent. They had also a very good trio of University bowlers in McCarthy, Warr, and Marlar. The great addition to Oxford's strength was the arrival of Cowdrey, who had immediate success as a freshman.

Oxford made 272 by early Monday morning and, by the evening, Cambridge, thanks to Sheppard, who hit the first hundred for his University since the War, were 14 ahead with four wickets in hand. This was an open position, but Subba Row was well supported by the later batsmen, and the score reached 408 for eight, of which he made 94. Sheppard then declared, and Oxford made a poor second showing, six of the side being out for 86. At that point Dowding and Coxon met the awkward lift and pace of McCarthy and Warr with a fine determination. Their stand, lasting two and a half hours, put Oxford ahead and the match into the extra half-hour. Cambridge captured the ninth Oxford wicket, but, as they still encountered a stout resistance, they had eventually to concede a draw.

For the first half of the season Middlesex played like champions, and at Lord's seemed invincible. By the end of the summer it was clear that they had flattered to deceive and, running second in the table in the early stages, seemed lucky to finish in fifth place. The explanation for this strange decline would seem to be that they enjoyed an undue share of good fortune at first, and were never quite as good as the result would argue. Later Compton lost form, and this seemed to spread, either by infection or coincidence, to several other batsmen. Young, given the Whitsun Bank holiday match as a Benefit, bowled splendidly to take 137 wickets. Compton and Edrich shared the captaincy, and this, on the whole, worked quite well. But it can never be a substitute for one well-established leader, and some thought that in the divided responsibility lay some of the causes of Middlesex's erratic performances.

In August "Joe" Murrell died. For forty-six of his seventy-one years he had been a devoted man of the Middlesex Club in several different capacities. He had started with Kent but, finding Fred Huish firmly established, returned to the county of his birth. He was a splendid keeper but, so far as ever keeping for England, he was again thwarted by the fact that Strudwick and E. J. Smith were both confirmed as prior choices when Joe was at his best. When his active days were done he used to run the Club and Ground sides, and was a rare good man to look after the young. Later he became scorer and was equally a paternal institution, teaching the uninitiated the game of bridge—that is, Auction, not the newfangled Contract, which he regarded with doubt and suspicion. He was a professional cricketer in the classic and exemplary mould, loyal, mannerly, and spirited. His eye was bright blue and direct, and his humour sharp and dry.

Far away in New Delhi the Nawab of Pataudi died of a heart attack at the age of forty-one. In the Varsity Match of 1931 Alan Ratcliffe made 201 for Cambridge to set a record. It must have been one of the shortest-lived of all cricket records, for "the Noob", having announced his intention of bettering it, went in and did so with 238 not out.

Less conspicuous in cricket circles was the death of Mr E. B. Shine in Hampshire. It was he who actually bowled the three balls (two of them no-balls) to produce 12 byes and prevent Oxford from following on in the match described at page 68.

12

The Games and the Players 1953

SIR LEONARD HUTTON once said that Don Bradman was worth three men to any side. When one thinks of the number of runs he made, the pace at which he made them, and his disrupting influence on any bowling side it is a fair statement. In addition the moral effect of his presence on his own side and on the opposition was incalculable. Now, in 1953, Australia would tour England without the aid of this enormous presence for the first time since 1930.

The first necessity, on his retirement, had been to find a worthy successor to the captaincy, and here Australia were very fortunate. In this connection it is tempting to digress briefly on the wider aspects of this appointment.

When Hassett succeeded Bradman he was the sixth Australian captain to lead his country against England since 1920, the year of the revival of Test Match cricket after the First World War. The Australian dynasty seemed to be automatic and untroubled. As the reigning captain announced his retirement, so his place was filled by a man qualified to lead, without controversy and with the confidence of all concerned. In every case he served his time until, of his own volition, he retired—the possible exception being in a rumour that Ryder wanted to lead the 1930 side but was outvoted by his fellow-selectors.

The history of English captaincy over the same period was rather different. Hutton, now to oppose Hassett, was the twelfth captain to appear against Australia in the same period. The various paths of his predecessors had on occasion been thorny. Three had suffered the censure of being deposed during a series, Jardine had signalized the end of his tenure, so far as Australia was concerned in a coldly ferocious telegram, and Hammond's Australian tour had ended sadly—indeed, dismally—in abdication. The causes and reasons behind this contrast are obviously manifold and complex and would call for prolonged analysis, not possible in a short space. The background is recalled here because it sheds an interesting light on the new contestants.

Hassett slipped into the Australian leadership with the unanimous approval of all parties and the welcoming warmth of the players. Competent, witty, and self-possessed, he stepped into the vast gap left by Bradman, and unobtrusively filled it.

Hutton's appointment was more controversial, as, indeed, was his handling of the post. The first professional to captain England since the days of Shaw and Shrewsbury, he was not unexpectedly the subject of suspicion and prejudice from diehard traditionalists. Nor did his enigmatic character commend him to all his fellow-professionals. His cautious methods in the West Indies were to be sharply criticized, and the tour had scarcely been an unqualified success. As he was the fourth English captain since the War and Hassett the second Australian the ratio of two to one was accurately maintained.

The Australian side was a very good one. Miller, Lindwall, and Johnston were still in top form, and the best trio of fast bowlers in the world. They were now joined by an exceedingly promising fast left-hander in Davidson. The spin division was still weak, but Benaud gave great promise of things to come. The batting was much less certain than in 1948. Bradman, even in his restrained mood of 1948, was irreplaceable, and without Barnes, it was not until Hassett himself opened that a suitable partner was found for Morris.

The prelude to the M.C.C. match at Lord's was a draw at Worcester followed by a series of innings victories, the losers including Yorkshire and Surrey. The weather for the match against M.C.C. prevented any play on Saturday, but on Monday Hassett sent his hosts in to bat on a fairly firm pitch. Five beautiful overs from Lindwall undermined the innings, as, with only 9 runs on the board, Simpson, Sheppard, and Compton were all out to him. Ring then took over, and M.C.C. made 80, being all out soon after lunch.

The Australians batted but moderately against Moss and Tattersall, but, owing to some bold hitting by Davidson and Benaud, gained a lead of 99. M.C.C. did better in the second innings, Compton getting 45 and Bailey a patient 64 not out, to make a total of 196. This virtually ended the match, as the Australians then lost two wickets for 13 in the remaining half-hour.

For a series which produced only one result in five matches, that of 1953 was one of the most varying and enthralling. The Lord's Test provided a perfect illustration of just how exciting a drawn cricket match can be.

On winning the toss Hassett went in first with Morris and, despite some trouble from a strained arm, played beautifully against some fine bowling from Alec Bedser. With good support from Morris and Harvey the score reached 220 for the loss of only two wickets, but when Hassett was compelled to retire for a spell Wardle took three wickets in quick succession, and Australia finished the day 263 for five. Hassett added only 3 next morning, but a cracking 76 by Davidson took the final score to 346. Lindwall then opened from what must have been one of his favourite vantage-points, the Pavilion end at Lord's. He may not have been as fast on average pace as in 1948, but he was now the complete master of pace, seam, flight, and variation. With the score at 9 he had Kenyon caught at short-leg. Hutton and Graveney then batted fluently and with complete assurance to make the score 177 for one at the close. Next morning Lindwall tried from the Nursery end, and his third ball, a rather slower yorker, deceived and bowled Graveney. This was a sad setback, but Compton and Hutton then added 102 for the fourth wicket. Thereafter Lindwall was too much for the later batsmen, and this promising start produced only a meagre lead of 26 runs.

Hassett was soon out in the second innings, but when Morris and Miller got Australia into a commanding position the later batsmen failed, and much of the advantage was lost. It was typical of this serpentine variation that Lindwall struck so bravely that he and Johnston added 54 for Australia's last wicket, to which sturdy effort Johnston contributed an unshakeable defence but not one run.

With the wicket lasting well the target of 343 was perfectly within England's reach, but always a very stiff task with Australia's wealth of top-class fast bowling. There was time in hand, for England had an hour's batting before the close of the fourth day. It was a most disastrous period for English hopes.

Lindwall, in a devastating burst, had Kenyon caught at mid-on and Hutton at slip. At the other end Graveney was brilliantly caught at the wicket by Langley, so England were 12 for three wickets. Compton and Watson saw the day out, but Watson ought to have been caught at short-leg off Ring in the last over of the day.

It was a depressing prospect which faced England on the sunny Tuesday morning of June 30. On the run of play to that point Australia could claim a slight edge as the better-equipped of two fairly well-matched teams. Should they get a lead at this early stage in the series it was difficult to see how England could catch up, unless blessed with a major slice of good fortune. This was the crucial day, and interest throughout the country was intense. But the general assessment of England's chances was reflected in an actual gate of no more than 14,000 people.

The thought of the 323 runs still needed for victory now seemed academic, and the possibility of survival remote. Watson and Compton met the first blast of pace on the fairly placid wicket confidently, but at 73 Compton was lbw to Johnston. Of all the remaining English wickets this was the one the Australians had wanted. But Bailey presented a dead bat of such determination that it seemed to be hewn out of granite rather than willow. Thus at lunch-time England had got to 116, Watson 54, Bailey 10.

It was during the hard-fought afternoon that Hassett's Achilles heel became apparent. His spinners were either too inexperienced or too lacking in consistent penetration to upset two batsmen dedicated to defence, usually an ideal state of affairs for the leg spinner. Thus, when the fifth-wicket partnership had survived the second new ball in the early afternoon, it boiled down to something of an endurance test, in which nervous control played a major role.

At tea-time the score was 183, with Watson 84 and Bailey 39, a position which prompted thoughts of a bid for victory amongst the optimistic and real hopes of survival amongst the sober-minded.

From this point there was a growing anxiety amongst the fielding side. Watson went on to his heroic century, and at 109 was caught in the slips off Ring. For five and three-quarter hours he had battled in the full knowledge that any misjudgment on his part, until the very late stages, would have meant the loss of the Ashes. It had been a great triumph of nervous stamina, apart from any other consideration. He was soon followed by Bailey, who had played an equally courageous and vital role. A pushing shot to the off aimed at Ring ended in a catch to the gully.

Brown and Evans took the sensible line of playing a natural game for the remaining half-hour, Brown, having struck boldly for 28, left Wardle with four balls (sufficient to end the match) to deal with from Benaud. These were safely negotiated, and one of the longest, tensest, and most absorbing days that anyone could recall having experienced at Lord's ended with the teams still all square.

In July the Gentlemen beat the Players for the first time since the War. It was predominantly a match of good bowling and superb fielding. A number of leading players were absent owing to injury, notably Hutton on one side and Cowdrey on the other. The Gentlemen were out for 129 on a drying pitch, Bedser and Tattersall each taking five wickets, but the Players fell short of this total by 6 runs. In improved conditions on the second day the Gentlemen made 311, Simpson making 117 and Edrich 98. This left the Players 318 to make on a damaged pitch and, although Emmett and Washbrook got 89 for the first wicket, they lost by 95 runs. Marlar took seven wickets for 79 in a prolonged spell, and was supported by a splendid close catching field. One of the features of the match was the fine bowling of Dooland, who gave the Gentlemen a most worrying time but was rewarded by only a single wicket.

Despite a first-innings century by Cowdrey, Oxford lost the University Match by two wickets. Oxford, with 312, led on first innings by 121 runs, but were shot out by Marlar for 116 in their second. A long, fighting innings of 116 not out by Silk brought Cambridge home close to time. Marlar took twelve Oxford wickets for 143 runs, so that there was little opportunity for glory amongst the other Cambridge men.

Middlesex again started the season with a successful burst, but, having led the table for a considerable period, fell away, as they had done in the previous year. Their eventual position was fifth, Lancs and Leicester sharing third place. They gave the Lord's crowds some good cricket in the earlier part of the season, but again lost the services of Compton as soon as the representative matches got under way. Moss was now a fine fast bowler, and Titmus got 94 wickets in his first full season.

In June "Billy" Findlay died in Kent. His good work and popularity as Secretary of the M.C.C. are written about elsewhere in this book, but he also had memories of Lord's as an active cricketer. He captained Eton and Oxford, and also kept wicket for Lancashire in their matches against Middlesex. He was a delightful cricketing companion in all circumstances.

Tom Wass died in his birthplace of Sutton-in-Ashfield, Nottinghamshire. He had been a picturesque character all his days and was the subject of a thousand stories. Sir Pelham Warner, who had a very soft spot for Tom, used to tell one of an encounter they had at Lord's. Sir Pelham's skilful blade, and a certain amount of ill-fortune, stood between Tom and what he considered his just rewards on a soft wicket in a Middlesex and Notts match. At this Tom swore, as was his way, fluently and mournfully. These imprecations catching his captain's ear, he was instructed to apologize, a mandate which coincided with a sudden downpour. As the players ran for cover Tom, who reciprocated Sir Pelham's affection, overtook him at the gallop and delivered his unreserved regrets. "Bludy sorry for swearin', sir," he bellowed, as he darted off in search of a comforting pint.

13

Tactics of Negation

THE thrill of recovering the Ashes in 1953 had given English cricket the accolade of a royal year. But the euphoria produced by success against the Australians was a dangerous smoke-screen camouflaging continuing apathy in the county game. Thanks to a financial shot in the arm injected from the profits of the Australian tour and the remission of entertainment tax, the counties enjoyed an artificial solvency which owed nothing to the entertainment value of championship cricket. In his maiden speech to the county secretaries Mr Aird delivered a warning against complacency—and the need for the warning was proved only too soon in the West Indies. He spoke also of the prejudicial effect of television on county cricket, adding a special plea for attractive play to draw into the grounds those who could become interested in cricket through broadcasting and television. "It is not healthy," he said, "for cricketers to play to empty stands; it is not healthy for counties to have their would-be supporters watching from their homes—and it is not healthy for the watchers either!" The danger to the counties of their spectators being induced to sit at home when Tests were televised was already very real; today, when the quality and quantity of television coverage has achieved such excellence, the temptation to exchange the vagaries of travel, the climate, and dull play for the comfort of an armchair and the freedom to switch off is often irresistible. In negotiating on behalf of the counties M.C.C. have sought to obtain realistic fees for Test coverage to compensate for loss of revenue on the grounds. But mere compensating fees do not meet the crux of the problem, which is the absence of live spectators. This is why M.C.C. have sought to limit the coverage of Tests. It would be a poor spectator who never saw a live game, but of the thousands who follow cricket relayed so magnificently on the box there must be a huge proportion who visit a cricket ground only once or twice a year. By contributing to the vacuum in which so much first-class cricket is played today they complete a vicious circle; dull, unadventurous cricket keeps the crowds away, but cricketers, like actors on the stage, need a live audience to make their performance come alive; with no spectator participation the game becomes dehumanized—no more than an academic exercise.

1953 ended with the dispatch by air of the second post-War team to the West Indies, under Len Hutton's captaincy. By the end of January England had suffered two humiliating defeats, and the general who was so recently the hero of the hour was castigated now for indecisive leadership. But in the third Test, in British Guiana, Hutton confounded his critics by superb batting and generalship of a well-knit England team which completely out-classed West Indies. This was the first, unhappy, occasion when tourists were subjected to the unpleasant hazards of bottle-throw-ing by sections of the crowd demonstrating against an umpire's decision, and Hutton was commended for his courage in standing firm and refusing to be intimidated. A predetermined draw at Trinidad on the docile mat which had failed to produce a result in any Test since it was laid in 1934 left England with the necessity of winning the final Test to square the rubber. That they did this in spite of losing the toss (Hutton had now called wrong in nine out of ten consecutive Tests) says much for the bowlers who, on a per-fect pitch, were able to dismiss such a fine batting side for a mere 139 runs. Bailey was the chief executioner; with a venom that could not be denied he took seven for 34. Hutton again derided his critics with a great innings of 205, to become the first England captain to make a double century in a Test overseas; E. R. Dexter alone has equalled the feat, with exactly the same score against Pakistan in 1961–62.

From the cricketing angle the tour was ultimately successful for England, and financially it was profitable for both countries. But from the point of view of good relations it was less happy, with the inflammable tensions of a hot climate twice flaring up into violence against the umpires. In this "needle" atmosphere frayed nerves led to unhappy incidents which, as always, lost nothing in the telling, and an exceptionally heavy burden fell on the M.C.C. captain's shoulders. It was an open secret that he and the whole team were not satisfied with the standard of umpiring. But the umpires were not helped by the noisy partisan interference of the crowds, whose vociferous criticism of unpopular decisions did not stop short of physical violence, threatening even the umpires' families.

Reports of the use by both sides of defensive bowling wide of the

leg stump in the first Test prompted the M.C.C. Committee to
send a letter to Hutton, promising him support if he should decide
to discontinue these tactics. Their apprehension about the harm
such bowling must inevitably do to the game was unanimous, but
they were determined that any decision to eliminate it from
M.C.C.'s tactics for the rest of the tour must be made by the
captain. The criticism was taken up by Sir Donald Bradman.
Writing from Australia, he postulated that as West Indies normally
played aggressive, entertaining cricket, for them to adopt such an
idea might have been in the nature of a reprisal. He was quick to
acclaim the outcome of the spring meeting of the A.C.C.C., when
Mr Altham, as spokesman for M.C.C., attacked not only defensive
bowling but also time-wasting in county cricket. In a statement
afterwards M.C.C. announced that, while it had been generally
resolved by the county representatives that legislation on defensive
leg-side bowling was not desirable, they had agreed that such
bowling was neither in the spirit nor in the interests of the game,
and all county clubs should point out to their respective captains
the undesirability of such tactics being employed in any circumstances. On slow play the counties decided that in 1954 a record
should be kept of the number of overs bowled per hour in each
innings of every county match.

    Negation was not the only bowling problem confronting the
Committee: 1954 was the year which saw the beginning of almost
interminable discussions, experiments, and negotiations aimed at
curbing bowlers' foot drag, which, though it was not a new problem, had become so prevalent that in England and Australia the
Governing Bodies felt compelled to act. While the two countries
were united in their determination to solve the problem, they were
widely divided on how to do it, with M.C.C. favouring the front-
foot rule in relation to the popping crease and Australia abiding
by the position of the back foot in relation to the bowling crease.
As an opening move the Secretary of M.C.C. discussed the situation with the first-class umpires at their spring meeting at Lord's
and reminded them of their duty to enforce the law. The outcome
was a decision to hold experiments at Lord's in the spring of 1955.

    At the Annual General Meeting in May Sir Norman Birkett, as
he then was, was elected an Honorary Life Member—a graceful
and appropriate tribute to a distinguished lawyer, who was one of
cricket's most ardent devotees and had contributed to it his own
particular gift of oratory. The felicity of his speech, delivered in his
peculiarly beautiful voice, was put to the test without delay at the

annual dinner, at which he had accepted the invitation to propose the health of the Committee.

In March a special sub-committee embarked on the task of considering the future election of M.C.C. members, with a special brief to solve the Gilbertian situation where, with the number of candidates entered each year already more than four times the normal wastage and increasing annually, the waiting period before election was approaching thirty years, and promised to reach a point where a would-be member could hardly expect to be elected during his lifetime. The rules for proposing and seconding candidates were now to be tightened up, with members limited to proposing and seconding one candidate per year. Contrary to the belief of many people—even today—the day was long past since the family butler called at Lord's to enter the name of the newborn son on his way to the registrar! The minimum age for entry was now raised from fourteen to seventeen years. The deliberations continued for two years, going hand in hand with the plans, already well advanced, to build a new stand on the site of the old "A" Enclosure—the modest single-decker stand portrayed in that imposing but fictional painting of a Lord's Test Match of the eighteen-eighties as the stronghold of the most élite socialites of their day and, until the day of its final closing, a much-loved haven of the more discerning friends and families of members and players. It was not until 1958 that Mr Kenneth Peacock's stand, seating 2900, was completed, though seating was provided on the lower terraces while the building was in its intermediate stages. By then the structure of M.C.C.'s membership had been revolutionized, by the progressive election of 3000 members in a new category of Associate members, paying a smaller subscription than full members and debarred from some of their privileges, including the use of the Pavilion in Test Matches, when its capacity is already filled by full members. The subscription rate for Associate members was fixed at £4 per annum, while the subscription of full members was raised from £4 to £6. All new members, except playing members, have to join as Associates, and the progression to full membership is compulsory.

Another long-overdue step in the embellishment and modernization of Lord's was the decision to redecorate the Long Room, unpainted since the ravages of war and ingrained with London soot and sulphur deposit from the as yet undwarfed stacks of St John's Wood Power Station. The old figured ceiling paper, which gave the impression of having been there since the Pavilion was

G

built in 1889, was stripped off, and bands of colour, with stripes of cream and rich Indian red, were introduced to pick out the moulding of the ceiling panels and relieve the rather sombre tones of the celadon walls. At the same time the old Victorian fireplaces, with their stucco architraves, in which no fire had burned since the installation of the central-heating system, were removed and illuminated display cases built into the chimney breasts.

At the end of the year Mr A. J. Howes retired from the Pavilion staff. He had been at Lord's since 1919 and, on the retirement of that unique character Jimmy Cannon, had stepped into his shoes as Head Clerk. A new office of Club Superintendent was now created and filled by Mr R. T. Gaby, once known as "Young Dick" to distinguish him from his father, "Old Dick", who worked at Lord's, man and boy, for sixty-two years. The Gabys are the last of a line of families, starting with the Darks, whose lives have been closely associated with Lord's and M.C.C. Of the present generation, two older brothers were on the staff before they lost their lives in the First World War; the other surviving brother, "Joe", is well known to thousands of members in his capacity as presiding genius at the back door of the Pavilion—or, as I should say, "the door at the rear of the Pavilion", as the main entrance has been called officially ever since Field-Marshal Lord Montgomery, on a rare visit to the ground, commented unfavourably on the indignity of broadcasting for a doctor to report at the back door, as though he were a tradesman! Joe Gaby has also earned the gratitude of many cricketers who have benefited from instruction at his cricket school.

Prophetically, one of the wettest seasons ever known was preceded by experiments in drying out cricket pitches with aero jet engines. Scorched earth would have seemed acceptable to the quartet of overseas teams which arrived in England in 1954 to face a season of rain-sodden pitches. Those among them who were making the trip for the first time might have been forgiven had they decided that an English summer was a travesty which, once experienced, could never be forgotten nor willingly endured a second time. Pakistan were the major tourists, whose appearances at Lord's, described elsewhere in this book by Ian Peebles, included a match against the Canadians. Both these countries were making their maiden representative appearance in England, both with substantial financial help, the Pakistanis from their Government, the Canadians from M.C.C., who underwrote the tour up to a limit of £4500. The other visitors were the Women of New

Zealand, making a full-scale Test tour, who practised in the nets at Lord's, and the Danish Kjøbenhavnsk Boldklub, who lost to M.C.C. by five wickets in August. Accustomed as they were to playing on the mat in their own country, their batsmen found themselves at a disadvantage on a wet pitch at Lord's. But their leading bowler, S. Morild, found it much to his liking and got a hat-trick, with A. Fairbairn, B. H. Lock, and A. G. W. Hill all clean bowled.

The Canadians, led by the Oxford old Blue Basil Robinson and stiffened by the inclusion of the expatriate West Indian Test batsmen Trestrail and Cameron and the ex-Glamorgan and Lancashire county player T. L. Brierley, had a great tour in spite of the alien pitches. At Lord's they won a highly entertaining match against M.C.C. in the last five minutes by 13 runs, and in the final match of the tour beat Middlesex by the even narrower margin of 3 runs. But, predictably, they were heavily defeated by a Pakistani team riding on the crest of the wave which had swept them to the peak of national ambition when they beat England at the Oval earlier in the week. The M.C.C. match was distinguished for the last appearance in a match at Lord's of Mr G. O. Allen, whose life had been so closely bound up with the ground from the time he first played there as a boy at Eton and carried his bat for 69 until, as an elder statesman and former President, he undertook the most senior as well as the most onerous permanent (but honorary) office M.C.C. has to offer—that of Treasurer. And in the years between ... the freshman bowling Cambridge to victory against Oxford; the Middlesex all-rounder attacking Lancashire to take all ten wickets; captain of England; Chairman of Selectors.

A crowd of 20,000 on Whit Monday were regaled with a superb innings by Denis Compton on a pitch which had been damaged by rain soaking under the covers. No one but Denis Compton could have run out his own brother in his Benefit match—but this he achieved, and for good measure ran out Titmus and Moss as well. He had a great Test season against Pakistan and with 453 runs and an average of over 90 in the four Tests he was easily the most successful batsman. So, with another M.C.C. Australian tour imminent and the Ashes at stake, there was national apprehension when it was announced after the final Test that he had synovitis in his knee and would not be able to sail in the *Orsova* on September 15. However, by the end of September he was enlivening the Cross Arrows matches at Lord's, batting and bowling in fine form to prove that the doctors' promises that he could join the team by air were not wishful thinking. His troubles were not yet over! Typically, on the eve of his departure his car, containing his cricket gear, was stolen near Lord's—and when he eventually arrived in Australia he had taken a week to get there because his plane had been held up in Karachi.

The Australian tour was anticipated with more than usual interest. To have regained the Ashes in England was fine, but the enemy had now to be beaten on their own ground, and this had not happened since 1933. Hutton was unfit for the second and third Tests against Pakistan, and it was argued in some quarters that the burden of captaincy, with all it implied for a touring captain on and off the field, was too heavy a load on the shoulders of our key batsman. There were those who regarded Hutton's tactics as more defensive than shrewd; they wanted the captaincy to go to David Sheppard, who had returned from his theological college to lead England at Lord's and Old Trafford. In the previous season he had spurred Sussex on to second place in the Championship, and his youthful zest and undoubted flair for leadership made him appear as a knight errant who would not fail to bring the Ashes home. The M.C.C. Selection Committee, with Mr Altham in the chair, were unanimous in choosing Hutton. With Compton's fitness in doubt, he led a party of eighteen players. For the first time a M.C.C. team in Australia were without the services of "Fergie", doyen of international scorers and baggage masters. George Duckworth now took his place, and if his score-books were less decorative than Fergie's, lacking his complicated diagrams and doodles, his long experience as a player and as manager of international tours made him a tower of strength; to experience he added his own incomparable humour as a heartening tonic whenever one was needed. For their physical wellbeing this team were accompanied for the first time by a professional physiotherapist, Mr Harold Dalton. The party of twenty-one was completed by Mr Geoffrey Howard as Manager and Mr Desmond Eagar as Assistant Manager. On the voyage through the Mediterranean the *Orsova* made a brief call at Naples, which enabled Hutton and some of the other players to make a pilgrimage to the grave of Hedley Verity, twenty miles away at Caserta.

That England, after a shattering defeat in the first Test at Brisbane, went on to win three matches off the reel hardly needs retelling. As that great-hearted American cricket enthusiast Mr Henry Sayen danced a victory fandango in the England dressing-room at Sydney, claiming that Len Hutton and his team owed the dramatic turn in fortune's wheel to his arrival from New York, his friend Mr Aird was too modest or too soft-hearted to assert his own claim that it was he who had brought inspiration from Lord's. His departure for New Zealand deprived him of the excitement of seeing England clinch the rubber at Adelaide and witnessing the receipt of a cable telling the team that the flags were hoisted at Lord's. Messages of congratulation received at Lord's included a cable from the Australian Prime Minister, Mr Menzies. England, who only a few years earlier were crying out for bowlers, now had such an *embarras de richesse* that Trueman, Lock, and Laker were left behind in England. And Bedser, the master, who had so recently bowled England to victory, was omitted from the second Test, after toiling at Brisbane, when barely recovered from an attack of shingles, for very little reward except dropped catches. It was now the sheer speed of Statham and Tyson which shattered the Australians' wickets, and the two youngest batsmen, May and Cowdrey, who made the runs for England. These four young players, all under twenty-five, were ushering in a new generation to replace the old guard of Hutton, Compton, Bedser, and Evans. Hutton's retirement after a summer of physical discontent in 1955 aggravated a problem which already existed. On the Australasian tour Simpson, Bailey, Edrich, and Graveney had all been tried as his partner to open the innings; the Selectors had now to look for a pair of openers.

14

The Games and the Players 1954

THE summer of 1954 achieved the melancholy distinction of being the wettest on record since 1903. It was a poor welcome to the most recent cricketing nation to join the international circle, Pakistan. Despite this bleak discouragement the Pakistanis did rather better than their neighbours the Indians had done. They won nine of their thirty first-class matches but, more importantly, won the last Test Match at the Oval, and so squared the series.

The Pakistanis had a more robust-looking batting order than the Indians and one absolutely top-class bowler in Fazal Mahmood. At the Oval Fazal took twelve wickets for 99 runs. He bowled at quick-medium pace with a pronounced turn from the leg as soon as he got any grip from the wicket, and he produced this effect with a sustained accuracy.

In the M.C.C. match Fazal bowled forty-two overs on the first day on an easy-paced wicket, whilst the Club scored 307 for seven wickets before declaring, Simpson scoring 126. The Pakistani batsmen did even better to declare at 310 for four, Imtiaz Ahmed and Maqsood Ahmed making 95 and 94. Bailey declared his second innings at the fall of the sixth wicket, leaving Pakistan 208 to win in two hours twenty minutes, but this time the batting failed against Marlar's off-spin, and the score was 85 for six at the close. At least the visitors had an opportunity of pitting their strength against strong opposition for three days without interruption.

The first Test Match played at Lord's in the second week of June, was a very different matter. Just over eight hours' play was possible during the five allotted days.

Play started on Monday afternoon, and lasted for two and a half hours before the intervention of bad light. In this time Pakistan scored 50 runs for the loss of three wickets. Next morning they were all out for 87. The drabness of the play was reflected in the bowling figures, which read 83 overs and five balls bowled for 81 runs scored from the bat.

England endeavoured to push along, but also found the going

very arduous, and at 117 for nine Hutton declared. Fazal and Khan Mohammad bowled unchanged and were, as the discerning pointed out, the first pair to do so in a Test Match since Gilligan and Tate bowled South Africa out for 30 at Edgbaston in 1924.

Hopes of an exciting finish rose when Bailey bowled Alim-ud-Din for nought, but Hanif's barndoor defence and some good stroke play by Waqar Hassan soon snuffed them out again. Pakistan finished 121 for three wickets.

Reinvigorated by their win at the Oval, Pakistan returned to Lord's in August to defeat Canada by an innings, and later beat Middlesex by 140 runs. The latter occasion was their last county match, and an easier win than the margin would argue as they declared both innings, the first at 303 for seven, the second at 232 for five. It was also achieved in the absence of the all-conquering Fazal.

The Gentlemen and Players match was also affected by the prevailing rain and fog, and turned out to be a very low-scoring affair. The Players, sent in on a damp pitch by Sheppard, scored 144 and 191, to which the Gentlemen replied with 126 and 160. In the circumstances the Players' win by 49 runs was a fairly substantial one.

There were two unusual features connected with this match. Bedser, whose selection for the forthcoming tour to Australia was all but certain, was left out of the Players' side in order that Loader might be tried. As the substitute took seven for 37 in the Gentlemen's first innings he also made pretty certain of his place, which he was duly accorded. The wicket-keeper on the Gentlemen's side was Benny Barnett, and the leg-break bowler for the Players Bruce Dooland. Thus the Green cap of Australia figured on both sides.

The balance of power had now swung to Oxford, who had much the best of a drawn game at Lord's. Oxford scored 401 for three wickets in their first innings, Mike Smith making 201, only the third double century in the history of the match. Cambridge made a very fair reply in getting to 344 for nine, and were grateful to Silk, whose second century in the University Match was 118, made as an opening batsman. Oxford, now in hard pursuit, put together 148 for nine wickets, at which Cowdrey made the third declaration of the game at five to four on the last day. Cambridge lost eight wickets in making 160, and there the day ended, with 36 runs still wanted.

Middlesex followed the pattern of the two previous years. A very good start suddenly petered out, and the season ended in a disappointing slump. It was difficult to see any clear reason for this repetition, but possibly their natural élan carried Middlesex forward by momentum as much as actual strength, and when this slackened the truth was apparent that they had considerable limitations as a side. On his comparatively few appearances Compton showed some of his best form, but, except for a number of fine performances by Edrich, the batting was disappointing, only these two averaging over 30. On the other hand Middlesex, with Young, Titmus, Warr, Moss, and a few auxiliaries, were a versatile and well-balanced bowling side. They slipped from fifth to seventh place in the table.

The whole nation mourned when George Hirst died at Kirkheaton, near where he had been born eighty-two years before. The *Daily Mail* had a leading article in which the writer saluted this simple, straightforward man, whose character and conduct had established him as a national figure beyond the credit he had brought to his profession. Indeed, had anyone sought the personification of the virtues which the old-fashioned regarded as being peculiarly British here was the man. Stalwart as the oak, generous, and complete master of his craft, he commanded an affection and respect in all who knew him personally or by repute. When M.C.C. elected the most illustrious professional cricketers as Honorary Cricket Members in 1949 he was naturally among the first to be nominated.

On January 20 Warren Bardsley died in Sydney. He had many great moments at Lord's, but his last Test Match there, in 1926, was one of his greatest. Going in as usual at No. 1, he batted through the innings for 193 not out.

On the same January day Fred Root died in Northampton. He had opened the bowling to Bardsley in that Lord's Test Match, his first for England.

15

The Bicentenary of Thomas Lord

IN 1955 M.C.C. joined with Yorkshiremen of Thirsk, where he was born, and men of Hampshire in West Meon, where he died, in celebrating the second centenary of the birth of Thomas Lord. To the cricketers of Thirsk, M.C.C. presented a carved oak plaque, which the President of M.C.C., Lord Cobham, unveiled in their cricket pavilion on July 24.

At West Meon, on a beautiful August day, a M.C.C. team walked in procession with the cricketers of West Meon and Warnford from the cricket pavilion to the churchyard to pay their respects at his grave and then on to drink a pint in the renamed Thomas Lord Inn and visit the house where he spent his last years. Afterwards, in front of a goodly crowd, comfortably ensconced on makeshift seating made of straw bales, they beat the local cricketers handsomely by a margin of 142 runs. On the actual day of the bicentenary I.T.A. broadcast live from Lord's an ambitious feature programme about the history of Thomas Lord's ground and of the M.C.C.

Lord might well have been astounded to see the metamorphosis of his ground, but his shrewd business head would have nodded approval of the building of stands to accommodate the paying public, and he would not have shed tears over the passing of the old "A" Enclosure—the only seating accommodation approaching the simplicity of his own modest benches—now about to be displaced by a modern two-tier stand with the object of supporting a bigger membership. He would also have approved the business acumen which lay behind the development of the new houses in Grove End Road, which were now taking shape—for had it not been his own ambition to speculate in building, even within the perimeter of the match ground, that had prompted William Ward to step in, in the interests of cricket, and buy him out? The houses, numbered 2–16 Grove End Road (even numbers), which had already been or were about to be demolished, had been bought freehold by the Committee in 1912 and 1929 for sums totalling

£98,500. The policy of acquiring property adjoining the ground had begun in 1880 with the purchase of J. H. Dark's house in St John's Wood Road. By 1929 the Club had become the owners, freehold, of the whole of the island site from St John's Wood Road, up Grove End Road, and along Elm Tree Road as far as the bend which converges with Cavendish Close. Many of the houses were (and some still are) delightful, with the rare luxury in London of gardens. But inevitably time, hastened by enemy action, had taken its toll, so that nearly all the properties in Grove End Road and several in Elm Tree Road, became uninhabitable. No. 12 Grove End Road was probably the most distinguished. With its fine central hall and musicians' gallery it was a fitting home for the talented and musical family who last lived in it. But it, like several of the others, was riddled with dry rot. Next door, No. 14 remained intact, as it is today, but the whole of the rest of the Grove End Road properties were demolished and the seven new houses which were built sold on ninety-nine-year leases, with priority given to members. Round the corner in Elm Tree Road two new houses for the Assistant Secretaries took the place of bombed-out houses at Nos. 4 and 6. Farther along, the old Secretary's house, No. 22, the spacious home of Sir Francis Lacey and his two successors in days when gracious living meant employing a butler, a footman, and a supporting retinue of domestic servants, had very reasonably been vacated, or, more accurately, never lived in by Mr Aird, who preferred the modern house next door built for him just before the War on the site of Thomas Hood's old home. No. 22, threatened with the axe in 1954 and then reprieved when a new tenant was found, was finally demolished in 1966; three small town villas now stand in its place.

In April Lord's had a new Head Groundsman: Austin Martin, who took over from Harry White in 1936, was succeeded by Mr E. C. Swannell, who had joined the ground staff in 1923. In the exceptionally wet season of 1954 the state of the ground had caused a good deal of disquiet, particularly in regard to the bumpiness of the outfield. Advice had been sought from the Sports Turf Research Institute at Bingley. The combination of consultation and hard work aided by better weather produced an enormous improvement, so that by July the Committee were able to congratulate the ground staff on the excellent state of the ground. This was the season when, to dispel the glare from the traditional brilliant-white sight-screens at the Nursery end (the Pavilion end was still without screens), pastel duck-egg blue paint was introduced.

At the A.G.M. the members warmly endorsed a unanimous decision of the Committee to elect the Right Hon. R. G. Menzies as an Honorary Member of the Club. His passion for cricket has been one of the major pleasures in a full and exacting public life. As Prime Minister of Australia he would have liked to educate successive English premiers in the creed that the most appropriate time for the Prime Ministers' Conference was coincidental with the Lord's Test. Now that he is Lord Warden of the Cinq Ports he has a special opportunity—and, indeed in Kent, a duty—to watch cricket in England and to visit the "Cathedral of Cricket", as he so gracefully nominated Lord's. On the same day the members agreed to broaden the rules for electing Honorary Life Members so as to open the doors to a distinguished band of international cricketers and overseas administrators, of whom the first was Sir Arthur Sims, elder Statesman at the Imperial Cricket Conference, where he represented his native New Zealand, but famous as a cricketer for having shared with Victor Trumper the world's record eighth-wicket partnership of 433 for an Australian XI *v.* Canterbury in 1914. The rule for electing as Honorary Cricket Members distinguished retired professional cricketers was modified to allow the election in exceptional circumstances of professionals who were still playing. The immediate exception was, of course, the victorious captain of the M.C.C. team in Australia, who was still on the high seas. When the *Oronsay* docked at Tilbury a few days later Hutton was met by Mr Aird, who handed him his M.C.C. pass and a member's tie. The team were entertained at a celebration dinner at the Dorchester Hotel on June 6.

The Selectors took the unprecedented step of announcing that Hutton had been chosen to lead England in all five Tests against South Africa, but before the first Test an attack of back trouble, which proved to be a more obstinate disability than plain lumbago, caused him to cry off and suffer a summer of miserable inactivity before announcing his retirement from first-class cricket in the following January. He had led England twenty-three times—more often than any captain before Peter May. His leadership at a time when English cricket at last rose from the slough of despond to reach its highest peak since the War brought him the unique distinction, the apogee of any captain's personal ambition, of beating the old enemy, Australia, at home and abroad.

The South Africans, departing from tradition, arrived in England by air, and M.C.C. departed from tradition by allowing this side, whose success under Jack Cheetham rested first and foremost on the excellence of their fielding, to hold their intensive fielding practices on the match ground, where they had the space they needed. It fell to the President of M.C.C., Lord Cobham, to welcome them to his native Worcestershire for their opening match. In his speech in the Guildhall he spoke for the realists who, unblinded by the glamour of winning the Ashes—though certainly not belittling the splendid young cricketers who had played so brilliantly in Australia—faced up to the grim economic fact that cricket was failing to attract the public, and that the fault lay squarely in the way the game was played. This extract from his speech still has the ring of truth:

> I do not think people will follow cricket much longer unless the game is reborn, but reborn it will be, and I think there are signs that the players will again hit the ball hard, high, and often. Can we get rid of these awful bores who prod doubtfully at half-volleys and let every long hop pass by? They are the ones who are emptying our cricket grounds. We must get rid of them!

The over-indulgence by both sides in defensive batting in the first Test at Nottingham, on a soft, easy pitch, goaded Lord Cobham into added protest, this time in the M.C.C. Committee, where he suggested that the time had come to set up an enquiry into the tempo of Test cricket. However, the second Test, played on a fast, fiery pitch at Lord's, was, in complete contrast, a splendid match, seeming to prove that the pitch was the governing factor and not the players. Middlesex's young off-break bowler, Fred Titmus, was brought into the England side to make his Test debut on his home ground. This was a wonderful year for him; it brought him his first "double", with 1235 runs and 191 wickets, with the added kudos of topping Albert Trott's record—now fifty-five years old—of 154 wickets for Middlesex in a season, and being the first Middlesex player since Robins and Haig in 1929 to complete the double. Middlesex suffered acutely from shaky batting, with fresh talent sorely needed. But from Norfolk came news that P. H. Parfitt had headed the batting and bowling averages at Fakenham Grammar School and had been awarded his county cap for Norfolk after making 131 against Kent II.

When M.C.C. entertained the Gentlemen of Ireland at Lord's at the beginning of September, Ireland were beaten and confounded by the leg breaks and googlies of Ian Bedford—just as the Essex batsmen had been confounded when, as a seventeen-year-old schoolboy, he made his debut for Middlesex in 1947. After his

National Service in the R.A.F. he fell out of county cricket until 1961, when he returned to captain the side for two seasons. But he had a highly successful career in club cricket and toured twice with M.C.C. teams in South America and once in Canada. Like another Middlesex player, the Rev. E. T. Killick, he collapsed and died at the wicket, while batting for his club, Finchley, at the early age of thirty-six. The Flamingos came too, and they too were beaten; the executioner this time was the Oxford University and Kent bowler A. W. H. Mallett.

Middlesex were now giving active thought to the idea of opening a cricket school, and they approached M.C.C. for a site at Lord's, and financial help towards building and maintaining it. The M.C.C. Committee did not, however, feel able to provide the site, and in view of their current very heavy commitments they felt compelled to refuse a grant. M.C.C.'s own Easter Cricket Classes underwent a radical change this year. The week of daily batting sessions limited to an hour in the nets, with bowling and wicket-keeping an optional extra, became a three days' intensive course, with instruction in every aspect of the game. Group coaching, already used with success in the courses of the Youth Cricket Association, was introduced to instil basic principles; every boy had batting, bowling, and fielding practice, and there were lectures and films on captaincy and tactics and on the history of cricket.

Tennis—real tennis—has been played at Lord's ever since the first court was built in 1835, presided over by some of the most distinguished professionals in the game. Jack Groom, the reigning professional in 1955, had come from Hatfield House as part-time assistant to Jimmy Fennell shortly after the First War. To mark his retirement after more than thirty years at Lord's, M.C.C. and his friends commissioned a medallion by Mr David Wynne, the sculptor whose fine portrait head of Peter Latham, by courtesy of its owner, Mr Michael Pugh, embellishes the dedans. David Wynne has also executed portrait figures of Alec Bedser and Denis Compton. The new head professional, Henry Johns, came to Lord's as an assistant in 1937–38 after playing as a boy at Prince's. He is five times winner of the Taylor Cup and winner of the Professional Handicap in 1938 at Hampton Court (the only time it was ever played there). In 1954 he won the first half of the British Open Championship at Lord's, but lost the second leg to Hughes at Manchester.

The A.C.C.C. had now given their blessing to M.C.C.'s idea of

sending "A" teams to countries where visits of full M.C.C. touring
teams were necessarily few and far between, and the overseas
representatives at the I.C.C. were invited to ask for teams to visit
their countries. In December the first "A" team sailed from Liver-
pool *en route* for Pakistan, with Derbyshire's new captain, Donald
Carr, in command and Geoffrey Howard as Manager. From the
point of view of English cricket such tours offered the chance to
give the experience of a tour to young players and those who were
on the fringe of Test honours. But the primary objective was to
bring good will and encouragement to the host country. It was a
tragedy that this first "A" tour, devised as an act of friendship,
should instead have been branded as a diplomatic disaster because
of an ill-judged rag perpetrated against the umpire Idris Begh.
Those involved soon found, to their dismay, that what had been
conceived as an innocent practical joke had overnight become an
international incident, cancelling out the goodwill achieved earlier
in the tour. So embittered were relations with Pakistan that, at the
instance of the Committee, the President of M.C.C., Lord
Alexander, telephoned the Governor-General of Pakistan, General
Iskander Mirza, who was also President of their Cricket Board of
Control, offering to recall the team. By the personal wish of General Mirza the programme was completed, M.C.C. winning the
last of the unofficial Tests in an atmosphere fraught with tension.

The idea of sending "A" teams as a substitute for full M.C.C.
touring teams to countries of Test Match status has not worked in
practice. A proposed tour to India in 1957–58 foundered because
their Board felt that they could not secure a "gate" unless India
fielded the strongest possible team in the unofficial Tests, and
M.C.C. guaranteed to send at least five or six of the top stars in
England. By contrast the sending of mainly amateur M.C.C.
teams to countries who are now Associate Members of the I.C.C.
has been tremendously successful.

At home the Board of Control and the A.C.C.C. held their usual
meetings in November and decided that in future the number of
Tests in England played against every country should be five. The
counties outvoted a proposal, strongly advocated by some of their
number, to increase the Championship programme to thirty-two
matches instead of twenty-eight, so that they all played each other
twice, home and away. Mr Aird referred to the proposal in his
speech to the county secretaries. He personally was convinced that
a superfluity of county cricket was impoverishing its quality, but
he suggested that counties might be allowed to arrange their own

programmes of as many matches as they liked above an agreed minimum; he saw no objection to the resulting reversion to the percentage system of points which was used quite successfully before the War. In March the Board of Control appointed Mr G. O. Allen to succeed Mr Altham as Chairman of the Selectors. With C. Washbrook appointed in place of A. B. Sellers the Committee now included, for the first time, two professional cricketers, L. E. G. Ames having been reappointed for the seventh year. At the suggestion of Northamptonshire, the counties agreed to see if evening attendances could be encouraged by an alteration in the playing hours of some matches so as to continue until 8 or 8.15 P.M. It was perhaps unfortunate that the experiment was made in a season which was more than usually wet and gloomy, not conducive to good light in the evenings; the home-going workers of Northants were not, as had been hoped, attracted into the grounds, and the experiment was disliked by their members. After a further season's trial the idea was dropped.

At the Annual Dinner Lord Montgomery, as the principal speaker, entrusted with the task of proposing the health of the Committee, used the occasion to offer some advice on the essentials of leadership—especially discipline—to the new England captain. Lord Alexander transferred his cricket baton to his fellow-Harrovian survivor of "Fowler's Match", Sir Walter Monckton, whose year in office was to be charged with the responsibility for far-reaching deliberations.

The Australians arrived at Tilbury on a rainy day, April 24. On the following Sunday, after a fleeting visit to the south downs for a pipe-opener on the Duke of Norfolk's beautiful ground at Arundel, they were back at Lord's practising at the nets *in camera* behind locked gates, the public not being admitted on the Sabbath. Their first match at Lord's, against M.C.C., presented the spectacle of a magnificent innings by Neil Harvey, who on the first day made 194 out of his final 225. Among the spectators was a distinguished and revered representative of the people of Fiji, Ratu Sir Lala Sukuna. At a short ceremony in the Memorial Gallery in the presence of the Australian team he presented on behalf of the Fiji Cricket Association a painting of their ground at Suva. During the match it was announced by the Selectors that Peter May would captain England. On the last day of the month the name of his predecessor appeared in the Queen's Birthday Honours—Sir Leonard Hutton, Knight Bachelor. To Parliament the Postmaster-General, Dr Charles Hill, had announced the inauguration of a new cricket telephone information service—the predecessor of the now digitalized "UMP"—on which, by dialling WEBber 8811, subscribers could obtain the latest scores at Lord's and the Oval. By the end of the 1957 season it was estimated that eleven million calls had been made, bringing the Post Office a revenue of £143,000, with the result that a royalty was sought—and obtained—for the Board of Control to distribute among the counties.

At the I.C.C. in July the representatives of India and Pakistan proposed that they should have equal voting rights with the founder members. At the same meeting Mr de Mello, the Indian representative, proposed that the name should be altered to the Commonwealth Cricket Conference. This proposal, though logical, would, if adopted, have caused confusion with the well-established Club Cricket Conference. However, now that the membership has been broadened into an international fraternity justifying the title International Cricket Conference, the question no longer arises. New Zealand and Australia both opposed India's proposals, and they were not put to the vote.

Middlesex now had Peter Parfitt specially registered from Norfolk, and in the year before his National Service he played regularly and with success for his new county. On the retirement of Leslie Compton, John Murray became the regular wicket-keeper. With Moss absent for a great part of the season, he had to wait a year for the fruitful partnership which made him the only keeper besides Leslie Ames to achieve the wicket-keeper's double of 100 victims and 1000 runs in a season. Another promising new-comer, T. Angus, had the thrill of taking all ten wickets for a M.C.C. "A" team against West Herts at Watford; his ten wickets cost 24 runs, in fifteen overs. The old Middlesex player Archie Fowler, who had for many years coached the young players on the ground staff, now took his place in the score-box, as official scorer to M.C.C. in the non-county matches at Lord's; the Middlesex scorer was Patsy Hendren.

The presence in England of the Australians gave the opportunity for a face-to-face discussion on the problem of drag, which had been magnified in the strong light of publicity surrounding the last M.C.C. tour, when Frank Tyson and the New South Wales fast bowler, Pat Crawford, had been spotlighted for criticism in the Australian Press. In the experiments carried out at Lord's in 1955 draggers had been subjected to the so-called front-foot rule (in use today), which penalized them if their front foot passed over the popping crease at the instant of delivery or if their back foot strayed

THE IMPERIAL
CRICKET MEMORIAL
GALLERY
Opened by H.R.H. the
Duke of Edinburgh, 1953.

AUSTRALIANS AT THE OPENING OF THE MEMORIAL GALLERY
H.R.H. the Duke of Edinburgh and the Duke of Beaufort (President of
M.C.C.) with W. J. O'Reilly, Arthur Mailey and W. A. Oldfield.

THE WARNER STAND, COMPLETED IN 1958
The Duke of Norfolk (President of M.C.C.) and Sir Pelham Warner at the
opening ceremony.

wide of an extended return crease; alternatively, they were made
to compensate for the estimated distance they gained by drag by
grounding their back foot in the delivery stride behind a mark
drawn eighteen inches to two feet behind the bowling crease. The
panel who had assisted at these experiments, consisting of members
of the M.C.C. Committee, the South African cricketer and Manager of their team, K. G. Viljoen, and the two Test umpires Frank
Lee and Laurie Gray, had adjudged the front-foot rule the easier
of the two on which to give a decision.

Subsequent exchanges between England and Australia having
failed to produce an agreement, the law as it affected the Australian tour was left unaltered. At a high-powered conference held at
Lord's immediately after the second Test the Australian delegates,
Sir Donald Bradman, Mr Jack Ledward, Secretary of their Board
of Control, and Mr W. J. Dowling, their team manager, made it
clear that they were against drawing arbitrary lines behind the
bowling crease—although later, in 1959, it was they who introduced the white disc to fulfil the same purpose. They were convinced that the best solution was to admit a measure of legalized
drag judging the fairness of a delivery on the position of the back
foot in relation to the bowling crease in the delivery stride and
amending the wording of the law to read, "in the *act* of delivering"
instead of "at the *instant* of delivery". Their main objection to the
front-foot rule was that Australian umpires felt it allowed insufficient time to watch the front foot and then raise their eyes to
the flight of the ball to give accurate decisions on lbw and caught
at the wicket. But Sir Donald conceded that their opinion might
alter in the light of further experiments with the front-foot rule
which he felt should be carried out in England, where there were
plenty of first-class umpires.

H

16

The Games and the Players 1955

THE early summer sun shone bravely to welcome the third South African team to visit England since the resumption of cricket. Although eventually beaten in the series, this side did as well as any previous South African team on tour in this country. After losing the first two Test Matches they won the third and fourth, and went down only after a good fight at the Oval.

There were several fine players to account for the team's success. The batting had a better-balanced air than that of 1951, and also had a more positive quality, McLean particularly being full of strokes. The fielding was keen and accurate. Perhaps the greatest advance was in the department of seam bowling. Two very tall fast bowlers, Adcock and Heine, led the way, and Fuller produced plenty of life at a shade less pace. For the first time, with Statham, Trueman, and Tyson in England, other countries were beginning to dispute an area which Australia had completely dominated for almost a decade.

From the first over he delivered at Worcester Heine made a fine impression. A very strong man of six foot four, he had a fine action which made the most of his height. As the tour progressed he developed in pace and, additionally, a marked ability to move the ball from the pitch. With Goddard's nagging left-handed accuracy and Tayfield's off-spin, this was a well-equipped bowling side in all circumstances.

The South Africans came to Lord's on May 21, having lost one and drawn three matches in a fairly easy programme up to that point. Their play in this match was a very much more accurate picture of their real powers.

The South Africans did not bat any too well to make 185 for nine declared, but M.C.C. put up a poor reply on an unhelpful pitch. Hutton had just got off the mark when he was assailed by lumbago, and took no further part in the game. The immediate effect upon his side was disastrous, and they were all out for 85. The South Africans made 184 in the second innings, but might have failed completely had it not been for a brilliant 85 from McLean, who drove and pulled with consistent determination. They seemed set for a long lead, but on the third morning five wickets fell for 8 runs, and the innings closed for 184. Titmus took eight wickets for 43. M.C.C. batted rather more respectably in their second innings, but, in face of good bowling supported by inspired fielding, lost by 93 runs. As neither Adcock nor Heine was playing, the South Africans still had something in hand.

The first Test Match, which England had won at Trent Bridge had been a rather dreary affair. The second was, in contrast, a most interesting and stimulating game. May, in the continued absence of Hutton, led England again, and both sides were obviously resolved to make a match of it from the very start. The wicket was a lively one, and May realized that in winning the toss he had not received an unmixed blessing, with Heine, in his first Test Match, to support Adcock.

Sure enough, England made a calamitous start. Kenyon and May were both out to the fast bowlers by the time the score was 8, Graveney went at 30, and Compton at 45. Although Barrington, favoured by a little luck, struggled bravely for 34, the innings closed at 133. Heine in his first session as a Test Match bowler had taken five for 60, producing a fine pace allied to steep lift and disconcerting movement from the pitch.

Statham had McGlew caught at the wicket off the first ball of South Africa's innings. When Trueman had Goddard similarly taken for o it seemed that the first innings might be a very close-run affair. But McLean, coming in at No. 5, showed the same strong, aggressive form as he had found in the M.C.C. match. South Africa passed England with six wickets in hand, and next morning McLean was missed more than once. These were extremely costly mistakes, and McLean hit resolutely to make 142. He was bowled by Statham last ball before lunch on the second day, and South Africa were 114 ahead at that point. A healthy tail raised this lead to 171, and England started their second innings with a fair problem before them.

Kenyon was lbw to Goddard at 9, but on a pitch which had lost much of its early fire Graveney and May were very soon established and scoring freely. By the close on Friday evening they had both passed the 50 mark, and when, early on Saturday morning, Graveney was out for 60 the second wicket had added 132. Compton helped to carry the score to 237, when May overbalanced and trod on his wicket. He had made 112 in four and a half hours, a century on his first appearance as captain of England at Lord's.

The remaining batsmen batted steadily if with no great distinction and, with 40 minutes to play, England were all out for 353.

McGlew was lbw to Statham second ball of the second innings, and at 17 Goddard edged Statham to Evans. The last ball of the day from Trueman brought further and serious trouble to South Africa. It took Cheetham on the point of the elbow, and an X-ray revealed a chipped bone, which meant his retirement for some time to come.

On Monday morning Statham carried all before him. A break for bad light between 12.30 and 2.30 gave him a breather, and he maintained a fine pace and control throughout his total of twenty-nine overs, in which he took seven wickets for 39 runs. The South African total of 111 was something of an anticlimax, coming at the end of four days of such evenly contested play. The match greatly pleased the large crowd who watched these exhilarating changes of fortune. The result seemed, if anything, to stimulate the South Africans to greater effort.

Indeed, when they returned to Lord's to play Middlesex the South Africans had beaten England at Manchester and Leeds. Although they lost the deciding match at the Oval this was a better record than any of their fellow-countrymen had achieved, with the possible exception of the 1935 team, whose one victory had won the rubber. Middlesex were well beaten by 235 runs after being bowled out by Heine for 108 in reply to a South African total of 254. McLean again evinced a liking for Lord's with a soundly hit 58 out of a second innings of 187. Once the ball started to turn sharply Middlesex came sadly apart against the off- and leg-spin of Tayfield and Smith, and were out for 98. One redeeming feature from the home team's point of view was the bowling of Titmus, who took eleven wickets for 54. He was once aptly described by his captain, John Warr, as a "fiddler" in that he "fiddled" batsmen out with a judicious mixture of spin, flight, change of pace, and native cunning.

There was another drawn University Match. Cambridge won the toss and, with 114 from Pretlove, made 304. Oxford were much beset by the spin of Singh and Goonesena and managed only 170, to which Cambridge were able to declare at 178 for eight. Oxford had four and a quarter hours to bat and, with Smith and Williams well on top, got to 175 for the fourth wicket. Smith batted splendidly for 104. When he was out there was no chance of winning the match, but Oxford were safe from defeat, having four wickets in hand at the close, by which time their score was 230.

The Gentlemen and Players, which had provided so much entertainment throughout the early fifties, was marred by injuries before and during the play. May, Bailey, Compton, Graveney, Evans, and Statham could not play owing to a variety of ailments, and during the match Cowdrey, Tyson, and Lock met with accidents. Bedser captained the Players and, given Watson as a replacement for Statham, at one moment found that only Titmus was fit enough to bowl from the opposite end.

The first innings was very even, the Players 316 and the Gentlemen 336 for eight. These highly respectable scores were largely due to the Leicestershire representatives, Tompkin making 115 for the Players and Palmer 154 for the Gentlemen. At least the finish was worthy of the recent tradition, for, set 201 to win, the Gentlemen lost by 20 runs in the last five minutes. Goonesena evidently found Lord's a suitable pitch for his leg breaks, for he followed up his good record in the Varsity Match by taking six for 83 in the Players' second innings of 220.

Middlesex had another strangely erratic season. With Titmus now a very fine bowler in all conditions, they had a well-balanced attack, but the batting was completely unpredictable. With injuries and representative matches Compton could take the field in only eleven matches, and this meant that there was no really dominating figure for most of the season.

At least Middlesex finished their matches. Of twenty-eight Championship fixtures fourteen were won and twelve lost, a remarkably high proportion of definite results, which earned the team fifth place in the table.

In May, Alan Fairfax, the quiet, generous Australian, died in London after a long and brave struggle against increasing illness. He had loved Lord's, making his first appearance for his country against M.C.C. in 1930. In after years he remarked that, so well behaved were the crowd of 30,000, his first impression was that he was playing on an empty ground. Personally I have always doubted if he ever got full credit for his powers as a bowler in that year. He remains in my memory as the best fast-medium Australian bowler of modern times, certainly amongst the right-handers.

G. L. Jessop died during the same month at the age of eighty. He had many glorious moments at Lord's, as elsewhere, but one has always to my mind epitomized his genius. In 1912 Nigel Haig sat with his uncle, Lord Harris, watching the victorious M.C.C.

team, returned from Australia, playing against the Rest of England at Lord's. Bill Hitch, at his very fastest, came on at the Pavilion end to bowl his first ball at Jessop. It was extremely fast, of good, full length, and pitched outside the off stump. The batsman got down on his right knee and mowed this formidable delivery to square leg so that it arrived half-way up the Mound Stand with a resounding thump. His lordship scratched his imperial, as he was wont to do in moments of deep thought. "That, my dear Nigel," he said, "is the best shot I have ever seen."

17

The Altham Committee 1956-1957

THE 150th Anniversary match of Gentlemen *v*. Players in 1956 was launched in soggy conditions on W. G. Grace's birthday, but Denis Compton at least was able to demonstrate that even minus his kneecap he could use his feet to "put the bat to the ball" (as W. G. defined the art of batting) and punish it more severely than most fitter batsmen. To digress, not so long ago I met the Sister who reigned over the private wing in the hospital where he had undergone this latest operation. She spoke in amazement of the physical courage that permitted anyone to play on such an agonized joint, and then related a delightful story against herself. As a devotee of horses she shared common ground with Denis on the subject of racing, but when it came to cricket she was a total ignoramus. So the names of the famous players who flocked to his bedside meant nothing to her, except that their inordinate number compelled her to give orders that nobody was to be admitted without permission. The news that Mr Godfrey Evans was asking to see Mr Compton, announced at a moment when she was deeply occupied with a patient who was so seriously ill that she was not expected to live, was not, therefore, received with enthusiasm. Infuriated by such a trivial interruption, she demanded irritably, "Who on earth is Mr Godfrey Evans?" From the bed, in a faint whisper, came the reply, "England wicket-keeper." In the whole of his exuberant career Godfrey Evans can never have administered a more potent tonic, for from that moment the patient never looked back.

The days of Gentlemen *v*. Players were numbered, and already the view that the distinction between amateurs and professionals should be abolished was being discussed widely in terms of restrained reason or violent vilification, according, by journalistic definition, to whether the argument was aimed at readers of the "heavies" or at readers of the "popular" Press. If M.C.C., as the Governing Body of cricket, strove to keep the true amateur in first-class cricket it was not, as was popularly stated, for the sake of the "old school tie", but with a sincere desire to regain and preserve the unfettered spirit of high adventure which, since the Golden Age, had been the amateur's priceless contribution to cricket. The modern game was gripped to the point of suffocation in an iron band imposed by the gospel of containment, shackling the players so that they could not break out of their prison even if they would. Never had a leaven of lightness and joy been more sorely needed, for, while there had been times in the past when cricket had been in the doldrums and survived, dullness had never before been allied in quite the same way with social and economic pressures. Enterprise was now a *sine qua non* for survival.

In February Sir Walter (soon to become Viscount) Monckton, the reigning President, had chaired a special sub-committee whose brief was to investigate the problems of amateur status and the current position of amateurs in cricket. As they saw it, their main objective was to consider how more amateurs could be enabled to play in first-class cricket. In the light of hind knowledge it is easy for people to say that the Monckton Committee were short-sighted in postponing the inevitable, but let those who do cast their minds back and consider for a moment the wealth of young amateur talent which was still available in 1956: it included the first three batsmen in the country—May, Cowdrey, and Sheppard —with Dexter and M. J. K. Smith in the wings. No wonder it was still possible to believe in amateur status! When, in 1962, the distinction between amateurs and professionals was abolished and all first-class players were called "cricketers", cricket was in the van, ahead of nearly every other sport, in accepting the facts of social and economic life. The Monckton Committee gave serious thought to the idea that first-class cricket should be confined to week-ends —an idea which has been mooted at intervals ever since. Their decision that the time was not yet ripe for making any alteration in amateur status was coupled with a recommendation that the whole structure of English cricket should be examined by a much more widely based Committee with regional representation. This recommendation took shape with the setting up of the Special Committee which sat under Mr Altham's chairmanship between October 1956 and January 1957 to consider and report on the future welfare of first-class cricket. In the intervening months an exceptionally wet summer had contributed to a drop in county attendances in a single year of half a million to a figure barely more than half the record total of 1947, so that the need for an enquiry was demonstrably acute. Towards the end of the season the non-party investigating body called Political and Economic Planning had turned a searchlight on the plight of the game and county finances in a pamphlet called *The Cricket Industry*. On rereading it I still find the contents slightly facile, but there is no doubt that at the time it stimulated interest by creating a talking point. Mr Altham discussed on the radio the implications of some of its findings—including the suggestion that first-class cricket should be confined to week-ends. The observation that "there is likely to be serious opposition to competitive cricket on Sunday" (with no mention of the Sunday Observance Act) was soon proved when the county representatives at the A.C.C.C. voted against Sunday cricket by an overwhelming majority and instructed the Special Committee not to consider it.

The Altham Committee of 1956–57 picked up at a sharper tempo the age-old motif of cricket ills and how to cure them. Their enquiry was, so to speak, only the first subject in a movement which culminated when the conclusions of the 1961 Cricket Enquiry Committee became effective in 1962. The second movement may be said to have ended with the setting up of the new framework of cricket administration under the Cricket Council, but the theme to which cricket will be played in the 1970s has still to be developed. In the course of five meetings the Committee not only considered every factor in the conduct of the game which might serve to enliven its tempo, but their discussions also ranged broadly over possible reforms in the structure of first-class cricket. The new Chairman of the M.C.C. Cricket Sub-committee, Mr Allen, met the county captains and reported back their views on such experimental reforms as extending the lbw law; limiting the number of fielders on the leg side; shortening the bowling crease to curb in-slant bowling; limiting the number of overs in the first innings, and amending the points scoring system to impart more urgency to the game. The Committee's report presented its findings in two sections, one on the conduct of the game and the other on the organization of the County Championship.

Firstly, they dealt with possible changes in lbw. No member of the Committee thought that a reversion to the "old" law would have the desired effect of bringing the game back to the off side; the "Bradman" extension giving a batsman out if he padded up and made no attempt to play a ball which would have hit the wicket, even if the point of impact were outside the line of wicket and wicket, was rejected also because of the difficulties it would present to umpires in interpreting the batsman's intentions.

Secondly, they explored the possibilities of discouraging the leg-side attack by limiting the number of fielders on the on side. While recognizing that this limitation might penalize off-spin bowlers on a turning wicket and some in-swing bowlers, they were neverthe-less agreed that the benefits outweighed the disadvantages. They recommended an experimental law limiting the on-side fieldsmen to five, of whom not more than two might be behind the *wicket* (afterwards amended to *popping crease*).

Thirdly, with considerable misgivings and against the opinion of the captains, they recommended that an experiment should be made for one season at least in limiting the number of overs in the first innings of county matches to eighty-five. The hope was to instil a sense of urgency into batsmen and to give the public attending the first day's play an opportunity of seeing something of both sides' batting and fielding. This recommendation was turned down by the counties. They decided instead, at the suggestion of Middle-sex, to offer a carrot for more urgency in the first innings by reducing the number of points gained for a lead from four to two and introducing two bonus points for a side leading on the first innings if they had scored faster than their opponents on a runs-per-over-basis. When this became effective in 1957 Surrey raced to their sixth Championship off the reel, finishing ninety-four points ahead of their nearest rivals and collecting no fewer than forty-eight bonus points.

The report next referred directly to the tempo of the game—the dominant theme of all their discussions—expressing particular concern at the growing tendency to waste time, above all by a progressive reduction in the number of overs bowled per hour. It was now proposed to strengthen Law 46 by instructing umpires to report offending players if time-wasting amounted to unfair play.

The last major reform was the introduction of the 75-yard boundary, aimed at encouraging attractive stroke play. With the same objective, the Committee condemned the slow, turning pitches which favoured bowlers on some grounds, and they made a fresh plea for the fast, true pitches which seem to be the gift most ardently prayed for by every cricket reformer within living memory and most seldom granted. Finally, it was agreed that the county captains should have regular meetings twice a year, in the autumn to review the previous season and in the early spring to discuss the future conduct of the game and make their views known to the A.C.C.C.

Turning to organization, the Committee did not recommend

any alteration in the Championship: suggestions for reducing the matches from three days to two, or playing one-innings matches, were rejected, and they were against splitting the counties into two divisions, with relegation and promotion. But they did recommend the introduction of a knock-out competition, for which a sub-committee had drawn up a set of conditions. Once more the image of a Cup for Cricket was welcomed and headlined in the Press, but once more it was first referred back by the counties and then shelved because they could see no answer to the problem of unfinished matches.

With the encouragement of young English cricketers in mind, there was a recommendation that a recent increase in the introduction of overseas cricketers should be halted by imposing a limit of two on each county's list of registered players in any one season. However, temporary registration was to be allowed for under-graduates in residence at Oxford and Cambridge Universities, playing first-class cricket as such.

Much hard work and deep thought had gone into the prepara-tion of the report. As always, in whatever he undertook, Mr Altham put his heart and soul into the enquiry and inspired all those who contributed to it in any way, in or out of the Committee, with his own enthusiasm. The report was well received, and only one of its recommendations for the conduct of the game—the eighty-five-over limit, on which the Committee itself had been least confident—was rejected by the counties. The other recom-mendations became effective in 1957. Only the knock-out com-petition remained on the shelf, until it was taken down and dusted in 1962.

While these weighty deliberations were in train in England, Peter May was leading a M.C.C. team in South Africa—his first tour as captain of England. He was in tremendous form in the pro-vincial matches, but in the Tests his luck deserted him, or else the responsibilities of leadership weighed too heavily, and he had a very moderate record. The Test scoring rate set a record "low", with England averaging less than 33 runs an hour and their opponents barely exceeding 29. The South Africans blamed England for setting the slow tempo in the first Test, when they made only 157 for three on the first day—sorry entertainment for the huge crowd who had flocked to see the inauguration of Test cricket on the new Wanderers ground outside the city of Johannes-burg. Three weeks earlier, when Transvaal entertained M.C.C. for the first "international" game on the ground, Statham enlivened the second day's play by opening with a hat-trick. This was a bowlers' tour, the highest honours going to "Toey" Tayfield, whose thirty-seven wickets in the Tests topped Vogler's record for South Africa. The first Test, particularly, was played out in a mood of turgid containment, with England winning by 131 runs. They went straight on to an overwhelming victory on a spinner's pitch at Cape Town. Here it was Wardle who bowled superbly in both innings, but outstandingly in the second, when he took seven for 36, South Africa being all out for the minimal total of 72. But now the tide receded for England; they could only draw at Durban. The fourth Test, at Johannesburg, was the match of the series. South Africa began auspiciously by winning the toss; at tea-time on the last day the result was still in the balance; fifty minutes later they had won their first Test on turf in South Africa, and the crowd were chairing Hugh Tayfield off the field, in honourable tribute for his nine wickets in the final innings. The final Test, at Port Elizabeth, was something of a farce because of the extraordinary state of the pitch as the result of being recently relaid with soil imported from Durban. Great cracks opened up and, with the ball behaving unpredictably, neither side could make runs. South Africa had the advantage of winning the toss, and won the match to square the series.

For this tour a new financial agreement with South Africa gave M.C.C. a profit of £26,500. Until now only tours to Australia had been run on a profit-making basis. It was a sign of the times that M.C.C. could no longer allow their Foreign Tours account to rely solely on the profits from one country, but decided that the time had come for all major tours to pay their own way and provide a margin of profit for the counties.

When the West Indies cricketers arrived at Waterloo Station in April the customary delegation of welcome was reinforced by two calypso bands and a vast throng of West Indian supporters. Their captain, John Goddard, accepted the new experimental rules for the 75-yard boundary and the control of time-wasting, but he would not agree to the limitation of leg-side fielders. A week before their arrival the death of Frank Chester brought tributes from every cricket-playing country. Their universal respect was summed up in Sir Donald Bradman's tribute: "Without hesitation I rank Frank Chester as the greatest umpire under whom I played."

West Indies' first match at Lord's was spoiled by rain. After a thrilling match at Edgbaston which ended in a draw they returned to H.Q. for the second Test, to suffer an innings defeat on a lively pitch which offered a feast to Statham, Trueman, and Bailey. Bailey, in his fiftieth Test, profited to the tune of eleven for 98. The pitch was the target for much criticism and discussion. When they came to review the season the M.C.C. Committee condemned it for having too much grass and being over-fiery, particularly at the Nursery end. They had wanted a fast, true pitch; what they got was fast enough, but most untrue, as bruised batsmen on both sides could testify.

At their Annual General Meeting in April, Middlesex members were told of the impending retirement at the end of the season of Denis Compton as a professional cricketer, and of W. J. Edrich from the captaincy. So ended an era. "The Middlesex twins" had striven mightily for their county and for England too, attracting spectators like a two-pronged magnet to cricket grounds all over the world. In their great season, 1947, they attacked the ball with a prodigal abandon, collecting runs and creating records which in these parsimonious days have almost ceased to be credible. Middlesex have not since produced players with the same magnetism, and Lord's has been the poorer. On his retirement Compton was honoured with the C.B.E., and he joined the select band of former professional cricketers who were elected Honorary Cricket Members of M.C.C.

The Lord's scene was now overshadowed by the scaffolded shell of the new stand, which obliterated completely the hallowed mound so much beloved by Sir Neville Cardus. Pending its completion the election of Associate members had been limited to 750. The new 75-yard-boundary boards were said by faithful Taverners to fix too wide a gulf between them and the cricket. With the winding up of the M.C.C. Catering Department, the Tavern itself was under new management, the whole responsibility for the catering having been let out to Messrs Ring and Brymer on a five-year contract.

At the Annual General Meeting Lord Monckton named as his successor the Duke of Norfolk, just home from Jamaica, where his team of county cricketers had had a highly successful tour both on and off the field, returning after six weeks with the Duke's colours unlowered. Mr Harry Crabtree was congratulated on the M.B.E. he had received in the previous year's Birthday Honours in recognition of his splendid work as Director of Coaching for the M.C.C. Y.C.A. The honour reflected the successful advances made by the Association in its task of providing better facilities for young underprivileged cricketers. In the Birthday Honours of 1957 the higher honour of C.B.E. went to Mr Altham. In the whole of his devoted service to the game his work as Chairman of the Y.C.A. was perhaps the facet which was nearest to his heart. In the years since the War he had worked indefatigably for cricket, as he would continue to do until the day of his death. Before his agile brain was directed towards administration he was cricket's historian, and in that capacity, as Chairman for eighteen years of the Art and Library Sub-committee (which he delighted to call the "Arts and Knitting"), he was entrusted with the task of building up the Club's historic treasures and presenting them to a public beyond the members in the Pavilion. In the summer of 1957 the Collection was enriched by treasures—books, prints, pottery, and other miscellaneous of "cricketana"—bequeathed by Mr Altham's lifelong friend and Winchester colleague, Mr E. R. Wilson. Rockley Wilson was one of those characters of rare vintage, beloved by all who know them. His store of knowledge of cricket's history and literature was equalled by a rich treasury of anecdotes which he recited with a special Wilsonian jerkiness and a minuscule spring-heeled jumping up and down as his fingers plucked nervously at his tie. He was, of course, in his prime, an admirable spin bowler who toured Australia, and in the long vacations away from Winchester he took many wickets for Yorkshire. As the result of his legacy the Committee agreed to the extension of the Memorial Gallery on the ground floor, where a showcase was installed in his memory. The extension was opened in 1959.

Material support for M.C.C.'s cultural activities was provided when the President's Fund was inaugurated in 1958 as the result of a legacy of £2000 from Mr E. E. Pool. The Fund's administration was vested in the reigning President, supported by his immediate predecessor, the Treasurer, and any other members he might invite to advise him in attaining the objects of the Fund, which are to support any project which would foster the game of cricket in any part of the world and to preserve and enhance the cricket heritage represented by the M.C.C. The most generous single disbursement from the Fund was for the completion of the purchase of the painting *Mr Hope of Amsterdam*. Other lesser sums have been spent on the M.C.C. Collection, but donations have been given to a multitude of other cricket causes and have helped cricketers in such widely separated places as St Helena, Corfu, the Student Cricket Club of Belgrade, Gambia, Papua, Bechuanaland (Botswana), the Solomon Islands, and Fiji.

In the "close season" of 1957-58 there was no major overseas tour, but on Boxing Day a M.C.C. amateur team of some strength, including several Test players, set out on a three weeks' tour of East Africa, under F. R. Brown's captaincy, with S. C. Griffith as player-manager. Two days later, in the extreme heat and humidity of Dar-es-Salaam, they found themselves playing on a matting wicket against a background of shimmering heat and getting somewhat the worse of a draw in a "representative match" against Tanganyika (as Tanzania was still called). In Kenya, after a brief courtesy visit to the Sultan of Zanzibar, they had a convincing victory on the beautiful ground of the Mombasa Sports Club, followed, up on the cooler heights of Nairobi, by a thrilling defeat off the last ball of the match against the Kenya Kongonis. On the Sikh Union Ground in Nairobi they met the strongest opposition of the tour in the Kenya Cricket Association and, thanks to a superb century by Hubert Doggart, they had the better of a draw. The final match, against Uganda at Kampala, ended in a win by ten wickets. This extraordinarily happy tour was M.C.C.'s first visit to East Africa. The team impressed and delighted their hosts not only by splendid batting, which sometimes reached as much as 100 runs an hour (Doggart was outstanding), but even more by smart fielding and running between the wickets.

18

The Games and the Players 1956

THE decisive wins in Australia and the good showing in the West
Indies had demonstrated the great advance in the strength of
English cricket in the first half of the fifties. The arrival of the
twenty-first Australian team to visit this country was awaited with
confidence. Australia had declined perceptibly from the peak of
1948, but, as always, were resilient, with a stream of young players
available from grade cricket, a training-ground in which the
novice learned from first-hand contact with the seasoned Test
Match veteran. If there was nothing to replace Lindwall, Miller,
and Johnston *in toto*, Davidson was a prospect of the highest class,
and in Ron Archer they had a very useful stock bowler. Benaud
was constantly improving the quality of his leg breaks, but there
was no match for the spin of Laker and Lock. The Australian
batting was now patchy, compared to the serried ranks of Bradman's last side. Because of this it was planned to use Miller chiefly
as a batsman, but injury to Lindwall and Davidson resulted in his
bowling a great deal more than had originally been intended.

The early summer weather was particularly wretched, and by
late May the Australians had succeeded in beating only Cambridge University. In the midst of a succession of draws they were
well beaten by Surrey at the Oval, where they had the disconcerting experience of losing all ten first-innings wickets to Laker.

The weather was still uncertain at Lord's, but the Australians
had a more reassuring match. Batting first, they made 413, but, as
Harvey made 225 and Rutherford 98, this handsome total still
reflected a disturbing unevenness. Lindwall pulled a muscle early
on, but the Australians bowled and fielded with much zest, and a
good M.C.C. side had reached only 203 for nine when rain washed
out almost the whole of the last day.

The first Test Match, at Trent Bridge, having ended in a fairly
even draw, both sides found themselves much beset by injury on
the eve of the second at Lord's, to be played from June 21 to 26.
The Australian losses, by virtue of the limited number of replace-

M.C.C. ADMINISTRATORS
H. S. Altham, Sir Hubert Ashton, G. O. Allen.

M.C.C. SECRETARIES
R. Aird and Colonel R. S. Rait Kerr.

LORD'S TAVERNERS' BANQUET IN THE LONG ROOM

ments, were the more serious, as Lindwall and Davidson, the main-stays of the attack, were both injured. England lacked Tyson and Lock, but had more adequate reserves in Statham and Wardle.

The whole tenor of the match was set by Miller. This mercurial, unpredictable performer demonstrated that, when required, he could still generate more fire than any of his contemporaries. The Lord's wicket was on the lively side when Australia won the toss and batted until bad light stopped play twenty minutes early on the first day. In that time they made 180 for three, a good per-formance against a formidable bowling combination—especially as Harvey had failed. Next morning seven wickets fell for 105.

When England batted Australia's new fast bowler, Crawford, retired with a strain after five overs. Miller then rose to the occasion. Richardson's fatal habit of sparring outside the off stump soon saw him caught at the wicket, and Graveney was clean bowled. Cowdrey and May had just about settled in when Cowdrey was out to a tremendous catch by Benaud in the gully. The stroke was a full-blooded slash out of the middle of the bat, and few except the catcher followed the flight of the ball. This seemed to crack the resistance, for only Bailey's patient defence was there to aid May's beautiful if restrained play. May made 63 out of the total of 171, and Miller bowled thirty-four overs and one ball to take five wickets for 72.

England struck back in the field, with Trueman working up his best pace, and at the end of the third day Australia were 115 for six. This was fairly even going, but next morning the young Benaud let fly. Whilst Mackay defended he swung the bat, to get 97 before being caught off a skier. Australia got to 257 and, with memories of their first innings, the task of getting 372 looked a very long haul for England.

Once again May got on top of the bowling in making 53. Miller again led the hunt, getting more life out of the pitch than any rival on either side. England were out for 186, and this time Miller had bowled thirty-six overs for 80 runs and another five wickets. As a souvenir he nipped one of the bails, but, with a characteristic ges-ture, tossed it to the crowd as he left the field.

Lindwall captained the side when the Australians played Mid-dlesex in July and decided to bat on a wet wicket. Only an eighth-wicket stand of 87 between Benaud and Lindwall saved his side from collapse before Titmus, and the total eventually reached 207. Middlesex then batted in the most erratic way on the Monday. There were 13 extras, and of 185 runs from the bat Compton made

I

61, Edrich 84, and Murray 35. The remaining batsmen made 5 runs between them, which, by some statistical formula, must be a record.

The conditions were very good for the second innings, in which Australia declared at 232 for three, and Middlesex once again put up a strange performance. Five wickets fell for 35, then Murray and Bennett added 70 without being parted, to make sure of a draw.

An attractive fixture in late August, the Australians *v.* the Gentlemen, was ruined by rain. In four hours before tea on the first day the Australians aided by a brilliantly hit 56 from David-son, made 226 for eight wickets, after which persistent rain prevented any further play in the match.

The University Match was drawn between two good sides. Cambridge, with Dexter, Barber, and Goonesena, were the stronger on paper, but when they had declared at 303 for seven M. J. K. Smith completed an extraordinary record by making his third successive hundred in the University Match. His side were 56 behind when they declared for nine wickets, but when Cambridge declared for the second time, leaving Oxford 191 to make in 65 minutes, the batsmen decided in favour of prudence and finished at 58 for five.

The Gentlemen *v.* Players was the 150th to be played at Lord's and, sadly enough, was spoiled by the weather. The Players made 236 and the Gentlemen 179 for six in the available time. Once the prospects of a result were eclipsed the chief interest lay in the form and fitness of Compton and Tyson, both reappearing after a spell of rehabilitation, one from removal of a knee-cap and the other from a fracture of a leg-bone. Neither did much in the light of figures, but Tyson had one tremendous burst of speed just before a storm ended the play.

For Middlesex it was a season of promise and hope. A large number of the older players had departed, but a younger genera-tion made a most encouraging showing. Particularly Murray in his first full season kept wicket splendidly, and was a most elegant and frequently successful batsman. Compton, though with knee-cap removed, played a few matches later on, whilst Edrich at forty captained the side with the assurance of experience and headed the batting averages. The team pleased their supporters and gave them good reason for faith in the future.

Charles Fry died in Hampstead in September at the age of eighty-four. He was much a man of Lord's in his active days and equally so in after years, when he might often be found in the Long Room discoursing upon the Greek poets or the technique of the long jump or, indeed, any subject under the sun. Perhaps his most remarkable moment at Lord's was not his most distinguished, but when he and Ranji were the only two wickets to fall in the second Test of 1902. Both were out before a run had been scored in the match.

At the beginning of the season "Chubby" Tate died at Wadhurst, in his native Sussex. He was the greatest fast-medium seam bowler of the era and probably of all time. His transition from a comparatively innocuous off-spinner to this pre-eminence was almost immediate and effected simply by abandoning spin and bowling at a consistently fast pace, instead of discharging the occasional fast ball by way of variation. The Lord's public had an early and convincing demonstration of this advance. In 1923 the Rest had made 200 for four by lunch-time on the second day. In a quarter of an hour after the interval Tate took five wickets without yielding a run, and the Rest were all out for 205.

Thereafter "Chubby" had many notable occasions at Lord's, some triumphant, some comic, but all consistent with a highly original personality. He was amongst the first Honorary Cricket Members to be elected to the M.C.C.

19

The Games and the Players 1957

THE great expectations, founded on their triumphs of 1951, led to some disappointment with the West Indies team of 1957. In the intervening six years West Indies had challenged strongly for "the World Championship" but, as with all successful teams, they had reached the stage where their best players were on the wane and the replacements still in the experimental stage. In this case several of the most promising experiments failed in the practical test.

The chief cause of the team's loss of positive strength was the decline in the potency of the spin combination of Valentine and Ramadhin. This was inevitable over the years, but was without doubt accelerated by overwork. Ramadhin was still a problem to most batsmen in his skilful disguise of finger spin but, after a magnificent spell in the first innings of the series at Birmingham, he seemed to lack the erstwhile life to exploit the immense advantage of this deception. Valentine had always relied on a tremendous power of spin, allied to great accuracy, and it was soon apparent that both these qualities had deserted him. The side still lacked pace of any considerable power, although Gilchrist astonished a number of people with his speed in the first Test Match.

The batting proved almost as great a disappointment. "The three Ws" had their moments, but injuries occurred to Walcott and Weekes at rather crucial moments, and Worrell alone averaged over 30 in the Test Matches. Of the newcomers O. G. Smith headed the Test Match figures, but the others, including Kanhai, did little. The fielding was on occasion rather below expected standards, and the overall record was fourteen wins in thirty-one first-class matches and three heavy defeats in the series.

This rather gloomy review does not mean that, given the opportunity in the variable weather of 1957, the team did not give some capital entertainment. In the M.C.C. match rain spoiled much of the first day, but the West Indians made a fine start with 337 for six wickets, with 117 from Walcott and 101 not out by Sobers. Worrell, in the role of opening bowler, was good enough to take six for 71, and M.C.C. were 53 behind on the first innings. Close made 108 in a robust two hours twenty minutes of hooking and driving. A blow on the foot in the field left him so lame that he had to have a runner throughout and was eventually forced to retire. There was little prospect of a result by this time, and the West Indians had a good bit of practice against Moss and Tyson in collecting 193 for three wickets.

The first Test Match, at Birmingham, had been the most astonishing game. On Saturday night, when Ramadhin had destroyed the English batting, it seemed that nothing except bad weather could frustrate West Indies. A prodigious second innings by England resulted in West Indies, far from winning, coming very near overwhelming defeat. Thus the odds for the Lord's match were very hard to assess. In the event a decisive English win reflected the true balance of power.

The match was played on a lively Lord's wicket upon which the splendid trio of seam bowlers, Trueman, Statham, and Bailey, dominated the match by taking nineteen wickets between them. Bailey bowled twenty-one overs, to disrupt the West Indian first innings by taking seven for 44 in a total of 127. There was still a bit of devil in the turf when England batted, and three wickets fell to Gilchrist and Worrell for 34 runs. Thereat Richardson and Cowdrey stemmed their progress and took the score to 129. The later batsmen took up the running and, with Cowdrey making 152, England got to 424, a position roughly equal to that of West Indies at Edgbaston at the same stage of the match.

There was no miraculous comeback by West Indies, but a Saturday crowd of 30,000 did see some wonderful cricket. The wicket seemed livelier than ever, and the English fast bowlers attacked with great relish. Three wickets fell for 32, but a fifth-wicket stand of 100 by Weekes and Sobers at least put a better face on things. It also produced some rare batting.

Weekes had a finger broken by a rising ball whilst already suffering from a slight leg-strain. Against some very testing fast bowling he showed his very best form, hooking the lifters with fine courage and judgment. Walter Robins thought it the best batting he had seen at Lord's since Bradman himself. When he was out for 90 Sobers, properly but unnaturally defensive, got to 66, but his departure was the end of official batting. West Indies were out for 261, and England had won by an innings and 36 runs.

In no first-class fixture do the relative strengths and fortunes of the contesting sides vary so rapidly as in the University Match.

This year it was the turn of Cambridge to dominate, which they did by an innings victory. Oxford made a mess of their first innings, and were all out for 92 on a green wicket. Wheatley had the notable analysis of five for 15 in fifteen overs. At the end of the day Cambridge were not so very far ahead, as five wickets, including that of Dexter, had fallen for 108 runs. The sixth wicket fell on Monday at 135, then Goonesena and Cook added 289 for the seventh. Goonesena was out for 211, when Cambridge declared, and Cook was not out for 111. On the last day Goonesena bowled splendidly to take four for 40, and Oxford lost by an innings and 186 runs.

The Gentlemen v. Players was a match so unlikely as to be almost peculiar. It afforded both contestants and spectators an abundance of surprise and diversion. The Gentlemen started boldly enough, passing 130 with only two wickets down, but rain brought about a collapse, and they were all out for 169. The Players had a truly lamentable hour in which they lost nine wickets for 46 before declaring. Dexter, who, with five wickets for 8, was the instrument of their destruction, had started the day with a total bag of eighteen wickets in first-class cricket. It was the Players' lowest score for over a hundred years. Insole attacked the bowling on an improving wicket, to make 79 not out, 20 off one over from Laker, and the Gentlemen declared at 167 for six. The Players set out in brisk pursuit of 291 runs, and with over 200 up for four were well on the way when Dexter brought about another untoward collapse. In the last ten minutes, 50 runs behind, Trueman and Hollies staved off defeat by one wicket.

Middlesex started the season with a strangely symmetrical pattern of wins and losses, no match being drawn until the end of June. The cricket was good, entertaining stuff with an occasional purple patch, as when Robertson and Gale put up 209 for the first wicket against Sussex. Moss bowled consistently well, and the team were happy under Edrich in his last year as captain. Compton found things more tiring, although his knee operation had been very successful, and had decided to end his career as a professional. It was apparent that, with the passage of time, several changes were imminent in the ranks and that other staunch members of the side had about run their race. In the Championship the team finished seventh, which was a drop of two places.

This year Clarence Bruce, third Baron Aberdare, was tragically drowned in Yugoslavia when his car overturned and pinned him down in three feet of water. He had played in three University matches, and for many years played for Middlesex whenever available. He batted in a free, swinging style, with the powerful and flexible wrists of the rackets-player, a game in which he also excelled.

In April Frank Chester died at the age of sixty-one. There is no saying what heights Chester might have reached from a most promising start as an active player, had he not lost an arm in the World War. His devotion to the game of cricket was rewarded when he achieved an eminence and reputation as an umpire quite unprecedented and still unrivalled. For many years the keenness of his senses, his power of sustained concentration, and his profound knowledge made him a seemingly infallible judge of any cricket situation. During that time his appointment for important occasions was as automatic as the selection of Jack Hobbs.

20

Seasons of Contrast

1958 was remarkable for the wettest June since 1903 and, as if the weather were not sufficient deterrent, the Lord's attendances were hit by a bus strike. Indeed, the whole "summer" was deplorably wet, and there was another half-million drop in the attendance aggregate. In May the New Zealanders beat M.C.C., but their modest resources suffered a body blow in that match when Bert Sutcliffe broke his wrist. They were a cheerful side whose good humour withstood "the slings and arrows of outrageous fortune". In the Lord's Test, which was England's hundredth since the War, their defeat by mid-afternoon on the Saturday meant that, for the second year running, a touring team's presentation to the Queen took place in the informal atmosphere of a cocktail party at Buckingham Palace instead of in line on the field at Lord's.

At the A.G.M. the Duke of Norfolk presented as his successor Marshal of the Royal Air Force Viscount Portal of Hungerford. The ranks of membership were swollen by 2000 new Associates and, as if to welcome (or perhaps camouflage) this throng, a discreet new tie was introduced as an alternative to the flamboyant red and yellow which used once to brand its wearer as "Non-U". The red-and-gold monogram on the navy-blue ground of the "city tie" was described by its manufacturer as "strictly speaking, marigold and buttercup"—a nice conceit had M.C.C. been a horticultural body. Members of sixty years' standing were now given the privilege of Honorary Life Membership. Before the year was out Douglas Wright retired from professional cricket and became an Honorary Cricket Member, and Honorary Life Membership was given to Sir Donald Bradman and to two county secretaries; to their doyen, Mr W. T. Taylor, now celebrating his Jubilee as Secretary of Derbyshire, and to Mr Harold Brown, the retiring Secretary of Notts, who had done much for Test Cricket at that famous ground. Another former county secretary, Lieut.-Colonel Hugh Henson, of Gloucestershire, died towards the end of the year. He was a delightful person, whose charm and ability endeared him to everyone at Lord's when he was deputy Assistant Secretary under Sir Pelham Warner. Towards the end of the War he had given invaluable service as a member of the Committee who re-drafted the Laws of Cricket.

Sir Pelham was still very much alive when he appeared in person at the ceremony when the Duke of Norfolk declared open officially the new stand and named it in his honour. It was as imposing as its predecessor had been modest; one of the few remaining rural corners of the ground had changed beyond recognition. The beautiful plane-tree, which the planners, to give them their due, had sought to preserve, sickened and died from the mortal blow dealt to it by the violation of its roots, but on the reconstituted mound was planted a flowering pyrus whose deep wine-red blossom has not, alas (to my eyes anyhow), been flattered in recent years by the enthusiastic planting of M.C.C. red and yellow tulips around it. But away with Lily Langtry's ghost and nostalgic sentiment! The stand provided seating for 3000 and offered improved amenities. The bar/cafeteria on the first floor has fine picture windows, enabling patrons to watch while they imbibe, and the "mod cons" are a great improvement on the Victorian austerity prevailing elsewhere. It was only the other day that I learned from an old friend who is a member that in the "con-veniences" to which Gentlemen may retire at either end of the bar, the usual fittings are each furnished with a window through which the occupant can watch the cricket. "How old 'Plum' would have loved this!" said my friend to his neighbour. "I bet the old boy thought of it himself" was the reply. Whoever the planning genius may have been, I need hardly add that he did not extend this particular piece of planning to the nose-powdering accommoda-tion provided for the wives and lady friends of members, which are sited discreetly at the rear so as to preclude any possibility of keeping in touch with the game.

Less pleased with their new quarters were the Press and the radio and television commentators, who preferred their former eyrie in the Pavilion, makeshift though it was, to the purpose-built, sound-proofed, and well-appointed boxes situated, as listeners and viewers are constantly reminded, in the general direction of deep extra cover.

The refashioning and modernization of the north-west corner of the ground was concluded by the completion of the seven new houses in Grove End Road.

This year Middlesex had a change of government. Off the field

Mr R. H. Twining, who had succeeded Sir Pelham Warner as President of the Club in 1957, handed over his wand of office to his friend and cricket contemporary Mr Gerald Crutchley; on the field John Warr took over the captaincy. Jack Robertson, now sole survivor of the Middlesex batting triumvirate, was still the best batsman in an otherwise very young side, but he dropped in the batting order to allow a newcomer, Eric Russell, to open with Gale. This year Middlesex joined the great majority of first-class counties by forming a Welfare Association and seeking to augment their income by running a football pool.

On Saturday June 28, during the tea interval of the Middlesex *v.* Somerset match, spectators had the then novel experience of assisting at the beating of the bounds by the parishioners of St Mark's Church, Hamilton Terrace. The Vicar, the Rev. W. H. Wilson, as an ardent cricket fan and a member of M.C.C., was particularly delighted that, in reviving this ancient custom, part of the ceremony could take place inside Lord's where the parish boundary line divides St Mark's from St John's Wood. In August the Royal Navy and the Army celebrated the fiftieth anniversary of their first encounter, and in honour of the occasion the score of the first match was printed on the match card.

For the first time since the War, a short M.C.C. tour of the Channel Islands was restored to the list of "out" matches. Desmond Eagar, with R. E. S. Wyatt and a team which included the Assistant Secretary of M.C.C., Jim Dunbar, plus their womenfolk, were "subjected" off the field to Channel Islands hospitality at its most fabulous. On the field they met and beat the combined Channel Island schools before meeting Jersey in a "representative" match which ended in an exciting draw. Sadly, the second match against Jersey was ruined by rain. The final game, against Guernsey on the beautiful Elizabeth College Ground, was won with five minutes to spare before a farewell cocktail party fortified the company for their return flight.

At the I.C.C. in July M.C.C. supported a proposal put forward by India's representative, the Maharaj Kumar of Vizianagram (known by long custom as "Vizzy"), with the backing of Australia, that, whereas the founder members had previously had two representatives while the younger members were limited to one, all countries should in future have equal status and equal representation and voting rights. This proposal was carried, but India's further suggestion that meetings should be held in the member countries in rotation received no support and was withdrawn.

Plans for the forthcoming M.C.C. Australia tour ran into troubled waters. M.C.C. had the support of the counties in seeking to curtail the duration of all the longer tours so that leading players might have some respite from the strain of a continuous round of six-days-a-week cricket and separation from their families, which was the peculiar lot of English cricketers. However, as the first to be affected, the Australians were not very sympathetic, and they viewed with concern the axing of up-country matches and the effects on profits. For some months there was a divergence of view amounting to deadlock. M.C.C. were unwilling to go back on their decision to shorten the tour and objected to a "bunching" of Test Matches, while the Australians regarded this as an inevitable outcome of the briefer schedule and financially expedient because of such extraneous matters as the celebration of Australia Day and the date of the Davis Cup tie.

In midsummer both J. C. Laker and J. H. Wardle informed the Selectors that for business and family reasons they would not be available. However, before the time came for the selection of the team the Chairman of Selectors was able to announce that both had changed their minds, and their names were included in the first fourteen players selected. Within three days the cricket world was startled to learn that the Yorkshire Committee had decided to terminate Wardle's engagement at the end of the season—an astonishing decision in the eyes of those who saw him as a great spin bowler and one of the most entertaining players in the game. Unhappily his dismissal was followed by a series of articles appearing under his name in *The Daily Mail*, highly critical of the York-shire Committee and his captain, Ronny Burnet. In face of this public criticism of the county, Yorkshire dismissed him forthwith. M.C.C. now had to consider whether or not to withdraw his invitation for the tour. Before making any decision the Committee invited him to Lord's, where at a prolonged meeting he was able to state his case. In announcing on the following day that they had decided to withdraw the invitation the M.C.C. Committee said they did so in support of the welfare of cricket as a whole in terms of loyalty and behaviour.

The M.C.C. team which sailed in the *Iberia*—the last to make the whole journey to Australia by sea—set out as cricket champions of the world, unbeaten since 1951, with no thought of defeat at the hands of Australia under their new captain, Richie Benaud. England were certainly unlucky, dogged by a whole chapter of accidents and injuries and with replacements (Dexter and

Mortimore) having to be flown out for the injured Subba Row and Watson. But the fact was that they were outplayed. England never found a satisfactory opening pair, and so the later batsmen were always struggling, with May thrown back on to defensive tactics. But the overriding memory is of a tour beset by controversial umpiring decisions and of complaints on the England side about the menace of a throwing epidemic which was pervading fast bowling in every grade in Australian cricket. Financially the tour was a success, with profits well up on 1954–55 and a sum of £16,500 for distribution to the English counties.

During the Christmas vacation a much more relaxed party of M.C.C. amateurs flew to South America on a highly enjoyable tour, with Hubert Doggart in command. A rain-ruined opening match seemed to the visitors to be more typical of their homeland than of Brazil, but a sumptuous Christmas in Rio and a convincing defeat of Brazil soon set the pattern of the tour. M.C.C. had paid the cricketers of Brazil and the Argentine the compliment of sending out a strong side, able to outplay their opponents in every department of the game. In countries where a small number of cricketers are knit in a limited community and batsmen and bowlers all know each other's foibles and weaknesses the visit of a team of unknown players gives a tremendous shot in the arm. The South Americans were devastated by the sheer speed of Sayer, by the accuracy of Bailey and Wheatley, and by the cunning of Ian Bedford, all in a class completely outside their experience. It was encouraging to find among the Argentine colts a good body of enthusiastic young players who profited enthusiastically from the coaching organized by M. H. Bushby in the team's spare moments. Two future Assistant Secretaries of M.C.C. played with great distinction, Donald Carr achieving a batting average of three figures and Jack Bailey a single-digit bowling average.

In late summer 1959 some of the same players, with Dennis Silk as captain this time, made the second post-War M.C.C. visit to Canada, rounding off the tour with matches in Philadelphia and Washington. In a great itinerary of single-day matches stretching right across the continent from Montreal to Vancouver the pattern was much as it had been in South America, with M.C.C. receiving a superb welcome wherever they went and winning most of their matches. Once more the bowlers, Bailey, Piachaud, and Bedford, outclassed their opponents. Even the wicket-keeper, Alan Smith, did the hat-trick. Once more M. H. Bushby devoted most of his spare time to coaching the young.

The value of sporting encounters at the highest level in cementing international friendships often seems at least arguable; the goodwill and encouragement produced by these less formal tours are undeniable. The only doubt lies in financial feasibility.

At home, in happy contrast to 1958, 1959 produced that rare phenomenon a superb English summer. Outside the Pavilion there was a great furore when shirtless men were seen at Lord's; inside, as I remember, binoculars were focused rather on a young lady whose sun dress, matching exactly her tan, gave an interesting deception of nudity. With attendances the best since 1955, the Secretary of M.C.C. was able to strike an optimistic note in his annual speech to the county secretaries, and the Editor of *Wisden* subtitled his Notes "English Cricket Thrives Again". Surrey's seven-year supremacy was broken at last, and the Championship pennant returned to Yorkshire. The visiting tourists, India, were beaten in the Tests by five matches to nil, and two almost unknown batsmen were saluted for their promise by *Wisden*, J. H. Edrich and A. A. Baig. The first was not yet considered ripe for international honours, but Baig, a first-year Blue at Oxford, was co-opted to take the injured Manjrekar's place in the Indian side. In the final match of the tour a Durham schoolboy called Colin Milburn made a century at their expense. Following the Australian humiliation, the England Selectors, G. O. Allen, H. Sutcliffe, D. J. Insole, and W. Wooller, made it known that they had embarked on a three-year plan to build up an England team worthy of the Australians' mettle in 1961. Established players made way for younger men. Laker was dropped, and at Lord's T. G. Evans made his farewell to Test cricket, securing the last of his 219 Test Match victims when he stumped S. P. Gupte off Greenhough.

The March meeting of the A.C.C.C. had decided on a more generous policy for covering pitches: during each night of a match, all day on Sunday if necessary, as well as on the eve of a match and as long as possible beforehand; also, from the moment when it was decided that no further play was possible on any day. The consequent need for more mobile equipment presented financial embarrassment to some counties and inspired much activity among manufacturers. Yorkshire spent over £2000 on glass-fibre covers, and at Lord's the old galvanized covers were re-roofed with Fibreglass. In addition the Grounds and Pitches Sub-Committee of M.C.C. spent a great deal of time in research to find practicable material to cover the whole square, with a small working committee carrying out experiments. Complaints had been

made that the polo-ground type of boundary boards used at
Lord's were dangerous—as, indeed, they were for any fielder
running full tilt towards them. A white rope was therefore introduced to mark the playing boundary, with boards outside the
rope to restrain spectators on big-match days. Another innovation
was the introduction of improvised canvas sight-screens suspended
from the Pavilion balcony; they were in use for the Test Match
against India and for all county matches. In September 1958 the
captains had requested that all counties should provide screens at
both ends, but at the end of the season the captain of Middlesex
opined that the additional screen at Lord's had been of very little
assistance, and the reaction of the players generally was so un-
enthusiastic that the Committee decided to discontinue them. The
players were much better pleased with the sliding screens which
were installed in 1964 (the year after the great match in which the
West Indies fast bowlers had demonstrated how hazardous batting
against a dark background could be in murky light) and have been
in use ever since. Surprisingly few members complained that they
blocked the view; but one distinguished champion of former
glories added a page to the Lord's folklore by declaring that he
elected to sit behind them to avoid the unwelcome sight of M.C.C.
batsmen toiling against the Australians. This year it was reported
for the first time that a ridge had appeared on the Lord's table—
more apparent at the top-side pitches than on those near the
Tavern. Nevertheless the Middlesex captain, J. J. Warr, thought
that the frequent incidence of shooters and balls that lifted high
might be caused by subsidence rather than a ridge.

The new President was Mr H. S. Altham, who for a year was
relieved of the full burden of responsibility for the Club's finances.
For the year of his Presidency my father became Acting Treasurer.
In the autumn the Club's finances received a considerable setback
as the result of a rise of £4476 in the rating assessment for the ground
and Tavern. Before 1956 the rateable value had been £3493. In
that year a threatened reassessment to £9663 had been alleviated
to £5000. Now, in 1959, the Valuation Officer was asking for as
much as £15,000—but added that he would agree to £9476.
M.C.C. appealed unsuccessfully to the Lands Tribunal for a
reduction to the pre-1956 valuation of £3500—pleading the
unremunerative nature of many of the matches such as schools and
Services fixtures. It was suggested by the representatives of the
Valuation Officer that M.C.C. should replenish its coffers by
arranging matches between male and female film-stars! Asked at

the Tribunal for his views on the future of cricket in Britain, Mr Altham had this to say:

Against the increased tempo of modern life cricket must be regarded as rather a slow-moving activity. Nevertheless I believe that cricket represents something traditional in the English way of life which will always command enough support to keep its head above water.

21

The Games and the Players 1958

SURVEYING the season of 1958, the Editor of *Wisden* sadly recalled that he had described 1956 as the wettest year within memory. He now ruefully decided that the summer just past took pride or shame of place. It was, in fact, a most dreary succession of rainy days interspersed with thunderous downpours.

The New Zealand team suffered with all others, but, being tourists, in a friendly but strange land, were at a greater disadvantage than the disillusioned natives. They were, as always, a most popular and sporting band, but could not be described as a great team. The injury so early in the tour to Sutcliffe, their one batsman of real international calibre, was a setback which threw the side out of balance in the early and vital stage of the trip. The results, in the circumstances, were not unexpectedly unimpressive: only seven matches were won, and the series brought overwhelming defeat by four lost matches and one draw.

The New Zealand first match at Lord's was one of their happiest. M.C.C. put a strong side into the field, but suffered defeat by 13 runs. Miller and Harford gave the visitors a fine start, but the later batting crumpled before Appleyard and Tyson, and the total fell just 10 short of the 200 mark. In the field the fast bowlers bowled well enough to make up for this collapse, and M.C.C. were out for 164. Miller and Harford again gave their side a fine start, and this time MacGibbon hit well for 66 not out, so that Reid could declare at 266 for eight. This time M.C.C. also batted very much better, but the fast bowlers again showed a fine tenacity. When the innings closed at 279 Hayes had taken seven for 49. The casualties had been heavy. It was in this match that Sutcliffe broke his wrist whilst fielding, Blair tore a shoulder muscle and could not bowl in the second innings, and Miller was unable to field because of a minor injury.

The second Test Match was as disastrous an occasion for the New Zealanders as the M.C.C. match had been encouraging. Defeated at Edgbaston, they lost the toss but put up another good

show in the field. At the end of the day England were only 237 for
seven on a goodish wicket, and that thanks mainly to Cowdrey. So
much rain fell overnight that play on Friday did not start till 3.20,
when MacGibbon finished off the English innings for 269. New
Zealand then batted on an awkward rather than dangerous pitch
and met with unrelieved calamity.

Trueman took the first wicket, then Laker and Lock went
straight through the rest of the batting. In just over two and a
quarter hours New Zealand were out for 47. Laker in taking four
for 13 and Lock with five for 17 were aided to some extent by mistaken tactics on the part of batsmen inexperienced in these conditions against bowling ideally suited to them.

Following on, they did little better. D'Arcy played an heroic
innings of 33, and Hayes at No. 11 struck 14, but this stretched the
total only as far as 74. The match was over with more than two
days to spare, and the margin of defeat was an innings and 148
runs.

One pleasing feature in this one-sided foray was the bowling of
MacGibbon, who had made such a good impression at Birmingham and was to take twenty wickets in the series. He was a great
character and immensely tall. Jack Phillipps, his manager, speaking at a dinner, remarked that if anyone wanted to know the real
meaning of discomfort he might try flying from New Zealand to
England with Tony MacGibbon in the adjoining seat.

The New Zealanders' return to play Middlesex in July was an
altogether happier occasion for them, although inevitably marred
by rain. Having got Middlesex out for 239, they headed this by 50
runs, largely through the agency of John Reid, who made 97 in a
couple of hours. Middlesex then made 174, and the New Zealanders
had a fairly easy task to get the 125 needed runs, as Moss was
unable to bowl owing to a sprained wrist. Only 3 of these had been
scored when heavy rain finished the day three hours before the
scheduled close.

Cambridge, led by Dexter, again won the University Match.
The start of the game was delayed for an hour through rain, after
which Cambridge batted tentatively to get to 161 for seven by the
close. Dexter made a surprise declaration next morning, and Oxford led on the first innings by 19 runs. Bailey, the Oxford captain,
who had bowled splendidly, suddenly tore a cartilage in his ankle,
and Cambridge recovered from an unpromising start. Green,
Cook, and Dexter, all got over 50, and the innings was declared at
269 for eight.

K

Oxford's last innings was somewhere between being lamentable and remarkable. Jowett made 56, and Eagar made 54. Nobody else made more than 7. When eight wickets had fallen for 134 Bailey hobbled to the wicket and battled manfully until only five minutes were left. At that point he was caught at the wicket, and Cambridge won by 99 runs.

The Gentlemen and Players fought an honourable draw, so far as the weather permitted. The first day was completely blank, but on the second the Players batted briskly to declare at 316 for five wickets. The Gentlemen lost three wickets for 63 before the close, but Subba Row batted through the entire innings bar the first run scored to make 102 not out. Insole declared 97 runs behind, when eight wickets were down, and in the limited time the Players declared at 70 for no wicket, after which the Gentlemen made 82 for three.

The chief benefit from the play was to the Selectors. Both Subba Row and Milton were prominent in their consideration, and a century from each was the sort of assurance Selectors welcome but do not always receive. On any specific trial there is ever an element of chance for both the Selector and the candidate. When Milton was 12 he played on to Wheatley, but the bails were undisturbed. He had his *quid pro quo* of bad luck, for, when fielding at short leg, he had his nose broken and retired for the rest of the game.

The departure of Compton and Edrich naturally had an immediate impact on the fortunes of Middlesex, who descended to tenth place in the table. There was no cause for despair, for the side was young and cheerful, and Warr soon showed he was the right man to lead them. Again they started well and were not beaten at Lord's until the end of June. A draw, in which they took four points for first-innings lead over Yorkshire, was worth many a win over lesser opposition.

On the morning of the Lord's Test Match the flags were flown at half-mast on the news of Douglas Jardine's death in Switzerland. He had led England for the first time against New Zealand at Lord's in 1931, and an eventful match had been a prelude to the most controversial captain in English cricket history. He was a fine cricketer and a character of granite-like texture. It was pleasant to observe that many fierce resentments caused by his tactics abated with the passage of time. As one who knew him well in his later years and saw much of him at public and private functions, I could not help observing that he had one revealing characteristic. Where any guest was diffident or neglected he would make a point of addressing his remarks to him and including him in the conversation. His heart was, in fact, very kind as well as very stout.

The two most original virtuosi of the era died within a few months of each other. George Gunn died in his sleep with, one would imagine from the legends he left behind, a gentle smile. He had originally been destined to be a musician, and he brought to cricket the art and imagination, not to say gentle eccentricity, of the musical profession. There were two remarkable points in his career which particularly concerned Lord's. His only Test Match in England was played there when he was sadly out of form in 1909. The second smacks of Sherlock Holmes's "curious incident of the dog in the night-time"—curious because it did nothing. In 1921, when the pace of Gregory and McDonald disrupted English batting, six new players were picked for the Lord's match, but the greatest existing master of fast bowling was omitted.

Lord's brought better luck to Charlie Macartney, who died in September. In 1912 he struck the irresistible Barnes and Foster for 99. In trying to convey to me Barnes's true quality he once told me that he had announced before this innings he was going to hit Barnes for six. Without trace of affectation he added, "I had to wait until I was 68."

In 1921 he received 22 balls and made 31. In 1926, in the second innings, he made 133 not out whilst five of his colleagues departed in making 43 between them. He enjoyed himself as much as everyone else did, especially when he playfully late cut a full toss for four. He was a confident but modest four-square cricketer, and a character who centres in almost as many evergreen cricket tales as George Gunn himself.

Frank Foster, who got Macartney out when he had made his 99 in 1912, died at Northampton. This was, in fact, the only occasion when the famous pair of Barnes and Foster played against Australia at Lord's. In contrast to his partner's Frank Foster's career was a short one, cut off by war, accident, and illness. He will be remembered chiefly as a bowler, with the same quality of making the ball fly from the pitch at redoubled pace which made Maurice Tate so devastating. From a short run he bowled mostly over the wicket with an easy left-handed action, moving the ball in to the batsman, but occasionally making one go the other way. Frank Woolley, who fielded second slip for most of the triumphant tour of Australia in 1911–12, said that taking a catch from Foster was "like being hit with a stick".

There was another memory of those great days when Vernon

Ransford, a fine Victorian left-hander, died in Melbourne. Perhaps his greatest feat during that series was in his home city when Barnes started the day by taking five wickets for 6 runs. Going in when four wickets had fallen for 11 runs, he, like the Abbé Siéyès, survived.

J. R. Mason, who died in October, was popularly regarded as the finest cricketer who never played for England. He was a cricketer in the widest sense of the term, and in Kent many will say he was also the finest captain who ever led his or any other county.

Mason had many great moments at Lord's and one truly awe-inspiring. Having put up 130 for the Gentlemen's first wicket with "W.G.", he momentarily forgot the problems of eighteen stone and a half-century of years and ran the "Old Man" out.

Philip Mead died in March. He was the soundest left-hander of his day, and deceptively progressive. Like all good old soldiers, so long as he was having a good grouse things were fine. My last memory of him in the middle at Lord's was a solid two and a half hours ensuring a draw on the last day. This was punctuated by bitter periodical references to the superb train leaving at that very moment for Southampton, but, despite my hopeful hints and commiserations, he was there at the end of the day. The next time I saw him at Lord's he was stone-blind, most cheerful, and without a grumble in the world.

22

The Games and the Players 1959

THE faith and patience of cricket-lovers was generously rewarded in 1959. The sun shone forth for the greater part of the season, and the players responded eagerly to its encouragement.

Only on the international plane was there disappointment. The Indians, although in some respects a better side than the previous one, lost all five Tests Matches by heavy margins, and were only moderately successful in the other first-class fixtures, winning six and losing eleven matches. Only the fourth Test at Manchester got into the fifth day, and three were lost by an innings. This caused some people to question the wisdom of five-day Tests with the lesser powers. Admittedly in the normal English climate even five days was no guarantee of a finished match, but the disruption to the domestic programme is considerable, and the disappointment to the public keen when the whole affair was over in three days. It is, however, a vexed problem involving national pride. One could not but reflect on the cheerful three-day games of pre-War days when England had to hustle to beat lesser opposition.

The M.C.C. match, as the traditional dress rehearsal for the series, foreshadowed its outcome. The Indians were outclassed by a good all-round home team. Milton and Dexter made centuries, and M.C.C. declared at 374 for four wickets. Umrigar and Borde made 82 and 88 respectively, but even so India could only manage 211. M.C.C. declared at 120 for one, then Illingworth bowled the Indians out for 136. On the last day there was only one wicket standing, so the match to all intents and purposes ended in two days.

In the Test India put up a better fight than in the innings defeat at Trent Bridge. They were beaten in three days, but made England struggle at one period, when, having made 168, they got seven English wickets down for 100. But Barrington made 80 and, with the somewhat unexpected support of 38 from Statham and 26 from Moss, England led by 58 runs. In their second innings India again batted in the same uneven pattern to make 165, so leaving England 107 to get, with, at least theoretically, over two and a half days to get them. Two wickets fell for 12, but Cowdrey and May collected the balance without being unduly pressed.

In July the Indians had the satisfaction of winning at Lord's, Middlesex going down by four wickets. They now had the services of Baig, the Oxford batsman, who made a particularly good hundred. The Indians were able to enforce the follow-on and were eventually set only 67 to win. Such was their impetuosity in the face of this warming prospect that they lost six wickets in the process and had some nervous moments.

Baig had materially helped in Oxford's first win over Cambridge since 1951. This was one match which started after heavy rain under a grey and cloudy sky. Oxford batted evenly but without great distinction to make 217, the second top scorer being C. A. Fry, grandson of "C.B.". Cambridge showed a lack of certainty against Sayer's lively pace and batted very unevenly to be out for 174. When Oxford were 154 for eight in their second innings, of which Baig had made 50, the game was very open, but the last two wickets added 84 and, on the form of the first innings, Cambridge were at a disadvantage. They lost Blofeld with 2 runs on the board, and therefrom were always short of the target, to lose by 85 runs.

The Gentlemen and Players both scored so freely that the Players had ten wickets in hand when the match ended in a draw. The Gentlemen's first innings did not presage this, for, apart from M. J. K. Smith, who made 79, no one did much, and the score was 194. Close and Illingworth then made centuries, and the Players reached 365. Sayer, after his successful Varsity Match, bowled at fine pace and took six for 69. At this point he promised to become a bowler of great if unsubtle pace rather in the pattern of H. D. Read, but these hopes were never quite fulfilled.

After losing an early wicket Smith and Subba Row replied by taking the score to 187, and Smith then went on to make 166. Declaring at 319 for five, May gave the Players eighty minutes to make 149, but his challenge was ignored. The Players were 49 for no wicket when it was decided not to claim the extra half-hour. This was a tame finish compared to the many alarms and excursions of recent years.

Middlesex found a splendid captain in Warr, an intelligent cricketer and a man of rare and original wit. They did not, however, have a great season, finishing tenth in the table. The batting was on paper good for the whole order, but seemed to be slow in developing. It was led by a very elegant opening pair in Eric Russell and the left-handed Gale. Russell made over 50 in six of his first eight innings, but thereafter was very variable. Once again hopes were raised by a good winning sequence in the early home session, but Middlesex were less successful when abroad. The future was promising in the number of young players, but so far there was naturally a great vacuum where Compton and Edrich had once dominated county cricket at Lord's.

In December there came the sad news that "Duleep" was dead. He was much loved by the Lord's crowd, and it was there he had played his greatest Test Match innings. In 1930 he had made 173 when, seeking to push the score along, he went to drive Grimmett and was caught off a skier to mid-on. His uncle, the great "Ranji", turned to his neighbour with some impatience. "I told you so," he said. "The boy's careless."

Farther afield Herbie Collins died in Sydney. He had known Lord's since he had made 127 against Middlesex for the Australian Imperial Forces on his first appearance. For a man so lucky as to be called "Horseshoe" Lord's brought him little fortune thereafter. Injury kept him out of the match in 1921, and in 1926 he made 1 and 24.

23

Illegal Bowling

AS the sixties overtook the fifties a new-look M.C.C. team returned from the West Indies, having achieved the hitherto unattainable feat of beating the West Indians on their own ground. But once more a tour had been marred by charges of time-wasting by England and bowling by their opponents that was both dangerous, because of a preponderance of short-pitched balls, and often illegal. Added to this the England captain, Peter May, was forced to fly home before the fourth Test, ill and exhausted from the reopening of an operation wound.

Financially the optimism of 1959 proved to be a flash in the pan, for, although in 1960 the counties increased their membership, most showed a loss in attendances. As for M.C.C., a surplus of £8885 in 1958 was converted in two years to a deficit of £9188—a figure which, however, was swollen by the transfer of £5000 to the Building Fund. In the autumn M.C.C. were asked once more by the counties to carry out an enquiry into their structure and future welfare.

But troubles other than finance were rocking the boat. As early as 1957 unofficial discussions at Lord's had led to the sinister word "throwing" reappearing after half a century on the agenda of the M.C.C. Cricket Sub-committee, with the result that Mr Allen passed on to the first-class umpires M.C.C.'s concern about the action of certain bowlers and urged them to enforce Law 26. But in spite of the admonitions no English bowler was called in 1958. As we have seen, throwing was soon to be blown up almost to the dimension of an international incident in the harsh light of criticism focused on such bowlers as Meckiff, Rorke, Burke, and Slater, playing against M.C.C. in Australia. Throwing now figured large in the discussions of every cricket board in the world, for all countries recognized the need to curb it. Already young bowlers in Australia, the West Indies, and South Africa were copying their elders and learning at an early age, almost before they were conscious of it, habits which they would find it hard to eradicate.

In England it was discussed at length by the A.C.C.C. In the close season of 1958–59 the search began for a definition of a throw, and the first-class umpires agreed to compile a list of bowlers with doubtful actions. In 1959 Lock, among others, was no-balled, and with great strength of mind and will he set about amending his action.

An article by Mr Harry Gee in the 1960 *Wisden* opened with an optimism which was shattered only too soon. "Will the summer of 1960 go down in cricket history as the season when the twin controversies of throw and drag were settled?" At the 1959 I.C.C. the members had made a unanimous declaration that they would seek all measures to eradicate throwing from the game. South Africa's representative, Mr Coy, went further, and declared that his country would not include any bowler with a suspect action in an international team. Yet it was a young South African bowler, Geoff Griffin, who was the unhappy victim a year later when, contrary to the hopes of Harry Gee, the whole problem exploded before the end of May. Griffin had been no-balled in provincial matches in South Africa, and his action had already excited much comment in England when he arrived at Lord's to play against M.C.C. and was no-balled by both umpires, Frank Lee and John Langridge. In his next match, against Notts at Trent Bridge, he was called no fewer than eleven times, an event which drove him to seek advice from Alf Gover. With a modified action, but erratic direction, he came through the first Test unscathed, only to be called again six times against Hampshire on the eve of the second Test. So came the historic match at Lord's; historic because of his hat-trick—a performance unique in a Lord's Test—but also, disastrously, because he was the first bowler to be no-balled for throwing in a Test Match in England. In all he was called eleven times, but the final blow came in the exhibition match, shortly before the arrival of H.M. the Queen and the Duke of Edinburgh to greet, for the last time, a South African team in England. Griffin's only over was extended by no-balls to eleven balls, and he could only complete the over by bowling lobs. He bowled no more on the tour, and an understandable coolness developed in the South African camp.

The affair lent urgency to the discussions at the I.C.C. in July. The proceedings were prolonged to two days instead of the usual one, and more high-ranking overseas delegates (as distinct from Englishmen representing their interests) were present than ever before. At the outset Mr Altham offered a solemn undertaking, on behalf of M.C.C., that England would exclude from international teams and tours all bowlers whose actions were considered suspect. However, two countries—West Indies and Australia—objected on the grounds that not to select a bowler would be to take authority out of the hands of the umpire and that selectors would be in an impossible position if they undermined respect for their own umpires by failing to select bowlers whom they had passed as fair. The countries reaffirmed unanimously their determination to eradicate throwing and, in the hope of securing a more uniform interpretation of what constitutes a throw, agreed on the following definition:

> *A ball shall be deemed to have been thrown if, in the opinion of either umpire, the bowling arm, having been bent at the elbow, whether the wrist is backward of the elbow or not, is suddenly straightened immediately prior to the instant of delivery. The bowler shall nevertheless be at liberty to use the wrist freely in the delivery action.*

The twin problem of drag continued, less explosively, to be the subject of discussion, experiment, and report in every country. It was agreed that the pulling back of draggers by the use of a disc had been internationally successful, though most delegates felt that ultimately the solution might be the front-foot principle and all member countries were commended to consider the possibility of adopting it as an experiment starting not before September 1962. In proposing a vote of thanks to the Chairman at the end of the two days Mr Dowling (Australia) said this was probably the most important meeting of the Conference since its inception.

In 1960 there was a ballot for the first time to fill the vacancies on the Committee, but the candidates recommended by the Committee were accepted. The President-elect was Sir Hubert Ashton, M.P. for Chelmsford, who added to his many responsibilities in public life a very active Presidency. The change from the old order was reflected in additions to the roll of Honorary Cricket Members: Godfrey Evans, Jim Laker, and Cyril Washbrook in 1960 and Alec Bedser in 1961. Unhappily, within a couple of months of his election Laker was the subject of a *cause célèbre*, having, in the opinion of his county club, overstepped the bounds of loyalty in misrepresenting their staff and officials in the inevitable book of memoirs which is the almost automatic appendix to every cricketer's career. Surrey withdrew his pass for the Oval, and it was with regret, after giving him a chance to state his case, that M.C.C. felt bound to support the principle of a player's loyalty to his county and suspend his M.C.C. membership. As in the case of Wardle, the affair caused something of a furore and left a bitter taste on the palate. But in the course of time Laker made his peace with Surrey and was reinstated. In July the President's personal invitation to a representative body of prominent overseas players and administrators resulted in the election of a further sixty-three Honorary Life Members.

The Committee were unflagging in their concern for the encouragement of young cricketers. The writer of a leading article in *The Times* at the end of the season mitigated the impact of poor attendances with the consolation that although fewer people were watching cricket more had been playing, and went on to say that by far the most cheerful feature of contemporary cricket was the admirable youth coaching scheme and subsequent encouragement of young entries to the fields. Under the reigning President's enthusiastic guidance the work of the M.C.C. Youth Cricket Association continued apace. Youth Cricket Councils had been set up at county level throughout the country, and there was now a large body of trained coaches, holders of the M.C.C. Coaching Certificates. At Lord's the reorganized Easter Cricket Classes gave intensive instruction to 450 pupils every year. But an examination of the costing of the classes now disclosed a formidable deficit, so that, not without reluctance, the Committee felt compelled to raise the fees to what was still a very modest sum.

Attempts were being made to prune the number of fixtures to which the Lord's pitch was subjected. It was not without some personal regrets that I saw the annual match between the Royal Artillery and the Royal Engineers banished to the fastnesses of Woolwich and Chatham, for in my extreme youth my father had appeared a number of times for the Sappers, and the matches in the years immediately before the War, when we first came to Lord's, were always occasions of keen rivalry and renewal of old friendships. Sir Neville Cardus was a fellow-mourner for the passing of this match—not, let me say, on account of the quality of the cricket, but because he so much enjoyed the band, which was supplied by the Gunners and the Sappers in alternate years. The Club Cricket Conference were another casualty, who, much to the chagrin of their genial Secretary, Major Woods, were banished in 1962 to Crouch End. In the past decade the number of out matches had increased by 25 per cent, and the 1960 list included another six-game tour of the Channel Islands and a "representative" match against Ireland at Dublin. With the preponderance of school fixtures in mind, steps were taken towards the delicate but very desirable policy of appointing younger match managers.

Because some counties had opted to play thirty-two matches the County Championship scoring system reverted to percentages. Middlesex, who abided by the limit of twenty-eight, gave John Warr a good parting present by improving their fortunes from a lowly tenth to third place, after Yorkshire and Lancashire. Some of his faithful admirers in "Q" Stand furbished the celebration by the gift of a wine decanter. The new captain, Ian Bedford, returned to county cricket after ten years in the relaxed atmosphere of club cricket.

A new responsibility laid upon Mr Griffith after his appointment as Assistant Secretary, responsible for cricket, was the role of Press Liaison Officer. M.C.C.'s attitude to the Press had been regarded at least in some quarters as less than helpful. Certainly it is true to say that my father, with his training in the school of Army discipline, took a cautious view of Press relations and did little to relax the reserve of his predecessors. There were those who thought M.C.C. made too little effort to present its own image in a favourable light. In 1960 the task of improving Press liaison was given to a newly appointed Standing Advisory Press Committee, which included Press representation nominated by the Cricket Writers' Club.

Inevitably the weight of the discussions at the A.C.C.C. centred on illegal bowling and the future of first-class cricket. Outside these topics it was agreed that, as an experiment in 1961, the follow-on should be abolished in county cricket and that the new ball should be available after eighty-five overs, instead of after seventy-five overs or 200 runs. A proposal to return to the old lbw law was turned down.

With the Australian tour of England imminent, 1960-61 was a blank winter for major English tours, but M.C.C. sent an "A" team to New Zealand. The team was led by Dennis Silk and included such Test potential as Roger Prideaux, Jim Parks, David Allen, Eric Russell, Bob Barber, and John Murray. As Manager they were fortunate to secure the services of Mr Jack Phillipps, a good friend of English cricket and Manager of two New Zealand teams in England. On the eve of the second unofficial Test Match at Wellington the team received a great welcome from Lord Cobham, lately President of M.C.C. and now Governor-General of New Zealand. Leading his own eleven at Auckland a fortnight later, he delighted 23,000 spectators by putting into practice his own doctrine of aggressive cricket to the tune of 44 runs in less than half as many minutes.

The 1961 Australians were awaited with rather more than the usual eager anticipation. Under the lively captaincy of Richie Benaud they had played in their own country against West Indies, whose own new captain, that prince of cricketers Frank Worrell, was as determined as Benaud to play the game as it should be played, with lively enjoyment. The result had been a series which revived interest in cricket throughout the world and added for good measure the intense thrill of the unique tied match at Brisbane.

But the eagerness was tempered with anxiety. Much preliminary thought was given to ensuring that during the Australian tour there should be no repetition of the fiasco of Griffin. Sir Donald Bradman, on the eve of his appointment to the chairmanship of the Australian Cricket Board of Control, was moved to say that if the controversy were allowed to get out of hand the Australian tour could lead to the greatest catastrophe in cricket history. Before he left for Australia after attending the 1960 I.C.C. he put forward a proposal which he was hopeful his Board would accept, that no Australian bowler should be called on the field, but that the Test Match umpires should have an early opportunity of seeing them and sending to the President of M.C.C. a confidential report on any bowler whose action they thought was suspect. In the event this sweeping moratorium was curtailed so as to end on the eve of the first Test, after which date umpires were instructed to "call" bowlers on the field. To avoid inegality the counties agreed to extend the moratorium to English bowlers in matches against the tourists. No unpleasant incident jarred the harmony between England and Australia in the centenary year of cricket tours between the two countries. The Australians left their suspect bowlers at home, and the only bowler on either side to be reported was Derbyshire's Harold Rhodes. Jack Fingleton, a better quali-fied judge than most, ranked this the happiest tour he had known in all his long experience as player and journalist—and this was not only because his own country won a rubber in England again after an interval of thirteen years. The credit lay very much with Richie Benaud, who during that summer became something of a knight errant in English eyes. Not every captain's promise to play attractive cricket is fulfilled, but Benaud's was, with a cheerful abandon and a determination to win matches which was soon demonstrated to the Lord's crowd in the match against M.C.C. Lawry's century—his third in a fortnight—was a signpost to the second Test, when, because of Benaud's unfitness, Neil Harvey led

Australia in his last Test at Lord's. In August Harvey captained the Australians again against the Gentlemen of England, as he paid his farewell to Lord's in a match which turned out to be the last of that time-honoured series, dating back to the days of Grace and Murdoch. Sadly, the occasion lacked lustre from the absence of May, Subba Row, and Cowdrey. Another Australian to make his farewell to international cricket at Lord's was their fast bowler Alan Davidson.

Peter May was fit enough to return to the England side at Lord's, though without resuming the captaincy until the third Test. But soon he announced his retirement from overseas tours; to ensure a continuity of leadership he added that he did not wish to be considered again for the England captaincy. As we shall see, his retirement led to lively conjecture and a copious flow of printing ink when the time came to select the M.C.C. captain for Australia in 1962.

The Lord's pitch was so much criticized for its excessive liveliness that immediately after the Test a consultant surveyor was called in to investigate the reputed ridge at the Nursery end. His findings indicated small variations in the height of the surface, and a more comprehensive survey at the end of the season showed a slight ridge where the ball pitched at the Nursery end and an even slighter corresponding ridge at the Pavilion end. It also transpired that the worst pitch was in the centre of the square. The experts thought that in the long term the square could be levelled successfully by top dressing, but the Committee decided on the more drastic cure of lifting the worst affected area and adjusting the soil level.

Some time before the 1961 season the balcony on the first floor of the Pavilion, which affords such an unrivalled view of the game, was found to be in danger of collapse. With regret, the Committee decided to replace the costly Victorian wrought-iron rails with a plain functional barrier, which offered the practical benefit of 70 additional seats and the possibility of electing 300 more members paying £1200 per annum. Hot weather in June made the extra seats outside most acceptable to certain members desiring to enjoy the sunshine in their shirt-sleeves. Complaints that members and their friends were appearing improperly dressed, jacketless and tieless, inside the Pavilion, had provoked a ruling that both should be worn inside the Pavilion, though no objection was made to their removal outside.

In August a representative team from Denmark played against

M.C.C. at Lord's, and were beaten by 115 runs in a one-day match. In the evening they were entertained to dinner, and they presented to M.C.C., as a previous Danish team had in pre-War days, a miniature silver flagpole bearing a Danish pennant.

This season Middlesex, under a new captain and partially deprived of the services of John Murray, who, for a season promised to become regular keeper for England, did well to make a strong challenge for the Championship, and eventually finish third, behind Hampshire and Yorkshire. Murray earned for himself a wicket-keeping prize of 100 guineas for the most victims; Peter Parfitt headed the batting averages and won the Cricket Writers' award of Young Cricketer of the Year. Two of the county's vintage players, Patsy Hendren and Jack Durston, who had once helped to fill the seats at Lord's and give hours of delight to the county's supporters, received a testimonial with a collection during the Middlesex *v.* Australia match. Needless to say, "Little Hampshire's" Championship, invoking the shades of Hambledon, brought particular joy to her President, the Treasurer of M.C.C.

For the second year running the meeting of the Imperial Cricket Conference was faced with a crucial problem, not on this occasion concerned with the conduct of the game, but with the status of one of the founder members. On May 31 the decision of South Africa to leave the Commonwealth had become effective, and although strictly speaking, this happening came too late for the status of the South African Cricket Association to appear on the Agenda, nevertheless her position was fully debated, without any decisions being taken. By definition, under the rules of the I.C.C., South Africa had ceased to be a member, but it was agreed by all the other members that her representative, Mr Foster Bowley, should attend as an observer, although he withdrew when the South African position was discussed. The newest member, Pakistan, was the first to say that any request by South Africa to be associated with the I.C.C. in the future would have to be accompanied by an undertaking to drop their attitude of exclusiveness and engage with all other Conference countries irrespective of colour. In a five-point written statement Mr Bowley met this by saying that the S.A.C.A. would gladly accept invitations to tour India, Pakistan, and the West Indies, but could not invite these countries to South Africa because the Government had stated it would not allow non-white teams from overseas to play against white teams in South Africa, but only against non-white teams. Other points were concerned with inter-racial cricket. The Board had held back from promoting official inter-racial matches because, although there was no law forbidding it, they felt that to do so might invite the Government to introduce one, thus preventing unofficial games which presently took place. When the Conference was founded in 1909 the objective had been the promotion of international tourneys between England, Australia, and South Africa. Until 1926 these three countries remained the sole members. However the policies of the Nationalist Government might be deplored, England and Australia could not but mourn the loss of their co-founder and seek at least to leave the door open for her readmission if and when more liberal policies prevailed. Meanwhile delegates were given the opportunity to report back to their Boards the general feeling of the Conference, and the question was left open for future consideration.

Evidence that the old order was changing came with the disappearance of familiar faces on the staff. More than one generation of cricketers had been served by Jack O'Shea, who retired from the post of Head Dressing-room Attendant after forty years at Lord's, and at the end of 1961 Mr C. Almond (known to his friends and colleagues as "Nutty") retired from the Ticket Office, where for years his precise, unruffled manner and unfailing courtesy had endeared him to members and staff alike.

The Ground and Fixtures Sub-committee were working on a new scheme for the M.C.C. professional staff to put to rights the lack of cricket progress and apparent waste of money being expended to produce county players as a contribution to the game. From time immemorial junior ground boys had been required to carry out a multiplicity of extra-cricket duties, notably ground-cleaning. Examination showed that their coaching was restricted to one or at most two afternoons a week; and the Sunday games— the only match play they got—for which M.C.C. paid expenses, were mostly of poor standard on bad pitches. The sort of cricket that boys of similar age at a public school enjoyed never came their way. In an age when life was more affluent and apprenticeship less harsh than in the boyhood of Hendren or Compton, recruitment on these terms was no longer fruitful. The life of the senior Grade A staff (nineteen to twenty years old) was spent being coached at the nets or bowling to members. Unlike young players attached to the counties, they had little or no opportunity for competitive cricket. The new plan was to eliminate the old Grade A staff and concentrate on the age group fifteen to nineteen. Gradually, over a transitional period, they were to be relieved entirely of ground-cleaning duties, which were henceforth performed by the secondment of labour from the Works Department, leaving the young cricketers ample time for cricket training and play. Arrangements were made for them to play mid-week matches against public schools, and a scheme was envisaged for attaching members of the staff to clubs in the London area. The cost of all this to M.C.C. was estimated at £1300 per annum. They would, of course, continue to provide staff to bowl to members in the nets, and the senior boys would play in M.C.C. out matches.

Before the end of 1960 Mr Ronny Aird had warned the Committee of his wish to retire after the 1962 season, and within a few weeks Mr S. C. Griffith was selected to succeed him. The pressure of modern administration had caused the virtual disappearance of the old Secretary's office, presided over, in turn, by Mr Henry Perkins (whose beard vied with W. G. Grace's and whose proverbial taste for whisky is belied by a couple of earthenware water-bottles which are reputed to have furnished his table), by the more ascetic and legalistic Sir Francis Lacey and his successor, Mr William Findlay; then, briefly, by my father, who, however, retired after the War to the modest but private sanctum which has been the Secretary's office ever since. Sadly, from the aesthetic point of view, this fine room with its lofty windows (allowing its occupants a splendid vista of comings and goings at the Grace Gates) had perforce to be partitioned to allow two Assistant Secretaries to carry out their respective duties in some privacy, if not in peace, in separate rooms. The illness of Mr Griffith shortly after his appointment became known was a serious blow and a great anxiety to his many friends, lest his health should be overtaxed by the strain of the ever more demanding office he was about to take up. It is as well, perhaps, that neither he nor they could see in the crystal ball the full extent of the crises and anxieties to which he would be subjected, greater far than those confronting any other Secretary before him.

In February Sir Pelham Warner, recovering from an operation and very conscious now of increasing age and declining health asked that he might be allowed to resign from the office of Trustee. In accepting his resignation with the deepest regret the Committee assured him that he could rely on an affectionate welcome in the Committee Room whenever he felt able to come to Lord's, and at the Annual Meeting he was elected the first Life Vice-President of the Club.

L

24

The Games and the Players 1960

THE weather reverted to the more normal "scattered showers" in the English summer of 1960. The cricket was correspondingly less inspiring, and the touring South Africans were, on the whole, a disappointment. The Editor of *Wisden* ruefully suggested that cricket-lovers would recall 1960 as "The Sad Season". It was not altogether uneventful.

The cricket world was still in a sensitive and controversial frame of mind concerning the great "throwing" controversy which had blown up in Australia on May's tour. The South African tour had not been long in progress when it was bedevilled by objections to Griffin, their new fast bowler, whose withdrawal after the second Test is recorded elsewhere in these pages.

Apart from this catastrophe the South Africans had certain other deficiencies which brought defeat by a strong England side in three straight matches. In the last two they did much better to achieve honourable draws, but by then interest had to some extent evaporated. Of thirty first-class matches in all they won fourteen and lost five. Adcock took twenty-six wickets in the series for 22·57 runs apiece, but he lacked the fiery support of Heine.

At Lord's in May McGlew put M.C.C. in to bat on a softish wicket, and could have been content to see them make 208. His peace of mind must have been greatly disturbed when, in his fifth over, Griffin was called by umpire Lee. When Griffin tried the other end Langridge twice no-balled him, and on one occasion Griffin had the unique experience of being no-balled by both umpires simultaneously for throwing and dragging. These incidents which were the culmination of much previous speculation, overshadowed the rest of the game.

The South Africans batted indifferently in unhelpful conditions to make 149, but Tayfield and Goddard bowled well enough to right the balance, and M.C.C. declared their second innings at 137 for nine. The South Africans had two hours and fifty minutes to get 197, but were always behind the clock. With 126 for seven at the close they were grateful to save the match.

The second Test Match started at Lord's on June 23. The umpires were Lee and Buller. England won the toss and compiled a total of 362 for eight wickets, at which Cowdrey declared. Griffin was the most successful bowler, and in taking four wickets for 87 he had become the first South African to do a hat-trick. But there was a very sizeable fly in this most pleasant ointment. Griffin bowled throughout from the Pavilion end, and was called no fewer than eleven times by Lee. It was sadly apparent that the cure had not been complete.

The South African batting twice broke down before Statham, who, at his very best, took eleven wickets for 97 runs. The South Africans made 152 and 137, so lost by an innings and 73 runs. This result coming early on Saturday, it was decided to play an exhibition match to entertain the large crowd sitting in the warm June sunshine.

Griffin again bowled from the Pavilion end, but this time Buller was the square-leg umpire. The first ball went by without incident, but the next four Buller "called". It was clear that do what he might Griffin could not satisfy the umpire's doubts, and on McGlew's advice he finished the over underarm. In delivering the first of these lobs he was no-balled by Lee for failing to notify the batsman of his intended change of style. It was one of the saddest moments I could recall on any cricket pitch, for it was obvious that Griffin's career was going to end at that moment, following so closely on the triumph of his hat-trick. It was a just but cruel situation, and the large crowd made every gesture of sympathy, clearly indicating its understanding that here was stark misfortune and no question of roguery. In the circumstances it was hard to derive much entertainment from the "exhibition".

It was interesting to see that when the South Africans returned to play Middlesex in mid-July the public gave Griffin a specially warm welcome when he appeared as "drinks waiter" or in any other capacity. This match was played in uncertain weather, and Middlesex batted with equal uncertainty against Adcock and Tay-field in making 191. The South Africans, led by 142 from Goddard, batted surely to declare at 397 for six. When Middlesex were 102 for four in the second innings the South Africans were well on the way to victory, but a violent storm flooded the ground and put an emphatic full-stop to the play.

The great names which had studded the University sides in the fifties now largely figured in the England teams. In the University Match of 1960 Oxford could boast two Indian Test Match players in Pataudi and Baig; and Prideaux, who opened for Cambridge, was later to do so for England. The match was drawn, greatly in favour of Oxford.

Corran bowled Cambridge out for 153, taking six for 48 in twenty-nine overs. When Oxford had lost three wickets for 32 things were very level, but Burki and Pataudi then took the score to 222, when Burki was out for 79. Pataudi went on to make 131, which must have delighted the shade of his father, and took Oxford to 310. A second fine effort by Corran brought him another six wickets for 70, but Cambridge, aided by time lost through rain, had still one wicket standing with 86 runs in hand at the end of the day.

The first day of the Gentlemen and Players match was washed out, but yet again it progressed to a really spectacular finish. When play was possible the Gentlemen fared poorly and made a modest 108. In much improved conditions the Players made 168 for two and declared. The Gentlemen now got into their stride and, with a flying start from Subba Row and Prideaux, they returned the compliment by declaring at 227 for four wickets. The Players blithely accepted the challenge of 168 at 96 an hour and arrived at 166 with eight wickets down, Allen and Moss having carried the score from 135. Allen then drove a ball to long-on, where Dexter ran in to gather it. One run was safely taken, making the match level, and the batsmen set out for a second which would bring victory. In this they might have been successful had not Dexter let fly and hit the middle stump at the bowler's end from 35 yards away. Moss was out by a fair margin, and, this being on the stroke of time, the match ended in a draw.

Warr's good captaincy was given a parting reward by Middle-sex running into third place. They were very close to Lancashire and with a bit of luck could have been second. They were not particularly powerful in either batting or bowling, but were a very good team and fielded superbly, a feature which made for good cricket to watch. In their opening sequence at Lord's they won their first five matches and drew the next two, but this time, for a change, they sustained their form over the season. Over the season four matches were lost, but only one, against Gloucester, at Lord's, a happy situation for their own supporters.

In January 1960 Donald Knight died aged sixty-five, and in September "Johnny" Evans. Both had played in the disastrous

Lord's Test Match of 1921, and to both it had brought disaster. Knight made 1 and 7 and was dropped, never to play for England again. Evans was a strange selection, on the strength of one innings of 69 not out for the M.C.C. against the Australians. A highly strung man, he suffered agonies of nerves, a state of mind which led to, and was not improved by, his dropping a couple of catches.

Erroll Holmes, who had a heart attack at the early age of fifty-four had played his only home Test Match at Lord's, against South Africa in 1935. He was on the losing side in a match which decided the series, making 10 and 8.

"Ben" Sherwell died whilst skiing in Switzerland. He was a delightful and amusing solicitor who had kept at Lord's for Tonbridge, Cambridge, Middlesex, and the Gentlemen. He surprised a good many people by standing right up to G. O. Allen, and *Wisden* adjudged him the finest amateur keeper of his day.

Alec Skelding died in April at Leicester. Raconteur, poet, philosopher, boxer, and character of great originality, he figured in a typically picturesque incident when umpiring the Australian Test of 1948 at Lord's. He wrote to Sydney Barnes, in reply to that gentleman's outspoken strictures concerning his eyesight, saying at Lord's he would leave his dog at the gate, but would retain his white stick and spectacles. It so happened that during the match a dog did stray on to the pitch, whereat the agile Mr Barnes scooped it up and, heaving it into Alec's arms, said, "Here's your dog—it must have broken away from the gateman."

25

The Games and the Players 1961

THERE was a very good cricket season in England in 1961. The weather was a good give-and-take summer to normal standards, and major cricket was fortunate in suffering little interruption. The Editor of *Wisden* expressed a warm satisfaction on reviewing the scene and paid tribute to the Australian touring side, not only on account of their skills but because of the splendid spirit they had brought wherever they played. It was a timely compliment.

Once again Australia had found an ideal captain. Richie Benaud had served the usual hard Australian apprenticeship, coming up through grade and state cricket to acquire an extensive experience of the international game. An observant and intelligent player, he had studied the craft in its wider aspects and turned his knowledge to best advantage on succeeding to the captaincy and later in his profession of journalism.

There were several new men in his side, for quite a number of the old guard had simultaneously come to the end of the road. The most heralded of the newcomers was Norman O'Neill. Few cricketers can ever have experienced the vast amount of publicity which developed after Don Bradman had expressed high hopes of his early promise. A modest, level-headed young man, O'Neill bore this embarrassment with remarkable equanimity, but it made his progress that much more difficult. Apart from his attraction as a batsman he had an overhand, hurling throw from the deep which propelled the ball far over the 100 yards and which would find little scope on the 70-yard English boundaries. Alan Davidson was now unchallenged leader in the fast field, and a fine support had emerged in McKenzie. A long, stubborn, left-handed opening batsman named Lawry aroused some curiosity in that his trade was stated to be that of a plumber and his hobby pigeon-fancying.

Benaud had stated that he meant to be aiming at victory every time he took the field, and when he arrived at Lord's on May 27 he had certainly made every endeavour to pursue this policy. He did so most successfully against M.C.C.

Before a crowd of 22,000 Lawry and O'Neill both hit centuries on their first appearance at Lord's. When Benaud declared at 381 for five Davidson removed Horton and Subba Row for 19. Cowdrey then batted admirably for 115, and was ably supported by Smith and Barrington, but when the fifth wicket fell at 222 there was a sad collapse, and the innings ended at 274. Davidson took six for 46. Lawry and Simpson then made 186 without being parted, so that, on the second declaration, the Australians had scored 567 runs for a loss of only five wickets all told.

Davidson had Horton lbw for o for the second time in the match, but the middle batting again did well. The same trio, this time aided by Subba Row, got the score to 176, at which the third wicket fell. Benaud brought about another collapse, and his side won by 63 runs with over half an hour to spare. It had been a well-timed affair.

The first Test Match had brought no result, and England gained the first advantage at Lord's by winning the toss. It was not an unqualified advantage, for the wicket was lively, and there was much talk of the legendary Lord's "ridge", supposedly the track of an old drain crossing the field about the good-length mark at the Nursery end. In these conditions Davidson repeated his earlier success in taking five for 42. Subba Row resisted with characteristic resolution but, although most got into double figures, no-one else got set. With over an hour to play England were all out for 206. McDonald and Simpson were out to the fast bowlers for 6, but Lawry and Harvey stayed until the close.

Next day Lawry also had a second Lord's success. When he was seventh out at 238 he had made 130, and England's troubles were seemingly near an end. But they had still to contend with Mackay, Grout, and Misson, who jointly raised the score to 340. The last two, McKenzie and Misson, added 49, thus topping Trueman and Statham, who had contributed 47 at the same stage.

England started their second innings briskly enough, but soon ran into trouble. Five vital wickets had fallen before the scores were equalled, and McKenzie was too much for the later batsmen. Despite a do-or-die 66 by Barrington, Australia on the last morning had only 69 to make. This turned out to be a very much more parlous exercise than anyone had thought possible. In a fiery spell Trueman and Statham had the first four Australian batsmen out for 19 runs. A hard chance to Lock from Burge went astray, or Australia would have been 35 for five at the lunch interval. Simpson kept Burge company until 58, after which the latter settled the day with two successive fours off Statham. It had been a good match and an exhilarating finish. My own view of the closing stages was somewhat distracted by the hair-raising antics of a couple of steeplejacks on top of the powerhouse chimney.

In the course of the match Statham took his 200th Test Match wicket and Grout his 100th behind the stumps. One earlier Lord's success not repeated was that of the unfortunate O'Neill, who, plumb out of form, made 1 and 0.

In July the Australians beat Middlesex by ten wickets. The great feature of the match was that Kenny Mackay opened the innings, not without a certain groaning and lamentation from the uninitiated. One over before lunch-time he had thrashed the bowling all over the field for 92, at which he unaccountably downed tools and played a maiden from Drybrough. The complete performance of 168 was very popular all round, for Mackay was the most generous of cricketers himself and a most arresting and rather droll figure in all he did. Middlesex did no more than moderately in making 153 and 185, but just managed to make the Australians bat again.

Lawry made another hundred when the Australians played the Gentlemen at the end of August. O'Neill, much restored, got 75 in the Australian reply of 422 to the Gentlemen's 195. At the second attempt the Gentlemen did much better and, with M. J. K. Smith contributing 90, made 325 for eight to draw the match.

The University Match was marred by the sad absence of the Oxford captain, Pataudi. Motoring quietly along Brighton front, he was rammed by a car coming from a side-street and, amongst other injuries, lost much of the sight of an eye. His recovery was, as is well known, remarkable, but there was no hope of any more play that year. Thus a depleted Oxford and a not very inspired Cambridge drew after losing some considerable time through thunderstorms. Cambridge, batting first, made 173, and Oxford declared at 232 for eight wickets. Cambridge then played out the match with 254 for six wickets. Craig, having made 0 in the first innings, made 105 in the second. If my recollection is accurate both he and his fellow-opener, Goodfellow, were double-firsts, a matter of great awe to the Blues of my day.

The Players beat the Gentlemen easily by 172 runs. In a comparatively low-scoring match the deciding factor was the bowling, which, on the one side, was distinctly professional and, on the other, plainly amateur, in the qualitative sense of the terms. The

Players had reached a total of 203; then Trueman took five for 47, to out the Gentlemen for 177, of which May made 79 and Prideaux 57. The Players declared in their second innings at 263 for six, after Close had hit well for 94 not out. Flavell then shot the first four Gentlemen out for 44 and, with no major recovery, they were all out for 117.

Middlesex had a good year under their new captain, Ian Bedford. He was a cheerful, intelligent leader, always prepared to experiment, and his young batsmen, Gale, Russell, Parfitt, and Titmus, throve. The county matches started with two defeats, but Middlesex shot from bottom to top of the table, where they remained for a considerable part of the season. Four matches were lost in the last weeks, but the county finished third, which could be accounted a good position.

R. H. Spooner was for many years the most polished of the great school of English amateur batsmen. It was in 1899, over sixty years before his death, that he played his first match for Lancashire, against Middlesex at Lord's. A lad of eighteen straight from Rugby, he made 44 and 83 against Albert Trott at his best. Not long before he died he described how he had hit Trott first bounce into the Committee Room. The most self-effacing of men, he obviously felt this was rather big talk and hastily added, "I think it was rather a good hit—for a boy."

It was just over thirty-one years before he died that Percy Chapman made his great century at Lord's against Australia which might have saved his side, and with it the series and his reign as captain of England. For him it was a period of muddled fortunes. Before he had reached double figures he popped the ball up between gully and cover so exactly within reach of either fielder that each stood looking at the other as the ball dropped gently between them. He later performed a less meritorious, less famous, but even more remarkable feat. For M.C.C. against the New Zealanders in 1931 he got two ducks, interspersed by a Greta Garbo film, all in the course of one rainy afternoon.

It was in the Lord's Test of 1930 that "Farmer" J. C. White, who died on May 2, made his last home appearance for England. He also had an unusual experience in this match. He bowled the first ball to Bradman to inaugurate the Don's own favourite innings of 254. It was met four yards down the pitch and slammed to long-on for four. It was not an experience to upset the "Farmer", who was a man of the most equable temperament and, with it, a rare good poker player.

The year was only two days old when Bob Catterall died in Johannesburg. In his first Test Match at Lord's he made 120, and returned to the same fixture in 1929 to be bowled by Larwood for 0. He was one of the fastest and tidiest outfielders I ever saw, and excellent company.

Colonel R. S. Rait Kerr died on April 2. His first active acquaintance with Lord's had been in 1908 and 1909 when he had made a half-century in each of the matches in which he had played for Rugby against Marlborough. In 1936, after a successful Army career, he was appointed Secretary to the M.C.C., a post which he occupied until 1952, apart from the war-time period, when he returned to his original profession. A man of fearless character and unusual clarity of mind, he conducted the Club's affairs with an almost proverbial efficiency. With his practical knowledge of every aspect of the game he was admirably qualified to redraft the Laws of Cricket, which he did shortly after the War. Sir Pelham Warner once remarked of him that he wrote the best minutes of anyone he had ever encountered.

26

Cricketers All

WHILE we have been following events of international import and domestic happenings at Lord's we have lost sight temporarily of the broad revolutionary current which was transforming the first-class game in England. We saw that early in 1956 Lord Monckton's Committee advised against any change in amateur status. In the wake of the Altham Committee's Report there followed a broader examination of amateur status by a new Committee under the chairmanship of the reigning President, the Duke of Norfolk. This Committee reported their findings to the M.C.C. Committee in February 1958, and then remained in being, making broader enquiries and issuing addenda, until their report was finally accepted by the counties in March 1960. The underlying concern to preserve the adventurous spirit of the amateur was extended in a practical way to considering how to iron out the anomalies of "shamateurism" while seeking means to ensure that leading amateurs should not be debarred on economic grounds from accepting invitations to tour overseas. At an early stage it was decided that amateurs on tour must have financial support. Discussions between members of the Committee and leading professionals showed that the professionals desired to see the true amateur retained, but understandably, not only on their own account but because they felt the amateur would lose prestige if the regulations were not tightened, they all agreed that existing anomalies should be cut out. As for the proposal to abolish the distinction between amateurs and professionals, they felt that, while this might appear to be a good idea on paper, it was not a workable proposition.

With this backing from the professionals, the Norfolk Committee's report rejected any solution on the lines of regarding all players as "cricketers". It recommended that at home amateurs were fully entitled to the repayment of genuine out-of-pocket expenses and suggested that the A.C.C.C. should give urgent consideration to working out a standard formula. More important, it stated for the first time that a clear distinction should be made between amateurs at home and on tour by accepting an agreed system of broken-time payment for loss of earnings.

In defining guiding lines for amateur status the report conceded that any cricketer carrying out full administrative duties for a county club could remain an amateur, but any cricketer who was paid directly or indirectly for playing cricket, either by a county club or by any associated organization, was a professional. The position of the pseudo Assistant Secretary was too complex and varied for any general formula, and individual cases would have to be considered on their merits. No restrictions were placed on writing or broadcasting other than those imposed by M.C.C. or the Board of Control with regard to tours and Tests, or by county clubs on their own players. The professionals had expressed doubts about advertising, but the Committee felt that as advertising affected so few players it might be left open to amateurs and professionals alike. It was suggested that a Standing Committee be set up to investigate and report on individual cases of players whose status was doubtful and, at the request of the A.C.C.C., M.C.C. set one up under my father's chairmanship in April 1958.

Grave doubts were expressed about the workability of the report's recommendations. A year after his Committee had issued it the Duke of Norfolk was moved to address its members in these words:

> Try as we may to retain it, amateur status as we have understood it is at an end; . . . the Special Committee had hoped the recommendations in their report would work, but, sadly enough, they have not. . . . Now is the time for reconsideration.

And at that meeting the Duke's Committee veered further than ever before in the direction of abandoning amateur status. In the light of these doubts a conference took place in October 1959 between the Special Committee and representatives of the county clubs, but only two counties voted for abolition, and a strong majority supported the report. As Mr Altham, presiding at the November meeting of the A.C.C.C., put it,

> they had had a most interesting, if at times baffling, discussion, in which most of those present had felt they were groping for a solution to a well-nigh impossible problem. At the end it had been agreed to vote upon five propositions, of which four were negatived, and the only proposition carried was in favour of maintaining the status of the amateur. In short, the buck had been firmly passed back to the Special Committee.

So, that Committee resumed its task and decided that the counties must now accept and respect the report, which was duly ratified at the 1960 spring meeting of the A.C.C.C., power being given to the Standing Committee to take action in cases of doubtful status. A tribunal was appointed to hear appeals against decisions of the Standing Committee, and Lord Birkett agreed to preside. However, the services of that great arbiter were not required, for the tribunal never met.

The decision of the counties to ask M.C.C. to set up a fresh Committee of Enquiry into the Welfare of Cricket was put into effect in December, when my father accepted the chairmanship of a Committee which included the President and the Treasurer of M.C.C. as *ex officio* members, with the Secretary of M.C.C., county captains and secretaries, players, both amateur and professional, as well as representatives of business and the Press. Their terms of reference were to examine, with particular regard to the financial situation of the county clubs, the current state of first-class cricket and consider whether any changes in its structure and/or in the general conduct of the game were needed. My father had prepared the ground by writing an appraisal which his Committee accepted as the basis of their enquiry and circulated to the counties with an invitation to send in comments and suggestions. The nub of the problem was seen to be financial: the lack of support for first-class cricket as it was currently played and organized, causing serious financial difficulties for the counties. Analysis of a comprehensive financial questionnaire completed by each county showed an aggregate excess of expenditure over normal cricket income amounting to an average of some £120,000 per annum over the previous five years. At the first meeting it was decided to prepare memoranda bringing two points to the immediate attention of the counties at the A.C.C.C. The first, repeating the now monotonous refrain of the tempo of the game and the need for fast, true pitches, drew approval from the county representatives and inspired a statement from the first-class captains expressing their unanimous determination to provide entertaining cricket during the 1961 season and to do their utmost to enliven the tempo of the game, especially on the first and second days of a match. This brings us to the second point, discussed in a memorandum prepared by Mr Hastilow and the Rev. David Sheppard, proposing a limitation of the first innings of county matches to enable spectators to see something of both sides batting on the first day. The counties turned this down for Championship matches, but accepted it as a desirable experiment for friendly games. From the second meeting of the Enquiry came an analysis of suggestions submitted by the public and the setting up of the very important Sub-committee to examine alternative structures for the game.

At this point the death of my father on April 2 interrupted the proceeding of the main Enquiry Committee, but throughout the summer the Structure Sub-committee, under Mr Robins's energetic guidance, considered numerous permutations and prepared a report for the Enquiry Committee when it was convened again in the autumn with Sir Hubert Ashton in the chair. By then the counties had come through a season in which, in spite of the captains' efforts to entertain, attendances were the lowest since the War. In November the Enquiry Committee circulated the Structure Sub-committee's recommendations with an interim report commending to the counties a modified version envisaging a reduction of the Championship programme to a uniform twenty-eight matches for each county and the introduction of a knock-out competition, but deferring a more revolutionary plan for each county to play one three-day match only against each other county and two one-day matches. The report and the Sub-committee's structural proposals were placed before the counties at a special meeting in December, when Mr Altham, as Chairman, asked their representatives to consider, first, whether they would wish to see any experiment made in 1962 and, secondly, what changes should be made in 1963. The counties voted against any experiments in 1962, but accepted the important recommendation for cutting their programme of three-day matches to a uniform twenty-eight and introducing a knock-out competition in 1963. By their decision the delegates had planted a milestone in the long history of county cricket. The meeting concluded with a discussion on Sunday cricket—the Home Office having approached sporting organizations for their views on amending the Lord's Day Observance Act. It was agreed cautiously by a majority vote to ask the Secretary of M.C.C. to inform the Home Office that the counties were in favour of the Act being changed to allow cricket, to which spectators could be admitted on payment, to take place on Sundays without committing the counties necessarily to take advantage of such a change.

The most significant subject discussed by the members of the Cricket Enquiry when they met again in February was amateur status and its corollary, broken time. Nobody voted against a resolution that broken time should not be paid in this country, and a substantial majority were in favour of asking the A.C.C.C. to reopen the whole question with a view to considering the desirability of calling all first-class players cricketers instead of amateurs and professionals. The counties' reaction was to throw the ball back to the Cricket Enquiry and ask them to prepare a memorandum on the subject. When the Enquiry Committee had the memorandum on the table before them a motion put forward by Messrs Warr and Hastilow recommending the abolition of the distinction between amateurs and professionals was lost, and it was agreed by a single vote to recommend retaining the *status quo*. However, when the memorandum reached the A.C.C.C. in November the Enquiry Committee's recommendation was defeated in favour of Glamorgan's resolution that all players in first-class cricket should in future be called cricketers and that any financial arrangements made with them would be the sole concern of their respective counties.

Six and a half years had passed since the Monckton Committee first recommended the retention of amateur status—six and a half years, many will say, of kicking against the pricks. The decision made on November 26, 1962, was without doubt realistic, but the occasional player who could once be relied upon to invigorate his county side has virtually disappeared from the first-class game. At the gateway to the new decade the first-class game in England has become wholly "professional", and the vitality which it so sorely needs is sought by the recruitment of stars from overseas, to the ultimate discouragement, one would think, of cricketers born and bred in Britain. Cricketers all, they arrive at Lord's like city commuters (only they don't have a five-day week). For what? Too often it is just another day's cricket; another day at the office. And who can blame them if, as they take the field in front of a handful of spectators, the edge of their enthusiasm is blunted and they play as soberly as city accountants balancing a ledger?

27

"A Gale of Change"

IN the winter of 1961–62 a M.C.C. team had toured India, Pakistan, and Ceylon, carrying out an exhausting programme of twenty-four matches, including eight Tests. In the absence of May's lieutenant, M. C. Cowdrey, who was unable to make the tour, E. R. Dexter led the side. For the first and only time to date, India won two Test matches and a rubber against England. The series against Pakistan, played in two legs, with the Indian tour sandwiched in the middle, resulted in England winning one match against two draws. When battle was rejoined in England the Pakistanis were outclassed.

The main interest in the summer of 1962 lay in the selection of the M.C.C. side for Australia, with special emphasis on the choice of captain. Having completed his sabbatical stretch as Chairman of Selectors, Mr G. O. Allen begged to be released, and a new Board of Control Selection Committee, under the chairmanship of Mr Walter Robins, made it known that they demanded enterprise. The candidates for the captaincy were Colin Cowdrey, Vice-Captain under May, but currently suffering from kidney trouble, which prevented him from captaining the Gentlemen, Ted Dexter, who had led the M.C.C. team in India with only moderate success, and an "outsider", the Rev. David Sheppard, who returned to international cricket after a gap of five years and was much fancied for his qualities of leadership. In the estimation of the popular Press and his many admirers his fine century for the Gentlemen clinched his selection, but their forecast was confounded only a day later when Dexter's appointment was announced. The last of the long series of 137 matches between the Gentlemen and the Players at Lord's assumed the status of a trial for selection for the tour. The game ended in an honourable draw when rain frustrated the Players' likely victory in the last half-hour. There was fine batting on both sides, and Prideaux as well as Sheppard contributed to the final tally of ninety centuries in the series. The Players had won

Left: LORD's
HOTEL RENAMED
LORD's TAVERN
New inn-sign unveiled
by the Duke of
Beaufort, 1953.

Right:
PRESENTATION
SEATS—A FEATURE
OF THE LORD's
GARDENS
G. C. Newman
(President of
Middlesex C.C.C.)
unveils seats in
memory of five
Middlesex amateurs,
A. J. Webb, F. T.
Mann, N. E. Haig,
G. E. V. Crutchley
and R. W. V. Robins.

THE LORD'S "RIDGE"
Surveyors at work, 1961.

THE LORD'S GROUNDSMAN
E. C. Swannell with motorized equipment.

sixty-eight times, the Gentlemen forty-one, and twenty-eight matches were drawn.

This was the first year in which the Lord's Taverners' tireless work of fund-raising for the National Playing Fields Association was rewarded by a fixture at Lord's. Their own team, star-studded with international Test cricketers and personalities from the world of entertainment, met a distinguished Old England side, and a crowd of 12,000 savoured again the audacity of the Compton leg sweep and the thrill of the Miller drive for six—though in the art of hitting sixes he was matched by Jack Ikin's three in a row on to the roof of the Mound Stand. A centenarian, Joe Filliston, was introduced to share the umpiring with Harry Sharp and Len Muncer. The play was lusciously carefree, but the fun introduced by the professional comedians was not allowed to debase it to the level of slapstick farce. In all, an enjoyable day was had by all but the most killjoy purists.

By May 1962 the membership had reached a record of 11,671, and although the waiting list had been reduced it remained pretty formidable. To keep the administration virile and up to date a rule was introduced limiting the terms of office of the Treasurer and the Trustees, which by long tradition were a lifelong sinecure, if such a word can be applied to an office which places such a burden on the shoulders of its holder as that of Treasurer. The retiring President, Sir William Worsley, had had an eventful year in an office which has come to demand much more of its holder than a graceful presence. He was the first President to fly out to visit a M.C.C. touring team, and he and Lady Worsley were royally entertained in India and Pakistan. September 30 was the day of the official departure of Mr Aird to his retirement in Kent, with the attendant opportunity of some splendid seaside golf on the incomparable links of the Kent and Sussex coast and the new experience of owning a horse called Sir Daniel to add zest to his passion for racing. Donald Carr had already been released from Derbyshire to fill the vacant office of Assistant Secretary in charge of cricket. In the hierarchy of Middlesex, Mr George Newman became President in the room of Mr Gerald Crutchley.

The Imperial Cricket Conference met as usual in July and received a memorandum prepared by Pakistan on the future admission of members outside the Commonwealth and the creation of a "Junior" section, but no steps were taken to bend the rules in favour of the readmission of South Africa. The subject of illegal bowling once more took up a great deal of time, with

M

discussions on both throwing and drag. M.C.C. were anxious to ensure good relations by extending the throwing moratorium for a limited period of up to seven years, but they received little support. West Indies, the next country to tour England, were opposed to it, and so, having served its purpose in 1961 and 1962, it was never revived. M.C.C. also made fresh efforts to encourage trials of the front-foot method of controlling drag, reminding delegates of their resolution of 1960 that this might be the ultimate solution. They finally agreed, subject to the approval of their Boards, that all countries should experiment in all first-class matches, including Tests, not later than 1963–64. West Indies, however, made it clear that they would not agree to play the experimental rule during their United Kingdom tour in 1963.

Deaths in 1962 included those two distinguished and graceful orators Lord Birkett and Mr George Lyttelton. George Lyttelton was a massive figure greatly beloved in the confabulations of the very select Sub-committee whose responsibility was the care of the Club's arts and library affairs. It was, I believe, in his honour that the members of that committee continued to be served with port and postprandial cigars long after these luxuries were denied to their less privileged brothers. Ian Peebles has written his memories of the Hendren brothers. The elder, Dennis, who died this year, was never a great cricketer, but in the forties he was a familiar figure in the white-coated uniform of umpire. My first memories of the unique "Patsy" are tied inextricably to my family's arrival at Lord's and my earliest regular cricket-watching: the recollection of a rotund, chirpy figure emerging from the players' gate between the Pavilion and "A" Enclosure. He was the idol of the Australian crowds and a "natural" for Arthur Mailey's graphic "googlies".

It was like old times to find three Middlesex men in a M.C.C. Australian team, and in spite of the county's cataclysmic descent to a lowly thirteenth place. Parfitt and Titmus, who proved to be one of the major successes of the tour, both earned the accolade of Cricketer of the Year in *Wisden*. Murray, recovering from an operation for varicose veins and fallen from his peak of the previous season, failed to regain his form and lost his place as No. 1 keeper to Alan Smith. Public conjecture about the captaincy was matched by conjecture as to who was to manage the team. Mr Griffith was widely favoured, but the moment of his succession to the Secretary's desk was hardly appropriate for an immediate absence of six months. M.C.C. achieved a *coup* of the first magnitude with the

dramatic and utterly unpredicted announcement of the appointment of the Duke of Norfolk, with Alec Bedser to assist him. In
December and January he was relieved for a few weeks by Mr
Griffith, who flew out with the new President, Lord Nugent, continuing the precedent begun by Sir William Worsley of visiting
host countries during M.C.C. tours.

The two captains' preliminary declaration and the high expectations of the Australian public that the series would be played in the
same spirit of enterprise which had raised the West Indies' matches
to such a peak were doomed to sterile non-fulfilment. M.C.C.
started well enough, but ran out of steam half-way through the tour.
Sydney proved to be their Waterloo: they were beaten there by an
innings by New South Wales early on—the first time a touring
team had lost by an innings to a state since 1883—but they
recovered from that early setback and returned for the third Test
one up after winning at Melbourne. England's loss of that third
Test and the levelling of the rubber seemed to deprive both sides of
the will to win, and the fourth match, at Adelaide, was a stalemate,
distinguished only by a bilateral determination not to lose. The
final Test, at Sydney again, should have been a great battle, with
the rubber in the balance and both sides making a supreme effort
to win, but it earned nothing but the anger and slow handclaps of
the spectators. In their eyes Mr Griffith's statement, "We have not
been altogether successful in maintaining in the minds of the
cricketing public the image of Test cricket as we hope it will be
played", was the understatement of the age.

In New Zealand England outmatched their opponents and won
three Tests in a row, the first two by an innings. Their score of 562
for seven at Auckland was the highest ever made against New
Zealand. The series earned the award of the newly inaugurated
Jordan Fruit Bowl, given by the New Zealand Apple and Pear
Marketing Panel for competition between England and New
Zealand.

In his inaugural speech to the county secretaries, delivered on
the eve of his departure for Australia, Mr Griffith had referred to
the rightness of the experiments that had been carried out to
encourage the casual spectator, but admitted candidly that they
had neither improved the character of the game nor succeeded in
their object. He made a plea for the restoration of one of the game's
chief virtues, simplicity, and he reminded county cricketers of the
immense satisfaction to players and spectators alike of another of
cricket's great virtues: the countless opportunities it offered to take

a chance. He had something also to say about county membership
—the foundation stone on which a county's success is built. Members and their families must be provided with amenities and
facilities to make the club a focal point for social activities.

Even though county attendances sank to a new "low", Mr
Griffith's first season as Secretary of M.C.C. proved to be an outstanding one, not least because the West Indies team, led by
Frank Worrell, brought with them, in the words of the Lord
Mayor of London as he bade them farewell at the Mansion House,
"a gale of change blowing through the hallowed halls of cricket".
In England, just as in Australia, they brought fresh vitality to the
game—and this in spite of a more than ordinarily wet summer.
The Lord's Test, without doubt one of the best matches ever
played on the ground, culminated, in threatening gloom and
dubious light, in a thrilling draw, with honours even when Colin
Cowdrey, batting with a broken arm, carried his bat for 19. By
winning three of the remaining matches and losing one West Indies
became the first holders of the Wisden Trophy, instituted by the
firm of Wisden to mark the publication of the 100th edition of the
Almanack which "the Little Wonder" (who had once taken all ten
wickets at Lord's) first published in 1864. The silver trophy, bearing a portrait in relief of John Wisden, flanked by figurines of an
English batsman and a West Indies bowler, was handed to the
President of M.C.C., Lord Nugent, at a short ceremony in the
Memorial Gallery. The winners, lacking any centre in their own
widely separated territories where it could be kept, requested that
it might remain in the Gallery. The award of a knighthood to
Frank Worrell was welcomed throughout the Commonwealth as a
well-deserved honour to a fine man, who was a great cricketer and
an outstanding leader.

The "gale of change" extended in other ways to our own
domestic season. The disappearance of the amateur and the consequent cancellation of Gentlemen *v.* Players left a vacancy for a
representative match which was filled by a game between the
M.C.C. Australian touring team and the Rest. In Australian years
the time-honoured match against the Gentlemen of England,
stamped indelibly with the personality of W.G., has been replaced
by a game against a side sponsored by the President of M.C.C. The
new knock-out competition got off to a good start, some lucky
charm or special favour from the Clerk of the Weather prevailing
to save the matches from serious interference. The Cup Final was
played between Sussex and Worcestershire on the first Saturday in

September before a capacity crowd, cheering on their favourites and flaunting banners and coloured rosettes as if they were at Wembley, not Lord's. However conservatively minded connoisseurs might deplore the wedge inching its way in to dismember the fabric of first-class cricket, and whatever criticisms might be levelled at the conception of limited-overs matches for putting a premium on defensive tactics and seam bowling, nevertheless there was no doubt that the public welcomed the competition. After seven years' trial the Cup Final has not lost its magnetism for the eager partisan crowds who flock to this grand finale to the Lord's season. The name of Gillette was soon attached to the competition, after the company who so generously sponsored it and whose fine silver trophy (the third major trophy offered for competition in 1963) designed by Mr Alec Styles and executed by Garrard's is awarded each year to the winners. Ted Dexter, captain of Sussex, was the first to receive it from the hands of Lord Nugent, carrying out his last public function at Lord's as President of M.C.C. before handing over to Mr G. O. Allen.

Such a season would have delighted the heart of Sir Pelham Warner, but while England played Australia at Adelaide on January 30 the captain of the first M.C.C. team to visit that country fifty-nine years earlier died in England. On the day when, as a thirteen-year-old schoolboy, newly arrived from Trinidad, he first visited the ground in the centennial year of M.C.C. to see the Club play Sussex and the Secretary of M.C.C., Sir Francis Lacey, clean bowled by "Round-the-corner" (Sir Aubrey) Smith, he lost his heart to Lord's. Cricket was to become his life, and cricket for him soon came to mean Lord's. It was not long before he was playing there; four years running for Rugby against Marlborough, then for Oxford, and from 1894 until 1920 for Middlesex. He succeeded Gregor MacGregor as captain in 1908, and in his last match he was chaired off the field, triumphant captain of the Champion county. His retirement from first-class cricket served to step up his career as writer and journalist: *The Cricketer*, of which he was Editor, first appeared in 1921, and he was successively cricket correspondent to *The Morning Post* and *The Daily Telegraph*. Meanwhile he served on the M.C.C. Committee off and on from 1904 for the rest of his life. He was Chairman of Selectors from 1935 to 1938, Deputy Secretary of M.C.C. during the War, President, Trustee, and, finally, in the last year of his life, Life Vice-President. In his will he charged his executors to convey this valediction:

I would like you to convey to the Committee of the M.C.C. and to all the staff at Lord's my grateful thanks for and sincere appreciation of the courtesy help and consideration they at all times showed to me during the years I acted as Deputy Secretary of the M.C.C. and during my period of office as President of the M.C.C.

His mention of the staff was typical, for he always treated them with the greatest courtesy and consideration, and he knew them as individuals and friends and cared deeply for their welfare. At a private ceremony in the summer his ashes were scattered on the ground he loved so well.

All domestic cricket this year was played in accordance with the experimental "front-foot" bowling rule, requiring the bowler to ground his front foot behind the popping crease in the delivery stride and the back foot inside the extended return crease. The West Indians had remained unshaken in their resolve not to take part in the experiment during the tour, so English bowlers were subjected to a double standard, the "back-foot" rule still applying to matches against West Indies. However, at the I.C.C. the West Indies representative, Mr Dare, gave an undertaking that the experiment would be tried in West Indies very shortly. Surprisingly few bowlers found much difficulty in adapting, and the rule has now been adopted by all countries of the International Cricket Conference. At the A.C.C.C. in the spring the counties decided to restore the follow-on rule, and to avoid tedium the captains agreed to a voluntary limitation of their bowlers' run up to twenty yards.

Old England played the Lord's Taverners again. Denis Compton's innings of 68 (in harness with his old partner W. J. Edrich, batting like old times at No. 3 and 4 after Sir Leonard Hutton and Cyril Washbrook had opened for England) was enlivened for T.V. spectators by a running commentary given by himself, describing each ball and what stroke he would play. Even more fascinating for armchair viewers was his earlier commentary on his bowling, telling them what kind of ball he would bowl and allowing them to see how well his strategy succeeded. This technical feat was made possible by the use of a mini microphone and transmitter. Gimmicky, perhaps, but rewarding entertainment if not too often repeated.

The Eton v. Harrow match was elevated by the undoubted distinction of the presence of the Prime Minister, Mr Harold Macmillan, but depressed by the more dubious one of a record "low" in attendances—attributable less to changes in the examination system and waning social prestige than to a downpour on the second day. The rain destroyed Eton's rosy hopes of beating their rivals for the first time since 1955 in a year when Richard Robins, the younger son of the Chairman of Selectors, was expected to take many wickets.

The invasion of England by West Indies was complemented by visits from two parties of young players from overseas, the South African Nuffield Schools team and the Canadian Colts; also by the Australian women. All three teams practised at the Lord's nets and were regaled to dinner in the Members' Dining-room. M.C.C. out matches included another Holland–Denmark tour in August, and in the autumn M. J. K. Smith led a highly successful five weeks' tour of East Africa. Middlesex were knocked out by Gloucester-shire in the first round of the Gillette Cup, but in the Champion-ship they fared considerably better than in 1962. Like those of most other counties, their attendances suffered from the rain, but a drop of 6000 was offset financially by the benefits of Pluvius insurance. Alan Moss retired at the end of the season, but John Price was already at hand as a promising replacement. In their away match against Kent at Tunbridge Wells they were the victims, or culprits, of an almost unparalleled débâcle when, at start of play on the Monday, only two of the team plus the twelfth man were on the ground, the rest having been caught in a snarl-up of traffic in the purlieus of South-east London. The promise of a commanding lead was nipped in the bud when the umpires rightly declared the innings closed at 121 for 3, and S. E. Russell and White with Clark, the twelfth man, had the odd experience of sharing the bowling and wicket-keeping while their opponents fielded out pending the arrival of the missing Middlesex men.

In July a novel match was played between teams composed of players of the highest repute, bringing back into use the old lbw law in conjunction with a four-stump wicket measuring eleven inches wide. The genesis of this game was the A.C.C.C.'s request to M.C.C. to consider such an amendment, which, it was sug-gested, would bring the line of play more to the off side and encourage attacking cricket, firstly, by improving the chances of out-swing and leg-break bowlers while discouraging inslant seam bowling and negative bowling directed at the leg stump, and secondly, by encouraging more play off the back foot, thus increas-ing the range of strokes. A special LBW Sub-committee, consisting of seven past and present England players and county captains with Mr G. O. Allen as Chairman, arranged a LBW Conference of twenty-three distinguished players in April to hear the case for reverting to the old law put by Mr R. E. S. Wyatt and the case against argued by Mr T. E. Bailey (who, however, made it known that he was not necessarily expressing his own convictions). The answers to the questions discussed by the delegates were inconclusive. Briefly, most of those who had played under both laws were in favour of reverting to the old one; current players preferred the *status quo*. But all but six agreed that there should be no reversion to the old lbw law without a widening of the wicket. Very little was learned either from net trials in April or from the experimental match in the middle; the players who gathered for a post-mortem afterwards showed little enthusiasm. The Chairman was disappointed in their reaction, which he felt was unimaginative, envisaging only the application of the proposed changes to present methods rather than the possibility of change. His Committee set out in full all the pros and cons, and on the strength of it M.C.C. recommended to the counties that no immediate change should be made. Critics of the proposed reform had laid the blame for the fashionable but dreary "forward defensive prod" less on the lbw law than on the prevalence of slow pitches, so once again the Committee urged the necessity for faster pitches. This problem had lately been the charge of a Faster Pitches Sub-committee working in consultation with the Sports Turf Research Institute at Bingley, and the advisory pamphlet which had been the child of their enquiry had been widely circulated.

Two more sub-committees were conceived at the meeting of the I.C.C., when West Indies raised the question of the infrequency of her visits to England and Australia, her representative pleading that, while his country did not want to see South Africa suffer, now that she was no longer a member West Indies might reasonably hope to receive a larger slice of the international cake. With her cricketers meriting the acclaim of the British public wherever they played, she could hardly have chosen a more auspicious moment for advancing such a claim. M.C.C. put forward the idea of twin tours, which was accepted in principle as the only means of achieving the desired end, and M.C.C. were asked to examine the practicalities, especially with regard to finance, and report as soon as possible to the various Boards. The result has been that since 1965, when South Africa and New Zealand toured in the same season, there have been twin tours every second year, one country touring from May to July and the second from late June to the end of the season. Each country plays three Tests against England, but there has been no attempt to use the month's overlap to stage anything like a triangular tournament. M.C.C.'s second task was to examine the question of Associate membership and the admission of members outside the Commonwealth on the basis of Pakistan's memorandum of the previous year.

Early in 1963 Mr Altham told the President that he felt the time had come for him to hand over his office to a younger man. The Committee accepted his resignation with the greatest reluctance and regret. At the A.G.M. members welcomed with acclaim the appointment of Lord Cobham as the new Treasurer—successor, only one step away, to his father. When Harry Altham attended his last meeting of the full M.C.C. Committee as Treasurer, Lord Nugent, the retiring President, spoke of the respect, affection, and gratitude which the Committee had felt for him during his term of office; he had found the secret of combining efficiency with courtesy, good humour, and friendliness.

The year ended, as it had begun, with the passing of one of cricket's Knights. Sir John Hobbs, the admired friend of Sir Pelham Warner, who had, under his captaincy, helped to recover the Ashes for England in 1904, died at his home in Hove on December 21. In Southwark Cathedral on February 20 Harry Altham delivered the memorial address, honouring, in his inimitably evocative prose, the character and prowess of a great man whom he had first seen in his first match for his county and afterwards joined as a fellow-cricketer for that county. In speaking of the Master's strength and of his deep conviction that the life he had chosen was indeed a life worth living, and that cricket, if played as it should be played, could and should make others feel the same, he might have been composing an epitaph for himself.

28

The Games and the Players 1962

THE most far-reaching event in the English cricket season of 1962 was the abolition of the amateur status. This was formally effected in November at a meeting of the Advisory County Cricket Committee, whose deliberations are recorded elsewhere in this book. For the ordinary workaday cricketer it was a timely move and one which many people had advocated for some years. It was, in fact, largely a change of name, for, over the years, the division between amateur and professional had become much eroded by writing, coaching, the endorsing of articles of equipment, and other practices which brought material gain from success as a cricketer. One great loss entailed was the Gentlemen and Players match, an occasion of particular fascination and picturesque title.

The season after that of 1961 was a lesser one and more than averagely wet. The Pakistanis toured with a lack of success which belied the promise of their original venture in 1954. Outplayed in the Test Matches, they won only four first-class games. They were unlucky in that they found that the style of English wickets had, in the interval, changed from "sporting" to heavy and enduring green. This was certainly not to their advantage.

Despite wintry weather the Pakistanis had a satisfactory match against the M.C.C. They were comprehensively thumped by Dexter, who made 79 in an hour and a half, but held the innings to 279 for eight wickets. Against a good seam attack they made 230, then fielded whilst Graveney made a graceful 110 out of 237 for five wickets. With four hours to bat they saved the game quite easily, making 152 for five.

The Test Match brought the second decisive defeat of the series. The Pakistan batting broke down against Trueman, and the first innings of the match just reached 100.

Graveney made 153, mostly on the second day, but again the bowlers did well to hold the score to 290 when the eighth wicket fell. At that point Trueman helped Graveney to add 76, and the situation then looked rather different. For once in a way Pakistan batted very well in these adverse circumstances. Burki, their captain, made a splendid 101, and lower down Nasim-ul-Ghani made exactly the same number. The total of 355 was highly satisfactory, but the bad start meant that England had only 86 to make, which they made for the loss of Cowdrey's wicket.

At least the Lord's weather was kind to the Pakistanis, and in July they played a free-scoring draw with Middlesex. Parfitt made 122 in the first innings and 114 in the second, so that Middlesex declared twice, at 294 for seven and 257 for six. Hanif replied with 191, a fine innings though not chanceless, and Pakistan topped Middlesex with 352 for seven. Set 200 to win, Hanif did not go in again, and the match ended when Pakistan were 143 for five wickets.

For the third year in succession the University Match was drawn. Cambridge made a very slow start, declaring at 259 for six near the end of the first day. Brearley made 113, a sound innings extending to almost four and a half hours. His task was eased by the fact that Pithey, Oxford's chief spinning hope, dislocated a finger when missing a catch in the slips. Next day Oxford got to 237, the innings being saved by 67 from the injured Pithey at No. 8.

Lewis made another century for Cambridge, 103 not out in a total of 190 for six, but only two and a half hours were left when the innings was closed. Oxford set out in pursuit of the required 213 runs, but when Mumtuza Baig twisted an ankle their chances were sharply lessened, and they were content to play out time, finishing with 136 for five wickets.

The last match in the traditional and historic series of Gentlemen v. Players ended in a fairly even draw. It was originally arranged that the captains were to be Cowdrey and Trueman, but as the former fell sick, it was accorded to Dexter to be the last captain of the Gentlemen.

Sheppard, opening the innings with a century, shared a second-wicket stand of 97 with Dexter, and their joint efforts sent their side on the way to the respectable total of 323.

The Players batted in humid conditions, which Bailey used with all his considerable skill. Six wickets fell for 104, but Titmus got 70, and Trueman, ever with a sense of occasion, made 63 to bring the final score to 260. Prideaux was promoted when the Gentlemen batted again, and responded by making 109 out of the total of 172 for five declared.

The Players were left to get 236 in three hours, and went about the job in a determined and entertaining style. Edrich and Parfitt put on 118 for the second wicket well in advance of the clock, their nimble running delighting the crowd and harassing the field. When the Players had reached 207 for three wickets and with over half an hour in hand there was every prospect of another grand finish. Unfortunately, at that point the rain came down in earnest and persisted, to finish the game.

The hopes engendered by the recent success of Middlesex that they might challenge strongly for the Championship were rudely dispelled. The county dropped from third to thirteenth place in the table and won only six county matches. This was a big disappointment, and the cause lay mostly in the shortage of bowling. Titmus did consistently well to take 110 wickets, but Moss had lean times. When this happened there was little of consistent attacking quality to substitute. The early spell at Lord's brought very mixed fortune, but a six-wicket victory over Yorkshire at the beginning of June was a good and encouraging performance.

Pat Hendren died in October. From his arrival as an orphan boy in 1905 until he sat watching the Cross Arrows as oblivion slowly overtook him, Lord's had been the main theme of his life. He had also been one of the great features of the life of Lord's. Having sold match-cards, fought for his county cap, and become the uncrowned king, in late life he returned in the modest but infinitely rewarding capacity of scorer, to be again where his heart lay. Few cricketers have so captured the imagination of every crowd in all the countries in which he played, but Lord's was his home ground and its habitués were his home crowd.

Earlier in the year Dennis Hendren, a devoted elder brother who had brought Pat to Lord's, died in hospital at the age of seventy-nine. There is something rather moving in the picture of him as an old man, without official connection, eagerly lending a hand with screen or roller as tangible evidence of the bond he shared with Pat for the days gone by.

Ernest Tyldesley, who also died this year, did not figure at Lord's as much as one might have expected of a cricketer of such prominence and reputation. He played but one Test Match, a minor one against the West Indies in 1928, and he had made 131 against the Gentlemen in 1926. His most notable day at Lord's was almost certainly in 1929, when he made 103 for Lancashire against Middlesex as G. O. Allen mowed down all ten of his side for 40 runs.

29

The Games and the Players 1963

1963 brought a really good cricket season. The weather was no more than fair give and take, but there were many satisfactory features in the domestic season, and West Indies, under the splendid captaincy of Frank Worrell, were a fine side and a great draw.

The year was saddened by the loss of the two greatest cricketing figures in the land. Sir Pelham Warner and Sir Jack Hobbs had both been knighted for services to the game which far exceeded their very great records as players.

Sir Pelham died at the age of eighty-nine on January 30. For the span of the century, so far as it had reached, "Plum" Warner had been a famous figure and his Harlequin cap a familiar emblem far beyond the actual realm of cricket. His devotion to the game has never been exceeded, and he had enhanced its credit in almost every part of the world in which cricket was played. He was an exceedingly good batsman, perhaps denied the ultimate greatness which his due, by a certain frailty of health. This he combated as far as possible by an impeccable technique allied to a sustained courage and determination.

He was a great captain. His methods were gently persuasive rather than fire-eating, but no tactician ever exceeded his shrewdness and his alert grip of the momentary situation, nor his knowledge of the foibles of friend and foe alike.

As Mary Tudor died with "Calais" written on her heart, so might he, for happier reasons, have died with "Lord's" written on his. His love of cricket and cricketers was catholic and all-embracing, but Lord's was the physical centre of all his affections. There he had served in every capacity—President, writer, selector, and player—and had revelled in the traditions and associations in every corner, which he knew so well. He had a happy knack of conveying this love and knowledge to others in plain but original terms, as when he measured the fall from one side of the playing area to the other as "a tall man in a top hat", which is one way of expressing a drop of six foot six inches.

One small but sharply indicative gesture epitomized his consideration for all men in general, and his respect for his "spiritual home" in particular. The most famous and recognizable figure at Lord's for half a century, he insisted on showing his membership card whenever he entered the ground or Pavilion, because he rightly thought that his example would greatly ease the task of the gatemen in carrying out their instructions. His influence in this, as in other matters, lives on, and it was an unashamed pleasure recently to cite this example to an unco-operative young member who thought the gatemen ought to know him—but was mistaken.

When Sir Jack Hobbs died in December at the age of eighty-one his surviving contemporaries, almost as a single voice, said he was the greatest batsman they had ever known. Most went so far as to assume that he was, in all circumstances, the greatest batsman of all time. It is an assumption which is difficult to refute.

There have been many players who have excelled in certain circumstances and in certain aspects of batsmanship, but Hobbs was the complete craftsman allied to the complete artist. Which is to say he was complete master of the mechanics of batsmanship, and he executed them with an unexcelled grace and fluency. Pace, spin, and swerve came alike to him, and he was at his greatest on bad wickets. It used to be remarked that it was only when his partner was called upon to tackle the same problems that the observer realized that it was a bad wicket.

Jack Hobbs was, of course, very much a man of the Oval, but cricket history might have been strangely affected had Essex had the prescience to grant him the trial for which he applied as a youth. His connections with Lord's were naturally very strong and lasting. It was said that when, in 1925, Percy Holmes made 315 not out for Yorkshire against Middlesex, to break the ground record which William Ward had set in 1820, Hobbs was moved to make a resolution. Whatever the truth of this, the following season he made 316 not out, again against Middlesex. He was not usually interested in records, often sacrificing his wicket when he had served the needs of his side, but on this occasion he seemed to persevere until his target was achieved—which would give support to the story.

To my mind the most fitting memorial to this great cricketer is a glass case in the Memorial Gallery which contains his cap, blazer, pads, and boots. On the opposite wall is an identical case containing the corresponding belongings of Victor Trumper.

It is appropriate that two cricketers of such genius, and men of such personal quality and modesty, should be thus jointly commemorated.

West Indies won the series comfortably by three matches to one, and generally were a most successful side. Worrell captained them with a firm but encouraging hand, and was endowed with fine batting and a well-balanced attack. The one point of contention was in the last-named department, and concerned the action of Griffith, which some thought doubtful and about which others were more outspoken.

The West Indians demonstrated their all-round strength in the M.C.C. match in May, but the result, a win by 93 runs, meant little, England declaring when still well behind. West Indies batted evenly and entertainingly on the Saturday, but play on Monday was interrupted by weather. By Tuesday morning the position was that M.C.C. were 120 for five wickets, in reply to a total of 306. Cowdrey in an effort to keep the match alive, declared, and Hunte, deputizing for an injured Worrell, co-operated by batting again and declaring at 79 for one. The M.C.C. made a good second start, but the batting collapsed against Gibbs. It might have occurred earlier, but Gibbs had been off the field for some time, and the umpires refused to let him bowl immediately he reappeared.

The second Test Match was a splendid game, which came to a most remarkable finish. Once again the West Indians, having won the toss, gave a very uniform performance in making 301. Kanhai made 73 and, of the regular batsmen, only Worrell himself failed to get into double figures. Shackleton finished the innings by taking three wickets in four balls on Friday, and at lunch-time England had lost Stewart and Edrich, both to Griffith, for 20 runs.

After lunch Dexter launched one of the most thrilling assaults ever seen at Lord's against real fast bowling. He reached his 50 in 48 minutes, and went on to score 70 before being lbw to Sobers. Seldom have bowlers of the type and calibre of Griffith and Hall been driven in front of the wicket with such power, or cut and hooked so easily and firmly, as Dexter countered speed with force. In all he received no more than 73 balls.

Barrington fought his way to 80, and England ended their first innings just 4 runs behind. In contrast to their first innings West Indies batting against Trueman and Shackleton was extremely uneven. Butcher played a grand innings of 133, supported manfully by Worrell, who made 33, to add 110 for the sixth wicket, but the rest failed, and the total reached only 229.

England now had a rare chance to level the series, but the weather and light were unpromising. The start was disastrous, with Stewart, Edrich, and Dexter out for 31 runs. Barrington and Cowdrey dug in, but, at 72, a decisive misfortune befell England. Cowdrey was struck a fearful blow on the lower forearm which broke his wrist and completely disabled him. When bad light and rain ended the play at 4.45 England had battled on to 116 for three.

The same conditions prevailed on Tuesday, and play could not be restarted until twenty minutes past two. Barrington was out at 130 for a brave innings of 60, and everything now depended on Close. Physically and morally Close played an heroic innings, taking many severe blows rather than risking a stroke. As his companions grew less competent he became more aggressive and, eventually on the attack, was caught at the wicket. When Shackleton joined Allen 15 runs were wanted in 19 minutes. When Hall started the last over the score was 226. The batsmen ran sharp singles off the first and third balls, but Shackleton was run out off the fourth. Cowdrey, intending to turn round and bat left-handed if called upon to take a ball, came to the wicket.

The position now made possible every known result of a finished cricket match. It could be a win for either side, a draw, or a tie. In the event Allen played the last two balls and the match was a draw, but, for most people, the most exciting draw they had ever seen.

In July West Indies beat Middlesex by nine wickets. This was a better match than the result would imply, but, after the excitements of the Test Match, was inevitably an anticlimax. The chief feature was a first-wicket stand for the touring side between Hunte and McMorris of 206. McMorris went on to bat through the innings, and was 190 not out when the last wicket fell.

The University Match was once again drawn, an altogether too frequent result in the post-War history of these encounters. It was, however, due almost entirely to interruptions on the part of the weather, for both sides did their best to get a result. Oxford declared 45 runs behind the Cambridge total of 246, then Cambridge followed their example on making 148 for eight wickets in the second innings. In two hours and twenty minutes Oxford got to 136 for six but, as one man was absent ill, they were in a somewhat ticklish position at the close.

Under the captaincy of Drybrough, Middlesex had a variable season, but advanced from thirteenth to sixth place in the Cham-

Left: THE LORD'S
DRAINAGE
Excavations on the
match ground, 1964.

Right: TWO
STAUNCH UMPIRES
S. J. Buller and
W. F. Price.

M.C.C. SELECTORS IN THE COMMITTEE ROOM, 1965
G. O. Allen, A. V. Bedser, M. J. K. Smith, S. C. Griffith, D. J. Insole and
P. B. H. May.

CRICKETERS OF THE FUTURE
Coaching at the Easter classes by W. F. Price.

pionship. Their record at Lord's was also very in and out, but in Russell, Gale, and Parfitt their supporters had three attractive batsmen to hold their interest, and Moss and Price were two fine, robust fast bowlers. Titmus supplied some good all-round cricket, and Murray, in addition to his wicket-keeping, was amongst the best-looking batsmen in the side.

In August C. M. Wells died at the age of ninety-two. He was affectionately known as "Father" Wells at Eton, where he spent many years. He had been a contemporary and warm friend of Sir Pelham, who had predeceased him by these seven months. He was a man of many talents and had a determination to master any subject which engaged his attention. Thus he became an authority on wine and acquired a stamp collection which aroused the admiration, not to say envy, of King George V.

N

30

150 Years in St John's Wood

FRESH memories of positive cricket in 1963 and the pleasant anticipation of a visit from the Australians were encouraging auguries for the 150th anniversary year of the present Lord's. As an introduction M.C.C. sent a team to India on an expedition which had been planned as an "A" tour, but at the pressing instance of India was upgraded to full international status with five Tests of five days each and five three-day "zonal" matches condensed into the space of eight weeks. Cowdrey, the chosen captain, having been declared unfit, M. J. K. Smith continued from the East African venture his initiation in leadership of England. The importation of food from Britain failed to save the players from the apparently inevitable tummy sickness which afflicts Europeans; by the end of January the simultaneous disablement through illness or injury of six of the team brought Cowdrey and Parfitt as reinforcements. Cowdrey flew out in company with Messrs Allen and Griffith, who for three weeks were the guests of the Indian Cricket Board of Control. From Bombay the President and Secretary made a flying visit to Karachi and thence on to Rawalpindi to meet the President of the Pakistan Board of Control, dine with members of the Pakistan Cabinet, and reach a final agreement on the arrangements for "twin" tours. Mr Griffith undertook an additional act of diplomacy by giving a helping hand to arrangements for the first ever visit to India of a team of English schoolboys, from London. Cowdrey had scarcely stepped off the plane before he was making a century in the third Test. But the cricket was ruined by inertia stemming from deadly slow clay pitches designed more to ensure five full days' gate money from a crowd who were crazy about cricket than to retain their enthusiasm. These pitches were the chief villains in robbing the games of any incentive or hope of a positive result. M.C.C. managed to beat South Zone by an innings, but all the other matches, including the five Tests, were drawn. Not a very positive start to 1964!

The Lord's anniversary was not heralded, as the opening of the ground had been, by the explosion of dynamite in the Tavern. That would have been to anticipate by several years the removal of that nostalgically popular but aesthetically unpleasing edifice from which, in this celebration year, the Anniversary Dinner was translated to the splendour of the Long Room. In proposing the toast of M.C.C. the President, Mr Allen, used the novel preamble "*Lady* and Gentlemen . . .", acknowledging the presence of your humble servant, who had the great privilege and unique honour of adding a small mite to Lord's history by her presence at this traditionally all-male gathering. Mr Altham was the Committee's choice to propose the toast of Lord's, and he was in tremendous form as he projected a verbal kaleidoscope recalling, as he put it, panels from the history of the ground, not forgetting to direct a fleeting glance back to the classic century by which the President-elect, Mr Twining, had ensured that, in the season after Sir Pelham's retirement, the Championship should remain with Middlesex. The evening was crowned by a speech in reply by the Prime Minister, Sir Alec Douglas-Home, himself a future President and a former Middlesex player and the first reigning Premier ever to speak at the Annual Dinner.

While the Marylebone Club celebrated a hundred and fifty years at Lord's, Middlesex commemorated the centenary of the county club, quite undeterred by the decision of Government that the County of Middlesex would shortly cease to exist. Their cricket record in this centenary year was adequate without being brilliant; stronger in batting than in bowling. Until July 14 they had the melancholy experience of never winning a match, but then their fortunes picked up with the better weather and the arrival of the Cambridge captain, Mike Brearley, who, fortified by his century in the Varsity Match, joined Eric Russell as his fellow-opener. With Russell first in the race for 2000 runs and Brearley close on his heels, they made a formidable opening pair, and at the end of the season Middlesex managed to hang on to their position in sixth place. Brearley was chosen to lead the President of M.C.C.'s Eleven against the Australians, and he was a very bright hope indeed in the eyes of Middlesex. Both he and Parfitt made centuries for the county against the Australians. On the Monday of that match, July 20, the Duke of Edinburgh came to watch the play, and afterwards, in a light-hearted speech in front of 1300 people who attended the centenary dinner at Grosvenor House, he proposed the health of the Club. The toast to the guests was proposed by Mr

Allen. The Prime Minister replied. During the evening the President of Middlesex, Mr George Newman, announced the setting up of a charitable trust which aimed to raise £60,000 to be spent in the field of youth activities. Other festivities included a cocktail party in the Long Room for the lady members and a reception in the Middlesex Guildhall given in honour of the Club by the Chairman of the Middlesex County Council. Sadly, before the year ended, the death occurred of Mr Frank Mann, Sir Pelham Warner's successor as captain; a vast, genial, kindly man, who swung a cricket bat with power and abandon, without fear or favour to the most distinguished bowler. Like his elder son, he had captained the county with distinction. Both had led remarkably happy and successful M.C.C. tours to South Africa.

The verdict on the Australian tour was one of disappointment at a failure to advance in the spirit of the West Indies series. The lack of initiative in the Tests was particularly disappointing, but the blame could hardly be laid entirely on the players when three out of the five Tests were ruined by rain. At Lord's there was no play on the Thursday and Friday, and a further downpour on the final day caused the match to be abandoned. The only silver lining to the cloud was a bonus of 3000 attendances in the Memorial Gallery. The waterlogged state of the ground, even when play looked possible on the second day, gave justification, if any were needed, of the Committee's decision to accept the advice of independent surveys carried out by the Sports Turf Research Institute and the National Association of Groundsmen to replace the old drains, laid in 1903, with an entirely new system of drainage at a cost which was estimated to be in the region of £5000. Immediately after the season ended the contractors moved in, and for a time the ground looked as though it was being prepared for trench warfare.

When Mr Allen relinquished the President's chair to Mr Twining he moved to the Treasurer's place at his right hand, succeeding in the select line of holders of this high office such distinguished figures as Sir Spencer Ponsonby Fane (to whom not the least part of M.C.C.'s debt is its artistic heritage), Lord Harris, and Lord Hawke. Lord Cobham, recently created a Knight of the Garter, had found the weight of his commitments since his return from New Zealand and his recent appointment as Lord Lieutenant of Worcestershire so heavy that he was reluctantly compelled to ask the Committee to release him from an office which was daily becoming more demanding. As Lord Lieutenant of Worcestershire he was the donor to M.C.C. of a handsome china punch-bowl, designed and executed by the Worcester Royal Porcelain Company in commemoration of the 150th anniversary of Lord's. The decorations by Mr Neil French included vignettes of the ground in the various ages of its life and emblems of cricket and M.C.C. Steps had been taken already to rationalize and ease the Treasurer's burden by a break-up of the old Finance and General Purposes Sub-committee. This Committee remained, but it was relieved of the responsibility for high finance and long-term planning by the creation of a new Financial Advisory Sub-committee. Although the Treasurer remained the titular Chairman of both these sub-committees, each was provided with a Vice-Chairman to take the chair if the Treasurer thought it unnecessary to preside in person.

Various Government changes were having effects on cricket quite unforeseen by the planners in the departments concerned. The deferment, for example, of the August Bank holiday until the brink of September, and the subsequent divorce between the religious and the secular Whitsun, disrupted traditional fixtures and made chaos of fixture lists arranged before the reforms were announced. An expression of protest addressed to the Secretary of State for Industry and Trade and Regional Development was unavailing. More disturbing, the whole future of youth cricket and the long-term education of cricketers seemed to be threatened by the advancement of examination dates and the consequent curtailment of the schools' summer term, reducing drastically their cricket programmes. The President and Secretary held talks with the Minister of Education, Sir Edward Boyle, and they discussed with him such broader issues as the lack of cricket education in Training and Physical Education Colleges, grants for tours of schoolboys overseas, and the formation of the M.C.C. National Cricket Association.

The encouragement given to all forms of sport by the Wolfenden Report, *Sport and the Community*, and the subsequent setting up of the National Sports Council had thrown in relief the lack of a representative national body for cricket, to which all clubs could be affiliated. Consultations between M.C.C. and the National Club Cricket Association confirmed that a need was felt for a patently national body to canalize the views and promote the interests of all cricketers and, above all, to negotiate with government in such fields as taxation, grant assistance, rating, and the extension of facilities for play. As a private members' club M.C.C.

felt they could not fully meet this need. The formation of the National Cricket Association was the first step towards the revolutionary modernization in cricket administration by which M.C.C. has now vested its authority as the Governing Body of Cricket in the Cricket Council, whose triple branches embrace M.C.C., the Test and County Cricket Board, and the N.C.A. The N.C.A.'s affiliation now includes all conceivable aspects of the game—too numerous to list. They aim, ultimately, to bring into their fold County Associations for every county, thus retaining county loyalties.

The future organization of international cricket marked time. As promised, M.C.C. presented to the I.C.C. proposed new rules, amended from Pakistan's memorandum, for the admission of Associate members, but, as delegates declared that their Boards had had insufficient time to discuss them, their adoption was put back until 1965. The counties decided on the novel procedure of balloting for Bank holiday fixtures against the tourists in years when there was only one tour. However, as Middlesex and Sussex (and "the Roses") were among six counties who opted out, preferring to preserve traditional fixtures, Lord's was not affected when the ballot was held in 1966.

That public and industrial sponsorship had taken the place of private wealth was evidenced by the familiar presence of the smart Rothmans luggage van conveying the tourists' gear from one venue to the next with smooth efficiency. The same service was shortly to be extended to the M.C.C. team in South Africa. The firm enriched the Board of Control receipts by fees of £1000 for the right to make a film of the Test Matches—a valuable tool for cricket education. And Lord's was the chosen stage for what was to have been the grand finale of a series of three matches promoted by Rothmans between a West Indies XI, led by Sir Frank Worrell, and an England XI. Alas, the final curtain proved to be a wet blanket, casting a depression which not even the presence of the Barbados Police Band could mitigate. Even more ambitious, in 1966 they presented the Rothmans World Cup, which was won by England in a three-cornered tournament with West Indies and the Rest of the World. One more international encounter took place at Lord's in 1964—on the Nursery ground, where Mr Ian Smith (still bi-laterally dependent) attended in a partisan capacity the Mashonaland Country Districts XI encounter with the Cross Arrows, whom they failed to beat by the narrowest of margins. They were the first Rhodesian senior side to tour England, and as a souvenir of their visit they presented for the Memorial Gallery a small copper figure of a bowler.

The adage "Beer is best" was substituted for "King Size" when the recently revived Single Wicket cricket was transferred from Scarborough to Lord's for the Carling Trophy competition. The tournament failed to reproduce the thrills of the old-time rivalries when Alfred Mynn was the unbeaten Champion or, to go back even further, when Lord Frederick Beauclerk was not above resorting to shady methods to maintain a comfortable income, but as an occasional entertainment the matches were a success. The rules are not, of course, the same as those governing the old single wicket when the fielders rarely exceeded five and no runs were allowed behind the wicket. The principals alone batted and bowled, but they had a full fielding side to support them. The winner of 1964's competition was the Essex all-rounder Barry Knight. After six years the competition was dropped in 1970.

Since the M.C.C. Collection has been organized under a full-time Curator as an independent department disseminating information and conserving cricket's heritage in a Gallery which has attained a recognized status as a museum, there has been a growing demand for loans for temporary exhibitions. One of the most interesting and ambitious I remember involved the dispatch to Australia in the autumn of 1964 of a generous collection of pictures and other objects for a F.B.I.-sponsored British Exhibition, in which the Long Room was ingeniously reproduced in facsimile in a department store in Sydney. The real Long Room had once more been rendered shabby by the action of the peculiarly virulent sulphur fumes and soot which seem to concentrate in St John's Wood (or at least they did until the local power station was closed down). The success of the Annual Dinner had drawn attention to the waste in allowing such a splendid room to remain deserted in the winter; so, with its potential for social functions in mind, plans for redecoration envisaged ambitious schemes for curtains, carpets, and new heating. These fine visions dissolved in the light of economic reality. Plans were also afoot for transforming the whole of Lord's into a lively and viable sports centre from September to March. A proposal to introduce a golf driving range on the practice ground had been turned down, but a new Club Facilities Sub-committee were exploring other possibilities and produced an optimistic report and plans for a sports centre on the Tennis Court site. For the time being their plans were deferred, but much more extensive planning was afoot. After three years of discussion and negotiation the Re-development Sub-committee had obtained planning permission for the development of the site running from the Tavern westwards along St John's Wood Road to the corner of Grove End Road. The Club's architects, Messrs Louis de Soissons and Partners, had been commissioned to design a new stand on the old Tavern site (for which Mr Kenneth Peacock was the architect) and a new Tavern, a 300-seater restaurant, and a tower block of flats (designed by Mr David Hodges) between Grove End Road and the Grace Gates. Of all the building operations ever undertaken by M.C.C. this was the most ambitious as well as the most costly; and there was no longer a William Nicholson to dip into his pocket for the capital. M.C.C. had themselves to meet the cost.

The question naturally arose whether or not to raise capital by the sale of the freehold of the corner site where the flats were to be built. This was turned down, though ultimately it was found necessary to grant a building lease of ninety-nine years to a contractor/developer rather than accept for M.C.C. the risks involved in a development project, whose cost had already been swollen by the planning authority's insistence on extra garages. Even so, the capital cost was an enormous burden on the Club's capital reserves, a burden which, as we shall see, some members thought unjustifiable.

The departure of the M.C.C. team for South Africa synchronized with a General Election, in which E. R. Dexter stood as a Conservative candidate for a South Wales constituency and was therefore not a candidate for the England captaincy. His reign was over, and although, having been unsuccessful in the Election, he joined the team, the crown passed to the victorious leader of Warwickshire, M. J. K. Smith, who became "the man in possession", as Mr Swanton would say, for a considerable spell. With him, as Manager, went Donald Carr, the Assistant Secretary (Cricket) of M.C.C. Smith and his team returned unbeaten, having won the rubber by a formidable victory in the first Test at Durban. A bid for victory in the second Test was thwarted by a magnificent innings by Colin Bland, who treated spectators to a fine display of the sadly neglected art of using his feet to kill the spin-bowling of Titmus and Allen. The third match was a marathon of slow play, but memorable for the "to walk, or not to walk" controversy centring upon the contrasting reactions of Barrington and Barlow to doubtful umpiring decisions. There followed two more drawn games in which England's backs were to the wall, and Graeme

Pollock gave a foretaste of his claim to be perhaps the finest left-handed batsman in the world.

The other Warwickshire Smith, Alan, was meanwhile engaged in South America, leading a M.C.C. side which visited Chile, Brazil, and the Argentine, winning all except one of their matches and enjoying themselves hugely, with the possible exception of Mike Griffith, who broke a toe and so was robbed of the chance of captaining Cambridge against Oxford in the Varsity hockey match.

A sad postscript to 1964: Peter, the Lord's cat, who had gambolled so joyfully on the outfield, stalking without discrimination sundry pigeons, sparrows, and mice, having survived the 150th anniversary celebrations, but sensing, perhaps, the imminent demolition of his ancestral home in the Tavern, was gathered to his fathers.

31

The Games and the Players 1964

AFTER a hesitant start the summer of 1964 blossomed forth into one of warmth and sunshine. It was rather an English caprice that the events which suffered chiefly from such rain as there was were the major ones of the series against Australia. Owing to this, and other causes, only one match was finished, and that in the Australians' favour.

This result was a disappointment to English hopes, for, with the departure of Benaud, Davidson, and Harvey, Australia was suddenly depleted, with no apparent reserve to fill this major loss. As so often, Australia was ready and prepared in one most important area. Benaud had been a very successful leader, enterprising and alert to every tactical problem, and was not an easy man to succeed. Even so, in Simpson there emerged another captain of the highest quality, and one who was to complete his "natural span" with equal success and certainty. By seizing his chances, and carefully husbanding their fruits, Simpson decided the outcome with his solitary Test victory at Leeds.

On their first appearance at Lord's the touring team had already had plenty of match practice to compensate for a short net preparation, further curtailed by rain. Against the strongest side Simpson could muster the M.C.C. got off to a good start when Boycott and Bolus put up 124 for the first wicket. But either the batsmen lost confidence as they proceeded or the bowlers found a more effective range, for the innings seemed to falter. By increasingly laborious play the score got to 193 for three, when Corling had a fine spell with the new ball, and the whole side were out for 229.

On Monday O'Neill, who had come in when the first wicket had gone at 14, batted superbly to make 151. Those who had watched him over the years were given further grounds for reflection. The mind went back to Perth in 1958, when this young man arrived to play against the M.C.C. in such a blast of publicity as few unproved cricketers have ever experienced. It was not of his seeking, and everyone who came into contact with him was delighted with his modest bearing and most pleasant demeanour. These characteristics remained constant through a career which gradually grew more enigmatic. Although punctuated by splendid moments his record never quite achieved the splendid hopes of his admirers, prominent amongst whom was Sir Donald Bradman.

On this Monday the Lord's crowd saw the Promised Land as O'Neill swept majestically on to 151. Simpson then took up the running, and the Australians closed at 358 for 6. Strangely inserted between the two centuries on the score-sheet were two successive ducks from Potter and Booth. No major reply came from the M.C.C., who were out again for 224. This total at least gave Simpson the opportunity of making his seventh successive innings of over 50, and so taking his side to a nine-wicket victory.

Whereas the first Test Match had suffered badly from the weather no play was possible on the first two days at Lord's at all. On Saturday Dexter won the toss and put Australia in to bat. Trueman, with five wickets for 42, upheld his judgment, and Australia had a struggle to reach 176. England lost Dexter on Saturday evening but, on Monday, topped Australia by 70 runs. This was almost entirely due to a fine 120 from Edrich, Sharpe coming next with 35.

England were in a promising position—given sufficient time—but rain and bad light allowed only two hours' play on the last day. The Australian batsmen had evinced a certain wariness against the spin of Titmus and Gifford, and the game could well have developed into an enthralling struggle. As it was Australia finished at 168 for four wickets.

The Lord's weather was much kinder when the Australians returned to play Middlesex in July, and a high-scoring match resulted. Parfitt made a century, and Middlesex declared at 285. Burge missed his hundred by 4 runs, but Booth got 132, and Australia in turn declared at 347 for eight. When Middlesex batted for the second time Brearley made 106 not out, and the match was drawn when the score reached 240 for three wickets. At least the crowd had seen some good, forceful batting in several various styles.

In August the Australians played the President's XI. G. O. Allen gave youth its fling, and a young side held a fully representative touring side to an honourable draw. They had the Australians out for 162, of which 60 came from the last two wickets. Declaring at 193 for nine, they met with rather stiffer second-innings batting.

Jarman, going in as "night-watchman", stayed to make 105, and Simpson declared with six wickets down, leaving the opposition 228 to get in two and a half hours. Boycott and Brearley made 121 in good time for the first wicket, but the batting then blew up and, at the close, had struggled to 179 for seven.

The most remarkable feature of the match was that Simpson registered his first "pair", bowled by Brown on both occasions, in the first over of the innings. Lord's had brought him some strangely varied fortune in his first visits as captain of Australia, but, with the Ashes in his keeping, he could afford to regard this setback philosophically.

The University Match was drawn for the fifth year in a row. It was unfortunate that no result had been achieved over a considerable period, during which public interest was clearly on the wane. Whether this period of indecision contributed to the decline to any great extent is a moot point, but it certainly did nothing to aid its arrest. In this case there was a certain element of irony and injustice, for the match itself was quite eventful.

Oxford once again lost the services of their fast bowler, Martin, through a shoulder strain on the eve of the match, and so took the field with eight new Blues. After a rainy delay of three hours Oxford finished the first day at 126 for five, but worse was to come, and the whole side was out for 142 on the second morning. Brearley led Cambridge with 119, Griffith and White made brisk eighties, and Cambridge, declaring at 363 for eight, left Oxford 221 to save the innings defeat with but forty minutes of the day gone. Three wickets fell for 79, but Manasseh, top scorer with 45 in the first innings, made an unbeaten hundred. With good support from Baig and Gilliat, Oxford were 243 for four and placed to make a fight of it when stumps were drawn.

1964 was the centenary of the Middlesex County Cricket Club. Originally the club had no immediate connection with Lord's, for its first corporate action was to hire a ground at Islington. Thence in 1869 it moved to Lilley Bridge, and two years later an abortive arrangement was made with Prince's Ground, near Knightsbridge Barracks. None of these schemes worked out to the satisfaction of the members, and in 1877 it was decided to approach the M.C.C. As a result Middlesex became tenants of Lord's in 1878, an association which has lasted harmoniously over the years, and is likely to do so during the lifetime of both institutions.

Middlesex had a fair, but not particularly distinguished, centenary season. They were again sixth in the County table, and at no time gave their supporters any material hopes of carrying off the Championship. In the good weather they certainly did give these same supporters some good entertainment. Russell and Parfitt averaged over 40, and Smith, Brearley, Clark, and Murray over 30. These were all good-looking strikers, and Smith showed great promise. The bowling was less convincing on the better pitches. Titmus took over 100 wickets for 16 apiece, and Hooker 70 at 22. Price, who got an England cap in the fourth Test Match, was unexpectedly costly in county matches, his 60 wickets costing 26 a time. Drybrough retired at the end of the season, and Titmus assumed the captaincy.

On January 12 C. R. Browne died in Georgetown, British Guiana. A popular cricketer, always known as "Snuffy", he played four times for West Indies, and was the first West Indian to be elected an Honorary Life Member of the M.C.C.

In February "Ronny" Stanyforth died whilst in office as a Trustee of the M.C.C. He had served the Club well in many capacities. As a cricketer he had come to his full power comparatively late in his career and proved a very able captain, particularly of touring sides. Beyond giving a slight initial impression of reserve, he was a most delightful, amusing, and considerate man. His exceptional quality as a speaker surprised and delighted General Smuts, who, replying to a speech made in Cape Town, said he had not come prepared for oratory on that plane.

Frank Mann died in October. He was an outstanding figure amongst the great personalities who had spanned the First War. In his case this was fairly remarkable in itself, as he was thrice wounded, and not only survived but showed little outward sign of his experiences. In this he was indebted to a physique which effected some of the biggest hits ever seen at Lord's. Four times in one match he struck the ball on to the roof of the Pavilion, and in another match made a straight drive (reputedly off George Macaulay) which cleared the screen and reached the arbours on the far side of the Nursery ground. He was a man of equally large character, and commanded a respect and affection amongst county captains unequalled in his day. He was perhaps best described by another man of great heart and physique. Bill Bestwick said he was "a toff".

George Brown, who died in December, boasted these same heroic qualities of heart and physique, but in a rather different mould of character. He was a man of considerable eccentricity with a love of practical jokes. One of these was a surreptitious pin in the calf of the leg accompanied by an astonishingly lifelike bark. It was said he had practised this innocent but nerve-jangling jest on every dignitary and nabob he had encountered in India, with somewhat varying results. He had long been on the Lord's staff, and had batted left-handed, bowled right-handed, kept wicket, and fielded brilliantly for the Club over the years. As an umpire in later years he made an official appearance before a very reluctant Committee to explain a certain eccentricity in his interpretation of the laws. On hearing that there had been any complaint he described himself as being "astounded", an orotund reply which was said to have deprived the Committee of any further will to proceed.

32

Throwing

THE Australians had barely returned from their English tour
before they set off again for the West Indies, an event which would
have had little bearing on the history of Lord's were it not for a
furore over the bowling of Charlie Griffith which escalated like
lightning to global proportions and eventually led some people to
question the integrity of the M.C.C. Committee.

In the English summer of 1963 Griffith had developed a
formidable yorker and an alarming bouncer. His action had passed
the scrutiny of the English umpires, but Alf Gover, who took him
to Pakistan in his Commonwealth side in the autumn of 1963,
reported a scepticism in the minds of umpires there, and opined
that he threw both the yorker and the bouncer. Now, as West
Indies and Australia met in the first Test in Jamaica, E. R. Dexter
put the cat among the pigeons by writing in his weekly column in
The Observer that if Griffith used the doubtful bowling action that
he had used in Barbados and in England in 1963, the result of the
game would be as meaningless to the Australian players as was the
result of the 1963 series in England to the English players. As
an ex-captain of England Dexter's remarks were bitterly criticized,
not least for the offence they gave in the West Indies. Dexter's
darts were fired at long range from another continent, but on-the-
spot castigation came from Richie Benaud, and before 1965 was
out two more Australian captains, present and future (Simpson
and Lawry), together with Norman O'Neill, had declared that they
regarded Griffith's action as so dangerous that they would neither
play against him nor in any team in which he played.

Whisperings of a Committee Room plot at Lord's to turn a
blind eye on illegality and instruct the umpires to pass the West
Indies bowlers (whose Board had declined the benefit of a
moratorium) were rendered audible in the summer of 1965 by
the publication in *The Daily Mail* of private correspondence
between the Australian-born umpire Mr G. C. Pepper and the

Assistant Secretary of M.C.C., Mr Donald Carr. In the previous September three matches had been played between an England Eleven and a West Indies Eleven at Scarborough, Edgbaston, and Lord's. From Edgbaston the umpire wrote that prior to the match he had been asked by Trevor Bailey (who captained the English XIs at Scarborough and Lord's, though not at Edgbaston) not to call any bowler and, in particular, to be lenient in applying the front-foot rule, which was still foreign to West Indies bowlers. He went on to say that had this been other than an exhibition match he would have had no hesitation at all in calling Griffith, whom he was seeing for the first time from the square-leg position. In the absence of the Secretary, Mr Carr replied to this letter approving the steps that had been taken on the grounds that to call Griffith would undoubtedly have caused unpleasantness in an exhibition match. The circumstances in which the letters reached *The Daily Mail* have never been fully explained; allegedly they were in a brief-case which was stolen from Mr Pepper at Taunton eight months after the event. That M.C.C. were made to appear to be party to a diplomatic bending of a law they had vowed to enforce could hardly have been more unfortunate, for all the hints and suspicions were given a semblance of truth. In July the Committee issued a statement denying all knowledge that any "influential member" of M.C.C. had advised the first-class umpires not to call Griffith, backing the statement with a categorical denial from each umpire on the first-class list that anyone had been so approached.

In the opening months of 1965 Britain and the Commonwealth mourned the passing of Sir Winston Churchill, who was an Honorary Life Member of M.C.C., elected in tribute to his leadership in the War. For M.C.C. the new year was rendered additionally melancholy by the deaths of three other great men who, each in his own way, had enriched the game. Lord Monckton of Brenchley died in January. Forty-six years after keeping wicket for Harrow against Eton in "Fowler's Match" he became President of M.C.C., nominated by his former team-mate, Field-Marshal Earl Alexander of Tunis. His acute legal brain allied with great charm of manner and the gift of diplomacy, priceless assets in the higher direction of the game, made him as deeply valued as a counsellor in Committee as he was sought after on less formal occasions as an orator. Of Harry Altham, who died in March, I have already written much. It was typical, and as he would have wished, that he died in harness, at the close of an

evening spent in delighting an audience of cricket-lovers at
Sheffield and keeping them spellbound by the liveliness and zest
of one of his incomparable talks. Within a week news came of
the death of Mr R. C. Robertson-Glasgow—"Crusoe" to his
friends. His gentle, evocative humour had never failed to light
up with smiles and chuckles the faces of cricketers and country-
folk, but his own life, in between the sunny periods when he
delighted his companions by his vivid wit, was clouded with
melancholy.

Harry Altham's great services to cricket and his devotion to
Lord's were acknowledged by the setting up of a memorial fund.
After much thought and putting aside with reluctance proposals
for a cricket school at Lord's—a project which many people
thought would have most delighted one whose first devotion was to
teaching cricket—the Committee announced that they hoped to
build a library in his honour. Unhappily the generous sum
collected was still inadequate to meet the building costs, and
so, instead, the capital has been vested in a fund to organize
cricket training for the young. I can imagine no memorial which
would have given more joy to one who, in the last years
of his life, tirelessly directed his keenest endeavours towards
encouraging young players who lacked the advantages of their
contemporaries at his beloved Winchester or any other public
school.

A simple tablet in the Memorial Gallery records the many
facets of his great services and devotion to the game.

The new season was the first since the Triangular Tournament
in 1912 in which a system of dual tours operated, with New
Zealand and South Africa as "guinea pigs". But the familiar refrain
of raindrops as the season opened at Lord's on May Day (deterring
all but the most hardy Tykes from supporting the white rose)
augured ill for the New Zealanders, whose twelve weeks' visit was
made dreary by incessant rain and low temperatures. John Reid's
young and largely inexperienced side was stiffened by the presence
of the veteran Bert Sutcliffe, emerged from retirement. Unluckily,
as in 1958, Sutcliffe was injured early on, so that, until he made a
century in the final match at Belfast, the support his presence gave
was moral rather than physical. Remembering the wet summer
their predecessors had suffered in 1958, the New Zealanders might
reasonably have felt that the dice was heavily loaded against them.
A deficit of £4000 was hardly an encouraging recommendation for
the policy of dual tours, even though, by visiting India and

o

Pakistan on the outward journey, they were able to return home not only enriched in experience but with a modest profit.

With the arrival of the South Africans in June a delighted public had the first glimpse of Colin Bland's fielding and Graeme Pollock's batting. Nevertheless, throughout the country attendances were severely hit, and pitches much criticized for their slowness and lack of vitality. As a grain of consolation for M.C.C., John Reid singled out Lord's as one of the very few grounds which could be called fast.

Middlesex delighted their supporters by beating Sussex, the twice unbeaten champions, in the third round of the Gillette Cup, thus ensuring that the Trophy would change hands in its third season. But any hope Middlesex and the faithful habitués of Lord's may have had of cheering them to victory in the Final were dashed by Surrey in a thrilling semi-final which, with 502 runs scored in the day, was lauded by *Wisden* as the best day's cricket seen at the Oval for some time. In the Championship, after being top of the table in July, Middlesex finished sixth for the second year running. Their new captain, Fred Titmus, chosen for England in all six Tests, achieved the distinction of becoming the first and only Middlesex bowler to take 100 wickets in Tests.

The Imperial Cricket Conference met as usual in July, and agreed on the new set of rules which have allowed its membership to be widened by opening the door to Associate members without Test Match status not necessarily members of the British Commonwealth. The first to be elected under the new rules were the United States of America, Ceylon, and Fiji. These national bodies have been joined by Bermuda, the Netherlands, Denmark, East Africa, Malaysia, Canada, Gibraltar, and Hong Kong. Logically it was decided that the Conference's name should be changed from Imperial to International Cricket Conference.

The principal other business was throwing, now, since the furore over Griffith, a problem more vexed and urgent than ever. After much discussion a new interim definition was commended to the Governing Bodies:

> *A ball shall be deemed to have been thrown if, in the opinion of either umpire, the bowling arm is straightened, whether partially or completely, immediately prior to the ball leaving the hand.*

This differed from the previous experimental definition in omitting any mention of the elbow having been bent, and *prior to the ball leaving the hand* was preferred to *prior to the instant of delivery*.

In October, M.C.C. appointed a special Sub-committee, with
Mr F. G. Mann as Chairman, to advise what further steps could be
taken to eliminate throwing from all grades of English cricket. The
other members of the Committee were Messrs G. O. Allen, D. J.
Insole, R. Subba Row, T. E. Bailey, E. R. Dexter, and two first-
class umpires, C. S. Elliott and W. F. Price.

In England the eye of the storm about throwing engulfed the
Derbyshire fast bowler Harold Rhodes, and earned for him the
doubtful distinction of owning the most photographed right arm
in the history of the game. From the day he was first no-balled by
P. A. Gibb in 1960 until he was finally cleared nine years later he
laboured under a cloud which only lifted in the last season of his
playing career, barring him meanwhile from the international
honours for which he had once appeared to be heading. The
public's sympathy was demonstrated by the warmth of the
farewell given him by a capacity crowd at Lord's, who stood and
cheered him as he bowed his way out of county cricket in the final
of the Gillette Cup in 1969.

The task allotted to Mr Mann's Committee was threefold: to
eliminate throwing from first-class cricket as fairly and as quickly
as possible; to eliminate it from other grades of cricket in the
United Kingdom; and, as a means of attaining these objectives,
to find an improved definition to help umpires in all grades of
cricket to apply a uniform interpretation of the law.

The existing procedure in first-class cricket was for an umpire to
call a bowler when he was satisfied that the ball had been thrown,
and for a report to be sent to the Secretary of M.C.C. on every
bowler after each match. Any bowler whose action was suspect was
reported to his county club. This procedure might possibly have
been successful in the long run, but it had not been entirely
satisfactory so far, and it was evident that there were still bowlers
with suspect actions. But difficulties in judging accurately and a
natural reluctance to become involved in unpleasant incidents
were causing a lack of uniformity in umpires' opinions and actions,
with the result that counties had continued to play bowlers who
may have been throwing consistently. The Throwing Sub-
committee recommended that this system should be supplemented
by the creation of a standing Sub-committee composed of Mr
Mann as Chairman and Mr Allen as Vice-Chairman, with
representation from retired umpires, members of the Board of
Control Selection Committee, current players, and county
committees; their task would be to adjudicate on bowlers who had

been called or reported, and they would have power to clear a bowler or to condemn him and, in the last resort and subject to the agreement of a two-thirds majority of a quorum of seven, to suspend a bowler until the end of the season. For other grades of cricket it was proposed to hold consultations with the umpiring organizations and to promote instruction of the correct bowling action.

Much time was spent studying films, assessing their value to the Adjudication Sub-committee, and deciding if they could be used in educating umpires and coaches and in helping to arrive at a better definition of a throw. Thought was given to the technical side of filming and the essential angles from which shots should be taken. It was discovered that these angles were long-on, long-off, from the eye of the batsman and the square-leg umpire. Black-and-white film was found to give better definition than colour, and slow-motion shots were desirable. The Committee's faith in the value of films was reflected in a recommendation that a new coaching film should be made, concerned principally with instruction in the correct bowling action, including shots of suspect actions, with pointers to the danger signs which a coach should look out for and correct before it was too late.

The I.C.C.'s most recent definition, as we saw, read that a ball should "be deemed to have been thrown if, in the opinion of either umpire, the bowling arm" was "straightened, whether partially or completely, immediately prior to the ball leaving the hand". The Australians objected to this on the grounds that the words "immediately prior to" were open to doubt, and that in some countries there were those who believed that the words implied that a bowler was fair provided his arm was straight at the instant of delivery. Mr Mann's Committee recognized some substance in Australia's objection, and, indeed, they regarded Sir Donald Bradman as one of their most valued advisers. Among the alternative definitions chosen for particular consideration was Ian Peebles' "horizontal law", which had been mooted in *The Cricketer* and commended for its simplicity by such good judges as Messrs R. W. V. Robins, R. E. S. Wyatt, A. R. Gover, and J. C. Laker. His formula read:

> *The ball shall be bowled, not thrown or jerked. That is to say that when, on the final swing, the bowler's arm reaches the horizontal, it shall be fully extended from the shoulder to the wrist until the ball is released. This does not preclude the use of the wrist.*

The Mann Committee preferred this:

A ball shall be deemed to have been thrown if, in the opinion of either umpire, the process of straightening the bowling arm, whether it be partial or complete, takes place during that part of the delivery swing which directly precedes the ball leaving the hand. This definition shall not debar the bowler from the use of the wrist in delivering the ball.

None of the definitions, of course, have ever precluded the free use of the wrist.

The Throwing Sub-committee's report was presented to the counties on March 1, 1966, sharing the agenda of a special meeting of the A.C.C.C. with the first report of the Clark Committee. The Adjudication Committee was duly set up, and the first candidate for their consideration was Harold Rhodes, whose unequivocal no-balling by umpires Buller and Elliott had cast him in the role of leading man, if not first villain. At a day-long session the experts watched him in action, saw him on film, caused more films and photographs to be taken, and heard medical evidence on the abnormality of his arm, with its double-jointed elbow, which, bending back beyond the horizontal, posed a special problem. At the end of the day the Committee's unanimous conclusion was that his basic action was fair, but they were divided on whether or not his action was occasionally suspect. Before May was out Charlie Griffith had been no-balled at Old Trafford—only the second tourist to be called for throwing in England—and Harold Rhodes was once more under scrutiny, with more films, more discussion, more demonstrations, before the Adjudication Committee referred his case back to the Committee of M.C.C. for a ruling on whether or not it was the intention that his very unusual form of delivery should be regarded as illegal.

At the I.C.C. all countries accepted the Mann Committee's definition for one year—1967. In 1968 M.C.C. sought to add a rider legalizing the action of double-jointed bowlers, but they received no support. The definition as it stood was confirmed for all countries, but Australia was still not happy, and her representative, Mr Bob Parish, argued strongly for the introduction of a preamble, emphasizing the basis of the law, which was that umpires should be satisfied that the ball was bowled. If they were satisfied, then there should be no reason to refer to any definition. Australia supported the continuance of a definition to which umpires should refer, but she had no wish to introduce one which might catch out a fair bowler. To meet this view the Conference agreed to introduce the definition with a preamble, stating that, "umpires must be satisfied beyond all doubt that the ball is bowled. If they are so satisfied no other question arises." The definition followed, "set out as a guide to umpires".

"Throwing" has been a dirty word in cricket parlance ever since Tom Walker was anathematized at Hambledon for attempting to modify underhand bowling, and the great sportsman who pioneered round arm was goaded into riding out of the game in fury and despair. In parenthesis, it is curious to recollect that Willes's disciples were denigrated as throwers or *straight-arm* bowlers! Not the least pernicious aspect of throwing is its power to stir up ill-will; other evils in cricket can be discussed calmly and dispassionately, but not throwing. It simmers like the brew in a witch's cauldron, ready to boil over at the touch of the feeblest tinder, and because it is both dangerous and inflammable it has been the determination of every country to eliminate it from the game. It is not so long since M.C.C. teams returning from Australia and the West Indies reported that all the young cricketers were throwing and revelling in it. Whether or not Australian and West Indies players reported similarly about English youth, it is obvious that if it is to be outlawed throwing must be shown to be wrong at the highest level, and the correct action must be taught at the lowest. Once a player is grooved into throwing he will be able to change only if he has an iron will, through a process of despair. Such a great and determined player as Tony Lock succeeded, but he is the exception rather than the rule.

33

The Games and the Players 1965

IN the season of 1965 there occurred the first "double event" designed to cope with the enormous increase of interest in international cricket in this country. It was arranged that the New Zealanders should tour during the first half of the season, and the South Africans should follow during the second.

The scheme was admittedly a compromise, and probably the only possible one in the circumstances. If the major and more attractive powers were to maintain a regular schedule at reasonable intervals, and the lesser to visit as frequently as they were anxious to do, the only apparent alternative was the introduction of a two-tier international system as far as England was concerned. Such a scheme was fraught with difficulties, not only physical and material, but also in the delicate area of national prestige.

Of the first practical experiment it might be said, as the Marquis de Dion said of his gear-box, "C'est brutale mais ça marche." The indifferent weather underlined the inherent disadvantages, and difficulty of maintaining a fair balance between the visitors. If there was a great disparity between the strength and attractions of the teams there was a danger that the lesser side would evoke very little interest from a public with fresh memories or awaiting better things to come.

In this case the New Zealanders were clearly the minor guest, and were immediately assailed by a disastrous spell of weather. They struggled bravely, and were gaining momentum by the end of the trip, but this illustrated the fact that a side in their predicament had not sufficient time to make a complete recovery. The three Test Matches were lost outright, and the only county to be beaten was Gloucestershire.

The M.C.C. match was a draw, but perhaps the happiest game of the tour. The toss was won against a side picked largely from the promising youth of English cricket, and Congdon and Dowling put up 130 for the first wicket. Sinclair at No. 3 made 63, and Congdon went on to 136. The New Zealanders declared at 318 for seven wickets, and then bowled M.C.C. out for 196. As Parfitt and Cowdrey made 125 between them none of the young did much to further their claims for the moment. Congdon and Sinclair had another splendid second-wicket stand, this time unparted, and New Zealand declared for the second time at 122 for one wicket. The never-long-absent rain spoilt what could have been a fine finish on the third day, and the match was drawn, with M.C.C. 175 for the loss of Hampshire, Barber, and Parfitt.

Further misfortune had befallen the team when they returned to play the second Test Match at Lord's starting on June 17. After an early collapse they had put up a splendid fight in the first match at Birmingham. Following on, they had scored 413 in their second innings, but had gone down by nine wickets. But the team was thrown out of balance when Sutcliffe was put out for most of the trip after being struck by a bouncer from Trueman. Reid had developed serious cartilage trouble, and was able to bowl only on rare occasions, and then with due caution.

The Lord's match was similar in pattern to Edgbaston. Despite a fine innings of 55 from Pollard, New Zealand never recovered from a disastrous start when Rumsey took four wickets with only 28 on the board. All out for 175, they were topped by 132 when England, led by Cowdrey with 119 and Dexter with 62, made 307. At the second attempt New Zealand were over 200 with only three wickets down, but, despite another fine 55 from Pollard, the total did not get beyond 347. This was a good recovery, but England coasted home by seven wickets. Although overwhelmed at the Oval the New Zealanders had shown that they were spirited opponents, especially in adverse circumstances.

The South Africans were such a success that there was much lamentation that they were to be seen for only half the season. A fine, enterprising phalanx of batsmen, under the direction of Van der Merwe, gave joy to the spectators wherever they played, and Graeme Pollock's grace and power raised visions of Frank Woolley in older memories. The fielding was uniformly superb, with Bland's brilliance also raising memories of times when people would go to matches to see Constantine catch and throw, apart from any other attraction.

There being no fixture with the M.C.C. in their truncated programme, the South Africans were seen at Lord's in the first of the three Tests. Although drawn it was a fine and very even cricket match. At the start the English fielders were seen to advantage when three magnificent catches disposed of Barlow, Lance, and Lindsay for 75 runs. Graeme Pollock and Bland then added 80 by attractive stroke play but, even with the last three wickets adding 102, the final total was only 280 on a good, plumb wicket. England made 338, Barrington being run out for 91 and Barber and Titmus both topping 50.

Graeme Pollock failed in the second innings, but Bland got 70 out of another moderate total of 248, which left England 190 to make in just under four hours. In the nature of the South African bowling, led by the long-running Peter Pollock, the over rate was slow, but it was, on paper, a very fair opportunity for England. Unfortunately the whole innings was upset when, at an early stage, Edrich was hit on the head by Peter Pollock and had to retire, severely hurt. Thereafter England steadily lost ground, and were fairly hard-pressed when seven wickets were down, and Edrich *hors de combat*, with 45 wanted at the close.

The South Africans had won the second and deciding Test Match when they returned to Lord's in August to beat Middlesex by five wickets. Middlesex owed the great proportion of a first-innings total of 335 for eight to Radley, who made 138, and Titmus, who made 101. The centurions set a Middlesex record of 227 for the sixth wicket, without which it would have been a somewhat ramshackle innings. As it was the South Africans fell short of this by 81 runs. The advantage was completely lost when Middlesex failed against the well-flighted off-spin of Crookes and were all out for 123. The South Africans made the necessary runs for five wickets, to complete their second win at Lord's. As they won the series and provided such attractive cricket on all occasions they had fair claim to being the most successful South African side to visit this country.

For the sixth year in a row the University Match ended in a draw. The early stages were somewhat tedious, but an eventful last day finished in a highly exciting situation. Oxford batted laboriously to declare at 176 for eight wickets, to which Cambridge replied with 153 for eight, their declaration at least striking an enterprising note. On the last day Gilliat hit well in the morning so that, when Cambridge went in for the second time, 220 runs were wanted in three and three-quarter hours. Martin and Watson bowled to such purpose that Cambridge were soon on the defensive and struggling to avoid defeat. There was still an over to come when the ninth wicket fell at 124, and an appeal against the light by Harvey, the last man, was turned down. Despite the failure of this desperate ploy, his partner survived the last over and Cambridge escaped.

Middlesex also seemed to be pursuing a set pattern in that, for the third year running, they finished sixth in the table. In this they were fairly lucky, for they won only two of the last seventeen matches. The weakness seemed once again to lie in the lack of a consistently penetrating bowling side. Titmus was always resourceful, and took 75 wickets for 16 apiece, but Hooker's 86 averaged 24. Two promising newcomers gave hope for the future. One was the son of "Lofty" Herman, of Hampshire, who bowled at a sharp pace, and the other H. C. Latchman, a leg spinner from the West Indies. It was also in pattern that Middlesex made a very fair start in their home matches, to give their supporters some good entertainment if no material hopes that the club would win the Championship.

Harry Altham died on March 11. He had been a member of the M.C.C. committee since 1941, Treasurer from 1951, and President in 1959. The game of cricket never had a more genuine devotee or more practical supporter. He was very much a man of Lord's, but even more a man of cricket in its widest aspects. He served the game as he had played it, generously and wholeheartedly.

Lord's lost another generous, unselfish cricketer when "Young Jack" Hearne died in September aged seventy-four. He was not a spectacular figure as a cricketer or as a man, but a steadfast and loyal member of his team, for which he would do his very best at all times whatever the circumstances. He is remembered chiefly as a batsman; it is sometimes forgotten that, until he broke his wrist, he bowled the best slow leg-breaks in England.

He had been preceded by his friend "Long John" Durston, a familiar and gigantic landmark standing beside him in the slips. For a dozen years he had bowled with unflagging gusto despite an injured right arm, and had played his only Test Match at Lord's. Like many giants, he had a gentle heart, and one can truly remark that the only injury he ever did any man was due to a mistaken belief in his power as a masseur—power being the operative word.

On October 17 another fast bowler died in Philadelphia at the ripe age of ninety-two. "Bart" King brought to cricket something of the baseball pitcher's art of "curving" the ball. At best he rated high amongst the bowlers of any country. He had made his last appearances at Lord's in 1908, when in taking six Middlesex wickets in a match that was all over in a day, he twice dispatched a youthful Hendren for nought. Three weeks later he had taken seven wickets when The Gentlemen of Philadelphia defeated M.C.C.

34

The Clark Committee and the Structure of County Cricket

IN the wake of the report of the Government-appointed Crathorne Committee on Sunday Observance there was a good deal of discussion on the pros and cons of first-class cricket on Sundays. At a special joint meeting of the A.C.C.C. and the Board of Control in June 1965 Glamorgan's representative, Mr Wooller, enquired if there would be any objection to two counties agreeing to play a week-end match on Saturday, Sunday, and Monday instead of Saturday, Monday, and Tuesday. His county felt that this might create considerable interest. So M.C.C. invited the counties to consider and report whether or not they would be prepared to play on Sundays, and laid the foundation stone for a new pattern in the social structure of the game. Middlesex meanwhile made history by inaugurating Sunday cricket at Lord's. On August 1 twelve of the county beat the Lord's Taverners, and 10,000 spectators contributed to the funds of the Middlesex C.C.C. Youth Trust and the National Playing Fields Association.

The first business of this joint meeting had been to consider a plan for playing eight one-day matches in place of four three-day matches within the County Championship in 1966. The germ of the scheme had arisen from a review by the M.C.C. Cricket Subcommittee of attendance figures since 1962. A partial recovery from the nadir of 1963, when County attendances were the lowest ever recorded, had left the figures for the relatively dry season of 1964 still well below 1962, and it was suggested that the success of the Gillette competition was a pointer, indicating a demand for one-day cricket, which should be followed up. The authors of the embryo scheme, a small sub-committee sitting under Mr Allen, were convinced that, with county receipts falling so rapidly, it was essential to try some form of experiment; such a limited experiment, they felt, would not undermine the three-day principle of county cricket, and if it failed there would be no difficulty in discontinuing it. Very few of the A.C.C.C. delegates were entirely against an extension of one-day cricket, but some feared the effect on the Gillette competition. The plan was heavily outvoted for 1966 and defeated, by a slim majority only, for 1967, but M.C.C. were asked to look into other possible changes in county cricket. So in the autumn yet another major cricket enquiry was launched under the chairmanship this time of Mr D. G. Clark.

The Clark Committee's terms of reference were to examine the future of county cricket in the widest possible terms and, if they thought fit, to recommend alterations in the structure and playing conditions of the Championship.

The current pattern of declining attendances, now more acutely apparent in cricket than in any other sport, seemed to demand a plan which would enable counties to reduce their running costs, but it was essential to try to discover from the counties themselves what they really wanted. So the Committee's first step was to send to every county a questionnaire asking for their views under four main headings: preparation of pitches; the players' conduct and approach to the game; playing conditions; and the future structure of county cricket. By November the replies had been analysed, and Mr Clark summarized them for the A.C.C.C. at their autumn meeting. He dwelt on the large measure of agreement on the cardinal subjects of pitches, the over rate, and the players' attitude to the game. Most counties paid lip service at least to the ideal of fast, true pitches, even though all but three admitted failure, blaming the weather or the nature of the soil. Whatever the cause, the general standard in 1965 had been extremely disappointing and Mr Clark and his Committee could not rid themselves of a suspicion that the counties were not all innocent of tailoring pitches for bowlers. There was scepticism, too, about most counties' claims that they were doing their best to reverse the steady decline in the over rate. In regard both to pitches and the tempo of the game the Committee made no secret of the fact that they felt county committees could and should have taken stronger action.

But the essence of the whole enquiry—the factor which must always govern how cricket is played, at any level—was contained in the questions on the players' conduct and approach. Predictably, nearly all counties were satisfied with their own players' conduct on the field, but few were happy about their approach to the game. It was now the Clark Committee's prime task to seek a way to rekindle the players' enthusiasm, to bring a sense of urgency to cricket, and to attract players who would play the game in that spirit.

The counties' replies to proposals for alternative structures for county cricket reflected their traditional reaction against any conception of change. Only a small minority expressed any dissatisfaction with the present structure, and none of the suggested innovations involving fewer three-day matches and the introduction of one-day matches received any firm support. However, there was support for limited experiments with Sunday cricket, and seven counties said they would play up to three of their home matches on Sundays in 1966. Middlesex were not of the number, so Lord's was not affected, but they played one Sunday match, against Surrey at the Oval. Opinions were equally divided on alterations in playing conditions, but a clear majority opted for discontinuing the 75-yard boundary restriction. At the A.C.C.C. the limited boundary became optional, and another of the Altham Committee's innovations, the rationing of fielders on the leg side was modified so that the only restriction was a limit of two behind the wicket.

Mr Clark's interim report was accepted by the counties with generous warmth, and it was heartening that they adopted a resolution stating that, while it was appreciated that Playing Conditions already ruled that time-wasting should be considered as unfair play, umpires should now be informed in the strongest terms that they had the counties' full support in implementing this regulation. An even tougher suggestion was that a Watchdog Committee should be instituted to act in cases of time-wasting and apply penalties, which might be extended to the umpires.

A positive step towards providing fast, true pitches, or, as the Committee preferred to define them, *hard*, true pitches, was an invitation to the counties to send their groundsmen to a conference at Lord's in December. Now it was the groundsmen's turn to answer a questionnaire, and from their replies it appeared that, out of the twenty-three who attended, twenty-two felt they knew how to produce a good pitch, though no more than three claimed success in 1965. All denied emphatically that they had ever received from their county committees instructions to provide other than fast and true pitches; most were given a completely free hand. Discussion of their individual methods disclosed a wide divergence, reflecting the practical impossibility of arriving at any standardized treatment for the variable factors of soil and climate prevailing from ground to ground and from year to year. In the five years which have elapsed since this meeting a great effort has been made to improve the status of groundsmen and to convince them that the importance of their work is appreciated. The groundsmen's conference is now an annual event in the Lord's calendar in early spring. Almost simultaneously with the 1965 conference a nicely timed approach was made by the Soil Science Unit of the University College of Wales at Aberystwyth for co-operation in a research project. The work of their unit has been of enormous benefit to cricket, and in January 1970 about thirty county groundsmen attended a week's residential course there, from which they returned much stimulated, with a great enthusiasm to go again.

Fortified by the counties' support, the Clark Committee faced the vexed question of what alterations, if any, should be made in the structure of county cricket. Each member was asked to submit his ideas in writing; the papers they produced were unanimous on the need for true pitches and a rejuvenation of the players' approach; most members agreed also that the future structure should involve some reduction in the existing programme and the introduction of one-day matches. In other respects their ideas were as varied as the flowers in June. A notable dissentient from the majority view about the curtailment of the existing programme was Surrey's forthright captain of the fifties, Stuart Surridge, who, heading his list of desiderata with the attitude of the players, followed by strong captaincy, contended that the complete answer to modern inertia was to be found in an aggressive approach. But he indulged in a little kite-flying by offering a novel alteration in the laws; the distance from the wicket to the popping crease should be increased by two feet. The batsman would still take guard in the normal way, but he would be enabled to move a further two feet to attack the ball without being stumped. The germ of the structural proposals eventually put forward to the counties was contained in the structure suggested by the Chairman, for one three-day match and one one-day match per week, plus the Gillette Trophy. Such a reduced programme, he argued, would cut out the financially non-effective days' play on Tuesdays and Fridays, when attendances were minimal. But in considering any reduction in the amount of cricket the Committee were deeply aware of the risk of antagonizing county members, who formed the backbone of cricket's economy. All structural alterations were, therefore, approached with extreme caution, with recommendations split into two categories: short-term recommendations, which would not imperil current membership, and long-term recommendations, focused on stimulating increased membership in the years to come.

As we saw, the first Clark Report was presented at a special joint meeting of the Board of Control and A.C.C.C. on March 1, 1966. Its preamble recited again the dismal catalogue of trends which had reduced county finances to such a parlous state: the negative approach of the players; a surfeit of cricket, sub-standard pitches, contributing to sub-standard batting and negative bowling; slow play; tactics of attrition in the first innings; loss of established players and potential talent because of the necessity of finding permanent employment, and the exclusion of the part-time player; finally, loss of spectator appeal. Reasons were given for rejecting a whole list of specific suggestions put forward for their consideration: the lengthening of the season to allow thirty-two three-day matches cut right across the Committee's belief that there was too much cricket and would not, anyhow, produce gates to meet the additional costs; they could envisage no spectator appeal in two-day single-innings matches; seven three-day Tests would seldom produce a result; one new ball only per innings would rob the game of a factor of spectator appeal and delay the dismissal of the "tail". They rejected also complete covering of pitches, on the grounds that rain-affected pitches were a traditional factor in English cricket, and because complete covering was impracticable on grounds with a small staff. Moreover, delays were only too often caused by water on the outfield. Short-term provisions for 1966 did, however, include a recommendation for fuller covering of the pitch, which was later rejected by the counties, so that, in effect, the degree of covering was left to the discretion of the home county. County committees were urged to take a much closer interest in the production of fast pitches, and once again there was a rap for their complacency about the over rate and admonishment to do more to encourage their players to adopt a positive approach and to appreciate that their livelihood was in jeopardy. As for Playing Conditions, by far the most controversial short-term recommendation was the experimental introduction of an over limit of 65 in the first innings of twelve out of each county's twenty-eight matches—an experiment which was greeted (if that is the word) with united damnation by the Press, who soon had the satisfaction of finding that they were seen to be wise before as well as after the event. After a single season the experiment was proved, as its critics foresaw, to favour defensive

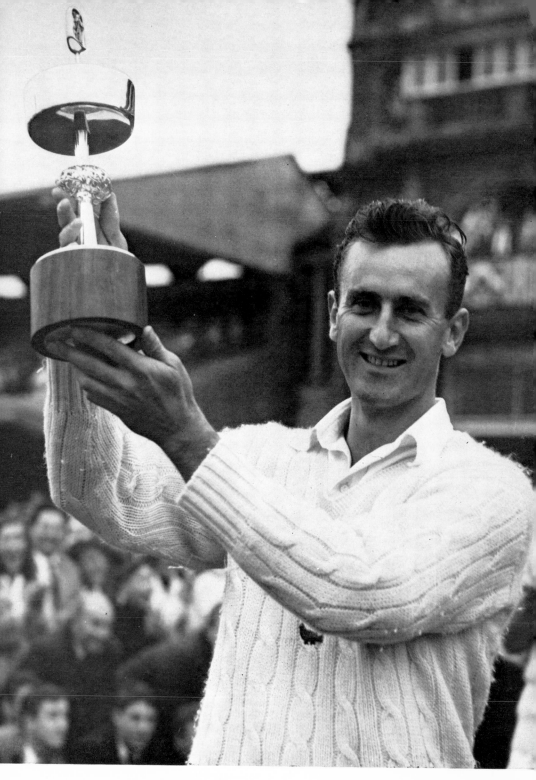

SUSSEX WIN THE KNOCK-OUT COMPETITION
E. R. Dexter with the Gillette Cup, 1963.

THE WISDEN TROPHY
West Indies were the first winners, 1963.

THE ROTHMANS TROPHY WON BY THE REST OF THE WORLD, 1967
Garfield Sobers receives the trophy from Mr A. E. R. Gilligan.

bowling rather than achieving its purpose of allowing the spectators to see something of both sides batting and bowling with a
sense of urgency on the first day. For traditionalists it seems
contrary to the laws of nature as well as the Laws of Cricket to
jettison the fundamental principle that a bowler's first objective is
(or should be) to destroy the batsman's "castle". But the rule of
limited overs, adopted with reasonable success in one-day Gillette
matches, had often been advocated for first-class cricket, and it
still had to be proved to be no good. As Mr Allen (who was very
sceptical of its merits) said in Committee: "Until it was tried in
competition county cricket its advantages and disadvantages would
never be known. The opportunity should be taken to make or
break it once and for all." With the primary object of discouraging
seam bowling, "interfering" with the ball was forbidden altogether,
either by polishing or raising the seam or rubbing on the ground.
A minor change in the scoring system allowed a team winning a
match to retain the two points they might have received for first
innings lead.

These, then, were the short-term proposals. For the long term,
two alternative schemes were offered for the future structure of
county cricket. Both retained the Gillette Cup in its existing form,
and both adhered to the principle of three-day cricket as the
cornerstone of the County Championship, while reducing the
number of three-day games to a minimum of sixteen, played at
week-ends. The first scheme envisaged sixteen three-day and sixteen one-day matches, to be played in a single championship; the
second offered twenty-three three-day and sixteen one-day matches
in separate championships. But before taking any decision
it was recommended that the counties should carry out an opinion
poll to ascertain the views of their members and supporters.

This first Clark Report was accepted in essence, and most of its
short-term recommendations became effective in 1966. During the
summer the counties made a survey of their members, and in the
winter M.C.C. canvassed the views of capped players. *The
Cricketer* magazine, too, sought the views of its readers. But an
enquiry on a far wider basis was carried out as a contribution to
cricket by *The Daily Mail*, who commissioned National Opinion
Polls to conduct a nation-wide survey with the triple object of
measuring the extent of public interest in cricket and other sports,
finding out how people spent their week-ends, and discovering
ways in which first-class cricket could be made more attractive to
spectators.

P

So when the Clark Committee came together again in the autumn they had a feast of evidence to digest. But as a bitter aperitif they had first to review the short-term experiments of 1966. Pitches, far from improving, got worse, and for once the weather could not be blamed; the suspicion lingered that some counties were interested in results rather than good cricket. It was decided to make a tough statement at the A.C.C.C., warning the counties of the possibility of banning certain grounds if the standard did not improve. Once again there was strong criticism of the over rate, whose infinitesimal improvement had done nothing to rouse the public from their *ennui*. Perhaps the bitterest disappointment was the counties' rejection by a single vote of the Public Relations Sub-committee's recommendation for the appointment of a Public Relations Officer for cricket, even though the Warwickshire C.C.C. Supporters Association had promised massive financial backing. This was a personal blow to Mr Clark, for as Chairman of that Sub-committee it had fallen to him to commend the appointment to the counties and to point out that an annual loss on direct cricket income amounting now to between £160,000 and £200,000 demanded urgent steps to sell the game more effectively.

The vast N.O.P. survey covered leisure activities of a representative section of the population during the last two weeks in May. including Whitsun. Of all those questioned 39 per cent professed an interest in cricket (third in the whole list of sports, after football and boxing). Of these, 7 per cent of the men said they took an active part in cricket—a higher proportion than for any other sport, including golf. Disastrous though the falling off in attendance was, the report indicated widespread interest in the game. The most cogent reasons given for not attending first-class cricket were: watching television, conflicting interests, dull play, and the weather—in that order. By contrast, of those who took part in *The Cricketer* poll a week or two earlier, 85 per cent claimed that they were not kept away by T.V.—indicating perhaps no more than the devotion and hardiness of that journal's readers. Sixty-nine per cent of them claimed that they were as interested in cricket as they had always been, though a significant majority were in favour of fewer three-day matches without the addition of one-day matches. The replies from the counties showed great disparity, with a strong bias towards structural changes but a lack of unanimity about their nature. There was, in every poll except the players' (in which the question was not included), massive support for Sunday cricket. The players' firmest support was for hard, true pitches, and even though almost all claimed to enjoy playing county cricket, a large majority thought modern first-class cricket produced poor entertainment. But they showed very little enthusiasm for the alternative structure offered for their consideration. Only the scheme for sixteen one-day and sixteen three-day matches in separate championships—which was to be the one recommended in the Clark Committee's second report—received something approaching 50 per cent support.

The Clark Committee's second report was presented at a special meeting of the A.C.C.C. in January. Having reviewed unfavourably the effect of the short-term recommendations, the Committee had perforce to say that nothing had occurred to reverse their criticisms of the previous year. It seemed certain that the 1966 figures would show a further financial decline, and if no action were taken to call a halt this trend would continue until some counties were forced to leave the Championship—a situation which, in view of the massive support for the game, could surely be avoided if appropriate steps were taken to institute changes in the playing programme. They named three principal objectives for the future: to produce the highest possible standard of play in all classes of cricket; to provide entertainment which would appeal to spectators and would be available when the majority were able to attend; and to improve the financial position in all counties.

After summarizing the views expressed in the various opinion polls the report proceeded to its main objective, the recommendations for the future, for which detailed reasons were given. The proposals came under five heads: the first, most important, most controversial, and dominating the others, was for a new structure to apply in 1968. There were to be two separate championships, comprising respectively sixteen three-day matches and sixteen one-day matches, plus the Gillette competition. It was also recommended that consideration should be given to playing a full 2nd XI competition of sixteen two-day matches. Secondly, playing conditions envisaged three-day matches on Saturday, Sunday, and Monday unless any county objected to playing on Sunday. A points system was suggested for the one-day championship; also a revision of the points for three-day matches, allowing an added incentive for the first innings. Thirdly, the registration rules were to be amended so as to allow one of the two overseas players who could be registered for each county to qualify after a residence of twelve months instead of twenty-four. Fourthly, it was recommended that the question of sponsorship should be examined for all three championships. Lastly, a firm recommendation was made towards banning county grounds on whose pitches a number of bad reports had been received.

In conclusion, the Committee repeated their conviction that the time was ripe for change; the vast public which was interested in cricket expected change and would welcome it. The weight of public opinion was clearly on the side of change, and they felt that if this did not take place the long-term effect on county cricket might well prove disastrous. They believed that the introduction of the proposed structure would cause a revival of enthusiasm as far as both the players and the public were concerned; but all the proposals would be worthless unless county committees ensured that the approach of captains and players to the actual playing of the game was positive and enthusiastic.

The report had a mixed reception. Broadly, the counties supported the lesser recommendations and rejected the basic structural reform. The revised points system was accepted; so were the relaxed qualification rules for overseas cricketers. A County Pitches Committee was appointed to operate machinery for adjudicating on pitches. Captains and umpires had henceforth to report on each ground, grading them into four categories from "very good" to "totally unfit for first-class cricket". Two reports in the lower grades brought a visit from the new Inspector of Pitches, Mr Bert Lock, the former Surrey groundsman, with the possibility that the ground might be banned. The institution of Watney's Groundsman of the Year Award has contributed to the campaign for encouraging groundsmen to regard their jobs as an important contribution to cricket, and in the last few years there has been a noticeable improvement.

In spite of this wide measure of acceptance the Clark Report was written off as "rejected" because its kernel, the revolutionary new structure, was decisively outvoted by the counties, the only reprieve being a reluctant decision to put it on the shelf and take it down and review it after the 1970 season. Never, perhaps, has so much thought been expended with such meagre results, and Mr Clark and his Committee might have been forgiven if they felt discouraged. Now, as the time approaches for a reassessment, the future of cricket in England is being discussed on a zonal basis. Meanwhile attendances at three-day matches in 1969 fell just under 327,000, whereas the Sunday League, in its first year, attracted 280,600 spectators. It would be premature to hail it as a resounding success before the novelty has worn off, and it has the serious objection from the players' point of view that it breaks into another match. By 1972, the earliest year when decisions taken in the close season of 1970–71 could become effective, the true worth of the Sunday League should be apparent, and it will be seen whether or not, with familiarity, the bonanza of cavalier-style cricket will have lost its charm.

35

Redevelopment of the South-western Corner

AS M.C.C. faced the close season of 1965–66 with two major enquiries on their hands—the Throwing Committee and the Clark Committee—the Secretary of M.C.C. was in Australia as Manager of a team who were renewing the challenge for the Ashes. During his absence the Committee were confronted in addition with the biggest domestic challenge which had ever occurred in the long history of the Club. The issue which, for the first time on record, threw into serious doubt the members' confidence in their Committee was the vast scheme for redeveloping the south-western corner of the ground from Grove End Road to the Mound Stand. Few members, probably, had the sense of history to review the economic growth in the hundred years since Mr R. A. FitzGerald became Secretary (Honorary) of a comparatively modest club of no more than a few hundred members. So meagre were the resources at the Committee's disposal then that the first grandstand could only be built thanks to the private enterprise of a band of members, and every other piece of capital development from the purchase of the freehold of the ground to the building of the Mound Stand was underwritten by a single member, Mr William Nicholson. To Mr FitzGerald the capital reserves of more than £300,000 at the Committee's disposal in 1965 would have appeared inconceivable. Now the Committee were proposing to expend a sum equivalent to the whole of these reserves, achieved by years of good husbandry and shrewd investment, on massive plans to sweep away existing buildings, including the cherished Tavern and Clock Tower and transform this side of the ground by erecting a towering stand. In the light of declining attendances a significant body of members regarded as an act of lunacy such prodigal expenditure on what might prove to be a white elephant.

A Committee of finance and property experts had spent three years considering this development. The paramount necessity which activated and accelerated all other considerations was the total obsolescence of the Tavern and its ancillary buildings as an effective control centre for the Lord's catering. Since Mr Portman's day successive M.C.C. caterers had incurred annual losses amounting to five-figure sums, and now an experienced firm with all the resources of a massive business were hardly more successful. It was clear that, under present conditions, Messrs Ring and Brymer would not renew their contract when it expired in 1967, and it was unlikely that any other professional caterer would be persuaded to take their place.

By the autumn of 1965 the Committee had approved highly integrated designs by Mr David Hodges and Mr Kenneth Peacock for the erection of flats, a new Tavern, and a stand which would engulf part of the old "Q" Enclosure and continue around the perimeter of the ground as far as the Main Gate.

The broad outline of these plans had appeared in the 1964 Annual Report, and members had been given fuller details in 1965, both in the Annual Report and at the Annual General Meeting. There was a warning of heavy capital expenditure and the likelihood of a rise in subscriptions. However, no estimates were given, and many members failed to appreciate fully the scope of the financial implications. Communication is, of course, a major problem in a club of such a huge membership, and on this issue much trouble arose from a failure to communicate effectively.

To forestall the probability of compulsory purchase, the first area to be considered had been the derelict Grove End Road corner site recently derequisitioned by the Water Board. Tenders were sought from contractor developers to build a multi-storey block of flats, and early in 1965 it was agreed to accept Messrs W. T. Chown's offer of £150,000 for a ninety-nine-year lease to erect a twelve-storey block of fifty-five flats and a penthouse, to plans approved by the Committee.

Faced with the imminent total collapse of the catering, the Committee next accepted the necessity for building a new Tavern, and they bowed to the united advice of architects and catering experts that, as the old Tavern site afforded too little space for an effective catering unit, the new Tavern should be built immediately to the west of the Grace Gates and adjoining the new flats. In such a restricted space it was obvious that much time and money could be saved by having one contract for the flats and the Tavern. Messrs Chown's contract was therefore extended to include the construction of the Tavern with its 300-seater restaurant and large reception-room/cafeteria at a cost to M.C.C.

estimated at £140,000. In round terms, therefore, the flats were to pay for the Tavern. Mr Hodges was the architect for both.

A decision had now to be made about the fate of the old Tavern, with the adjoining Members' Dining-room and the Clock Tower, whose boxes, behind their charming wrought-iron balustrades, had been honoured by the presence of kings and queens, prime ministers, and the most illustrious figures in the British Commonwealth. Sentiment and affection were overwhelmingly on the side of conservation, for to pull them down was to drop the curtain for ever on romantic rendezvous under the Clock, to silence the bucolic "Old Met" humorists on the Tavern promenade, and to deprive loyal taverners of their home. Economy as well as sentiment seemed to argue for their preservation, adapted as far as practicable for bars and cafeteria. But practicability was the key to the argument for demolition. Preserving the shells of these buildings would have involved heavy outlay on conversion and repairs to crumbling fabric for an end product of limited functional value. As for the Clock Tower, it was doomed already by the plans for the new Tavern, which involved sidestepping the Grace Gates thirteen feet to the east, thus making the Tower an obstacle in the way of a dignified driveway up to the Pavilion. The Committee concluded, not without heart-searching, that it would be false economy to pour money into the sieve represented by obsolete buildings, thereby abandoning an opportunity of completing the modernization of the ground, which might be lost for ever. So they now approved, as the third stage, Mr Peacock's four-decker stand, in which the needs of taverners were met by a fine concourse and bar. The remainder of the ground-level terrace and the top tier was designed for members and their friends (to support a larger membership), and the two middle tiers provided twenty large twenty-four-seater boxes with moveable partitions to convert each to two smaller units if desired.

By the members' assent at successive Annual Meetings, the Committee had a mandate to go ahead with the plans and to enter contractually into an agreement, but the members' approval at a special general meeting was needed to secure the "ways and means". This meeting was held at Lord's on October 20 with a threefold agenda, to ratify the sale of the tender of the building lease of ninety-nine years to Messrs Chown; to authorize the Trustees to sell investments and exercise their powers of borrowing to the extent necessary to implement the proposals and to increase the number of full members and raise the subscription rates by

50 per cent from £6 to £9 for full members and from £4 to £6 for Associate members.

As was customary, the meeting had been summoned by notices in *The Times* and *The Daily Telegraph*, but a body of members complained that there had been insufficient notice and that, on such complicated issues, a full written explanation should have been given. A notice inserted by a member in the personal column of *The Times*, urging members to attend, "to oppose the proposals to provide funds for grandiose building programme", foretold that this meeting would be no formal rubber stamping of the Committee's proposals. Those who attended heard a very lucid explanation of these proposals from the President, Sir Oliver Leese, supported by the Treasurer and Messrs G. C. Newman and M. J. C. Allom, Chairmen respectively of the sub-committees responsible for redevelopment and catering. The first resolution, ratifying the sale of the building lease for the flats, was passed by a substantial majority, but on the other two an amendment was carried demanding that a second special general meeting be convened in writing, giving twenty-one days' notice, accompanied by an explanation of the Committee's proposals. The feeling of the meeting was that, regardless of the merits of these two resolutions, they should be referred back on the grounds that members had received insufficient information and that the announcement of the meeting had not been seen by enough members to secure a representative attendance.

Such a barrage of criticism aimed at an establishment hitherto unchallenged did not pass unnoticed by the Press. In *The Daily Mail* Mr Alex Bannister drew a word picture of the President, General Leese, and his staff with their backs to the Long Room wall. It is fair to say that the Committee were considerably shaken by the strength of the opposition, and meticulous preparations were made for the second meeting, convened for January 11, 1966. A booklet explained every aspect of the scheme, with descriptions, plans, and drawings of the new buildings and estimates of cost. The required capital, £305,000, could have been met from the resources of the M.C.C. Trust Fund, but, rather than denude the Club of all its readily realizable assets, the Committee proposed to raise a third from the sale of investments and borrow the balance on a bank loan repayable over thirty years. Finally, there was an explanation of the proposed new structure for subscriptions and membership, designed to provide substantial additional income to cover the loss of revenue from investments and the cost of servicing the loan, and leaving a balance to meet rising costs. The standard subscriptions were raised by 50 per cent, but a concessionary rate was introduced for "country" members living outside a radius of a hundred miles from Hyde Park Corner and for members under twenty-five or over sixty-five years old, whose subscriptions remained at the old rate. The addition of 1000 Associate members and the election of full members up to the permitted maximum of 10,000 by January 1967 promised a new total of 14,000.

Some 750 members had notified their intention to attend (though no more than 550 turned up). Such a throng exceeded the capacity of the Long Room, and the venue was transferred to the more commodious Seymour Hall, where formality was added to the occasion by the elevation of the Committee and their advisers to a platform raised well above the floor of the hall. News had just been received of England's victory in the third Test, and in his opening speech the President referred to it, saying:

> The reputation and standing of Lord's is second to none in cricketing circles in the world. It is the Mecca of cricketers of all nations and the Headquarters of cricket from which come forth the Laws of Cricket, the spirit in which it should be played, and the encouragement to men of all ages and all nations to play what we believe to be the finest game of all. And what better example than the manner in which our team have gone about their tour from the moment they set foot in Australia, bringing them this brilliant victory today. Would you like me to send a telegram of congratulations from this meeting to the team?

Needless to say, whatever disagreements there may have been about the formal resolutions on the Agenda, this impromptu resolution was passed with acclamation. The President went on to plead that, if M.C.C. were to maintain their prestige, they must move with the times and provide accommodation, buildings, catering facilities, and match and practice grounds second to none. This was a wonderful opportunity for M.C.C. to show that they had faith in the game of cricket and in the future of Lord's.

Again there were three resolutions. The first concerned the Trustees' powers of borrowing and charging the property and assets of the Club to the extent necessary to implement the redevelopment. The other two resolutions sought approval for the new subscription and membership structure. The main debate focused on Resolution 1. The plans for the flats and the Tavern were accepted almost without demur, but there was lively criticism of the proposed outlay on the stand. The President and the Chairman of the Redevelopment Sub-committee explained the reasons why the Committee had hastened to sign an agreement in April, foreseeing accurately new legislation which would otherwise have necessitated building licences. The nature of the scheme, with every part of the operation dovetailing into another, was so highly integrated that it had been essential to have a single contract for the whole. But until September 30 there had been an option not to build the stand, and in fact the Committee's final decision to build it had only been taken on July 28.

The most extreme opposition came from a group of members whose amendment excluded altogether the rebuilding and modern-ization of the Clock Tower and Tavern, specifically limiting the Trustee's powers to raising money for the new Tavern. However, this amendment was heavily defeated. It was pointed out that failure to build the stand now would attract a claim for breach of contract of not less than £20,000, to which must be added £7750 for fees. The demolition of the Clock Tower, with the consequent loss of its boxes and 500 seats above, could not be avoided if the Tavern project was accepted, so only the old Tavern and Members' Dining-room would remain. The transformation of these buildings into a viable proposition by extensive repairs, new drainage, and conversion would bring the total cost of retaining them to well over £50,000, without taking account of the loss of income from the Clock Tower and a sizeable reduction in the new catering contract offered by Messrs Watney, Mann.

The subsequent debate, well argued on both sides, devolved upon the enormous cost of the stand, which its critics said was out of all proportion to the Club's requirements. The day was won by Sir Bernard Waley-Cohen, whose well-reasoned amendment asked that consideration be given to a modified new stand, costing less than the £280,000 at present envisaged.

In order to adhere to the building programme the Committee now had to act fast to consider possible modifications. On the very day after the General Meeting they considered whether to omit the top terrace, thus saving £20,000 at the expense of 1500 seats, or whether to limit the boxes to one tier, saving £33,600 and losing twenty boxes and their revenue. They chose the latter, and aesthetically I personally believe this has improved the stand, whose additional height would have dwarfed every other building on the ground.

Work on the flats began without making any profound impact on Lord's. Now, in the spring, the first visible sign that the main

development was about to begin was evident with the re-siting of
the Grace Gates. Work on the Tavern block, scheduled for
completion in 1967, was screened behind a lofty barrier. The
destruction of the old Tavern and Clock Tower began only after
Lord's had closed its gates to the last spectator in the autumn, and
there were few to witness the sorry devastation and feel the sharp
nostalgic pang as these well-loved buildings crumbled under the
weight of bulldozers. Even so, they nearly had an eleventh-hour
reprieve when the Committee, learning that there was, without
satisfactory explanation, a substantial increase in the cost of the
Tavern, paused to think again about the stand.

June 13, 1967, a week before the Test Match against India, was
the day fixed for the formal opening of the new Tavern. Mr
Griffith drew the first pint as he had drawn the last in the old
Tavern the previous autumn. The bar, with its rough-hewn
décor with the unadorned oak pillars and white brickwork
(synthetic!), is pleasant to sit in and has stood up well to several
years of heavy wear and tear. For this Tavern, unlike its predecessor in its latter days, attracts a brisk trade at all seasons, and
the bar lunches are good enough at the right prices to hold a
regular clientele. Upstairs the two fine reception rooms can cater
for banquets, meetings, and receptions on a scale to dwarf utterly
the capacity of the old Tavern. The long stretches of wall made
shallow by the inevitable low ceilings of modern architecture,
have posed a problem for pictorial decoration which has been
solved by the use of blown-up photographs of old prints, and the
lightness of the black-and-white prints has successfully enlivened
the (to my taste) over-sombre combination of olive-green walls and
a heavy red-and-black carpet. My own most severe criticism of
an otherwise successful building is the hideous, though functional,
I suppose, staircase which protrudes into the Harris Garden.

The demolition squads had now done their worst, and some
semblance of order was emerging above the barricades which hid
the new stand. From time to time huge pre-cast units rose up into
the sky, hovered, and then settled as the new phoenix arose from
the ashes. The stand was ready on schedule for the Australian
Test in 1968, and there were moments before the notorious hail-
storm blanched the ground, concentrating its carpet in front of the
stand, when its occupants basked in glorious sun. The boxes are a
vast improvement on their predecessors as a viewpoint for the
cricket, for they are less remote than the Clock Tower and,
whether you are an avid watcher or prefer to engage in social

chatter, they are a great deal more comfortable. The gay but rather aseptic-looking red-and-yellow polypropylene chairs are surprisingly resilient and comfortable to sit in. But such a fine structure is far too little used.

The major redevelopment brought in its wake other lesser schemes which were, to a greater or lesser degree, complementary to it. The loss to the new Tavern of the old "Garden" Restaurant near the Grace Gates created a need for a new under-cover centre for the Easter Coaching Classes, and so, at considerable cost, the covered coaching area was built on part of the cinder car-park on the Nursery area. The first nets were held there in April 1967.

Then, in 1967, it was agreed with Watney's to "gut" the old Players' Dining-room and servery above the visitors' dressing-rooms in the Pavilion and to build in their place a smaller, but better-furnished dining-room for the players and a dining-room for the Committee, both served by a new kitchen manned by M.C.C. staff, who, under the supervision of the Club Super-intendent, are now entirely responsible for catering for the players and Committee. This has eliminated the hazardous task of bringing food from distant kitchens and has improved beyond recognition the quality of food served to the players. The montonous diet of cold meat and salad has vanished in favour of a freshly cooked hot joint, most welcome after a morning spent fielding out on an English May day! The Committee Dining-room has not only benefited the Committee, though I sometimes wonder if they miss the breath of fresh air afforded by the walk to the Tavern, but it has provided an admirable venue for the small Club dinners which were introduced in the close season of 1968–69. These dinners are, of course, all "stag" occasions, but I was fortunate enough to be entertained there to dinner by Sir Oliver Leese and members of the Arts and Library Sub-committee, when I retired as Curator, and so I can testify personally to the delightful setting which the room affords for a small dinner or cocktail party.

The high cost of the Tavern Stand, as it has been named by a majority vote of the members, has of necessity raised the question of further development of a non-cricketing nature to replenish capital. For sixteen years, while my father was Secretary, we lived in No. 22 Elm Tree Road, which had been the home of Mr and Mrs Findlay and of Sir Francis Lacey. Once upon a time the house was known less prosaically as Clunberry Lodge. It was a gracious house, enlarged from a mere "cottage" consisting of two rooms up and two down with two more in a semi-basement, by the addition of gable-ended extensions, providing a lavish drawing-room and dining-room, with bedrooms, dressing-rooms, and basement rooms to match. But this was a plan which demanded a staff of Edwardian dimensions; menservants in the basement and women-servants in the attics. Had the foundations been sound it might have been converted into charming flats, but, sadly, it had become a white elephant. One of the charms of the house had been the garden, spacious by London standards, and the Committee wisely decided that such a valuable site must be made to earn a better reward than the uncertain rent for a crumbling house. And so as the demolition squads moved in I tried not to see what was happening until three modern villas arose set back from the road in a small semicircular close. They are sold to their new occupants on long leases for a sum which was unfortunately rather less than had been hoped.

The Redevelopment Sub-committee, having completed their main task, were merged with the Property and Works, and the amalgamation was renamed the Property and Development Sub-committee. For several years they have been actively engaged in considering a feasibility plan produced by Mr E. K. Smart which, if carried through, will result in major development at the Nursery end, with the possibility in mind of a block of flats, a hotel, and flats for M.C.C. staff.

36

Plans for the Close Season

WHILE M.C.C. members argued the pros and cons of the redevelopment at Lord's, half a globe away in Australia Mr Griffith suffered an agony of divided loyalties, torn between his duty to be at Lord's at a time of crisis and his commission as Manager of the M.C.C. team. But the M.C.C. Committee were steadfastly determined to leave the helm at home in the hands of the Deputy Secretary, Mr Dunbar, who, as Assistant Secretary responsible for the redevelopment, needed no briefing. As team manager Mr Griffith was vested with unprecedented authority, comparable to that given to Sir Alf Ramsey in the realms of football, to direct the policy of the cricket and command a positive approach. Under his guidance the captain and team early made great strides towards obeying the selectors' command to play with aggression, and England came very near to recovering the Ashes. As the most dynamic opening batsman England had produced in years, Bob Barber soon became a major hero. Of the four-man Middlesex contingent, Russell, Murray, Parfitt, and Titmus, Titmus alone enjoyed success, less for his bowling, which lacked some of its former penetration, than for his spirited batting. Russell unluckily suffered a broken finger early in the first Test, which, failing to mend in time for the second, lost him his place to Boycott. Behind the stumps Murray played second fiddle to Parks, whose superior batting kept him in favour with the selectors even after a cardinal error in the second Test had probably cost England the match. Parfitt's batting lost all its punch, so that he ended up miserably among the bowlers at the foot of the table. On the eve of their great win in the third Test the team received news of the death of George Duckworth, that great England wicket-keeper whom one of his captains once described as "one of the smallest but noisiest of all cricketing artists". He was not only a great-hearted cricketer and a delightful companion and a true friend, but also an extremely shrewd judge of the game. Shortly before the fourth Test the President of M.C.C. arrived in Australia, with high hopes of seeing England, led by the captain of his own county (Warwickshire), regain the Ashes. But his hope was not to be fulfilled, for a revitalized Australian side beat England by an innings at Adelaide, and the final Test, on which, once more, all depended, was doomed already when rain came to clinch a draw. The President's visit was in one respect historic, for it enabled the President and the Secretary of M.C.C. to be present together at a meeting of the Australian Cricket Board of Control, and hear at first hand the Australians' views, *inter alia*, on the vexed problem of throwing.

On the homeward journey, after drawing all three Tests against New Zealand, they had two days' cricket in Hong Kong. The first of these one-day games was spoilt by rain, but in the second M.C.C. beat Hong Kong comprehensively, with a Boycott century and astonishing bowling averages of four for 5 by Jones and four for 28 by Allen. They arrived home only a little ahead of the West Indies, whose first engagement was a Press conference at which the Wisden Trophy, won by West Indies in the year of its inauguration, 1963, was handed to Gary Sobers, now captain, in the room of Sir Frank Worrell. At the end of the season, having led his team to victory, he received the trophy once more from the President of M.C.C., Sir Oliver Leese. By the wish of West Indies, the Wisden Trophy is permanently housed in the Memorial Gallery at Lord's, in trust for the holders. Only in the winter of 1967–68 it travelled with the M.C.C. team to the West Indies, to be seen in all their territories before returning to Lord's with the victorious English team.

When M.C.C. entertained the tourists to dinner during their first match at Lord's, the principal speech of the evening, the toast to Cricket and the West Indies, was proposed by Sir Alec Douglas-Home, now president-elect.

Advance bookings for the tour were quite unprecedented. At Lord's, for the fiftieth Test played on the ground since England met Australia there in 1884, the total gate receipts reached a record sum of £58,602—£2000 up on the previous West Indies tour of 1963. The five Tests yielded a record aggregate profit of £188,400. This was the first year in which a team of professional broadcasters, led by Mr John Snagge, manned the Public Address System. During the match both teams were entertained to a cocktail party in the Memorial Gallery, to which ladies were invited. The choice of venue was particularly appropriate in the Presidency of Sir Oliver Leese, who is also Chairman of the Arts

THE 200TH TEST BETWEEN ENGLAND AND AUSTRALIA
Sir Robert Menzies presents an 1880 sovereign to the President of M.C.C. and
the England captain, Mr A. E. R. Gilligan and M. C. Cowdrey.

PRIME MINISTERS PAST AND PRESENT
Sir Alec Douglas-Home, President of M.C.C., host to Mr and Mrs Harold
Wilson in 1967.

ETON *v.* HARROW

A lonely survivor of a multitude of coaches.

and Library Sub-committee. Warwickshire commemorated his
dual office of President of M.C.C. and of their county by presenting
for the Memorial Gallery a splendid showcase for displaying the
most celebrated of M.C.C.'s collection of historic bats. He had also
the great personal satisfaction and pleasure of crowning the season
by presenting the Gillette Trophy to the captain of his own county
team.

The modern contribution of big business in sponsoring and
promoting cricket was exemplified in 1966 by the inauguration of
the Horlicks awards of £200 for the best batting and bowling in
each Test, plus £500 to the side winning the series. Gary Sobers
demonstrated his towering supremacy by winning the batting
awards in the first, second, and fourth Tests, to which he added the
award for bowling in the fourth. Only Graveney and Murray, who
shared the award in the final Test, won batting honours for England, but at Lord's and Trent Bridge Higgs won the bowling
award, and the final Test was all England's, with Jones nominated
as the bowler of the match. Murray's century at the Oval was
some consolation for his earlier rejection by the Selectors, and,
having collected his thousandth "scalp" in first-class cricket, he
now received from *Wisden* the accolade of Cricketer of the Year.
His Benefit match at Whitsun brought Middlesex their first win of
the season; his total collections earned him £8010, which, in the
Middlesex Benefit stakes, was second only to Denis Compton. As if
to celebrate the impending Middlesex victory there was a short
ceremony in the Harris Garden during the tea interval on Whit
Monday, when a seat was unveiled in memory of J. W. Hearne.
Walter Robins, in a short speech in Hearne's honour, described
him as the best all-rounder Middlesex ever produced. When he
bowled his prodigious leg breaks it was said that the ball could be
heard humming in the air.

Rothmans added to their bounty by inaugurating the World
Cup—an extension of the matches between England and Sir
Frank Worrell's Eleven and England and the Rest of the World in
1964 and 1965. Three teams now competed in a triangular
tournament of one-day matches under Gillette rules, played at
Lord's as a pendant to the season. The contestants were England,
West Indies, and the Rest of the World, the last a combination led
by Bobby Simpson, whose team was composed of Test cricketers
from Australia, India, South Africa, and Pakistan, plus a former
West Indies wicketkeeper, now up at Cambridge, Deryck Murray.
The World at large lacked match practice, and were outplayed by

Q

both West Indies and England, so the tournament developed into a renewed battle between the protagonists in the Test series, with England this time the victors. For the second season Rothmans enriched the coffers of cricket by handing over to M.C.C. substantial sums from the televising of the highly popular Sunday Cavalier matches, for the benefit of the central fund being created for the new-style administration of cricket. Their next contribution was to be a film of the England v. West Indies Tests.

At the Annual General Meeting the Treasurer announced a deficit of £9600, after transferring £5000 to the Building Fund. The picture for the future was made gloomier still by the forthcoming introduction of Selective Employment Tax—a devastating blow to the county clubs, as well as to M.C.C. Predictably, representations were made to the Chancellor of the Exchequer for some alleviation, but with no success.

Increasing pressure on the Treasurer brought a decision to relieve him altogether of responsibility for the non-financial business of the Finance and General Purposes Sub-committee by divorcing absolutely that Committee from its offspring, the Financial Policy Sub-committee. This was now absorbed in a new Finance Sub-committee, a tightly knit body consisting of the Treasurer, as Chairman, with one of the Trustees, the Chairman of the Property and Development Sub-committee, and a small band of highly experienced experts in banking, investment, and business, together with the Club's Accountant. Their concern was and is financial policy, development, the preparation of the annual accounts, and investment policy, leaving the General Purposes Sub-committee to deal with all other normal business of the old "F. and G.P.". A minor financial windfall was a bequest of just under £500 from a Mr E. S. Murphy, of South Africa. During his lifetime Mr Murphy had wished to present an electrically operated scoreboard, but as this was not practicable he decided on the legacy, which was now donated to the M.C.C. Y.C.A.

The Middlesex accounts also showed a substantial deficit, for the first time since 1960. For reasons of economy they decided to abandon their club and ground fixtures. With the retirement of Mr F. G. Mann after fifteen years as Honorary Secretary, the appointment ceased to be honorary. The new Secretary was Mr Arthur Flower, who, coming to Lord's shortly after the War, was already the senior member of the resident Middlesex staff. Thus his appointment involved no drastic change in the personnel of the Middlesex office. George Mann has for many years been an active

M.C.C. Committee man, working indefatigably as Chairman of the Cricket Sub-committee of M.C.C. and, now, of the Test and County Cricket Board's Cricket Sub-committee.

At their meeting in July the I.C.C., now for the first time International rather than Imperial, underlined this new status by electing as Associate members the Netherlands and Denmark as well as Bermuda and East Africa. They still sought, without agreement, an acceptable definition of a throw, but agreement was reached on a miscellany of other laws. A captain might now forfeit his second innings; M.C.C.'s experimental rule prohibiting a catcher from stepping over the boundary after making the catch was commended for acceptance; general satisfaction was expressed with the front-foot rule; it was agreed that for two years a new ball should be taken after a stipulated number of overs; efforts were to be made towards encouraging young bowlers to take a shorter run-up; and time-wasting was again condemned. A new conception, born at this meeting, was the responsibility of the senior members towards the Associate members. A proposal to inaugurate a fund to which Test-playing countries would subscribe to provide coaches had later to be modified, but spheres of assistance have since been agreed upon, so that every Associate member comes under the umbrella of a full member, and it is envisaged that help from the parent countries should include supplying qualified coaches. M.C.C.'s protégés are Denmark, Holland, Canada, and Gibraltar.

When it was first suggested as a means of enabling all countries to make more frequent visits to the U.K., the new principle of double tours, for which New Zealand and South Africa had acted as pilots, had been readily accepted, but, now that they were immediately involved, some countries were reluctant to fall in with the revised programme. Pakistan accepted a short tour for 1967, but the other guests, India, made strong objections, which were only overcome after the President of M.C.C. had halted his journey to Australia for a personal meeting with members of their Board and India had been promised two more short tours and a full tour before 1979. West Indies, at great strength and assured of an enthusiastic welcome from the British public, reinforced by their own expatriates, now expressed disgust at being scheduled for a shared tour (with New Zealand) in 1969. Even before it was released, forecasts of the revised programme had received such a hostile reception in the West Indies Press that the Secretary of M.C.C. was moved to issue a full Press statement putting the whole

question in its proper light. For West Indies had originally agreed
with enthusiasm to the new schedule, which gave them another
full tour only three years after their triumph of 1963—"a wonderful
gesture", their Board had called it. Now the idea of being asked to
share an English season with another country was being seen as an
affront, and it was even suggested that the proposal for a short tour
in 1969, so soon after two full tours, was a calculated insult,
because the long-established pattern of Australian visits had not
been disturbed. However, the Secretary was able to persuade the
West Indies cricket authorities that this was very far from being
the case, but that the M.C.C. Committee, firmly believing in the
policy of double tours, were determined not to let them drop after
a single season, but to adhere to a programme which, including as
it did all countries except the oldest rivals, Australia, should be
seen to be fair.

From November until March, under the pall of fog, snow, and
blizzards, Lord's can be a cheerless place, dead and often bitterly
cold. The promise of fine new buildings and the necessity to raise
income brought to a head once more its wasted potential during
the close season. "What on earth do you do in the winter?" has
almost ceased to be a sick joke suffered by the staff with varying
degrees of impatience, according to their temperament, for it must
by now be apparent to the merest tyro where cricket is concerned
that the Committee Room, if not the ground, is a hive of activity.
But all this activity in the dead season is aimed towards promoting
what is to happen in the summers to come. Only tennis and squash
attract a steady clientele, and that limited to the small number
who can be accommodated in one real-tennis court and two
squash-rackets courts. In October 1966 a new Club Facilities Sub-
committee was appointed to review their predecessors' schemes
and consider once more what better use could be made of the
ground all the year through. The first project put up for the
consideration was the lease of the practice ground to Bertram Mills'
Circus—a possibility which offered lively scope for the imagination, but which foundered because of a wide differential between
the rent which was offered and what M.C.C. felt they should
demand. The nearest substitute was the very temporary lease of a
caravan site for a troupe of film stars, Sally, Pancho, Lulu,
Spanio, and Freddie, the Lenz chimps. Freddie had a reputation
as a formidable left-arm bowler!

The use of the match ground for winter games has always been
inhibited by the certainty of damage to the turf on this heavy clay

soil. Our Australian friends are often amazed that it is not used for football, "to aerate the ground" as they do in Australia, where turf recovers in a matter of days. But anyone who advocates football at Lord's should take a look at the pitches in near-by Regent's Park. The longest-established outdoor winter game has been lacrosse, dating back to 1876, when the Committee extended a warm invitation to a pioneer Canadian team. Lacrosse continued spasmodically until 1953, when the groundsman pleaded success-fully that matches played on Saturday afternoons in autumn and spring on a pitch across the Nursery end of the ground interfered with his treatment of the turf. It was now agreed to lease the ground to the Hockey Association for an international pre-Olympic hockey tournament in October 1967. The matches, played on two pitches marked out to the east and west of the table, were a tremendous success. The highlight was a dramatic defeat of India by Pakistan. All the players were delighted with the splendid state of the ground, and in the following April senior and junior matches were played between Great Britain and Belgium.

Profit is, of course, one motive, and a very important one, in developing facilities, but it is not the sole objective. A serious effort is being made to find means of creating an integrated club, catering for young married members and offering attractions for the whole family all the year round; and there is a sense of responsi-bility to benefit the local community. Ways and means have been thrashed out for developing Lord's as a sports centre, with an indoor cricket school as the prime objective, and such additional amenities as a health centre, an international squash-rackets court with spectator accommodation, a bar, changing rooms, and showers. Such plans are to some extent in conflict with purely financial considerations, which could mean their modification or even drastic pruning in favour of more remunerative schemes being considered by the Development Sub-committee. The hope is that both may be able to live together. Meanwhile a modest start has been made by the inauguration in the winter of 1968–69 of monthly Club dinners in the new Committee Dining-room. These comparatively small gatherings of fifty or sixty members have been extremely popular, especially with the younger members. About twice in the winter a speaker is invited; often there is a film show in the lecture-room; and on some nights members may introduce guests. The Committee Dining-room has also been made available after play for members to entertain lady guests. Whether or not the introduction of fruit machines into the long bar is an amenity or not is open to divided opinions; *chacun son goût*! The Facilities Committee have also worked hard to promote more support for the Annual Dinner, and a record attendance of 250 in 1970 bore witness to the success of their industry.

Between Australia 1965–66 and West Indies 1967–68 there was a respite from major tours, but a M.C.C. under-twenty-five team went to Pakistan, with the Middlesex player J. M. Brearley as captain and L. E. G. Ames as Manager. The tour was a personal triumph for Brearley, whose 793 runs, including a triple century, put him head and shoulders above all the other batsmen. The present England wicketkeeper, Alan Knott, also covered himself with glory and showed the calibre which brought him top international honours at a very early age. In a gruelling five weeks' programme, in which there was hardly a day when they were not either playing or travelling, they did well to return unbeaten, winning all but the three representative matches which, in the pattern of Tests in India and Pakistan, were drawn.

In December and January Mr Griffith spent a fortnight in South Africa as the guest of the South African Cricket Association, discussing the future of Tests between England and South Africa and seeing Australia defeated for the first time in South Africa. At Newlands he saw Graeme Pollock play one of the greatest Test innings since the War.

He returned within a matter of days of the momentous meeting when the Clark Report was referred back by the counties. Arising from its penultimate paragraph urging county committees to ensure that the approach of their captains and players was wholly positive and enthusiastic, he was persuaded to make a personal approach to a representative group of players at the start of the new season. So in April three representatives—usually the captain, the senior player, and one of the younger players—from each of sixteen counties gathered at Lord's to hear him preach again the gospel of enterprise and purpose, and to discuss together how to put his words into practice. The seventeenth county, Somerset, though unrepresented, received him in person at Taunton. It is a sad reflection that, in spite of all the Secretary's powers of persuasion and the great personal effort he made in presenting his arguments, at the end of the season the verdict was that the cricket had been, in the main, more torpid than ever.

When he made his annual speech to the county secretaries in December, the counties had just decided to glamorize their teams by allowing immediate registration of a limited number of overseas stars. Mr Griffith made a plea for club cricketers to be given a chance to play alongside the Cowdreys, the Graveneys, and the Titmuses, and for counties to prune their permanent staff so as to be able to pay the top players a remuneration related to their worth to the county club and the spectator.

Although the counties had turned down the appointment of a P.R.O., they supported M.C.C.'s decision to appoint the former Chief of the B.B.C. Light Programme, Mr Denis Morris, as Public Relations Adviser, on a year's assignment to examine the presentation of cricket to the paying public. Implicit in his approach was the Clark Committee's belief that the time was ripe for a change in structure. He visited all the counties, discovering their reaction to questions concerning their relations with the public, the dissemination of information, facilities for members and the public, and co-operation between counties. His report, which was circulated to the counties in the spring of 1968, contained some frank criticism and much constructive advice. In June 1967 M.C.C. announced the appointment of the former Oxford University and Essex fast bowler, Mr Jack Bailey, as an additional Assistant Secretary at Lord's, with special responsibility for public relations and Press liaison.

1967 was Canada's year and a season of many minor tours. As part of the centennial celebrations of the Canadian Cricket Association, Mr Dunbar, with his wife, Sheila, made a lecture tour right across the country, travelling, in three weeks, more than 6000 miles and meeting cricketers and talking cricket in twelve different centres. They were, of course, taken to the 1967 "Expo", erected on a site on St Helen's Island in the St James River, where cricket had been played between Montreal and a Garrison team in 1829. Everywhere they went they were enthusiastically received as ambassadors of M.C.C. and overwhelmed with hospitality. In July a Canadian colts team arrived in England and practised in the nets at Lord's and visited the Memorial Gallery before setting out on a tour of English public schools. An Indian schools team, making a maiden appearance at Lord's, had a last-over victory against a M.C.C. Schools XI which bordered on melodrama. Three other overseas teams visited Lord's without playing there; the Zambian Eaglets, who were the first Zambian team to visit U.K., and two South African sides, representative of their schools and universities. But, to return to Canadian happenings, their cricket year was completed by a M.C.C. tour to Canada and U.S.A. from late July until early September. This popular cosmopolitan side led by the American-born Dennis Silk and including Everton Weekes and the Middlesex players Bob Gale (as Vice-captain), Don Bennett, Ted Clarke, and Alan Moss, returned unbeaten, having played twenty-five games in five weeks, with twenty-one matches won. To this record—"fabulous", in the modern idiom—Don Bennett contributed 768 runs, topping the averages with 70.

In August M.C.C. entertained a representative Dutch team and, having bowled out their visitors for 226 on a good wicket, they were left with three hours to get the runs. After Russell Endean was out with 15 still needed, it fell to Kees Bakker to score the last two runs needed off the last ball to beat his compatriots. It is hard to imagine a better finish to a fine day's cricket, with 553 runs on the board.

It seems to be the fate of those who are allocated the first "leg" in dual tours to suffer deplorable weather. Poor India! May 1967 offered a sad welcome to her young and inexperienced side. The fixture against M.C.C. was no exception from the dismal pattern. The first day was the Saturday of the F.A. Cup Final, and the meagreness of a "crowd" of no more than 2000 made the occasion even more gloomy than it might otherwise have been.

Weatherwise, Pakistan, who shared the season with India, were more fortunate. Their captain, Hanif, a veteran already at thirty-three years old, was well known in England. Of those who were newcomers the one who made the greatest impact was Majid Jahangir Khan, son of the Cambridge University and All-India seam bowler, notorious at Lord's for having demolished an innocent London sparrow in his undergraduate days. Soon Majid became a bright star in the firmament of Wales, as represented by Glamorgan. Then, like his father, he went up to Cambridge, for whom in the 1970 Varsity Match he scored a double century of much distinction.

At the I.C.C., New Zealand's representative, their former Governor-General, Lord Cobham, made a plea for countries who had visited the U.K. in the first half of a season of dual tours being given the second half the next time, and in 1969 they profited splendidly by being the second to arrive, whereas the unfortunate West Indians endured the same fate as India and New Zealand before them. Out of contrariety, the spring of 1970, when there was no tour, seemed to start off where the magnificent late summer of 1969 left off.

It was agreed, on the proposal of Australia, that in future, when arranging Playing Conditions before a Test series, participating countries might, by mutual consent, extend the playing hours of the final Test if, after the penultimate match, neither side led by more than one match. West Indies raised the question of the effectiveness of the Conference, to which delegates came without authority to make decisions, so that any matter of importance had to be referred back. After a discussion it was agreed to recommend that delegates should in future be given more power and flexibility in their negotiations at the I.C.C.

Middlesex's introduction of county cricket to Sunday spectators at Lord's was utterly disappointing and, if a former member of the staff may be forgiven for saying so, a sad disillusionment for the "back-room boys" who sacrificed precious days of rest to make it possible. In fairness it must be said that in the first of these Sunday matches it was the opponents, Hampshire, who set the sluggish pace by allowing a commanding innings built upon a great Marshall century on Saturday to labour on well into Sunday afternoon without evident purpose. But the Middlesex batsmen seemed incapable of emerging from their shells, and the result was one of the most moribund day's cricket that anyone who had the misfortune to witness it can ever remember. When Northants and Surrey played on later Sundays the gate was noticeably less and the fare offered to those who came equally stodgy. Only on the Monday of the Northants match, when Middlesex woke up and routed their opponents, a flaming *crêpe Suzette* was proffered to the faithful *cognoscenti*.

More festive altogether was the one-day game against the International Cavaliers on the last Sunday in August, when the biggest Lord's crowd of the season saw Middlesex beat the international stars by 10 runs. The receipts, £2300, were a record for the Cavaliers. On the Nursery ground on the same afternoon twenty finalists competed for the Fred Titmus Bowling Cup, devised to improve accuracy and variation in schoolboy bowlers. The winner was Geoffrey Roan, a colt from the Ealing Cricket Club. Most of Middlesex's other matches were as lifeless as their Sunday games, but against Pakistan, Russell and Harris revived memories of Robertson and Brown, by beating by two runs that famous pair's opening partnership record of 310. In the Lord's Test against India, Murray, so soon to be ousted by the youthful Alan Knott, equalled the world record by holding six catches in an innings. Murray's beautiful innings at Birmingham was followed at Lord's against Pakistan by an "Imperial Pair" which proved to be his swan song in Tests.

The pitches at Lord's were well reported on. Nevertheless, the match ground suffered an outbreak of fusarium disease, germinated on the new plastic covers. Effective though these sheets were for protecting large areas of the square, when they were rolled back for storage on the perimeter the long plastic snakes made an ideal breeding-ground for fungus growth. A season later Lord's was to suffer the ignominy of incurring enough grade three and four reports to bring a visitation from Mr Lock, which was followed by his appointment by the Committee as consultant to the Head Groundsman.

M.C.C.'s affairs in 1966–67 were presided over by Sir Alec Douglas-Home, who is reported as saying that as much paper passed through his hands as President of M.C.C. as he ever had to read when he was Prime Minister. Whether, in the years which have followed his comparatively untroubled tenure, the output from the mills of cricket has surpassed those of State is a matter for speculation.

The new President-elect was Mr Arthur Gilligan. As a former captain of England it was particularly appropriate that it should have fallen to him, as one of his most happy duties, to preside at the dinner at which England and Australian players, past and present, celebrate together the two hundredth Test between their two countries. Primarily a fast bowler, Mr Gilligan had delighted to swing the bat lustily near the bottom of the order, and it was at No. 11 that he made his first century in first-class cricket. As he entered on a term of office which was to be more troubled than that of any of his predecessors, he suffered a major operation, from which he recovered splendidly to face the anxieties which culminated in the cancellation of the M.C.C. tour in South Africa.

Meanwhile, in the summer of 1967, the England captaincy made the headlines again. In 1966, in continuity from the Australian tour, the leadership had started in the hands of M. J. K. Smith, then passed to M. C. Cowdrey, and finally, in the last Test, to D. B. Close. It was seventeen years since his youthful debut in Tests; now, as captain of England, he met and beat West Indies, rewarding the selectors in their urgent search for aggression. By mid-August 1967, after he had led a revitalized English side to victory in six Tests in a row, his selection for the captaincy of M.C.C. in West Indies seemed no more than a formality. But at Birmingham on August 18 one of those incidents occurred which split public opinion and whose consequences outpace their immediate significance. On the final day of Yorkshire's match against Warwickshire, when Warwickshire were chasing 142 runs in 102 minutes, Yorkshire were accused and afterwards convicted by the Executive Committee of the A.C.C.C., composed of ex-captains, of using delaying tactics amounting to unfair play, and Close himself was held responsible. For England's captain to be severely censured by his peers clearly placed the M.C.C. Selectors in a position of deep embarrassment. None of the facts of the case were denied, and Yorkshire accepted the Executive Committee's rebuke, but Close himself emerged from a meeting with the Committee at Lord's convinced of the rightness of his tactics. For the Selectors he remained number one choice as tour captain, but the M.C.C. Committee felt unable to endorse a choice which would have made them appear to condone tactics which they deemed unfair. With Mike Smith no longer in the running, having announced his retirement from first-class cricket, Colin Cowdrey became the undisputed choice.

If Cowdrey had ever felt hurt at being dropped from the captaincy or selected as second best, he never allowed himself to complain. In West Indies his batting and his leadership recovered their old sparkle, and he and the M.C.C. team returned to England in the spring unbeaten, and victors in the rubber. There were an unconscionable number of drawn matches, including four out of the five Tests, and if it might be said that England only won the fourth Test at Port of Spain thanks to an over-generous declaration, they nevertheless accepted the challenge of 215 in two and three-quarter hours, with a nicely timed finish within three minutes of time. Once more an England team in the West Indies were subjected to riots and bottle-throwing, sparked off by crowd disagreement with the umpire. An added hazard was unleashed this time by the forces of law and order in the form of tear gas, intended to disperse the rioters, but taken by a contrary wind in a cloud across the ground, away from the public enclosures, to engulf the fleeing cricketers and innocent spectators in the pavilion.

The tour brought near tragedy to one member of the team, the Middlesex captain, Fred Titmus, whose foot became entangled with the screw of a small pleasure boat; the loss of four toes on his left foot was serious enough, but how much worse it might have been! As it was, he made a miraculous recovery and was soon bowling again for Middlesex with his former skill. During the tour the team were supported in person by the presence of numerous friends and members of M.C.C. on "package" tours. The President, now happily recovered from his operation, was able to fly out, and he and the Secretary had personal meetings with the West Indies Board, which enabled points of difference to be ironed out and discussions to take place which were extremely beneficial.

37

The Games and the Players 1966

1966 was a year of great activity in the administrative and legislative spheres of cricket. The appropriate committees examined many and diverse subjects, ranging from the problems of "throwing", or illegal bowling, to the experiment of limiting the first innings to sixty-five overs. The Advisory County Cricket Committee busied themselves with a comprehensive survey of the future of county cricket. All these matters are duly recorded in the part of this book concerned with the problems of administration and legislation.

The season was a fair one in the actual playing area, but again handicapped by an undue amount of wet weather. The seventh West Indian team toured under Sobers and, although clear winners in three Tests to England's one, they were not generally as successful as they had been under Worrell three years previously. In a heavy programme they won only eight of their twenty-seven first-class matches.

The four West Indian matches played at Lord's were drawn, but, none the less, provided some very good cricket. In the M.C.C. match Butcher led the way with a fine innings of 137, which enabled his side to declare at 349 for nine wickets. The M.C.C. side made an unpromising start by losing five wickets for 157, but M. J. K. Smith and J. T. Murray both made centuries to add 200 exactly for the sixth. It looked as though there might be a clear-cut decision when West Indies were 37 for four in their second innings, but Butcher was missed early on and saw his side out of danger with another good innings of 56.

West Indies returned to Lord's on June 16 with all the confidence afforded by the crushing defeat of England in the first Test Match at Nottingham. England were at the same time assailed by one of those moments of uncertainty which tend to result in a change of captain. Cowdrey now succeeded Smith, who was dropped from the side.

Sobers won the toss, but Higgs bowled with such spirit and

accuracy that West Indies had to work hard to get to 269. Thanks to Boycott, Graveney, and Parks, England passed this total with three wickets in hand, and a splendid stand between Parks and Higgs of 59 for the ninth wicket gave England a most welcome lead of 86. Higgs continued his leading role by helping to dispatch the first five West Indian wickets for 95 and raised visions of an early English win. At that point Sobers and his cousin, David Holford, came together, and were unparted when, five hours and twenty minutes later, Sobers declared at ten-past one on the last day. The unbroken stand had added 274, of which Sobers had made 163 and Holford 105.

Set 284 to make in four hours, England lost four wickets for 67, but Graveney, handicapped by a bruised thumb, came in at No. 6 to support Milburn, who was going well in his usual robust style. These two added 130 without being defeated, so that England, without claiming the extra half-hour, were within 87 of the West Indies at the close. Despite the lack of a decision it had been an eventful match. It was to be seen that Hall, although willing as ever, had lost some edge and that Griffith, having been at pains to keep his action up to the required standards, was now a useful rather than deadly fast bowler.

At Trent Bridge the West Indians once again heavily defeated England, but, reappearing at Lord's to play Middlesex, made a somewhat indifferent impression. Once more they won the toss, but in five hours, during which ninety-five overs were bowled, could manage only 187 for eight wickets, at which the innings was declared. Middlesex lost half their side for 42, but, thanks to Clark and Hooker, who made 99 and 81, they declared at 243 for eight, made off sixty-three overs. Another cautious innings by West Indies left Middlesex 187 to make in two hours and twenty minutes. As the first three overs took over a quarter of an hour to bowl, and as there was a ten-minute stoppage for light, all hope soon evaporated and, with two men out for 85, the result was a dull draw. It was not the real stuff of Caribbean cricket.

On July 27 West Indies went forth to play against the President's XI. This was composed of cricketers of under twenty-five years old, a very good idea which was spoilt to some extent by injuries and changes in the original selections. It was, in fact, a rather unlucky match in several respects. The President's side batted without any great spirit, the exception being Amiss, who made 69 out of the total of 164. Sadly enough, West Indies failed to give the young men a timely object-lesson in enterprise when they made a very sedate 227. The President's side had reached 182 for five wickets when rain ended the match, an intervention which no-one greatly regretted.

Oxford were not considered to be a very great University side, but their captain, R. M. C. Gilliat, having won the toss, made 86 in an attacking innings which infused the same commendable outlook into his team. The result was that he declared at 300 for seven. Cambridge were subdued in contrast, and the spin of Ridley and Elviss was allowed to dominate the match from then on. After an hour's play on the third morning they had been bowled out for 140 and 151, to lose by an innings and 9 runs. This result mercifully broke the run of six draws, the longest in the history of the Match.

Middlesex had a disappointing season. Having finished in sixth place for three successive seasons, they abruptly descended to twelfth. Price made a return to his best form, but otherwise the bowling lacked force. The batting maintained a fair level of competence, but there was no dominating power to pave the way.

In contrast to most previous seasons the opening spell at Lord's was rather dismal, and no match was won until the Bank holiday, when, for Murray's Benefit, Sussex were comfortably defeated. In the second half of the season no home match was won after July, and Middlesex retired from the scene with hopes of better times to come.

In January M.C.C. lost a most distinguished member with the death of George Duckworth. Apart from his fame when active as a wicket-keeper, he had been a tower of strength on several M.C.C. tours when he acted as scorer, luggage master, and Father Confessor. He made one of the more original remarks about Lord's, where he was as popular as on his native Old Trafford. When Middlesex played Lancashire in the leather-jacket era very much on the Tavern side of the ground a batsman remarked to George that the pitch was behaving in an odd way. "I'm not surprised," replied the keeper, "being right on't doorstep of Poob."

This adjacency had some point for Tom Goddard, who died in May. He naturally liked to bowl his off-spinners from the Pavilion end to gain the help of the slope, whilst Charlie Parker liked the Nursery end for the same reason. Strangely enough, the Gloucester match always seemed to be played on the extreme Southern fringe, which caused Tom to make some salty comments on the short leg boundary. One year, presumably owing to a fit of compassion on the part of the ground staff, the wicket was pitched right under the

Grand Stand. So great was Tom's elation at the vast expanse to the on that he rushed up with such impetuosity that he sprained his back in his first over. Reg Sinfield, a fellow off-spinner, took over and captured nine wickets—mostly caught on the leg boundary.

Claude Taylor died in January, still the holder of a Lord's record. In 1923 he opened the innings for Oxford and made a century as a freshman against Cambridge.

In February Jack Massie, the grandson of H. H. Massie, died in Sydney.

Roger Blunt died in June. A quiet, steadfast man, he still has claims to being the best all-rounder his country has produced. In the first Test Match between England and New Zealand which was played at Lord's he made 96, and so contributed to a very honourable draw.

Bernard Atkinson, who died in September, made one of the most remarkable and original strikes ever seen at Lord's. Playing for Middlesex against Surrey in 1934, he met a bouncer from Alf Gover with an overhead tennis smash which sent the ball straight back over the bowler's head for six.

In the same month Lord's lost a very popular captain of Middlesex when Ian Bedford died suddenly, aged thirty-six. He had appeared at Lord's in a war-time match in his early teens, not much taller than the stumps, but a model leg-spin bowler in miniature. If he never quite fulfilled his promise he was a most popular member and, ever cheerful, almost unduly modest for a bowling captain.

Having survived several illnesses, Nigel Haig died in October. He was a very fine all-round athlete and games-player, but cricket had ever been the true essence of his life, and Lord's was the centre of his cricket. The game had many personalities in his times, but none richer than he. Raconteur, wit, and man of many parts, he was an endless source of anecdote and reminiscence. Not a few of the incidents recorded in this book were first heard from him in vivid and arresting terms.

38

The Games and the Players 1967

THE season of 1967 started by setting an unwelcome record. The opening month was the wettest May to be recorded since 1873. It could be claimed that this was the most rain-stricken early period known in the whole history of English cricket as a national game.

Every cricketer in the realm suffered in the prevailing frustration, but the Indian tourists, who were to precede the Pakistanis under the new arrangements, were harder hit than anyone else. They were inclined to be a brittle side in normal English conditions, and the lack of match practice, and the discouraging circumstances when play was possible, stifled spirit and talent at a most vital time. When injuries caused further disruption it was not surprising that the tour was a sad disappointment. In eighteen first-class matches only two were won, against Cambridge and Derby. All three Test Matches were lost outright. The match against M.C.C. at Lord's was a relatively happy one. Pataudi made 70 and Hanumant Singh 38 out of a total of 134, and the Indians then did well to get the Club out for 211. When heavy rain ended the match at lunch-time on the third day the Indians had made the respectable total of 108 for two wickets.

The second Test Match was a crushing defeat by an innings and 124 runs, ending with a day and a half's play in hand. India batted first on a hard, fast wicket, and fell to Snow and Brown for 152. England made 386, of which Graveney made 151, and on a damp pitch India went down to Illingworth for 110.

The Pakistanis were luckier with the weather and, without a very much better record, put up a stouter fight. They won three and lost three of their seventeen first-class matches, saved the first of the three Tests, and made a very fair showing in the last before going down by eight wickets.

On a perfect Lord's pitch scoring in their match against Middlesex was high. When Pakistan were out for 237 Russell and Harris put up 312 for the first wicket, a record for their county and the highest for any wicket against the Pakistanis. At 452 for three Middlesex declared, but Burki and Jahangir then made centuries, so that their side were 301 for four at the close.

Although the closing stages were something of an anticlimax Pakistan emerged from the first Test Match at Lord's with considerable credit. England made 369 on a good wicket, Barrington going in at No. 3 to make 148. Pakistan made a poor start against Higgs and, when the seventh wicket fell at 139, seemed destined for a heavy defeat. Asif Iqbal then joined his captain, Hanif Mohammad, and together they added 130 for the eighth wicket. When Asif was out for 76 Hanif went on to score 187 not out, and carried the score to 354.

England declared at 241 for nine wickets, leaving Pakistan 257 to make in three and a half hours. This meant a perfectly possible rate of 73 runs an hour, but regrettably the Pakistanis did not make any gesture in reply to this challenge. At the end of the day three wickets had been lost for 88 runs.

The University Match was once again a draw. A comparatively high-scoring match was graced by a century by Toft in Oxford's first innings of 316 for seven wickets, and by Cosh in a Cambridge reply of 258. Oxford declared at 159 for seven wickets, leaving Cambridge 218 to get in two and three-quarter hours. Cosh and Malalsekera put up 50 in 28 minutes for the first wicket, but the later batsmen were unequal to sustaining this pace, and Cambridge ended with five men out for 152.

Middlesex had a somewhat peculiar season. They ascended from twelfth to seventh place in the county table, but the manner of their progress caused some criticism. There was a negative quality about their play which was seen at its worst in the match against Hampshire at Lord's in early July. This was an occasion of some significance as it saw the inauguration of Sunday cricket at Lord's.

Although only twenty minutes play was lost through rain neither side completed an innings. Hampshire declared at 421 for seven on the second day, and Middlesex finished the match with 371 for seven wickets. One remarkable outcome of this prevailing caution was that Middlesex were unbeaten at Lord's until the last match of the season, when Somerset won by ten wickets.

In September the competition for the World Cricket Cup was played at Lord's, sponsored by Rothmans. The Rest of the World, even though many of the great players came in very short of practice, easily defeated an England XI and Pakistan, and the

England XI beat Pakistan. The matches were all on a one-day basis and provided some very good entertainment.

In 1930 a young G. O. Allen, returning from a net with a senior professional, paused to look at the match in progress in the middle. "My goodness," said he on seeing the first ball bowled, "that's a pretty good action." His companion eyed him quizzically. "So it should be," he said. "That's Syd Barnes."

It was the great man's last appearance at Lord's, playing for Wales against the M.C.C. It was, indeed, his last appearance in a first-class match.

As in every cricketing centre in the world the name of Barnes is hallowed, and his picture hangs in the Long Room. It is rather curious that the world's greatest bowler had so little active connection with the greatest of grounds. He played but twice for England at Lord's—in the Triangular Tournament of 1912. Against South Africa he took eleven wickets for 110, and, a fortnight later, was his side's least successful bowler with 0 for 74 against Australia.

In 1957 he had a great day at Lord's when the surviving members of the triumphant team of 1911–12 gathered with Sir Robert Menzies. Sir Pelham Warner was joined by Wilfred Rhodes, George Gunn, Frank Woolley, and Philip Mead. Barnes was the senior present and a striking, erect, and dominating figure in his eighty-fifth year. He died on December 26, 1967, aged ninety-four.

This year Sir Frank Worrell died a young man of forty-two. He had been a particular favourite of the Lord's crowd since the days of '51 when his grace and dash had caught the imagination of the crowd. His last Test Match was in 1963 and ended in the extraordinary situation where England's last wicket was defended by Cowdrey with a broken arm going to join Allen with 6 runs wanted for victory. The last injunction Worrell issued at Lord's to the side he led so well was to Hall, who bowled the final over. It was "Whatever you do don't bowl a no-ball."

The first day of the year brought a major loss to the cricket world with the death of Maurice Leyland. He had played at Lord's for Yorkshire, the Players, England, and, as Sergeant Leyland, for the Army v. the Navy in war-time. His was the last wicket the writer ever took at Lord's.

Arthur Mailey, amongst the first honorary members to be elected to the M.C.C. under the scheme, died in Sydney on December 31. No-one could have more richly deserved this honour, for he was a great *cricketer*. He spun the ball till it buzzed like a bee, and released it with the detached joy of the artist. As such he begrudged no batsman and, if hit for six, felt that he had at least achieved something. He once told Neville Cardus that in a Test Match he had unaccountably been allowed to bowl three maidens in a row. His increasing boredom was relieved by Warwick Armstrong, who had him off with the terse observation that he had plenty of people who could bowl maiden overs.

He was a man of deep and dry humour and of much talent. He greatly loved the old country, and one would suspect that Lord's had a very special place in this affection.

39

The Cricket Council

1968 was my last season at Lord's. In the previous autumn I had told the Committee of my wish to retire, and in July Mr Stephen Green arrived to learn what was in store for him when he became Curator in October. The twenty-fifth Australian team playing the two hundredth Test against England, at Lord's, on a ground refurbished with brand-new buildings offered the ingredients for a great season. Climatically such hopes had an early setback, for by the Saturday in mid-May when the Australians surveyed a watery scene from the shelter of the Pavilion, wondering when they would begin their match against M.C.C., they had lost already no fewer than forty-nine playing hours out of a possible sixty. For the two hundredth Test, Cowdrey tossed for the first time with the 1880 sovereign presented by the Lord's Taverners for Tests between England and Australia, and Lawry misjudged his call. But a bombardment of rain and hail, reducing the match to half its allotted span, ensured that the weather, rather than either team, would be the victor. As Sir Robert Menzies put it, "Lord's was in liquidation". Even so, in purple patches between the storms there were glimpses of what might have been, and hopes rose in loyal English hearts that the Ashes were within our grasp as Milburn demonstrated first that an England batsman could strike the ball with might and main, and then, dramatically, Australia crumbled before the combined assault of Messrs Brown, Knight, and Snow.

As a celebration for the two hundredth Test, the dinner to the tourists was postponed from its usual date during the match against M.C.C. to the Saturday of the Lord's Test. It brought together the most distinguished company who had yet gathered in the new Tavern Restaurant. As a prelude to the speeches the President, Mr Gilligan, presented a silver ashtray to each member of the two teams and the umpires. Then the assembled company, which included a host of former England and Australia captains and players, were privileged to hear Sir Robert Menzies, at his most felicitous, crown the occasion by proposing the toast to Cricket between England and Australia. The reigning captains of England and Australia replied in turn, Colin Cowdrey paying a graceful tribute to Sir Robert and Bill Lawry declaring a resolve on behalf of all the players to give the people of England the cricket they deserved.

Two lesser international visits had been planned, but the first, the maiden tour of England by a representative Ceylon side, having been in a state of "off-on" for several months because of selection and financial difficulties, was finally cancelled. In July the first representative team of the United States Cricket Association arrived, accompanied by their President, Mr John Marder, and their Secretary (as Manager), Dr Tony Verity. They had several long practices in the Lord's nets in preparation for their one-day match against M.C.C., but, lacking match practice so early in their two months' tour, they were overawed by the occasion and lost by the rather large margin of nine wickets.

In July, Jack Bailey took a strong M.C.C. team to Holland. With two former Test cricketers, Russell Endean and Alan Moss, they were a tough proposition for their opponents. They beat Holland and de Flamingos and drew with The Hague and the Royal Netherlands Cricket Association. One player, Graham Chidgey, made a century (against The Hague), and Alan Moss and the captain had some notable bowling figures.

The A.C.C.C.'s decision to allow the immediate registration of players from overseas triggered off a race for the top stars. Middlesex held back, but in August they enlisted Australia's A. N. Connolly. At their Annual General Meeting it was announced that it had been decided to found a Supporters' Club, called the Seaxe Club, after the three seaxes on the Middlesex badge. In the hope of persuading forward prodders and negative bowlers to forsake defence and switch to attack, the A.C.C.C. had introduced to the Championship a new, mathematically intricate, incentive-points system for the first innings. Each 25 runs over 150 and each two wickets in the first eighty-five overs earned a bonus point for the batting or bowling side, as the case might be. In the batting stakes, with no more than 21 points, Middlesex came last. Nevertheless in the Gillette competition they beat Surrey at Lord's for the first time in seven years and, encouraged by a series of home draws, proceeded to the semi-final, when they fell to the eventual winners, Warwickshire.

At the end of the year Jack Robertson retired from the office of Head Coach, and Don Bennett was appointed to succeed him.

The M.C.C. Committee had recently asked the counties to make it known that their contracted players would be welcome as members. Jack Robertson and Don Bennett, with the most senior current Middlesex players, Peter Parfitt, Fred Titmus, and John Murray, were among the first to be elected.

As Mr Allen's first five-year stint in the M.C.C. Treasurer's hot seat drew to a close he had the melancholy task of declaring a record deficit of £14,200 on the 1967 accounts. With the new concessionary rates costing £11,500, the additional income from subscriptions and entrance fees had fallen well below the sum hoped for, and had been largely offset by heavy reductions in receipts from matches. A formidable rise in wages and salaries reflected the spiral of activity which had been mounting steadily since the War, but now gathered momentum as the government of the game became more highly organized. Some two years earlier M.C.C. had declined a proffered contribution from the counties, but in February 1968, with the formation of the T.C.C.B. in prospect, the Secretary had told the representatives of the A.C.C.C. and the Board of Control that, while M.C.C. considered it a privilege to help the counties to administer the first-class game, the time had come when the Club could no longer afford to carry the whole of the financial burden. As a result the counties had agreed that each should contribute a sum of £250 annually.

In the annual report members learned officially that, as the outcome of negotiations with the Sports Council and the Department of Education and Science, M.C.C. had been asked to set up a Governing Body for cricket, to be known as the M.C.C. Council. At the same time it was announced that, as the result of this administrative reorganization, the constitution of the National Cricket Association was to be substantially extended, with the aim of setting up in every county, with the help of the county clubs, County Cricket Associations, to which clubs could be affiliated.

It will be remembered that the N.C.A. was founded to canalize the interests of cricket below first-class level, and that one of its cardinal objectives was to offer to Government a body, patently national, who would qualify to negotiate for concessions and grants from public funds. Early in 1966 at a discussion between the N.C.A.'s Chairman, Lord Nugent, and the Department of Education and Science about the possibility of a grant being given towards the cost of a M.C.C. Schools' tour to South Africa, doubt was expressed by the Government officials as to the national status of the N.C.A. because it had no control or jurisdiction over the first-class game. When Lord Nugent reported this to the M.C.C. Committee they appointed a sub-committee, with the rather unwieldy title "To consider certain matters connected with the organisation of cricket throughout the United Kingdom". The Minister for Sport made it clear that he considered M.C.C. should be the body responsible for cricket—the one with which Government should deal—and he invited the Secretary of M.C.C. to prepare a blueprint for a future organization. It was realized that if M.C.C. were to be accepted as the Governing Body the Ministry would insist on representatives being nominated from the M.C.C., the A.C.C.C., the Board of Control, the N.C.A., and the Y.C.A. The M.C.C. Committee decided that, rather than add nominated members to the existing Committee, it would be preferable to form a separate Council in which members of the M.C.C. Committee joined the nominees of the other bodies.

This was the picture which the Secretary painted for the A.C.C.C. in March 1967, adding that the new administration would require their amalgamation with the Board of Control in a single body, advisory to the M.C.C. Council. This new body, christened the Test and County Cricket Board, held its inaugural meeting at Lord's on July 19, 1968. They were cordially received by the President of M.C.C., who presided pending the election of Mr C. G. A. Paris as Chairman. To their existing responsibilities towards county cricket and Test Matches at home has been added the organization of official representative tours overseas, even though these teams still bear the name of M.C.C. The Board operates through Standing Sub-committees (twelve in 1970). If any of their recommendations are not approved the Board refers them back rather than taking a contrary decision. This new method of working will, it is hoped, lead to greater efficiency and achieve more continuity and consistency of policy than in the past.

The Cricket Council, from whose title the name of M.C.C. was subsequently dropped, is composed of the President and Treasurer and nine nominees of the M.C.C. Committee; the Chairman and nine nominees of the National Cricket Association (of whom three represent coaching organizations and youth cricket); the Chairman and three nominees of the Test and County Cricket Board plus the Chairmen of their Finance and General Purposes and Cricket Sub-committees; and the Chairman of the Minor Counties Cricket Association. The Secretary of M.C.C. is Secretary of the Council. The new set-up forms a pyramid. At its base, the N.C.A. shelters under its wing the huge network of club cricket, youth, coaching, women's cricket, etc. Above them comes the T.C.C.B., responsible for first-class cricket. Finally, at the pinnacle, is the Cricket Council, the national Governing Body and titular head of all the lower strata. M.C.C. itself retains responsibility for the Laws of Cricket.

Inevitably all these changes in the machinery of cricket resulted in the operation of Parkinson's Law in the office administration at Lord's. Mr Dunbar was already wholly engaged with the work of the N.C.A. and the Y.C.A.; now Mr Carr was allocated to the T.C.C.B. The old M.C.C. Cricket Office, familiar to playing members as the repository of the Match Book, was divided by the creation of a new First-class Cricket Office up in the gods of the Pavilion, where Mr Brian Langley presides as right-hand man to Mr Carr, leaving Mr Bailey in charge of Club and domestic cricket affairs, including the maintenance of the ground. In his public relations hat Mr Bailey was charged with the promotion of cricket, and Mr R. J. Roe was appointed by the T.C.C.B. as Promotions Officer to assist him. The Secretary of M.C.C. is *ex officio* Secretary of both the M.C.C. Council and the T.C.C.B. On the setting up of the T.C.C.B., M.C.C.'s Club Superintendent, Mr R. T. Gaby, relinquished an association of twenty-one years with the Board of Control and the A.C.C.C. To the warm tributes he received was added a cheque to mark appreciation for his valuable contribution to cricket's administration over so many years. M.C.C.'s most recent appointment, now that the existing secretariat are so heavily occupied with higher administration, is a Club Business Manager, Group Captain Ronald Ford.

Apart from considering their own demise and rebirth, the A.C.C.C., in common with the I.C.C., had spent two active years in seeking means to enliven the game. As we have seen, the County Championship was given a new incentive points system. In 1967 the captains' right to forfeit their second innings was incorporated in the Laws of Cricket and, for county matches, an experimental rule was introduced the following year stating that if, due to weather, less than eight playing hours remained, the first innings of each side should automatically be forfeited, with no bonus points for either side. In 1968, too, the counties struck another blow at time-wasting by ruling that the final hour of play should be extended to a minimum of twenty overs unless the match finished earlier. At international level the I.C.C. supported M.C.C. in recommending a modification of the absolute ban on polishing the ball. This had been applied experimentally in all grades of cricket in the United Kingdom in 1967, but the N.C.A. had reported that it had been condemned universally by club cricketers. Now, the bowler alone was allowed to polish the ball, but nobody, not even the bowler, was allowed to scuff it on the ground.

Both the I.C.C. and the counties were concerned with excessive pad play, and, in continuing arguments about lbw, opinions veered between the school of thought, favoured by a majority of the counties in 1967, which advocated a return to the old law, and the opposite extreme—Mr Stollmeyer's proposal, backed by the West Indies Board, to extend the law to cover balls pitching on the leg side. But by 1968 the counties had modified their ideas, and they turned down M.C.C.'s proposal to commend the old law to the I.C.C. The 1969 I.C.C. referred back for the consideration of their Boards no fewer than four variations. Australia and West Indies recommended the retention of the existing law, but added notes, requiring the striker to make an attempt to hit the ball and, in the case of West Indies, extending the law to the leg side. Pakistan offered an original approach by suggesting that padding off balls pitched on the offside constituted unfair play, meriting, at the third offence, after two warnings, dismissal by the umpire under Law 46 without an appeal. M.C.C.'s formula, based on Australian thinking, was introduced experimentally in the U.K. in 1970, having first found favour in Australia and West Indies. Once more, as when the very first law of lbw was introduced in 1774, umpires are asked to add to their other duties the power to read the mind of the batsman. It remains to be seen how difficult they will find it to interpret his intentions and to administer an experimental law which reads:

a batsman will be out if, with any part of his body except his hand, he intercepts a ball which has not first touched his bat or hand which, in the opinion of the umpire, would have hit his wicket, provided that, either, the ball pitched or would have pitched in a straight line between wicket and wicket, or, the ball pitched outside the batsman's off stump and, in the opinion of the umpire, he made no genuine attempt to play the ball with his bat.

The law on leg byes also received attention, and an amendment was introduced allowing the batsman to score if he has tried to avoid being hit—a piece of legislation which had in mind being hit by a bouncer.

As an amendment to the Clark Report, Hampshire had success-fully proposed that no alteration in the structure of cricket should be implemented before 1970. Nevertheless, so soon after the rejection of the Clark plan as November 1967, Hampshire's representatives took the initiative in advocating a Sunday League on the model of the International Cavaliers' matches. Their proposal was accepted in principle by a substantial majority, and Mr Clark's services were enlisted once more as Chairman of a Structure Sub-committee to examine the idea and submit recommendations which could be implemented in 1969. The players, represented by the newly formed Cricketers' Association, were not very enthusiastic when the project was explained to them by the Secretary of M.C.C. at their Annual General Meeting. Nevertheless, the counties accepted the programme outlined for the Sunday League and the consequent curtailment of the Championship schedule to twenty-four matches. An unhappy outcome was that Rothmans, who had contributed such wonderful largesse in terms of money and entertainment, saw the introduction of the Sunday League as a rebuff to the International Cavaliers, and have largely transferred their patronage to other fields. They were particularly disappointed at the curtailment of their financial support for cricket caused by the counties' decision to bar registered players from Sunday T.V. appearances outside the League. At a Press conference Mr Griffith defended the T.C.C.B. against the charge that they were determined to put an end to the Cavaliers, who had shown how to make Sunday cricket a success. Everyone, he said, connected with the game, would want these matches to continue, and long experience had shown that such matches, run for charity, could be a success for a charity or beneficiary without television fees. The only real point at issue was whether or not the Cavaliers matches involving registered players should be televised. While conceding that the Cavaliers' financial returns would be affected by the loss of fees, he claimed that the overall financial benefits to the counties and their players would be increased by the best possible promotion of the Sunday League, and that criticisms levelled at the T.C.C.B. had been totally unjustified. Sponsorship was not hard to enlist, and eventually another tobacco firm, John Player, took the league under their wing. The financial awards consist of prizes of £1000, £500, and £250 to the top three teams, plus a bonus of £50 to the winners of each match. Individual awards are a Batting Jackpot of £1000 for sixes, a Bowling Jackpot for players taking four wickets, and a special prize of £50 offered by the B.B.C. (who were awarded the television rights) for the fastest 50. Playing conditions are similar to those for the Gillette matches, but with less time, there are fewer overs and the bowlers' run-up is limited to fifteen yards. The winners in the first year were Lancashire, with Hampshire as runners up. Middlesex finished seventh, and one of their batsmen, C. T. Radley, distinguished himself by making the highest individual score, 133 not out against Glamorgan.

Those who are dedicated to the traditional image of first-class cricket are resentful of this projection of the village green on to county grounds. They regard the type of carefree cricket popularized by the Cavaliers as bordering on slapstick comedy, unworthy of serious players. The fact remains that three-day cricket today is in a state of ennui, affording much less enjoyment than it should to players and spectators alike. Whereas first-class cricket has become a speciality for devotees, the League is an entertainment for the whole family. If the one-day game on Sundays can give players back the feeling of unwinding and overcoming their addiction to defence, then the three-day game may be the better for it. But this is for the future; the immediate evidence is that the Sunday League has alienated spectators still further from the first-class championship, and this is a situation which is filling the game's administrators with grave concern.

For the twin series of Tests against West Indies and New Zealand, the T.C.C.B. appointed a new team of selectors. D. J. Insole handed over the Chairman's seat to the erstwhile Surrey and England bowler Alec Bedser, whose colleagues were Don Kenyon and two newcomers, Alan Smith, the Warwickshire captain, and Yorkshire's W. H. H. Sutcliffe. They had the distasteful duty of participating in disciplinary action against one of the most senior members of the England side, Tom Graveney. On the Sunday of the first Test he had flouted the rules of the T.C.C.B. by appearing in a match arranged for his benefit at Luton, for which he received £1000, and the Disciplinary Sub-committee of the T.C.C.B. decided to suspend him for three Tests. His suspension brought to a sad close the international career of one who, for nearly a generation, had contributed largely to the quality of English batting and given pleasure to thousands by his fine stroke play.

In an attempt to fit in with Board Meetings in member countries the date of the I.C.C. this year was advanced to June. In an agenda which was largely monopolized by debates on lbw and amendments to other laws time was found to consider the import of the metric system, expected to come into force in England in the near future. They were reassured by the Danish representative that its use for cricket raised no great problems; but it has been announced that the equivalent of 22 yards runs into three decimal figures, 20.117 metres.

A tribute was paid at the Conference to Sir Arthur Sims, who had died in April at the age of ninety-one. As New Zealand's representative for many years, he had attained the status of a doyen. He had a deep affection for Lord's and was a welcome and familiar figure there; one of the kindest men I remember, for whom wealth, earned by personal enterprise and hard work, was a passport to philanthropy. Since his retirement New Zealand have been represented with distinction by their former Governor-General, Lord Cobham, and their High Commissioner in London, Sir Dennis Blundell, once, as E. D. Blundell, a Blue at Cambridge in company with M.C.C.'s President of 1969–70, Maurice Allom, and such famous players as Duleepsinhji, Walter Robins, and Maurice Turnbull.

Among other distinguished members who have died in recent years are two of the surviving war-time leaders, Marshal of the Royal Air Force Viscount Tedder and Field-Marshal Earl Alexander. Both had given notable service to cricket, the first as President of Surrey and the second as President of M.C.C. Another whose loss was deeply felt, both for the warmth of his personality and for his unstinting services as an administrator, was Mr G. O. Shelmerdine. He was first elected to the Committee in 1953, and at the time of his death he was Chairman of the Grounds and Fixtures and the General Purposes Sub-committees of M.C.C. and also of the Committee which administers the Gillette Cricket Cup. Losses in the ranks of those who may be called, without disparagement, I hope, the "ordinary members", included four who had been deeply concerned with club cricket. Mr Robin Buckston and Mr Ivor Gilliat were both enthusiastic match managers for M.C.C.; their interests lay particularly in encouraging young players. Lieut.-Colonel K. B. Stanley and Brigadier W. E. Clark gave their chief service to the peripatetic clubs, Ken Stanley as Honorary Secretary for many years of Free Foresters and Willie Clark in tireless work for I Zingari and the Band of Brothers. His devotion to the arts as a connoisseur, primarily, of Georgian furniture, enabled him to contribute invaluable expertise to the deliberations of the Arts and Library Sub-committee, and it was he who presented the interesting picture of a cricket match in the grounds of Deepdene House, afterwards the home of Thomas Hope of Amsterdam, and the repository for his treasures. By the death of Mr A. A. Thomson, the devotees of Lord's and wearers of the white rose everywhere mourned a friend, whose speeches were as hilariously funny to listen to as his books were a delight to read. Few men of letters have combined more felicitously the arts of speech and prose-writing. His loss has been felt most nearly, perhaps, by the members of the Cricket Society, over whom he presided with such dignity and wit.

At this moment of transition and diplomatic stress the M.C.C. Annual General Meeting was one of the longest on record. The huge deficit reported a year earlier on the 1967 accounts was substantially reduced, but even so, Mr Allen, now re-elected for a further term as Treasurer, was unable to regard with equanimity a still formidable adverse balance. A year earlier it had been agreed to increase the number of full members to 11,000; in 1969 there was a further increase to 13,000 full and 2000 Associate members, and by the spring of 1971 this figure is likely to rise by another 1000, to reach a total of 16,000 members. The decade closed on a happier financial note with a modest surplus in 1969.

After completing eighteen years as a Trustee, Mr R. H. Twining asked to be excused from re-election. He had first served on the Committee in 1933, and as a mark of appreciation for his long and outstanding services to the Club he was elected a Life Vice-President, the only member to be so honoured since the death of Sir Pelham Warner, with whom he shared the triple distinction of having served as President of Middlesex and President and Vice-President of M.C.C. His place as Trustee was filled by Mr G. C. Newman, a M.C.C. Committee man of long seniority, Chairman of the various sub-committees who have been responsible for property, works, and development and the reigning President of Middlesex.

As the season opened I learned with deep personal sadness of the sudden death of the Museum Attendant, Mr Denis Rons. He had been to me, as Curator, a loyal and imaginative right-hand man, using his manual skills to the great benefit of the displays in the Memorial Gallery. During the few months in which they had worked together he had been an invaluable assistant to my successor, Stephen Green, and his loss has been keenly felt in the department of the arts.

On the cricket field the decade closed with the retirement of the Head Groundsman, Mr E. C. Swannell. His successor is Mr James Farebrother, who came to Lord's from Trent Bridge as Assistant Head Groundsman in 1968.

The spring of 1970 witnessed the crossing of the last "t" and the dotting of the final "i" in the modernization of Lord's carried out in the last two decades. The venerable scoreboard at the Main Gate and its slightly less elderly master on the grandstand have been replaced. But the new boards, being of similar design to the old, are unobtrusive innovations. Not for Lord's the encyclopaedic electrically operated boards so popular overseas! Finally, after much thought about whether or not Lord Ebury's clock could be re-erected and exactly where it should be sited, a new clock was introduced on the Tavern Stand.

40

The Games and the Players 1968

REVIEWING the events of 1968, the Editor of *Wisden* headed his notes "An Exasperating Year". There was solid ground for this august irritation, but a large proportion was not directly connected with the actual play. There had been the inauspicious start with a riot in Jamaica, and later the controversy concerning D'Oliveira which led to the cancellation of the tour to South Africa. Arising out of this last dispute was the attack upon the M.C.C.

There were, however, matters to complain of in the field of play. There was once again a miserably wet opening to the season. In some measure owing to this, the twenty-fifth Australian side to visit England was a disappointment, despite the fact that they retained the "Ashes". As in the case of the Indians in the previous summer, a great deal was lost because of rain at the beginning of the tour, when match practice was, as always, most desirable.

The side was led by W. M. Lawry, by now a veteran amongst Test Match batsmen, and contained several newcomers of high promise. To support McKenzie there was a remodelled Connolly, who, from a short run, was an entirely different proposition from the indifferent fastish bowler of the previous tour. The fielding and throwing were up to the highest Australian standards.

The first match of the tour at Worcester was completely washed out, and the matches against Leicestershire and Lancs were much curtailed. No play was possible on the first day in the M.C.C. match at Lord's.

On Monday the Australians enjoyed their first full day's cricket, and were able to declare at 246 for nine wickets. Lawry made 66, and Sheahan made a splendid first impression in getting 46. M.C.C. batted laboriously to make 142, at which, it now being a two-day match, Lawry forced the follow-on. There was never a real chance of a finish, and at the close the score had reached 56 for one wicket. With four for 21 in the first innings and one for 8 in the second Connolly was the outstanding Australian bowler, with swing and lively movement from the pitch.

THE TAVERN, 1868–1966
A full house for the 1948 Test.

NEW TAVERN STAND IN EMBRYO, 1967
High-rise flats have ousted Regency villas from St John's Wood Road.

NEW TAVERN STAND CROWDED FOR A TEST

Having beaten England decisively at Old Trafford earlier in the month, the Australians came to Lord's for the second Test Match on June 20. There were five changes in the England side, the inclusion of Milburn, Barrington, and Knight proving particularly successful selections. Cowdrey won the toss, but only 85 minutes' play was possible on the first day. From the first over on Friday morning Milburn deployed his full power of stroke, and in two and a half hours made 83, hitting twelve fours and two sixes. This was a splendid lead, but England failed to press home the advantage. At the end of the day the score was 314 for seven wickets but, as 53 had been collected overnight and only a quarter of an hour's play had been lost, this was no great achievement after such a brisk start. On Saturday only fourteen overs were bowled, and England raised the score to 351 without further loss.

On Monday the Australian batting disintegrated before Snow, Brown, and Knight on a green Lord's pitch. Only Walters and Gleeson reached double figures in the total of 78, Brown taking five wickets for 42. In the follow-on Lawry and Redpath got the total to 50 by the close of play, but England had a rare chance of evening the series. This was thwarted by another wet day which precluded any play until 3.15. Australia, no longer in acute danger, reached 127 for four wickets by the close of play.

The Middlesex match in July got off to a good start, but was also spoilt by rain on the last day. Parfitt made a century, as he had done in the same match four years previously, in this case 110 not out. With Radley also undefeated with 70, Middlesex were able to declare at 277 for four wickets. The Australians batted indifferently against the off-spin of Titmus and Parfitt, and managed no more than 227. Having acquired this advantage, Middlesex pressed on, but now their batting wilted under pressure. Eight wickets had fallen for 108 when rain put an end to the match after 85 minutes' play. Thus what could have been a most exciting match was ended at its most interesting point.

Once again lovers of University cricket had to face the unpalatable fact that the annual match at Lord's, once such a gay and eagerly awaited meeting, was now of limited and parochial interest. The match of 1968 was yet another draw, but, in its course, provided some capital cricket. The sad measure of public support was unimproved in that, over the three days, a total of just over 2000 people paid to watch it.

The first day was dominated by a magnificent attacking innings by Goldstein, the Oxford captain, who made 155 out of 206 runs

s

when he was the second wicket to fall. His side raised the score thence to 363 for eight wickets but, by slow and cautious play, dissipated their advantage. Their bowlers recovered some of this lost ground by taking the first three Cambridge wickets for 39, but the later batsmen, more enterprising than their opposite numbers, got the score to 306.

Goldstein once again set the pace, and had made 32 of the first 34 runs when hit in the face by a bouncer. His temporary retirement robbed the innings of its momentum, although he later returned to complete his 50. Eventually Cambridge were set 242 to make in two and three-quarter hours. When six wickets had fallen for 78 with over an hour to play it seemed that defeat was at hand. Cosh and Jorden then played with judgment and resolution to add 53 runs in the last 70 minutes without being separated. An interesting example of the effects of the stimulation born of hope and urgency was provided by the fact that Oxford, in their exertions to dislodge them, bowled twenty-six and a half overs in the last hour.

Middlesex, first under the captaincy of Titmus and then of Parfitt, had a rather uninspired and uninspiring season. A burst of success which brought victory in each of the last four matches raised them from the depths to tenth place in the Championship. The difficulties of the season ahead were foreshadowed by all three matches at Lord's in May being drawn. The final results were reflected in the batting averages, in which Titmus led with the very modest figure of 25. Russell and Parfitt just succeeded in topping the thousand runs, to average fractionally less. At least Middlesex had an attractive bowling side with the pace of Price, the off-spin of Titmus, and the welcome and promising leg breaks and googlies of Latchman.

On December 12 Walter Robins died after a long and distressing illness. He had been connected with Lord's for over forty of his sixty-two years. No cricketer ever brought to the game a more propitious mixture of devotion, enthusiasm, knowledge, and humour. Nor did anyone ever strive harder to serve it in every sphere, not least by playing it as he believed it ought to be played— with joy and enterprise—on all occasions. He was a splendid captain and wonderful company, for he not only knew cricket, practically and historically, but he had a vast knowledge of cricketers of all eras and a fund of anecdote concerning them. A character in his own right, he was and remains the subject of many stories himself, a form of obituary he would have favoured.

41

"Stop the Seventy Tour"

WE must now retrace our steps to the beginning of one of the sorriest chapters in cricket's history, the sequence of events which culminated in the severance of Test cricket between England and South Africa.

Already, in 1960, David Sheppard had registered a personal protest against Apartheid by refusing to play against the South African cricketers, and their 1960 and 1965 teams had been faced with demonstrations and protest marches, which, however, never threatened to disrupt play. The emergence of Basil D'Oliveira as an established England player raised widespread speculation about the projected M.C.C. tour to South Africa in 1968. In February 1967 policy statements by Mr Pieter le Roux, South Africa's Minister of the Interior, made it clear that D'Oliveira would be unacceptable, and smouldering speculation flared up into a blaze of antagonism. Promptly it was reported that about half the Labour M.P.s and many Conservatives were expected to sign a motion calling on M.C.C. to cancel the tour, and within a few days Mr Denis Howell, the Minister responsible for Sport, made a statement in the House saying that informal discussions had taken place between the Government and representatives of M.C.C., and, indeed, some months earlier the Secretary had outlined M.C.C.'s policy. M.C.C. had informed the Government that the team to tour South Africa would be chosen on merit, and in this respect any preconditions that the host country laid down would be totally disregarded. The Government were confident that if, when the time came, any player chosen for the touring side were to be rejected by the host country, then there would be no question that the M.C.C. would find such a condition wholly unacceptable and the projected tour would be abandoned.

The Minister's statement was welcomed by an overwhelming majority of M.P.s, irrespective of party. Earlier, in his statement, Mr Howell had assured the House that the Government had no responsibility—nor did they wish to have responsibility—for the activities of the Governing Bodies of sport, and the debate ended with a nice exchange with the Member for St Marylebone. "Does not the independent and proper attitude of the Marylebone Cricket Club," asked Mr Hogg, "endorse the view that it is independent not merely of the South African Government, but also of the British Government, and should remain so?" To this the Minister replied, "I do not know whether that question was intended to be a long hop or a full toss. We all recognize the Right Honourable and Learned Gentleman's special responsibilities, and I think that his declaration of independence is warmly accepted."

In April the doubts raised by Mr le Roux's statements were partially dispelled when his Prime Minister Mr Vorster, announced that racially mixed sports teams from countries with whom South Africa already had friendly relations would henceforth be warmly received. This was taken to mean that the arrangements for the M.C.C. tour could go ahead. However, a rider to the Prime Minister's statement, later to be used as the excuse for banning D'Oliveira, placed an embargo on any visiting sportsman whose presence was judged to be liable to cause civil disorder.

In January 1968 the M.C.C. Committee sent a letter to the South African Cricket Association seeking an assurance that no restrictive preconditions would be imposed on the selection of the M.C.C. team. No immediate reply was received, but it was decided to take no further action pending the return from South Africa of Sir Alec Douglas-Home, who was having talks with South African Ministers and the South African Cricket Association. It had also to be decided whether or not to include a visit to Rhodesia. On Sir Alec's advice it was agreed that, if the Government's view was that the M.C.C. team should not go to Rhodesia, that part of the tour should be called off, but that arrangements for the main South Africa tour should go ahead on the assumption that the selected team would be accepted by their Government when the time came. When, in May, it was announced that, on Government advice, the team would not go to Rhodesia, there was vocal criticism in some quarters of M.C.C.'s "abject surrender to Government".

While these discussions were in train Basil D'Oliveira was enduring a deeply discouraging tour in the West Indies; and back in England, even though he played in the first Test against Australia and made top score for England, his form for several months was so poor that he lost his place, and his selection for the South African tour looked more and more improbable. However, fate took a hand when Tom Cartwright fell out of the final Test against Australia. The Selectors decided to replace him with a batsman, but, with their first choice, Prideaux, also unfit, the captain's preference for an all-rounder led to the eleventh-hour substitution of D'Oliveira. Now, recovered from the miserable form which had dogged him and spurred on by the great ambition to tour in the country of his birth, he played a great innings of 158 and became the hero of the match.

On the evening of the final day the M.C.C. Selectors, Messrs D. J. Insole, A. V. Bedser, D. Kenyon, P. B. H. May, with the team captain and manager, M. C. Cowdrey and L. E. G. Ames, together with the President and Treasurer of M.C.C., gathered at 8 P.M. to make the final choice for South Africa. At ten to two the following morning they rose, having decided, on cricket grounds, not to include Basil D'Oliveira. The M.C.C. Committee's announcement that they had approved a team from which he was omitted exposed the Selectors to a charge that they were guilty, at best, of lack of judgment and, at worst, of bowing to political expediency. Lord's was inundated with letters and phone calls, M.P.s added their voices to those of the protesters, about a dozen M.C.C. members resigned, and others, in a group led by the Rev. David Sheppard, demanded a Special General Meeting at which they would table motions of censure.

The News of the World now announced that they were sending D'Oliveira to South Africa as a reporter to cover the tour, and there were rumours that the South African Government would adopt the attitude that this assignment was designed to embarrass them and would refuse to allow him to enter the country.

With doubt persisting about the fitness of Tom Cartwright, the Selectors had stated, when the names of the team were released, that D'Oliveira and Don Wilson might be called upon if any of those selected were unable to tour. When Cartwright's injury failed to mend the M.C.C. Selectors felt, as the T.C.C.B.'s had for the Oval Test, that no other bowler could equate with his nagging accuracy, with the early swing, or with the late movement off the seam which had so tricked the South African batsmen at Nottingham in 1965. So once more D'Oliveira, having been rejected as a batsman, was called upon as an all-rounder to take his place, with I. J. Jones brought in as an additional bowler. Mr Vorster's reaction was sharp and hostile. In a speech to Nationalist Party members at Bloemfontein, calculated to woo the support of the

hard-line Verkrampte dissidents, he claimed that the team as
constituted was not the team of the M.C.C., but the team of the
anti-Apartheid movement, the team of the South African Non-
Racial Olympic Committee, and the team of Bishop Reeves.
D'Oliveira, he said, had become a political cricket ball, and the
team had become the team of South Africa's political opponents,
the team of people who didn't care about sport or sporting
relations. On September 24, Mr Arthur Coy and Mr Jack Cheetham attended a special meeting of the M.C.C. Committee. But
their long journey achieved no more than to allow them to express
in person regret at the train of events and to reaffirm that there was
nothing they could do to alter the fact that the M.C.C. side, as
constituted, was unacceptable to the South African Government;
the matter had been taken out of their hands. Both sides expressed
the hope that, in spite of the South African Government's attitude,
friendly relations could be maintained between the cricket
authorities of the two countries. The following statement was
issued after the meeting:

> The M.C.C. Committee met with representatives of the South
> African Cricket Association this afternoon. The Committee were
> informed that the team selected to represent M.C.C. in South Africa
> is not acceptable for reasons beyond the control of the South African
> Cricket Association. The M.C.C. Committee therefore decided
> unanimously that the tour will not take place.

It was understandable that those outside the inner conclaves of
cricket should have suspected M.C.C. of political thumduggery.
First had come the omission of D'Oliveira at the moment of his
splendid return to form; then an interim statement by the Chairman of the Selectors that he had been considered as a batsman
rather than as an all-rounder; finally, his inclusion in place of a
bowler. It requires no deep imagination to appreciate the crushing
disappointment suffered by D'Oliveira himself. At the end of a
season when the cherished ambition of selection for the South
African tour seemed to be vanishing into the shades the prize had
suddenly reappeared, almost within the grasp, only to be snatched
away as he was reaching out to take it; the final disillusionment was
to find there was no prize to grasp. As we now know, he had borne
an additional load of personal anxiety, torn between the promise of
financial security offered by a highly lucrative contract with the
South African Sports Federation for a coaching engagement in
South Africa and his ambition to represent England in the country

of his birth. Acceptance of the contract involved an immediate decision, abandoning the hope of touring with M.C.C. or continuing in English cricket. Some months later, long after D'Oliveira had decided to remain in England and go all out for the chance to play for M.C.C. in South Africa, the Director of the South African Sports Federation claimed that their offer, just before the team for South Africa was picked, was a coincidence, and that it was not the intention, through the offer, to remove him from the list of people available for the M.C.C. tour. This was not the impression D'Oliveira received at the time, and it is clear that, whether they did it intentionally or not, those who subjected him to such pressures had much to answer for.

In the second week in September the M.C.C. Committee met David Sheppard and five other representatives of his group to discuss the views they wanted to put at the Special General Meeting and explain to them the Committee's actions regarding the South Africa tour over the past eighteen months. Sir Alec Douglas-Home was the leading spokesman in arguing the good sense of the Committee's policy and their reluctance to press for answers to hypothetical questions which would be likely to push the South African Government into giving an unfavourable reply. The basis of M.C.C.'s policy towards South Africa had always been the desirability of preserving bridges of contact, so that their cricketers, whether white or non-white, should not be isolated from the incentives offered by international competition.

The meeting with Mr Sheppard's group had not, as the Committee hoped, averted the need for the Special General Meeting, which was held at Church House, Westminster, on December 5; the rotunda of the Assembly Hall was filled to capacity with 1000 or more M.C.C. members, overflowing into an adjoining room. In the chair was M.C.C.'s new President, the former Secretary, Mr Ronald Aird. Members had been summoned by a notice, circulated to the 10,000 full members, in which the formal notice of the meeting and the recital of the resolutions of the requisitioners was followed by their arguments for their resolutions and those of the Committee against. The Rev. David Sheppard was himself the dominant figure of the evening; the former Sussex and England batsman now opened the innings for his side in debate, by moving the first resolution:

That the Members of M.C.C. regret the Committee's mishandling of affairs leading up to the selection of the team for the intended tour of South Africa in 1968–1969.

He argued his case in measured terms with cool reasoning, expressing belief, as did all their critics, in the integrity of the Committee and the Selectors, but putting much emphasis on the Committee's failure to press for the assurance they had sought in their letter to the South African Cricket Association in January. His seconder, the Middlesex and England batsman Mr J. M. Brearley, who had toured South Africa with M.C.C. in 1964–65, spoke of his own change of heart, and argued that the Committee were mistaken in their priorities: that the importance of keeping links with South Africa was outweighed by M.C.C.'s wider responsibilities towards non-white cricketers at home and in other countries. Secondly he argued that there was a discrepancy between M.C.C.'s image in the eyes of the public and the Committee's idea of what that image was and the image they were projecting.

Until now the temperature of debate had been cool and rational. Being no longer a member of the M.C.C. staff, I was not privileged to be present in the hall, but, on the evidence of those who were and of reports in the Press, it seems to be the opinion of friend and foe alike that at this point the heat was turned on by the advocates of the Committee. First, the Chairman brought on his head criticism from both sides by entering the debate to declare that there was a fundamental difference between the views of the M.C.C. Committee and those of Mr Sheppard and his supporters: that the Committee were very anxious indeed to send a team to South Africa, on the clear understanding that any player selected would automatically be accepted and accorded the usual courtesies extended to a member of a visiting team, but that Mr Sheppard and some of his supporters never wanted us to send a team to South Africa at all. Then Mr Dennis Silk, the first spokesman for the Committee, was criticized for introducing a note of acrimony which reflected, perhaps, the stresses and anxieties to which the Committee had been subjected during the past months. M.C.C. had hoped to have, as their principal speaker, Sir Alec Douglas-Home, whose expertise in debate would have added weight and diplomacy to their arguments. It has been widely said that those who spoke for the Committee did not present their case as well as the speakers for the opposition, and that they failed to read accurately the weight of sincere concern of the ordinary member on an issue of great moment; that they were outplayed by a team who included a formidable array of practised orators.

The first resolution had been in the nature of a post-mortem on the past. The meeting now turned to resolutions two and three, which were concerned with policy for the future, and read:

2. That no further tours to or from South Africa be undertaken until evidence can be given of actual progress by South Africa towards non-racial cricket.

3. That a Special Committee be set up to examine such proposals as are submitted by the S.A.C.A. towards non-racial cricket; the M.C.C. to report on progress to the Annual General Meeting of the club; and to the Governing Body for Cricket—the M.C.C. Council.

These two resolutions were debated together. The proposer, Mr Peter Howell, made the point that it was no longer enough merely to hope that South Africa would some day relax their policies towards non-white cricketers; the time had come to ask for and secure a measure of progress. For the Committee Mr Aidan Crawley repeated what had been argued in the pamphlet convening the meeting, that they were motivated by a continuing desire to promote cricket between England and other countries with which this country has diplomatic relations. The implications of the resolution were political dynamite. However much the policies and actions of other Governments might be objected to, it was almost always better to maintain contacts across deep divisions so that it was possible to continue, in however humble a way, to try to influence events in the way you wanted them to go.

The debate in all had lasted from 6.30 P.M. until nearly ten o'clock. It had been anticipated that, when the votes were counted, the Committee would have a commanding majority, but, though this was assured by the votes already cast by post, the very much narrower margin of confidence shown in the voting on the night by the mightiest turnout of members who had ever attended a general meeting reflected their deep concern over the greatest issue they had ever been called upon to face. At the end of the day the Committee had secured a vote of confidence, and their opponents could claim not a little success for gaining a platform and earning a measure of support for their views. But the real triumph was that these issues should have been talked out in a forum which encompassed such an unprecedented representation of members.

Before he declared the meeting closed Mr Aird paid a warm public tribute to Basil D'Oliveira for the great dignity he had shown throughout this unhappy affair. Mr Aird, in his turn, was acclaimed from every side of the house for the way he had conducted a very difficult meeting.

One of the "Sheppard Group's" charges had been that the Selectors had been put in an intolerable position, under threat that, if D'Oliveira were selected, the South African Government would object—a charge which Colin Cowdrey, speaking for the Selectors, strongly denied. That the chief officers of M.C.C. had not been unmindful of the danger of the Selectors being influenced by political pressure was revealed in April, when it became known that in March 1968 Lord Cobham, on the eve of his return from a visit to South Africa, had been told by Mr Vorster that it was extremely unlikely that D'Oliveira would be acceptable to his Government. This attitude, very different from the impression gained by Sir Alec Douglas-Home only a week or so before, was reported by Lord Cobham to the Secretary of M.C.C., who discussed it with the President (Mr Gilligan) and the Treasurer (Mr Allen). Because they felt it was imperative not to prejudice the members of the M.C.C. Committee who were also Selectors they decided to keep the information to themselves. This revelation, made almost at the exact moment that the South African Sports Federation's offer to Basil D'Oliveira was divulged, aroused a fresh wave of hostility and caused M.C.C. to issue a long Press statement not only setting in perspective the facts connected with Lord Cobham's interview and the reasons for the action that had been taken, but also giving an assurance that there was absolutely no evidence that any offer had been made to D'Oliveira by the South African Cricket Association or by the South African Government. Once again M.C.C. were the target for heavy criticism, levelled this time principally at the President, Treasurer, and Secretary. The pressure on Mr Griffith was so intolerable that he was driven to announce that he felt the best interests of cricket might be served if he were to resign. The Committee, however, would not hear of this. They gave him personally a warm vote of confidence and endorsed the action of their three senior officers.

By the accident of fate the great Church House meeting had been the last scene in an era, the ringing down of the curtain on M.C.C.'s direct responsibility as the Governing Body of cricket in the United Kingdom. Power was now transferred to the M.C.C. Council, to whom the T.C.C.B., meeting at Lord's less than a week later, recommended that the South African tour of 1970 should proceed as planned. In a statement announcing their decision they confirmed their aversion to racial discrimination of any kind and declared that, while they respected the rights of those who wished to demonstrate peacefully, they were resolved to uphold the rights of individuals in this country to take part in lawful pursuits, particularly when those pursuits had the support of the majority. Because of the special factors surrounding the tour a sub-committee was appointed to examine the situation and advise the Council through the T.C.C.B. on the feasibility of playing against the South Africans. So the historic inauguration of the M.C.C. Council was rendered doubly historic by the weight of their decision to confirm the wish of the T.C.C.B. to proceed with the tour. With their decision began that long-drawn-out agony which culminated in the tour's final cancellation on May 22, 1970.

I was in Cape Town when the news was announced; in fact, I heard it from members of the South African Board of Control and a group of non-white cricketers with whom I was spending the evening, giving them a talk about cricket history. There had recently been attacks against a dozen or so county grounds. Except at Cardiff, where a pit was dug on the table and filled with tin-tacks, and at Bristol, where the turf was attacked with weed-killer, the opposition was confined to slogans and posters. Later a more imaginative group attempted to invade Lord's with the intention of staging a non-racial game of cricket, but, baulked by the gateman, they set up their stumps in the road, to the great entertainment of pedestrians and the exasperation of motorists. My hosts at Cape Town were much interested in the defence of Lord's and the introduction of barbed wire, festooning the table, and artificial pitches, but nobody raised his voice to object to the tour. I have since regretted that, in respect to their obvious determination to avoid controversial topics, I neglected to ask the direct question whether or not they wanted the tour to go ahead.

By mid-March I returned to England to find all the forces of modern communications media heavily involved in the controversy. The most militant opposition came from the Stop the Seventy Tour Committee, whose leader, Mr Peter Hain, made it known immediately after the T.C.C.B.'s announcement in December that the battle was on. David Sheppard, now Bishop of Woolwich, had, with the Bishops of Southwark and Stepney, led a protest march against the Springboks rugger team at Twickenham. Having at first allied himself with the Stop the Seventy Tour movement, he now disowned their overt promise of violence and with the former Conservative Minister for Education, Sir Edward Boyle, as his Vice-Chairman, formed a new group, the Fair Cricket Campaign, dedicated to non-violent protest.

Political pressure from overseas was brought to bear with a threatened crippling of the Commonwealth Games at Edinburgh, from which the African and some Asian countries vowed to withdraw if the tour went ahead. Faced with the evident vulnerability of most county grounds, the Cricket Council now accepted the advice of the T.C.C.B. Sub-committee that the itinerary should be curtailed to twelve matches only, played between June 6th and August 18th at venues limited to eight grounds which could most easily be protected. To offset the loss of profit and provide the vast sums needed for additional protection, policing, and insurance, a group of cricket patrons led by Lieut.-Colonel A. C. Newman, V.C., war-time hero of the raid on St Nazaire, launched a fund with the object of raising £200,000. After the cancellation of the tour the relatively small sum collected was handed over to the Cricket Council to be used for the good of cricket generally, and it has been applied to the welfare of small clubs.

The President of the South African Cricket Association, Mr Jack Cheetham, had given an undertaking that future South African teams would be selected on merit, irrespective of colour. His announcement was hailed in many quarters over-optimistically as a complete answer to the charges of racialism levelled against his Board. In practice, in terms of the 1970 tour, the promise was scarcely more than a gesture, coolly received by the South African Cricket Board of Control, for though the selectors contended with Government regulations for permission to watch non-white players in the Super League, these players' most optimistic champions scarcely expected that any one of them would be found to measure up to the very high standard achieved by the South Africans in the Tests against Australia. The gesture of the S.A.C.A. was hardly matched by the Nationalist Government, who, in the hectic weeks preceding a General Election in which they were seeking to woo back the extreme right-wing supporters of Dr Hertzog, seemed determined to do everything possible to exacerbate world opinion and to secure South Africa's isolation from international sport. The refusal of a visa to the American lawn-tennis player, Arthur Ashe, led immediately to their expulsion from the Davis Cup. Cricket received a direct blow by a ban on the International Cavaliers, and a visa was even denied temporarily to a "courtesy white" Japanese jockey.

England as well as South Africa was in the thralls of pre-Election fever; with Ministers and Members on the Government side making oppositionist pronouncements against the tour, cricket was in danger of becoming a party political issue, affecting the Election. The Home Secretary, Mr James Callaghan, while expressing his personal opposition, had nevertheless given an undertaking that cricket grounds would be protected from violent attack, but a statement by the Prime Minister in a television programme in which he seemed not to discourage the demonstrators, was received with deep indignation by those who thought the tour should continue. The standpoint taken by the Cricket Council was that their job was to promote cricket and to resist threats of violence aimed at depriving the public of a lawful pursuit. In their view, if the Government wanted the tour stopped, it was for them to say so, and it was in response to a direct request by the Home Secretary that the final decision was taken, on May 22, to cancel the tour.

It is too soon to forecast the long-term effect of the sanctions against South Africa. I first went there in the winter of 1966–67, when Mr Vorster had recently taken office and there was talk of a more relaxed policy. Returning in 1970 after three years, I sensed a closing of the ranks in the face of world hostility. Now the initial reaction to the cancellation seemed to be one of bitterness coupled with the charge that the decision was dictated by mob rule. However, the forces of the Verkrampte were discomfited in the Election, and Clyde van Ryneveld has written that the political situation is more fluid than it has been for a long time. He instances the admission of Maoris in the All Blacks rugger team and says that sportsmen are increasingly speaking out in favour of the inclusion of non-white sportsmen. He is confident, too, that the South African Cricket Association will persevere with their efforts to establish contact with the non-white cricketers and find means to implement the policy of picking touring teams on merit. But the South African Cricket Board of Control are not easily to be wooed. Their claim is that, as a completely non-racial body, they have achieved integration and should be regarded as the representative body of South African cricket. Having, however, failed to attract into their fold the Johannesburg-based South African African Cricket Board of Control, their effective influence is therefore confined to those who may be termed, broadly, in the idiom of South Africa, coloured cricketers—Indians, Malayans, and those of mixed blood, together with a handful of Africans. The greatest need of non-white cricketers is for better opportunities: better pitches, more and better coaching, and more competition, for which not only money is needed, but also endeavour. It is common knowledge that the S.A.C.A.'s offer of 50,000 Rand (rather more than £25,000), which could have helped towards these needs, was turned down mainly because it was objected that the administration of the fund was to be vested in the hands of Trustees. It is very easy to sympathize with this attitude; it is also easy to see that, as a responsible body, the S.A.C.A. feel they have a duty in the administration of the funds entrusted to them. The non-white cricketers have constantly declared that the isolation of South Africa from international competition would reflect disastrously on their own standards. If this is proved to be true it will be the saddest result of a wholly tragic situation.

The impact of the disruption of cricket with South Africa on England and M.C.C. encounters at home and abroad was threefold. A tour to Pakistan and Ceylon replaced M.C.C.'s South African visit, only to break up in disaster; a world-wide M.C.C. "junior" tour was curtailed; and a new trophy was introduced for an international series at home.

Immediately M.C.C.'s South African visit was cancelled negotiations started for a short tour to India, Pakistan, and Ceylon after Christmas. But the evil spirit which foredoomed the South African trip seemed determined to ensure that, whatever its destination, the last major tour for which M.C.C. were responsible in fact as well as in name should be fraught with disaster. In spite of the special pleading of Mr Carr, on two personal visits, and the promise of £20,000 in sterling from the Burmah Oil Company, the Indian Government felt unable to release currency unless the tour to their country was extended to include more than two Tests. So, as a prelude to a gruelling journey through Pakistan, M.C.C. opened with eleven pleasant days in Ceylon, giving initial satisfaction locally in Colombo by conceding victory, on the scoring rate, in a limited innings match with the Ceylon Board's Eleven. From the peace of Ceylon they plunged into a barrage of political strife in Pakistan which had nothing whatever to say to cricket. At Lahore and Dacca civil disorder made a nonsense of the first two Tests. Nevertheless, against this deplorable background of disturbance, Cowdrey at Lahore and D'Oliveira at Dacca played innings of power and grandeur. At Karachi the final curtain was rung down early on the third day as uncontrolled riots disrupted play. England had made the commanding score of 502 for 7, to which Colin Milburn, happily unaware that he was playing his final innings in a Test career which was soon to be so tragically curtailed, had contributed a lusty opening century which earned him the Lawrence Trophy for the fastest hundred for England in Tests during the calendar year of 1969. Amid the maelstrom the team had soldiered on, trying not to put a foot wrong, until the utter breakdown of law and order caused the President of the Pakistan Board of Control, Mr Fida Hassan, to declare that stumps must be drawn. England had been sustained throughout by the wisdom and patience of their Manager, Mr Ames, who had been a tower of strength and diplomacy in intolerable circumstances.

Early in their reign the T.C.C.B. had agreed in principle to try to send a M.C.C. "B" team to minor cricketing countries, and an ambitious programme of matches, in a semi-global tour, from Africa to the Far East, was eventually arranged for February and March 1970. In the event, as a demonstration of displeasure against the South African tour, the African countries, Zambia, Kenya, and Uganda, withdrew their invitations, leaving a residue of eight matches in Ceylon, Singapore, Malaysia, Thailand, and Hong Kong. This so-called "B" team, led by A. R. Lewis, was of near Test calibre, including as it did a galaxy of stars who had already played, or would soon play, for England. With them went the doyen of Test umpires, Mr Syd Buller, who added coaching and lecturing sessions to his umpiring duties. In fact, the team as a whole went out to teach as well as to play. In Ceylon, cricket has always been strong in the schools and colleges, and Alan Smith, who found time to visit them, confirmed the enormous enthusiasm which persists at school level. On the Colombo Oval a 10,000 crowd roared their delight when Boycott was bowled with the second ball of the match—a failure which was entirely out of character on a tour when "seeing Boycott make a hundred" was a spectacle anticipated with joyful confidence wherever he played.

Wherever they went the team played in colourful surroundings and enjoyed lavish entertainment. Their captain has said that the batting of Boycott and Alan Jones was an object-lesson, fulfilling the reason for the tour. Of the bowlers Don Wilson was the most feared; he earned for himself the name of the "Malayan Mauler". The achievement of the whole team was not so much the winning of six out of eight matches, with two drawn heavily in their favour, as in teaching the skills of cricket in centres where the impetus of international competition is lacking. Such a tour, as may be imagined, cost far more than the receipts which could be expected from attendances; it was made possible by the combined sponsorship of British-American Tobacco and Burmah Oil, with a further generous contribution from the Warwickshire C.C.C. Supporters Association.

Sponsorship was in evidence again in the announcement, accompanying the news of the cancellation of the South African tour, that the gap in representative cricket would be filled by a series of matches played between England and the Rest of the World for a handsome trophy consisting of a silver Irish Harp set on a plinth of Connemara marble, presented by Messrs Arthur Guinness. In addition they gave a total of £20,000 in prize money, of which £7000 was for distribution to the county clubs through the T.C.C.B. Of the balance £2000 went to the winning side in each Test and £3000, plus the prize money for any drawn matches, to the winners of the series.

The captain of the World was Gary Sobers, whose team of players from Australia, West Indies, India, and Pakistan included a strong contingent of South Africans, Ed Barlow and the Pollocks having flown over to join their compatriots Barry Richards and Mike Procter, who were already in county cricket.

Sixty-seven years after M.C.C. players first donned the fighting emblem of St George slaying the dragon, the Cricket Council prepared for *their* first venture in Australia. Externally their team do not reflect the change of government, for they wear the same colours and engage in the same battle—the fight to recover the Ashes. The first M.C.C. team returned victorious. The early form of Ray Illingworth and his men offered no promise that they would do likewise. Nevertheless, by beating the Australians twice at Sydney they, like Sir Pelham Warner's side, recaptured for England that much-coveted though mythical prize—the urn containing the Ashes.

DISSOLUTION, 1966
Dismemberment of the old Tavern and Clock Tower.

THE NEW TAVERN BESIDE THE GRACE GATES

"STOP THE SEVENTY TOUR"
Defensive illumination of the ground.

CANCELLATION OF THE SOUTH AFRICAN TOUR

42

The Games and the Players 1969

THE last cricket season of the sixties could hardly have opened in worse conditions, wet and miserable. Nor could the decade be said to go out in a blaze of glory, for it was never an exhilarating summer's play.

Two touring sides shared the available time and amenities. The West Indies were well below their accepted post-War standards. All great teams must eventually complete their appointed cycle and be rejuvenated, not always a continuous nor immediate process and quite likely to result in a temporary depression. Such was rather the case of the West Indians, their form impaired at the same time by too much cricket, collectively and individually. In particular, their leader and hope of inspiration, Sobers, looked tired and stale. When a cricketer is surfeited, try as he may he cannot flog a tired spirit to give of its physical best. The powerful combination of Hall and Griffith was no more, and Gibbs clearly on the wane. There was a certain amount of good cricket on both sides, but England ran out winners by two matches to nil.

The New Zealanders ran much to their accepted pattern, keen, popular, and courageous, but departed still without a victorious Test Match to their credit.

The County Championship was quite a spirited affair, with Glamorgan coming home with a rush in the latter part of the season. It was twenty-one years since they had, for the first time, topped the table, and the enthusiasm in Wales was unbounded.

One-day matches were increasingly popular and well supported. Lancashire, trailing sadly in the County Table proper, won the new John Player League, with, one would hope, stimulating effect on cricket at Old Trafford. This event, sponsored by the famous tobacco firm, was a major success and could well be a pointer to the nature of county cricket in the future. Their neighbours, Yorkshire, won the Gillette Cup, which was also some compensation for a moderate showing at No. 13 in the County Championship.

T

West Indies came to Lord's at the end of May, to draw with the M.C.C. It was not an outstanding match except for the superb batting of Edrich and a good innings by Sobers. Out of a first innings of 200 Edrich made 125, and impressed everyone by his timing and confidence. When West Indies topped M.C.C. Sobers made 74 in his very different left-handed style, with, on this occasion, no hint of staleness. Rain restricted the last day's play to less than three hours, during which time Edrich and Boycott scored 127 without being parted. Of these Edrich scored 77 with the same sure touch which he had shown in the first innings.

The West Indies came to the second Test Match already one down, to play a very even draw. At one moment they seemed well on the way to winning, but were thwarted by good Yorkshire grit. Batting first they scored 380, led by a century from Davis. This might have been a really big total but for a sad mishap which befell Sobers. When he had made 29, and was showing signs of his best form, a ball bounced off his pads in the direction of short-leg. He took off and was half-way down the pitch before he realized that his partner was either unaware or unwilling. As he stood helplessly ten yards from home Boycott ran up and broke the wicket.

Sobers was afforded some compensation when England batted, for, so well did he and his fast bowlers use the new ball, England lost five wickets for 61 runs. There then followed a fine and attractive stand of 128 for the sixth wicket. John Hampshire had for some years caught the eye as a fine free stroke player, but his record had perhaps not kept pace with his style. It was variously said that he was a fast-wicket player, that he lacked concentration, and that he was unable to pace himself over a long innings. Not one of these comments could have been urged against him in this his first Test Match. Coming in at 37 for four wickets, he played with perfect judgment from the start. When Knott who had played equally well, was out at 189, Hampshire went on to make 107. Even so England were 219 when Snow joined his captain. Illingworth now started to play to his very best form, and by the close the pair had taken the score to 321. On Monday Illingworth also completed his hundred and, with Snow undefeated for 9, the total reached 344. The pitch still being very good, time was now an acute factor, but Sobers' declaration at 295 for nine made a definite result more than a possibility. England wanted 322 in five hours, and in fact got to 295 for seven wickets. Boycott got 106, but failed to pitch the early scoring rate high enough to enable his successors to seize the advantage. Not the least feature of the game was the magnificent slip fielding of Sharpe.

In late July England won the first Test at Lord's against New Zealand. Following the occasional pattern of these events in other years, New Zealand held the opposition up to a point, but lacked the basic strength to sustain the pressure. They did well to get England out on a green pitch for 190, but even so were 21 runs behind on the first innings. Edrich, now in a fine spell, made 115 in the second innings, and New Zealand were left 361 to get. Against Underwood's subtle variety of pace, flight, and spin their batting failed, and England ran out winners by 231 runs.

Once again the University Match was drawn, but after some very good cricket. Cambridge declared at 273 for eight, after a good, even batting performance, in contrast to Oxford's uncertain reply of 235. Cambridge, with a second fine innings by Knight, of 88 not out, declared at 210 for two, and Oxford accepted the challenge of chasing 249 in three hours. Goldstein, noticeably below form in the first innings, now found his touch and got 69 out of 106 in 98 minutes. But the Oxford effort spent itself, and they were reduced to playing out time at 221 for seven wickets.

Middlesex had a moderate season under the captaincy of Peter Parfitt. The early matches at Lord's were marred by rain, two probable and much-needed victories ending instead in draws, so that Middlesex finished at No. 11 in the table, one down on 1968. Much hope had been placed in Connolly after his splendid bowling on the Australian tour. He was always an interesting performer, but seemed unable to produce the fire and movement of the previous year. Even so he took seventy-four wickets, a greater bag than anyone else, and added a nice cosmopolitan note to the cricket at Lord's.

In the John Player League Middlesex were much more successful, finishing at No. 7. The one-day Sunday matches were a very popular innovation and provided some entertaining if not wholly authentic play.

The older generation of cricketers and cricket-followers at Lord's were saddened to hear that Reg Bettington had been killed in a motor accident in New Zealand. Large in body and personality, he had arrived from New South Wales to play in four University Matches for Oxford, and in 1928 played for Middlesex. He bowled his buzzing leg breaks and googlies with a fine, high-stepping, wheeling action from which the ball left his powerful fingers with a snap audible in the deep field. He batted with a fierce, robust power, and (being a most outspoken man) if he never sought popularity, he acquired it in an extraordinary measure wherever he played.

In Colombo Dr Churchill Hector Gunasekara died at the age of seventy-four. When Oriental names were less commonplace than in the present age he lent a picturesque air to the Middlesex team, for whom he bowled a crafty leg break. Unless his parents were unusually prophetic they can scarcely have realized how truly heroic were the names they had bestowed upon their son.

Gerald Crutchley had been in poor health sometime before his death in August. He had been intimately connected with Lord's ever since his days at Harrow. Having played against Eton, he went up to Oxford, and had the extraordinary experience of being 99 not out against Cambridge at the close of play and in bed with measles before nightfall—and so out of the match. For many years he graced the Middlesex batting order with his fluent driving and cutting, to become, in after years, President of the club.

Every cricket ground had reason to mourn Emmott Robinson, for within his breast burnt the clear, fierce flame of devotion. He was a *Yorkshire* cricketer, and all else he might approve but not without reservation. Lord's, one suspects, he regarded as faintly Babylonian and all Southerners as inclined to flippancy. He never played for England, whom again he probably thought something of a mixed bag. But he has claims to being, in the widest sense of the term, the greatest county cricketer of his day. As such his shade must be enshrined at Lord's—however uneasy in its surroundings.

On October 29 Victor York Richardson, an honorary member of the M.C.C., died in South Australia at the age of seventy-five. He had been a very notable athlete in a variety of spheres, but was chiefly known in England as a fine, robust cricketer. His batting was brave and dashing, and he must have been one of the very few ever to hook Larwood, at full power, for six. He also had a grand, robust humour and a wealth of salty Australian anecdotes. His last years were warmed and gladdened by the cricketing ability of his grandsons, Ian and Greg Chappell, both of them now Test players.

43

The Games and the Players 1970

THE cricket season of 1970 was unique in the history of the game. Only once before had an international cricket tour become directly involved in politics, and then it had been to a limited and discreet extent. When feeling had risen to great heat over the Body Line tactics of the 1932–33 tour in Australia there had been concern about its effect upon Commonwealth relations, and Mr J. H. Thomas, Secretary of State for the Dominions, had sought to bring his influence to bear on the disputants. King George V himself, although in no sense a cricketer, studied the technical aspects of the situation and, in the opinion of one eminent cricketer, talked more sense than many more closely concerned. When harmony was restored the only remaining scars were upon those personally or physically involved in the actual play.

The political forces leading to the cancellation of the 1970 South African Tour were very different in origin, and infinitely deeper and wider in implication. These have been dealt with elsewhere in this book, and this chapter is rather concerned with the practical effects on the season's play at Lord's.

When, under Governmental pressure, the Cricket Council withdrew their invitation to the South Africans there was an enormous hiatus in the programme arranged some time before the controversy arose. The South African team promised to be the best ever to come from that country and, fresh from trouncing Australia, would have been a tremendous draw. Their absence left much bitterness amongst cricketers, who were very doubtful if it was to the benefit of non-white South Africans and felt that, in a free country, approval or otherwise of the actual team was a matter for the individual judgment and conscience.

It also left the cricket authorities with the problem of finding some substitute to fill the void thus suddenly created. With commendable enterprise and energy the series of matches against a World XI (which had naturally been considered during the dispute) was organized into a practical proposition.

The first 'Test' of the series, played at Lord's on June 17th, 19th, 20th, and 22nd, was a somewhat one-sided affair. The World assembled a side of great all-round strength under the captaincy of Sobers. From the West Indies came, in addition to the captain, Kanhai, Lloyd, and Gibbs, from South Africa Richards, Barlow, R. G. Pollock, and Procter, with McKenzie, Engineer, and Intikhab Alam the sole representatives of Australia, India, and Pakistan. For various reasons England were without Boycott, Edrich, Graveney, and Cowdrey, and still sorely missing Milburn and Barrington. Thus the side had a rather immature and inexperienced air, with D'Oliveira batting at No. 4. This was emphasized when Sobers, having lost the toss, bowled his seamers in such irresistible form that seven English wickets fell for 44. Total disaster was averted by a fine innings by Illingworth, who made 63, and was courageously supported by Underwood and Ward in raising the final score to 127.

England then felt the full weight of a batting order which started Richards, Barlow, Kanhai, Pollock, and Lloyd. When the fourth wicket fell at 237, after a day's break for the General Election, the stage was set for Sobers, who showed his best form in scoring 183. Barlow had the rare experience of making a century under the auspices of two Prime Ministers (Mr Wilson on Wednesday and Mr Heath on Friday), and the World batted on until all out for 546. England in reply lost their first wicket for 0, but Luckhurst and D'Oliveira replied with spirit, making 67 and 78 respectively, and Illingworth again batted splendidly to make 94. The resulting total of 339 was highly creditable in the circumstances, but the margin of defeat was an innings and 80 runs.

This reverse caused some foreboding that England had taken on an opposition far beyond their current resources, but ten days later at Trent Bridge they started on their way to a fine eight-wicket victory, and thereafter more than held their own. One pleasing feature of the whole series was the wonderful camaraderie of the World XI. Their manager, F. R. Brown, said that never in his whole experience had he known such a happy dressing-room, a state of affairs for consideration by students of race relations.

Middlesex finished second from the bottom of the County Championship, the lowest position they had ever occupied and one worse than that of the disastrous season of 1930. This was a setback as unexpected as it was unwelcome, for there was apparently quite an abundance of individual skills. An injury to Connolly's back was possibly the first link in a chain of misfortunes, for

without his best form the out-cricket seemed to lack sufficient force
to clinch any favourable situation. Thus, what with occasional
interference from the weather, six of the first seven Middlesex
matches were drawn. The balance of play was such that definite
results might have meant an equal number of gains and losses, but
this would have been infinitely preferable and of greater material
value in the matter of points.

At least in July Middlesex had a great moment at Lord's in the
defeat of Yorkshire. This event lent the Club's supporters some
confidence in the belief that their team had considerable potential
strength which might well blossom under the new captain, J. M.
Brearley, who succeeded Peter Parfitt at the end of the season.

The final of the Gillette Cup was played at Lord's on September
5th, the finalists being Lancashire and Sussex. The outcome was
a fairly easy win for Lancashire, although they had moments of
anxiety. Sussex started the day uncertainly, losing two wickets for
34, but Buss and Parks batted sufficiently well to give hopes of a
good total on a rather sluggish pitch. Good Lancashire fielding
and accurate bowling contained the scoring rate to 184 for nine in
sixty overs, a readily attainable target for the pursuers. When
Lancashire had lost four wickets for 113 the game seemed evenly
poised, especially as Lloyd had just departed, but Pilling was
unshakeable. With Engineer equally resolute the runs were struck
off in one ball over fifty-five overs without further loss.

The result must have been extremely satisfactory to all cricket-
lovers. Not long since it had seemed that Lancashire might fade
from the cricket scene altogether and leave Manchester's fame to
its successful football teams. Now Lancashire had won the Gillette
Cup, the John Player League, and given Kent a hard fight for the
County Championship, Lord's must have rejoiced to see Old
Trafford once again a thriving as well as a historic cricket centre.

Herbert Strudwick died in February at the age of ninety-one.
For many years before and after the First World War he had been
the most famous and probably the best of English wicket-keepers.
It was therefore strange that it was not until he was forty-one that
he kept wicket for the first time for his country at home. This was
at Trent Bridge in 1921. He was a familiar and popular visitor to
Lord's throughout his career and one of the original Life Members
of the M.C.C. under the system inaugurated in 1949.

"Syd" Buller died during the first week of August whilst
umpiring in the Warwickshire v. Notts match at Edgbaston. A
Yorkshireman who emigrated to Worcestershire, he achieved

greater fame as an umpire than he had done as a successful county
player. In the first role he achieved a pre-eminence which had only
been rivalled by Chester in a previous generation. A most respected
figure at Lord's, it fell to him on that ground to "call" the young
South African Griffin, in an almost tragic scene, which must have
severely taxed even his courage and integrity.

Greville Stevens, who died in September, first appeared at
Lord's in senior company as Midshipman Stevens in 1918. The
next year, whilst still a schoolboy, he played for the Gentlemen
and hit the Players' best bowler, Cecil Parkin, into the Pavilion
for six. He played for Middlesex for a decade, and captained
Oxford in his third University match. He did not actually play for
England at Lord's, but, for Middlesex, he made 149 against the
Australians in 1926. He was a man of great acumen, considerable
wit, and strong personality, as successful in the City as in the
cricket world and equally liked and respected in both.

44

Highlights of 1946-1970

CRICKET statistics over an adequate period are a fair guide to
efficiency, individual and collective. Even so, like all statistics, they
call for very careful interpretation, especially in the case of the
individual. The range of play covered by the term "first class" in
England is a very wide one. A century against a University in a
lean year and one made against Lindwall and Miller or Valentine
and Ramadhin are both first-class hundreds so far as the seasonal
averages are concerned. Even if these two performances could be
numerically equated the result would still ignore many essential
factors in making comparison, such as the conditions of play,
time, and the number of chances offered. Thus perhaps the best—
indeed, the only true—measurement of any cricket performance is
made by that notoriously fallible and variable computer, human
judgment.

In trying to recall the highlights and major feats in twenty-five
years of cricket at Lord's the writer admits that the selection is
personal. As such it is easily assailable and may be prey to many
omissions and guilty of controversial inclusions. In brief it is, as the
lawyers say, "without prejudice" and in no way intended as a
work of reference. It can also be suspect of bias to the extent that
many of the greatest moments have for me been created by
bowlers.

It was the batsmen who led the way. In the season of 1947
Compton, Edrich, and Robertson made a score of centuries
between them at Lord's. In every case the natural bent of these
stroke-playing batsmen was encouraged and urged on to its full
by Robins's inspiring captaincy. Admittedly English and South
African bowling, which also came in for some rough treatment
from this trio, was still in the process of redevelopment; but it was
a festival summer. As the sun shone down it seemed that cricket
had shed all its problems and that another golden age was at hand.

The second Test Match saw "the Middlesex twins" at their best
and most devastating. When England had lost two wickets after

a rather unenterprising start they added 370 for the third wicket, a record against South Africa and only 12 short of the partnership between Hutton and Leyland at the Oval against Australia in 1939. But the capacity crowd was less interested in figures than in the torrent of strokes and, despite Compton's erratic reputation as a runner, the splendid understanding between the partners.

The greatest spectacle of the whole season of 1948 was, for me, a first sight of Lindwall in the Lord's Test Match. It was almost exactly ten years since McCormick had for one hour achieved real greatness from the same attacking position, the Pavilion end at Lord's. Both these bowlers I had watched from the same point of vantage, a box on the Father Time stand, which is the most impressive if not the most instructive angle from which to view fast bowling. If from the broadside view one cannot follow the movement of the ball in the air and off the pitch one is compensated by the greater impression of speed and a generally more pleasing view of the bowler's action.

McCormick had, in his hour, achieved a greater pace than any Australian bowler to visit this country since Gregory and McDonald. He had struck one as a fine fast bowler of good action and hostile speed unrelated to any great subtlety. The clear memory of his triumphant hour made a good yardstick for comparison with his successor. Lindwall had only to bowl one ball to reveal the classic beauty of his run-up and delivery. As he progressed his command of tactics and his shrewd variations of pace and flight were a joy to the beholder, if less so to the recipient. He was an object-lesson in the art of attacking the incoming batsman, employing that most dangerous ball to the unattuned eye, the fast, straight half-volley. The two balls delivered to Tom Dollery, taking strike against Australia for the first time and in poor light, were as devastating as one could imagine in the circumstances. They were both near-yorkers of ferocious pace, and both plumb straight. The batsman did well to get the toe of the bat to the first and was in no way disgraced when utterly shattered by the second.

It was two years later that, within an hour, a little-known Ramadhin established himself as the most baffling spinner of his day. No reputation in my experience has advanced so rapidly from almost complete obscurity to international fame. There was a certain irony in the fact that the man to predict this success was almost its first victim. Bill Edrich on his way to the first Test at Manchester had said, when visiting his friend Denis Compton nursing his crocked knee, that this chap Ramadhin could well be a major problem. Looking at the scores from Manchester, the listener could well have doubted the truth of this judgment.

It was when Edrich joined Washbrook in the second Test Match that Ramadhin found his length and confidence, and soon had both batsmen in a considerable tangle. Neither could tell the direction of his spin, and both found themselves like the batsmen of a previous era when faced with the first efficient googly bowlers. Seldom can Lord's ever have seen batsmen of international calibre so dominated by slow bowling on a good pitch, for Valentine bowled superbly at the other end. In stark figures the details of the play were that England, having got to 62 before losing a wicket, were 86 for five wickets after an hour and a half of uphill struggle. The ninth wicket fell at 122, at which Wardle swung the bat to raise the score to 151. Ramadhin's figures of five for 66 were matched by Valentine with four for 48, but it was Ramadhin who destroyed the batsman's morale. Watching fine batsmen deceived time after time by the direction of his spin, one felt he had introduced a new dimension into spin bowling. Part of the difficulty of identifying the break arose from his very quick action, only a momentary glimpse of a dark hand being available to the striker. The effect was aptly described by one victim as that of a man throwing a bunch of confetti at him.

Against a considerably stronger English batting side at Lord's in 1956 Keith Miller bowled Australia to victory. The absence of Lindwall and Davidson had laid a heavy responsibility upon him, and he carried it triumphantly. The impression remains of the ball, delivered with the perfect elastic action and powerful roll of the shoulders, hitting the hard Lord's wicket with a bang and sailing through to the wicketkeeper chest-high. With ten wickets in the match this was as good a piece of sustained attack as this extraordinary and mercurial bowler ever achieved.

Two innings played at Lord's remain vividly in the mind's eye, not for the magnitude of the scores they achieved, but for their unique quality. In 1957 West Indies followed on almost 300 runs behind. The wicket was fast and inclined to be fiery, whilst the ridge at the Nursery end seemed to aid the tendency of the ball to fly. In such conditions Trueman and Statham, supported by Bailey, made a formidable attack.

Everton Weekes was suffering from a cracked bone in one finger when he came to bat a second time. When four wickets had gone for 80 runs he and Sobers added 100 for the fifth. Weekes struck sixteen fours in making 90 from superb and courageous strokes. Despite the sharp and erratic lift of the ball he constantly hooked with fine judgment and effect. Walter Robins watched the whole performance with enthusiasm and, when it was done, pronounced it the finest batting he had seen since Bradman in full flight.

It was six years later, when West Indies had produced the immense pace of Hall and Griffith, that Dexter played an equally remarkable but very different innings in the same fixture. In answer to a West Indian total of 301 England found themselves at lunch-time on the Saturday 20 for 2. Hall and Griffith had a fast Lord's wicket, from which they extracted as good a pace as had been seen since Lindwall and Miller and looked like having a real field day. It was a daunting prospect for the two batsmen in possession, Dexter and Barrington.

The next hour was the greatest onslaught on fast bowling of this calibre that I have ever seen at Lord's or elsewhere. Dexter made 70 runs off seventy-three balls received and 40 of them in bound-aries. The overpitched ball he thumped with immense power in front of the wicket, and anything short he cut or hooked fearlessly. Very few batsmen come to mind who are so poised and speedy of reflex that they can play this game, most players against this pace concentrating on the back foot and content to push the half-volley. Stan McCabe comes to mind as a supreme master of the attack against pace, and Dexter was his equal on that day.

The Test Matches of 1969 saw some very notable play at Lord's. Hampshire, going in for England for the first time when four wickets were down for 37, played a very fine maiden century. Despite a couple of hard knocks from Holder he played with capital judgment, a factor in his batting which had hitherto occasionally been suspect. He had the major misfortune to be run out in the second innings when a respectable score might have ensured his selection in both series of 1969.

The same innings ended with a great showing from Illingworth, who completed his hundred in the course of a last-wicket stand of 83, of which Snow made a gallant 9 not out. Illingworth's previous best in Test cricket had been 50, and he also was suspect, his weakness being against the slow flighted ball. There was no evidence of this during a beautifully free innings, but, admittedly, there was no Ramadhin to tease him.

When the New Zealanders came to Lord's for the first Test they were overwhelmed by Underwood, who took eleven wickets for 70 runs. This was a model piece of left-handed bowling, accurate, intelligent, and deadly. One could appreciate the true bowler's instinct in the way in which Underwood adjusted to the varying conditions in changeable weather, always finding the right pace and length.

Finally, a hundred dazzling catches rise to mind in over twenty years of cricket at Lord's, making this the most difficult area of all from which to choose. The most sensational catch in that considerable time must surely have been made by Benaud in the gully, taking Colin Cowdrey in the second Test of 1956. The bowler being Mackay, gully stood fairly close. The stroke was one of Cowdrey's exceptionally powerful slashes, which frequently beat third man, and the ball came from the middle of the bat. Taking the ball one-handed above his head, Benaud was toppled backwards by the force of the blow. It is doubtful if any eye from the ringside followed the course of the ball.

There have been several visiting teams whose fielding has been a joy in itself. The Australians always seem to excel collectively, and their fielding has the air of a well-organized mass attack rather than a passive or individual exercise. Always to be remembered is their tremendous throwing, as exemplified by O'Neill, Harvey, and Sheahan. The South Africans have always been efficient and recently brilliant, with Bland truly spectacular. West Indies strike as being more variable, with several, notably Sobers, of great versatility. England, despite the weight of their seasonal domestic programme, have of recent years been well up to international form, and the slip fielding of Sharpe was one of the grandest features of 1969.

It was in the last season of the decade that Lord's saw one of its more remarkable all-round feats there or on any other cricket ground. As Sobers' performance in the first match between England and the World XI has already been mentioned in the preceding chapter it is not necessary to do more than remind the reader that having bowled his fastish "seamers" as well as ever in his career he followed up this success with a devastating innings of 183. Seldom can any captain have had a greater practical hand in the defeat of the opposing side in international cricket. This resounding achievement was also satisfactory in that it stayed any fears that length and intensity of service was threatening to bring Sobers' grand career to a premature end.

45

Patterns of the Past and Trends of the Future

IN this chronicle of Lord's I have taken a widely catholic view of my brief, for the headquarters of cricket reaches out its arms to embrace the whole cricket universe. It is the story of a generation in which Lord's has been the cockpit of a revolution; in this short span profound changes have occurred whose closest parallels were the growing pains of the formative years of the mid-nineteenth century.

Lord's itself has suffered a transformation in its whole aspect. A few friendly landmarks—even the obsolete stacks of the power station—remain to offer reassurance in a still relatively pleasant residential neighbourhood, but the former semi-rural atmosphere has become utterly metropolitan. St John's Wood has lost the character of a quiet suburb with the cricket ground as an island in the midst of Regency villas only one step removed from farmland. Their sites have been invaded by great blocks of flats, towering above the ground to house a population multiplied a thousandfold, and heavy traffic grinds along St John's Wood Road so that those who seek to cross over to the ground do so at their peril. And inside, cherished landmarks have vanished; the Tavern, the Clock Tower, and the friendly "A" Enclosure no longer offer rendezvous for friends. Since the Eton and Harrow match has shed all its glamour as the grand finale to the London season, it matters little that the most favoured pitches for the gay coaches are engulfed by the vast new stands which hem in the Pavilion on either side. Now, since the disappearance of the Tavern, its seniority is properly advanced to patriarchal status. Once it was hard pushed to accommodate a membership of 7500; now, anachronistically, it supports a membership of twice that number, but it is splitting at the seams to house a staff which, to match the escalation of modern administration, has doubled its pre-War strength.

There is no fixed date when M.C.C. became the Governing

Body of cricket, any more than the exact day is known when the Club was founded. The situation just happened; the leading patrons of cricket formed the Club, and so the Club became paramount, and cricketers everywhere looked to M.C.C. for leadership. But 1970 can be pinpointed as the year when M.C.C.'s authority was delegated to the Cricket Council. By their abdication from national sovereignty they have become citizens of a private members' club—a club which, with a new ceiling of 16,000, must surely be the largest cricket club in the world. However, in the new administration M.C.C. have retained their world-wide authority as administrators of the Laws, and they are still the owners of the ground which cricketers everywhere regard as the greatest in the world. Lord's is now the centre of a vast administrative network which is more complex than ever before.

A review of M.C.C.'s endeavours in the realm of first-class cricket since the War must appear as a catalogue of losing battles against financial pricks and of unavailing struggles to come to grips with stagnation in the game. The post-War honeymoon was soon over, leaving English cricket face to face with the economic facts of a new pattern of life and leisure which, hand in hand with the malaise of lifeless play, dragged attendances down to a small fraction of their 1947 bonanza.

Numerous committees of enquiry have worked almost ceaselessly to diagnose the nature of the ills which have beset the game and advise on what the remedy should be. Seemingly endless changes and experiments have been prescribed with very little success. The counties, always more conservative than M.C.C., have resisted radical alterations in the structure of first-class cricket, but in the last few years the county game has undergone a minor revolution by the introduction of one-day fixtures for the Gillette Cup and the Player's County League. The future structure is still *sub judice*. It may be that the T.C.C.B. will eventually decide to reduce the First-class Championship to one match a week. Whether or not the matches are then confined to week-ends could be a matter of local preference, for there are some provincial grounds in holiday centres which, unlike Lord's, command their best attendances in mid-week.

The root causes of the ills which have beset the game in recent years seem to me to stem from social economy. Financial insecurity, it could be argued, lay behind the "go canny" attitude which captivated the players, and economic pressure kept away the amateurs who might have corrected the trend. Since the sham of spurious amateurism has been swept away cricketers may have improved their status, but seven-days-a-week professionalism has surely robbed the game of spontaneous enjoyment.

The financial decline of county finances has accelerated to landslide proportions; more than half the counties are in serious difficulty, and their combined deficit of the last five years is a quarter of a million pounds. The prosperous clubs are those whose supporters clubs have enriched them with revenue gained from football pools. The outstanding example is, of course, Warwickshire, whose Supporters Association, having provided all the capital required by their own county, have directed their considerable resources towards helping poorer counties and financing the central administration of cricket. So one salient characteristic of this generation is the dependence of cricket on football for finance. Another is industrial sponsorship. Not long ago M.C.C. would have looked askance at this type of commercial promotion; now, in common with charitable causes and a host of other games, they have learnt to accept it gratefully. In their own finances M.C.C. have offset declining match receipts and rising costs by 100 per cent increase in the number of members, for whom capital reserves have been expended to provide accommodation.

Life, thank goodness, is never static; it is the proverbial hallmark of the aged to say that things aren't what they were. If I stick my neck out and say that I doubt very much that the first-class player today gets as much fun from the game as his father did, I know that I may be influenced by my own exceptional good fortune in having been introduced to cricket-watching at Lord's as "Patsy" Hendren bowed out and Edrich and Compton were launched like a pair of meteors. Walter Robins and Jim Sims spun their leg breaks and googlies uninhibited by any charge of prodigality, and, on any evening, big Jim Smith could empty the Tavern with his mighty drives. Middlesex were an exciting side under an exuberant captain, and the excitement was revived in the first post-War seasons.

Whatever one-day cricket may have to offer in terms of instant enjoyment, the two-innings match is still the backbone of the game. Millions are avidly interested in Test Matches, whether they watch in person or as television viewers, or merely follow progress on radio or in the Press. Cricketers cannot become international players without training in first-class matches—and, incidentally, "instant" cricket will cease to have any advantage over the village green if its players are not of first-class potential. It is a cliché to say that first-class cricket in England is at the crossroads, but so it is, as never before. While respecting the sincere efforts of the many good and wise men who have worked unsparingly to cure the ills of this generation, I believe the game has suffered from a super-fluity of doctoring, which has disconcerted spectators and un-settled the players. On the road forward into a new decade it is the players, I believe, who must take the initiative to recover their eagerness under determined leadership on the field rather than through legislation from the committee room.

Appendix 1

A Statistical Survey

.compiled by Bill Frindall
First-class matches only

TEAM RECORDS

Highest Innings Totals (600 and over)

729 for 6	Australia *v.* England	1930
665	West Indies *v.* Middlesex	1939
612 for 8	Middlesex *v.* Nottinghamshire	1921
610 for 5	Australians *v.* Gentlemen	1948
609 for 8	Cambridge University *v.* M.C.C.	1913
608 for 7	Middlesex *v.* Hampshire	1919
607	M.C.C. *v.* Cambridge University	1902

Lowest Innings Totals

Under 20:

15	M.C.C. *v.* Surrey	1839
16	M.C.C. *v.* Surrey	1872
17	Gentlemen of Kent *v.* Gentlemen of England	1850
18	The B's *v.* England	1831
18	Australians *v.* M.C.C.	1896
19	M.C.C. *v.* Australians	1878

Lowest total this century:

27	M.C.C. *v.* Yorkshire	1902

Totals under 50 since 1945:

43	M.C.C. *v.* Cambridge University	1951
43	Kent *v.* Middlesex	1953
47	New Zealand *v.* England	1958

Highest Match Aggregates

1601	England (425 and 375) *v.* Australia (729 for 6 and 72 for 3)	1930
1502	M.C.C. (392 and 426 for 4) *v.* New Zealanders (460 and 224 for 4)	1927
1443	Middlesex (478 and 244 for 7) *v.* Gloucestershire (478 and 243 for 7)	1938

Lowest Match Aggregates (completed matches)

105¹M.C.C. (33 and 19) *v.* Australians (41 and 12 for 1)	1878
134 England (81) *v.* The B's (18 and 35)	1831
149 England (73 and 2 for no wicket) *v.* Kent (33 and 41)	1858

¹ World record.

Tie Matches

M.C.C. (69 and 107) *v.* Oxford and Cambridge Universities
(115 and 61)   1839
The first recorded tie in first-class cricket
Middlesex (272 and 225) *v.* South Africans (287 and 210)   1904
Middlesex (371 and 69) *v.* Leicestershire (239 and 201)   1907

Matches completed in One Day

Up to the end of the 1970 English season there were only 52 recorded instances of first-class matches anywhere in the world being completed in a single day. Almost half of these (23) have occurred at Lord's, including the shortest match on record, which was completed in just over three hours' actual play:

Somerset (35 and 44) *v.* Middlesex (86)   May 23, 1899

PLAYERS' RECORDS: BATTING

Highest Individual Innings (300 and over)

316 not out J. B. Hobbs: Surrey *v.* Middlesex	1926
315 not out P. Holmes: Yorkshire *v.* Middlesex	1925

Highest Career Aggregates (15,000 and over)

	Innings	Not out	Runs	Highest score	Average
E. Hendren	589	75	25,097	277 not out	48.82
W. J. Edrich	457	42	17,019	245	41.00
D. C. S. Compton	381	33	16,732	252 not out	48.08
J. W. Hearne	469	52	15,844	234 not out	37.99
J. D. Robertson	430	24	15,741	229	38.77

Most Hundreds (25 and over)

E. Hendren	74		P. F. Warner	32
D. C. S. Compton	48		W. G. Grace	29
W. J. Edrich	37		J. W. Hearne	28
J. D. Robertson	34			

Hundred in Each Innings of a Match

Prior to 1946 there were 18 instances (by 15 players) of a batsman scoring a hundred in each innings of a first-class match at Lord's: B. J. T. Bosanquet, K. S. Duleepsinhji, and E. Hendren did so twice. Instances 1946–70:

J. D. Robertson	147 and 137 Middlesex v. Sussex	1948
R. J. Christiani	131 not out and 100 not out West Indians v. Middlesex	1950
P. H. Parfitt	122 and 114 Middlesex v. Pakistanis	1962
B. J. Booth	109 and 104 Leicestershire v. Middlesex	1965

Fast Scoring

Fastest 50
14 minutes, F. T. Mann (53): Middlesex v. Nottinghamshire   1921
Fastest 100's
55 minutes, F. G. J. Ford (112): Middlesex v. Philadelphians   1897
57 minutes, G. L. Jessop (124): Gloucestershire v. Middlesex   1901
Fastest 200
135 minutes, G. L. Jessop (233): Rest v. Yorkshire   1901
Century before Lunch
On First Day
Pre-1946   W. H. B. Evans, P. V. Williams, J. D. Robertson
1957   J. D. Robertson (119): Middlesex v. Sussex
On Other Days
Pre-1946   W. W. Read, J. B. Hobbs, J. N. Grover, D. C. S. Compton, K. R. Miller
1948   W. J. Edrich (128): Gentlemen v. Australians
1962   R. M. Prideaux (109): Gentlemen v. Players

Carrying Bat through a Completed Innings

Prior to 1946 this feat was achieved on 63 occasions by 47 players, P. F. Warner doing so 8 times and W. G. Grace 4.

1947	B. Mitchell	103 (198) South Africans v. M.C.C.
1949	M. B. Hofmeyr	64 (169) Oxford U. v. Cambridge U.
1951	F. A. Lowson	76 (218) Yorkshire v. M.C.C.
1951	A. H. Phebey	54 (126) Kent v. Middlesex
1954	N. H. Rogers	56 (126) M.C.C. v. Surrey
1963	E. D. A. McMorris	190 (383) West Indians v. Middlesex
1965	J. M. Brearley	90 (197) M.C.C. v. Yorkshire
1969	G. M. Turner	43 (131) New Zealand v. England

Highest Partnerships for Each Wicket

1st:	312, W. E. Russell and M. J. Harris: Middlesex *v.* Pakistanis	1967
2nd:	380, F. A. Tarrant and J. W. Hearne: Middlesex *v.* Lancashire	1914
3rd:	424*, W. J. Edrich and D. C. S. Compton: Middlesex *v.* Somerset	1948
	The highest third-wicket partnership in England	
4th:	330, W. Barnes and W. Gunn: M.C.C. *v.* Yorkshire	1885
5th:	289*, Nawab of Pataudi (Snr) and L. E. G. Ames: England *v.* Rest	1934
6th:	274*, G. St A. Sobers and D. A. J. Holford: West Indies *v.* England	1966
7th:	289, G. Goonesena and G. W. Cook: Cambridge U. *v.* Oxford U.	1957
8th:	246, L. E. G. Ames and G. O. Allen: England *v.* New Zealand	1931
9th:	184, A. C. Russell and L. C. Eastman: Essex *v.* Middlesex	1920
10th:	230, R. W. Nicholls and W. Roche: Middlesex *v.* Kent	1899
	* Unbroken partnership.	

PLAYERS' RECORDS: BOWLING

Ten Wickets in an Innings

E. Hinkly	Kent *v.* England[1]	1848
	on his first appearance at Lord's	
J. Wisden	North *v.* South[1]	1850
	all bowled	
S. E. Butler	10 for 38 Oxford U. *v.* Cambridge U.	1871
A. Shaw	10 for 73 M.C.C. *v.* North	1874
A. Fielder	10 for 90 Players *v.* Gentlemen	1906
G. O. Allen	10 for 40 Middlesex *v.* Lancashire	1929

[1] *No analysis was preserved for either of the two earlier instances*

Sixteen Wickets in a Match

E. Hinkly	Kent *v.* England	1848
	on his first appearance at Lord's	
C. D. Marsham	16 for 93 Gentlemen of England *v.* Gentlemen of M.C.C.	1855
J. Southerton	16 for 52 South *v.* North	1875
	16 wickets in one day	
W. G. Grace	16 for 60 M.C.C. *v.* Nottinghamshire	1885
Best post-War match analysis		
J. C. Laker	15 for 97 Surrey *v.* M.C.C.	1954

Most Wickets in a Career

J. T. Hearne   1719 wickets (average 16.42)
F. J. Titmus has been easily the most successful post-War bowler at
Lord's. At the end of the 1970 season his total number of wickets stood
at 974, average 21.61.

Four Wickets with Consecutive Balls

J. B. Hide	Sussex *v*. M.C.C.	1890
F. Martin	M.C.C. *v*. Derbyshire	1895
A. E. Trott	Middlesex *v*. Somerset	1907

His Benefit match; he performed a second hat-trick in the same innings

Hat-tricks

Pre-1946	40 instances of the hat-trick; 5 bowlers achieved the feat twice:	
	H. J. Enthoven in 1926 and 1934	
	J. T. Hearne in 1902 and 1912	
	J. W. Hearne in 1911 and 1914	
	R. W. V. Robins in 1929 and 1937	
	A. E. Trott twice in one innings in 1907	
1947	J. M. Sims	Middlesex *v*. South Africans
1948	A. E. G. Rhodes	M.C.C. *v*. Surrey
1950	C. J. Knott	Gentlemen *v*. Players
1951	J. A. Young	Middlesex *v*. Lancashire
1956	A. E. Moss	Middlesex *v*. Gloucestershire
1956	D. V. Smith	M.C.C. *v*. Oxford University
1958	F. S. Trueman	Yorkshire *v*. M.C.C.
1960	G. Griffin	South Africa *v*. England

PLAYERS' RECORDS: ALL-ROUND CRICKET

All-round Cricket in a Match

Hundred in Each Innings and 10 Wickets:
B. J. T. Bosanquet (103 and 100 not out, 3 for 75 and 8 for 53)
   Middlesex *v*. Sussex   1905
100 Runs and 10 Wickets:
The following 13 players have achieved this rare match double at
Lord's, but no-one has done so since 1930:
G. O. Allen, W. W. Armstrong, R. H. B. Bettington, B. J. T.
Bosanquet, F. M. Buckland, W. Flowers (twice), W. G. Grace
(thrice), R. J. Gregory, J. W. Hearne (4 times), G. H. Hirst, P. R. Le
Couteur, H. W. Lee, and A. E. Trott (thrice).

Leading All-round Career Records

	Runs	Average	Wickets	Average
J. W. Hearne	15,844	37.99	883	22.54
W. G. Grace	12,690	36.78	654	14.73
F. J. Titmus	9,118	23.80	974	21.61

PLAYERS' RECORDS: WICKET-KEEPING

Most Dismissals in an Innings

7   W. F. Price   (7 caught) Middlesex *v.* Yorkshire   1937

Most Dismissals in a Match

9   A. E. Newton   (6 caught, 3 stumped) Somerset *v.*
    Middlesex   1901
9   G. L. Langley   (8 caught, 1 stumped) Australia *v.*
    England   1956
9   J. T. Murray   (8 caught, 1 stumped) Middlesex *v.*
    Hampshire   1965

PLAYERS' RECORDS: FIELDING

Most Catches in an Innings

6   A. J. Webbe   Gentlemen *v.* Players   1877

Most Catches in a Match

7   A. F. J. Ford   Middlesex *v.* Gloucestershire   1882

POST-WAR MEMORABILIA

D. C. S. Compton: Scored 1000 runs in a season at Lord's on six
occasions (plus three pre-War). His aggregate of 2052 (average
76.00) in 1947 is an all-time Lord's record as is his total of eight
hundreds for that season, when he reached 50 in 16 of his 30 innings.

W. J. Edrich: Scored 1000 runs in a season at Lord's on eight occasions
(plus three pre-War), including his highest aggregate: 1592, average
63.68, in 1938).

J. D. Robertson: Scored 1000 runs in a season at Lord's on nine
occasions. His best season was 1947, when he totalled 1691 runs
(average 58.31) with seven hundreds.

F. J. Titmus: Took 108 wickets (average 16.02) in 1958, and is the only
bowler to take 100 wickets in a post-War season at Lord's.

TEST MATCHES AT LORD'S

Lord's has staged 57 Test Matches since 1884, including one between Australia and South Africa during the Triangular Tournament of 1912. England's record is as follows:

Opponents	Played	Won	Lost	Drawn
Australia	22	5	8	9
South Africa	10	6	1	3
West Indies	8	4	1	3
New Zealand	6	3	—	3
India	6	6	—	—
Pakistan	3	1	—	2
Rest of the World	1	—	1	—
Totals	56	25	11	20

Results of Post-War Tests

Season	Opponents	Result	Captains England	Opponents
1946	India	England: 10 wickets	W. R. Hammond	Nawab of Pataudi, Snr
1947	South Africa	England: 10 wickets	N. W. D. Yardley	A. Melville
1948	Australia	Australia: 409 runs	N. W. D. Yardley	D. G. Bradman
1949	New Zealand	Drawn	F. G. Mann	W. A. Hadlee
1950	West Indies	West Indies: 326 runs	N. W. D. Yardley	J. D. C. Goddard
1951	South Africa	England: 10 wickets	F. R. Brown	A. D. Nourse
1952	India	England: 8 wickets	L. Hutton	Vijay Hazare
1953	Australia	Drawn	L. Hutton	A. L. Hassett
1954	Pakistan	Drawn	L. Hutton	A. H. Kardar
1955	South Africa	England: 71 runs	P. B. H. May	J. E. Cheetham
1956	Australia	Australia: 185 runs	P. B. H. May	I. W. Johnson
1957	West Indies	England: innings and 36 runs	P. B. H. May	J. D. C. Goddard
1958	New Zealand	England: innings and 148 runs	P. B. H. May	J. R. Reid
1959	India	England: 8 wickets	P. B. H. May	P. Roy
1960	South Africa	England: innings and 73 runs	M. C. Cowdrey	D. J. McGlew
1961	Australia	Australia: 5 wickets	M. C. Cowdrey	R. N. Harvey
1962	Pakistan	England: 9 wickets	E. R. Dexter	Javed Burki
1963	West Indies	Drawn	E. R. Dexter	F. M. M. Worrell
1964	Australia	Drawn	E. R. Dexter	R. B. Simpson
1965	New Zealand	England: 7 wickets	M. J. K. Smith	J. R. Reid
	South Africa	Drawn	M. J. K. Smith	P. L. van der Merwe
1966	West Indies	Drawn	M. C. Cowdrey	G. St A. Sobers
1967	India	England: innings and 124 runs	D. B. Close	Nawab of Pataudi, Jnr
	Pakistan	Drawn	D. B. Close	Hanif Mohammad
1968	Australia	Drawn	M. C. Cowdrey	W. M. Lawry
1969	West Indies	Drawn	R. Illingworth	G. St A. Sobers
	New Zealand	England: 230 runs	R. Illingworth	G. T. Dowling
1970	RW	RW-Inns and 80	R. Illingworth	G. St A. Sobers

Summary of Test Match Records

Highest innings total: 729 for 6 Australia 1930
Lowest innings total: 47 New Zealand 1958
Highest individual score: 254 D. G. Bradman (Australia) 1930
Best innings analysis: 8 for 43 H. Verity v. Australia 1934
Best match analysis: 15 for 104 H. Verity v. Australia 1934
Hundred on Test debut: H. Graham (107) (Australia) 1893
J. H. Hampshire (107) v. West Indies 1969
Hundred in each innings: G. A. Headley 106 and 107 (West Indies) 1939
Hundred before lunch: J. B. Hobbs v. South Africa 1924
Fastest 50: 36 minutes J. J. Lyons (Australia) 1890
Fastest 100: 95 minutes P. W. Sherwell (South Africa) 1907
Fastest 200: 234 minutes D. G. Bradman (Australia) 1930
Carrying bat through completed innings:
J. E. Barrett 67 (176) for Australia 1890
W. Bardsley 193 (383) for Australia 1926
W. A. Brown 206 (422) for Australia 1938
G. M. Turner 43 (131) for New Zealand 1969
Highest partnership for any wicket:
370 (3rd) W. J. Edrich (189) and D. C. S. Compton (208) v. South Africa 1947
Hat-trick: G. Griffin (South Africa) 1960

Middlesex Players Capped by England since 1945

The following list includes all post-War Tests and not just those played at Lord's. The total number of post-War appearances is given in parenthesis.

G. O. Allen (3)	A. E. Moss (9)	W. E. Russell (10)
D. C. S. Compton (70)	J. T. Murray (21)	F. J. Titmus (49)
J. G. Dewes (5)	P. H. Parfitt (34)	J. J. Warr (2)
W. J. Edrich (30)	J. S. E. Price (10)	J. A. Young (8)
F. G. Mann (7)	J. D. Robertson (11)	

Gentlemen v. Players at Lord's (1806-1962)

Played	Gentlemen	Players	Drawn
137	41	68	28

Results since 1945

		Captains	
Season	Result	Gentlemen	Players
1946	Players: innings and 140	W. R. Hammond	J. Hardstaff, Jnr
1947	Drawn	N. W. D. Yardley	L. E. G. Ames

Captains

Season	Result	Gentlemen	Players
1948	Players: 7 wickets	N. W. D. Yardley	L. Hutton
1949	Players: 4 wickets	F. G. Mann	D. C. S. Compton
1950	Drawn	F. R. Brown	H. E. Dollery
1951	Players: 21 runs	N. D. Howard	D. C. S. Compton
1952	Players: 2 runs	F. R. Brown	L. Hutton
1953	Gentlemen: 95 runs	F. R. Brown	C. Washbrook
1954	Players: 49 runs	D. S. Sheppard	D. C. S. Compton
1955	Players: 20 runs	D. J. Insole	A. V. Bedser
1956	Drawn	C. H. Palmer	C. Washbrook
1957	Drawn	P. B. H. May	D. C. S. Compton
1958	Drawn	D. J. Insole	T. G. Evans
1959	Drawn	P. B. H. May	D. Brookes
1960	Drawn	M. C. Cowdrey	J. B. Statham
1961	Players: 172 runs	P. B. H. May	W. Watson
1962	Drawn	E. R. Dexter	F. S. Trueman

Summary of Records

Highest innings total	579	Players	1926
Lowest innings total:	24	Players	1829
Highest individual score:	232 not out	C. B. Fry (Gentlemen)	1903
Best innings analysis	10 for 90	A. Fielder (Players)	1906

Highest partnership for any wicket:

309 not out (3rd) C. B. Fry (232 not out) and A. C. MacLaren (168 not out) for Gentlemen 1903

Most post-War appearances: 12, T. G. Evans (Players)

W. R. Hammond and W. J. Edrich shared the distinction of appearing for both the Gentlemen and the Players at Lord's.

UNIVERSITY MATCH (1827-1970)

The following results table includes the five matches played away from Lord's in the mid-nineteenth century:

Played	Cambridge	Oxford	Drawn
126	50	44	32

Results since 1945

Captains

Season	Result	Cambridge	Oxford
1946	Oxford: 6 wickets	P. E. Bodkin	D. H. Macindoe
1947	Drawn	G. L. Willatt	M. P. Donnelly
1948	Oxford: innings and 8 runs	J. M. Mills	H. A. Pawson

Captains

Season	Result	Cambridge	Oxford
1949	Cambridge: 7 wickets	D. J. Insole	C. B. van Ryneveld
1950	Drawn	G. H. G. Doggart	D. B. Carr
1951	Oxford: 21 runs	J. J. Warr	M. B. Hofmeyr
1952	Drawn	D. S. Sheppard	P. D. S. Blake
1953	Cambridge: 2 wickets	R. G. Marlar	A. L. Dowding
1954	Drawn	M. H. Bushby	M. C. Cowdrey
1955	Drawn	D. R. W. Silk	C. C. P. Williams
1956	Drawn	M. E. L. Melluish	M. J. K. Smith
1957	Cambridge: innings and 186 runs	G. Goonesena	A. C. Walton
1958	Cambridge: 99 runs	E. R. Dexter	J. A. Bailey
1959	Oxford: 85 runs	D. J. Green	A. C. Smith
1960	Drawn	C. B. Howland	A. C. Smith
1961	Drawn	D. Kirby	C. D. Drybrough
1962	Drawn	A. R. Lewis	C. D. Drybrough
1963	Drawn	J. M. Brearley	Nawab of Pataudi, Jnr
1964	Drawn	J. M. Brearley	D. R. Worsley
1965	Drawn	R. C. White	J. D. Martin
1966	Oxford: innings and 9 runs	D. L. Murray	R. M. C. Gilliat
1967	Drawn	S. G. Russell	G. N. S. Ridley
1968	Drawn	G. A. Cottrell	F. S. Goldstein
1969	Drawn	A. M. Jorden	F. S. Goldstein
1970	Drawn	A. M. Jorden	M. St J. W. Burton

Summary of Records

Highest innings total:	503	Oxford	1900
Lowest innings total:	32	Oxford	1878
Highest individual score:	238 not out	Nawab of Pataudi, Snr (Oxford)	1931
Best innings analysis:	10 for 38	S. E. Butler (Oxford)	1871
Best match analysis:	15 for 95	S. E. Butler (Oxford)	1871

Highest partnership for any wicket:

289 (7th) G. Goonesena (211) and G. W. Cook (111 not out) for Cambridge   1957

Appendix 2

M.C.C. and Youth

M.C.C.'s first active participation in coaching young cricketers was the inauguration of the Easter Cricket Classes by Sir Francis Lacey. Not only has the curriculum of these classes been extended, but the net has been thrown wider to include boys outside the privileged ranks of members' sons and even to admit girls.

In 1970 tradition was struck a shattering blow by the temporary banishment of the time-honoured Eton *v.* Harrow match—ousted when the need arose to rearrange the fixture list to suit a South African tour which was shortened and condensed. Of the traditional schools matches, Cheltenham and Haileybury, Clifton and Tonbridge, and Beaumont and Oratory have all disappeared, leaving Rugby and Marlborough as sole survivors. This need not be taken as an indication of some falling off in M.C.C.'s interest in the schools; indeed, the reverse is the case. For a variety of reasons—social, economic, and educational—support for the schools matches at Lord's has declined catastrophically. Eton *v.* Harrow has become a sad occasion, an insubstantial shadow of former glories. It may well be that interest in all the Lord's Schools matches will be sharpened if they are played at the schools, even though the boys will miss the honour of playing at Lord's. For M.C.C. the balance of priorities has shifted towards reviving the ground from its fatigued condition induced by years of overwork. But generous compensation is offered to the schools in the stupendous programme of out matches; in the two and a half months from May until mid-July no fewer than 142 matches are currently played against schools and colleges, out of a total of 174 matches in the same period. The best schoolboy players, both from the public and the State schools, are still brought to Lord's for representative matches, and in 1965–66 M.C.C. sent a schools team, captained by D. R. Walsh from Marlborough, on a tour to South Africa.

Since 1948, however, M.C.C.'s greatest endeavour has been towards the grass roots—the boys who lack the privileges of their brothers at the public schools—believing that all should be given the chance to receive what cricket has to offer in terms of physical wellbeing, fun, character-building, enjoyment, and fellowship. It was the role of the 1949 Cricket Enquiry to discover how cricket might be encouraged where opportunities were lacking, and their achievement was the founding of the M.C.C.

Youth Cricket Association, whose energies have been chiefly directed
towards the advancement of coaching. Their first task was to standard-
ize technique and the basic skills of coaching and to introduce the art of
group coaching as developed by Mr Harry Crabtree. By "standard-
ization" it was not intended to enchain a budding Compton in a rigid
groove. The aim was rather to train schoolmasters and youth leaders to
give basic instruction in schools and clubs where facilities for individual
coaching were non-existent. In 1952, after several years of careful
preparation by Mr Altham, Mr Allen, and their advisers, the first
edition of the *M.C.C. Cricket Coaching Book* was published as a "Bible"
for cricket coaches. Their pupils were catered for by a pocket-sized
handbook called *Cricket—play the game*. Royalties from these and other
publications sponsored by the Association have been ploughed back to
further its aims. The written word was supplemented by visual aids:
batting and bowling films, film loops, film strips, and wall charts. At
Lilleshall Mr Altham regularly presided over the courses at which
senior coaches qualified for the Advanced Coaching Certificate,
inspiring students and staff alike by his own avid enthusiasm. These
were the coaches—many of them professional cricketers—who would
train youth coaches under the direction of the Area Youth Councils,
which were set up in a network covering the whole country. In the first
ten years more than 15,000 schoolmasters, youth leaders, and others
attended these "county courses", and senior coaches and holders of the
Advanced Certificate conducted courses in at least a dozen overseas
countries, including East and West Africa.

Parallel with the Y.C.A.'s campaign for coaching, the Cricket
Enquiry's plea for better facilities led to research in the field of artificial
pitches. On the personal suggestion of the Duke of Edinburgh, in the
year in which he was President both of M.C.C. and the National
Playing Fields Association, these two bodies undertook a joint enquiry
which resulted in two invaluable reports giving specifications for non-
turf pitches at widely different prices, to cater for every type of condition
and usage. Their work has now been taken up by the Wrigley Foundation, whose object is to stimulate and encourage in the young an interest
in playing cricket and achieving greater efficiency and skill at the game.
The great bulk of M.C.C.'s work for young cricketers has now passed to
the National Cricket Association, whose Secretary, Mr Dunbar, is
currently pressing with great enthusiasm the case for the artificial pitch.
On May 31, 1970, M.C.C. finally dissolved the Y.C.A. and handed
over its assets of some £10,000 to the Altham Memorial Fund as
working capital for the fund's objects of running courses for young
cricketers. The N.C.A. have vested responsibility for the work of the
Youth Cricket Association in their own National Coaching Committee
and Junior Youth Standing Committee.

Appendix 3

M.C.C. and the Arts

SIR PELHAM WARNER'S story of Lord's had an appendix in which Lord Ullswater escorted the reader on an imaginary tour around the pictures in the Long Room, and wrote of the inestimable benefit bestowed upon posterity by Sir Spencer Ponsonby Fane when he formed the nucleus of the Collection. Between the Wars the Collection had been cared for devotedly as a labour of love by Captain T. H. Carlton Levick, who strengthened the debt M.C.C. already owed him by his typically generous help and courtesy to the young and inexperienced curator who was appointed in 1945. The Collection, as I remember it then, with the bulk of the Library packed away in lockers and the pictures hung Victorian-style, almost touching each other from floor to ceiling, seemed extensive. Now, reviewing the list of accessions which have piled up since, I am amazed by what a comparatively large proportion has been added. There can be no doubt that this influx has been attracted by the creation of the Memorial Gallery and the Committee's heightened sense of responsibility, as trustees of cricket heritage, to preserve for the public, at the headquarters of cricket, a record of the game's history and traditions.

During this century there have been four major gifts or bequests which have made the Collection what it is. The Library's initial claim to be anything like representative of cricket literature came with the bequest of Mr A. L. Ford's Library in 1930. Then, during the War, on the death of Sir Julien Cahn, Lady Cahn gave M.C.C. one copy of every book in his very extensive cricket library, into which the library of Mr F. S. Ashley-Cooper had been absorbed. These two main gifts dovetailed in such a way as to make the M.C.C. Library the most comprehensive specialized cricket library in the world, and every effort has since been made to maintain and improve the standard by adding newly published works and filling gaps in the past. The most important single gift of pictures came from the collection of Sir Jeremiah Colman, the first Baronet. In 1947 his son, the younger Sir Jeremiah, gave M.C.C. twenty of the choicest pictures, and then, with the Memorial Gallery in view, allowed them to take the pick of the remainder. In respect to the collector's wish that the pictures should be kept together, nearly all are hung in the Memorial Gallery, where the public can enjoy, amongst others, three of the most important in the whole collection, the *Cricket Match at Brading, Isle of Wight* (*c.* 1760), *The Game of Cricket* (once wrongly described as Hambledon), painted about 1790, and John Ritchie's *Village Cricket* (1855).

In 1967 the Rockley Wilson bequest of books, pictures, and ceramics further enriched every branch of the Collection, and a showcase was installed to commemorate his generosity.

The Memorial Gallery is almost wholly furnished with gifts of showcases and fittings in memory of club cricketers or individuals. The interesting series of paintings of cricket abroad, which form a girdle round the earth, are largely the offerings of the many overseas bodies whose grounds they represent. Because they were given specifically for the Memorial, this is where they are normally hung. But their numbers have multiplied so generously, far beyond the compass of the walls, that the changes have to be rung annually, with emphasis placed each year on the countries who are currently our guests. It would be idle to pretend that, as works of art, they all touch the heights. The best are probably the Sydney Cricket Ground by Lloyd Rees and, a late addition, Peter McIntyre's Auckland. Cricket is an unrewarding subject for an artist, and the number of modern painters who have portrayed it successfully is very small indeed. M.C.C., it must be confessed, have not been over-enthusiastic about acquiring, let alone sponsoring, modern works; cricket, not art, is after all their business. Sir William Worsley, who, as any visitor to Hovingham will have discovered, has a very discriminating taste, marked his presidency by the gift of Adrian Allinson's earthy portrayal of backyard cricket against a backcloth of the smoky chimneys of Stoke-on-Trent. The gift, he said, was intended as an incentive to M.C.C. to collect modern works. A few years ago, with the help of a grant in aid from the Victoria and Albert Museum Purchase Fund, the Committee bought Lawrence Toynbee's fluent portrayal of a West Indian batsman, called *Hit to Leg*.

Perhaps the most important, though not the most spectacular, development has been the build-up of three-dimensional objects. For instance, nearly all the famous players' bats have been acquired, mainly by gift, since 1945. The holding of ceramics and the other items we conveniently call "cricketana" was minimal until a conscious effort was made at my father's instigation to collect pottery. This side of the collection still lacks such really choice examples as the Lowestoft jug with the Boitard decoration or the, probably unique, bowl decorated after Gravelot's print of 1739 (which was loaned to M.C.C. for a season before its owner, Mr Anthony Baer, sent it to Melbourne). Nevertheless, purchases and gifts have made it reasonably representative.

This impressive expansion has put M.C.C. in the position of being able to offer a considerable service outside their direct responsibility for promoting cricket. The Curator is in constant demand to answer, verbally and by correspondence, a diversity of queries about cricket's history and records. Sometimes he is confronted by questions which would involve a lifetime of work—I remember being asked by one hopeful correspondent to send him the full score of every county match that had ever been played! Often it is only possible to supply a reading list or to invite the enquirer to use the Library. This in itself is a service which has developed since the War, and the Library is constantly occupied by authors and students. An extensive library of copy-photographs has been built up and grows almost daily to match the requirements of authors and publishers. All through the year visitors, often from overseas, ask to be shown round, and M.C.C. make what they hope is a worth-while contribution to education by arranging out-of-season conducted tours for schools and societies. Extramurally, the present Curator is prodigally generous in giving up his spare time for talks and lectures.

One of the benefits of this escalation of M.C.C.'s cultural activities—particularly the founding of a public gallery—has been recognition of its status as a specialized museum of national importance. A few years ago, when the Committee examined the pros and cons of creating an Educational Trust, there was no difficulty in securing Government acceptance of the draft deed; the Committee themselves withdrew because they felt that the time was inopportune. The status of a Trust would have been useful when, in 1968, the Trustees of the seventh Duke of Newcastle decided to sell the very interesting and attractive portrait of Mr Hope of Amsterdam, which had been loaned to M.C.C. The picture fetched £9975 at auction, and was afterwards bought by M.C.C. for the purchase price. Thanks to the standing of the M.C.C. Collection in public esteem, only £854 of this sum had to be found from the M.C.C.'s general funds; the balance was secured by generous donations from the Victoria and Albert Purchase Fund and the National Art Collectors Fund, from private subscriptions, and from the resources of the President's Fund.

Now that the M.C.C. Collection has achieved such generous proportions, much discrimination must be exercised in acquiring accessions; purchases must be restricted to items of exceptional interest or merit and to maintaining the continuity of the Library. There is one field in which the Collection is weak and might be strengthened at comparatively low cost—cricket dress. Some years ago when Don Bradman was induced to give his cricket boots there were those who thought that such an exhibit was inappropriate. How misguided were their objections, for history is created by the mundane things of today. How delighted M.C.C. would now be to be able to exhibit a pair of buckled shoes worn, say, by William Beldham at Lord's in 1787! Quite one of the most interesting recent gifts has been a costume of the eighteen-twenties worn by a cricketer called Henry Daw, of Christchurch, Hampshire.

Appendix 4

Tennis and Squash Rackets

Tennis

GOLD AND SILVER RACKETS

Tournament instituted for members, 1867; opened to non-members, 1870
Winners of Gold Racket from 1946

1946	W. M. Ross-Skinner	1954–58	Hon. M. G. L. Bruce
1947–49	W. D. Macpherson		(fourth Lord Aberdare)
1950	R. C. Riseley	1959	P. Kershaw
1951–52	W. D. Macpherson	1960–65	D. J. Warburg
1953	D. J. Warburg	1966–70	H. R. Angus

The winner holds the James Byng Gribble Cup, presented by Lady Pontifex, 1904.

Winners of Silver Racket from 1946

1946	W. D. Macpherson	1956–59	D. J. Warburg
1947–49	R. Aird	1960–61	P. Kershaw
1950	W. D. Macpherson	1962	Lord Aberdare
1951	R. C. Riseley	1963	P. Kershaw
1952–53	Hon. M. G. L. Bruce	1964–65	A. C. S. Tufton
1954	D. J. Warburg	1966–68	D. J. Warburg
1955	P. Kershaw	1969–70	A. C. S. Tufton

M.C.C. Members' Handicap
D. P. Henry Cup instituted 1953

1953	P. D. L. Cazenove	1962	F. C. S. Tufton
1954	J. H. Pawle	1963	C. B. R. Featherstonhaugh
1955	J. D. Whatman	1964	E. C. Pemberton
1956	F. C. S. Tufton	1965	Hon. I. H. Lawson-Johnson
1957	J. S. O. Haslewood	1966	W. H. Ollis
1958	D. M. Beadle	1967	D. M. F. Harvey
1959	C. H. W. Robson	1968	B. B. Waddy
1960	W. H. Ollis	1969	D. F. Sharpe
1961	D. A. L. Camm	1970	R. A. B. Gowland

M.C.C. Doubles Handicap
Instituted 1957
Ronald Aird Cup presented by J. D. Whatman, 1967

1957   M. M. Morton and C. J. Harrisson
1958   P. D. L. Cazenove and B. H. Bliss
1959   P. B. Greenwood and H. N. E. Alston
1960   P. D. L. Cazenove and W. H. Ollis
1961   J. W. Leonard and R. G. Gibbs
1962   J. W. Leonard and P. E. Matthews
1963   C. A. A. Black and R. Graham
1964   W. M. Ross-Skinner and Lord Kinnoull
1965   J. R. Greenwood and D. B. Carr
1966   D. B. Carr and P. de Lisle
1967   Major A. J. S. Griffin and M. G. Griffith
1968   M. A. Pugh and A. Wagg
1969   W. M. Ross-Skinner and D. A. de la B. Pritchett
1970   M. A. Pugh and A. R. Wagg

Professional Handicap—Taylor Cup
Presented to the Tennis and Rackets Association by General Taylor, 1934
Originally played at Prince's; restarted at Lord's, 1950

1950	R. Hughes (Manchester)	1963	D. Cull (Lord's)
1951	W. Holmes (Queen's)	1964	P. Dawes (Oxford)
1952–53	H. Johns (Lord's)	1965	I. B. Church (Leamington)
1954	W. Tutt (Cambridge)	1966	F. Willis (Manchester)
1955	R. Hughes (Manchester)	1967	I. B. Church (Leamington)
1956–57	H. Johns	1968	N. A. R. Cripps (Queen's)
1958–59	in abeyance	1969	F. Willis (Manchester)
1960	R. Hughes (Manchester)	1970	D. Cull (Lord's)
1961–62	in abeyance		

Amateur Tennis Singles Championship
Played at Lord's in 1958

Won by the American, Northrup R. Knox; Lord Aberdare was runner-up.

Squash Rackets

BATH CLUB CUP

For competition between London clubs

M.C.C., playing in Division I, won the Cup in 1949, 1954, 1955, and 1959.

Appendix 5

Office-holders of M.C.C.

Presidents

1946	General Sir Ronald F. Adam, Bart
1947	Captain Lord Cornwallis
1948	Brig.-General the Earl of Gowrie
1949	H.R.H. the Duke of Edinburgh
1950	Sir Pelham Warner
1951–52	W. Findlay
1952–53	The Duke of Beaufort
1953–54	The Earl of Rosebery
1954–55	Viscount Cobham
1955–56	Field-Marshal Earl Alexander of Tunis
1956–57	Viscount Monckton of Brenchley
1957–58	The Duke of Norfolk
1958–59	Marshal of the R.A.F. Viscount Portal of Hungerford
1959–60	H. S. Altham
1960–61	Sir Hubert Ashton
1961–62	Lieut.-Colonel Sir William Worsley, Bart
1962–63	Lieut.-Colonel Lord Nugent
1963–64	G. O. Allen
1964–65	R. H. Twining
1965–66	Lieut.-General Sir Oliver Leese, Bart
1966–67	Sir Alec Douglas-Home
1967–68	A. E. R. Gilligan
1968–69	R. Aird
1969–70	M. J. C. Allom
1970–71	Sir Cyril Hawker

Treasurers

1938–49	Ninth Viscount Cobham
1950–63	H. S. Altham
1963–64	Tenth Viscount Cobham
1965–	G. O. Allen

Trustees

1926–46	Sir Francis Lacey
1936–47	Colonel Sir Stanley F. Jackson
1938–50	Seventh Earl of Dartmouth
1946–49	S. Christopherson
1946–60	Sir Pelham Warner
1948–53	W. Findlay
1950–	Captain Lord Cornwallis
1954–69	R. H. Twining
1955–64	Lieut.-Colonel R. T. Stanyforth
1965–	Lieut.-Colonel Sir Terence Nugent
1969–	G. C. Newman

Secretaries

1936–52	Colonel R. S. Rait Kerr
1953–62	R. Aird
1962–	S. C. Griffith

Assistant Secretaries

1926–52	R. Aird
1949–	J. G. Dunbar
1952–62	S. C. Griffith
1962–	D. B. Carr
1967–	J. A. Bailey

Appendix 6

M.C.C. Tours

TEST TOURS

Australia and New Zealand

1946–47

W. R. Hammond*	L. B. Fishlock	R. Pollard
N. W. D. Yardley†	P. A. Gibb	T. P. B. Smith
A. V. Bedser	J. Hardstaff	W. Voce
D. C. S. Compton	L. Hutton	C. Washbrook
W. J. Edrich	J. T. Ikin	D. V. P. Wright
T. G. Evans	James Langridge	

Major R. Howard   (Manager)
W. Ferguson   (Scorer and Baggage Master)

1950–51

F. R. Brown*	J. G. Dewes	D. S. Sheppard
D. C. S. Compton†	T. G. Evans	R. T. Simpson
T. E. Bailey	W. E. Hollies	J. B. Statham
A. V. Bedser	L. Hutton	R. Tattersall
R. Berry	A. J. McIntyre	J. J. Warr
D. B. Close	W. G. Parkhouse	C. Washbrook
		D. V. P. Wright

Brigadier M. A. Green, J. A. Nash   (Joint Managers)
W. Ferguson   (Scorer and Baggage Master)

1954–55

L. Hutton*	D. C. S. Compton	J. E. McConnon
P. B. H. May†	M. C. Cowdrey	R. T. Simpson
K. V. Andrew	W. J. Edrich	J. B. Statham
R. Appleyard	T. G. Evans	F. H. Tyson
T. E. Bailey	T. W. Graveney	J. H. Wardle
A. V. Bedser	P. J. Loader	J. V. Wilson

C. G. Howard   (Manager)
G. Duckworth   (Scorer and Baggage Master)
H. W. Dalton   (Masseur)

* Captain   † Vice-captain

1958–59

P. B. H. May*	J. C. Laker	J. B. Statham
M. C. Cowdrey†	P. J. Loader	R. Subba Row
T. E. Bailey	G. A. R. Lock	R. Swetman
E. R. Dexter	C. A. Milton	F. S. Trueman
T. G. Evans	J. B. Mortimore	F. H. Tyson
T. W. Graveney	P. E. Richardson	W. Watson

F. R. Brown (Manager)
E. D. R. Eagar (Assistant Manager)
G. Duckworth (Scorer and Baggage Master)
D. Montague (Masseur)

1962–63

E. R. Dexter*	R. Illingworth	Rev. D. S. Sheppard
M. C. Cowdrey†	B. R. Knight	A. C. Smith
D. A. Allen	J. D. F. Larter	J. B. Statham
K. F. Barrington	J. T. Murray	F. J. Titmus
L. J. Coldwell	P. H. Parfitt	F. S. Trueman
T. W. Graveney	G. Pullar	

The Duke of Norfolk (Manager)
A. V. Bedser (Assistant Manager)
W. R. Watkins (Scorer and Baggage Master)
S. Cowan (Masseur)

1965–66

M. J. K. Smith*	D. J. Brown	J. T. Murray
M. C. Cowdrey†	J. H. Edrich	P. H. Parfitt
D. A. Allen	K. Higgs	J. M. Parks
R. W. Barber	I. J. Jones	W. E. Russell
K. F. Barrington	B. R. Knight	F. J. Titmus
G. Boycott	J. D. F. Larter	

S. C. Griffith (Manager)
J. T. Ikin (Assistant Manager)
J. Jennings (Physiotherapist)

1970–71

R. Illingworth*	J. H. Hampshire	R. W. Taylor
M. C. Cowdrey†	A. P. E. Knott	D. L. Underwood
G. Boycott	P. Lever	A. Ward
B. L. D'Oliveira	B. W. Luckhurst	R. G. D. Willis
J. H. Edrich	K. Shuttleworth	D. Wilson
K. W. R. Fletcher	J. A. Snow	

D. G. Clark (Manager)
B. W. Thomas (Assistant to Manager and Physiotherapist)

South Africa

1948-49

F. G. Mann*	C. Gladwin	M. F. Tremlett
S. C. Griffith†	L. Hutton	C. Washbrook
A. V. Bedser	R. O. Jenkins	A. Watkins
D. C. S. Compton	C. H. Palmer	D. V. P. Wright
J. F. Crapp	R. T. Simpson	J. A. Young
T. G. Evans		

Brigadier M. A. Green   (Manager)
W. Ferguson   (Scorer and Baggage Master)

1956-57

P. B. H. May*	J. C. Laker	P. E. Richardson
D. J. Insole†	P. J. Loader	J. B. Statham
T. E. Bailey	G. A. R. Lock	B. Taylor
D. C. S. Compton	A. S. M. Oakman	F. H. Tyson
M. C. Cowdrey	J. M. Parks	J. H. Wardle
T. G. Evans		

F. R. Brown   (Manager)
G. Duckworth   (Scorer and Baggage Master)
H. W. Dalton   (Masseur)

1964-65

M. J. K. Smith*	J. M. Brearley	P. H. Parfitt
E. R. Dexter†	D. J. Brown	J. M. Parks
D. A. Allen	T. W. Cartwright	J. S. E. Price
R. W. Barber	R. N. S. Hobbs	N. I. Thomson
K. F. Barrington	J. T. Murray	F. J. Titmus
G. Boycott		

D. B. Carr   (Manager)
M. McLennan   (Scorer and Baggage Master)
R. I. A. Nicholas   (Physiotherapist)

West Indies

1947-48

G. O. Allen*	J. Hardstaff	W. Place
K. Cranston†	R. Howorth	J. D. Robertson
D. Brookes	L. Hutton	G. A. Smithson
H. J. Butler	J. T. Ikin	M. F. Tremlett
T. G. Evans	J. C. Laker	J. H. Wardle

G. O. Allen   (Manager)
S. C. Griffith   (Assistant Manager)

1953-54

L. Hutton*	J. C. Laker	K. G. Suttle
C. H. Palmer	G. A. R. Lock	F. S. Trueman
T. E. Bailey	P. B. H. May	J. H. Wardle
D. C. S. Compton	A. E. Moss	W. Watson
T. G. Evans	R. T. Spooner	
T. W. Graveney	J. B. Statham	

C. H. Palmer (Player/Manager)

1959-60

P. B. H. May*	E. R. Dexter	M. J. K. Smith
M. C. Cowdrey†	T. Greenhough	J. B. Statham
D. A. Allen	R. Illingworth	R. Subba Row
K. V. Andrew	A. E. Moss	R. Swetman
K. F. Barrington	G. Pullar	F. S. Trueman

R. W. V. Robins (Manager)

1967-68

M. C. Cowdrey*	J. H. Edrich	G. A. R. Lock
F. J. Titmus†	T. W. Graveney	C. Milburn
K. F. Barrington	K. Higgs	J. M. Parks
G. Boycott	R. N. S. Hobbs	P. I. Pocock
D. J. Brown	I. J. Jones	J. A. Snow
B. L. D'Oliveira	A. P. E. Knott	

L. E. G. Ames (Manager)
J. Jennings (Physiotherapist)

India, Pakistan, and Ceylon

1951-52

N. D. Howard*	E. Leadbeater	D. Shackleton
D. B. Carr†	F. A. Lowson	R. T. Spooner
D. V. Brennan	C. J. Poole	J. B. Statham
T. W. Graveney	A. E. G. Rhodes	R. Tattersall
M. J. Hilton	F. Ridgway	A. Watkins
D. Kenyon	J. D. Robertson	

1961-62

E. R. Dexter*	A. Brown	G. Pullar
M. J. K. Smith†	B. R. Knight	P. E. Richardson
D. A. Allen	G. A. R. Lock	W. E. Russell
R. W. Barber	G. Millman	D. R. Smith
K. F. Barrington	J. T. Murray	D. W. White
J. Binks	P. H. Parfitt	

T. N. Pearce (Manager)
H. W. Dalton (Masseur)

India only

1963–64

M. J. K. Smith*   J. H. Edrich   J. M. Parks
M. J. Stewart†   I. J. Jones   J. S. E. Price
K. F. Barrington   B. R. Knight   P. J. Sharpe
J. G. Binks   J. D. F. Larter   F. J. Titmus
J. B. Bolus   J. B. Mortimore   D. Wilson
M. C. Cowdrey   P. H. Parfitt

D. G. Clark   (Manager)

Pakistan and Ceylon only

1968–69

M. C. Cowdrey*   J. H. Edrich   J. T. Murray
T. W. Graveney†   K. W. R. Fletcher   P. I. Pocock
D. J. Brown   R. N. S. Hobbs   R. M. Prideaux
R. M. H. Cottam   A. P. E. Knott   J. A. Snow
B. L. D'Oliveira   C. Milburn   D. L. Underwood

L. E. G. Ames   (Manager)
B. W. Thomas   (Physiotherapist)

OTHER TOURS (OUTSIDE EUROPE)

Canada and U.S.A.

1951

R. W. V. Robins*   W. G. Keighley   E. K. Scott
J. N. Bartlett   A. McCorquodale   J. R. Thompson
A. H. Broadhurst   A. W. H. Mallett   M. M. Walford
I. P. Campbell   A. G. Powell   J. J. Warr
G. H. Chesterton   C. R. D. Rudd

1959

D. R. W. Silk*   M. H. Bushby   J. F. Pretlove
J. R. Thompson   D. J. Green   R. M. Prideaux
J. A. Bailey   C. B. Howland   A. C. Smith
R. W. Barber   D. J. Mordaunt
P. I. Bedford   J. D. Piachaud

J. R. Thompson   (Player/Manager)

1967

D. R. W. Silk*   R. C. Kerslake   C. J. Saunders
R. A. Gale†   D. J. Mordaunt   J. P. Fellows-Smith
D. Bennett   A. E. Moss   E. D. Weekes
E. A. Clark   J. D. Piachaud
A. R. Duff   G. N. S. Ridley

Ceylon and Far East
1969–70

A. R. Lewis*
A. C. Smith
G. G. Arnold
W. Blenkiron
G. Boycott

K. W. R. Fletcher
R. M. C. Gilliat
J. H. Hampshire
A. Jones
P. I. Pocock

G. R. J. Roope
D. J. Shepherd
R. W. Taylor
D. Wilson

A. C. Smith   (Player/Manager)
J. S. Buller   (Umpire)

East Africa
1957–58

F. R. Brown*
S. C. Griffith
J. A. Bailey
G. W. Cook
G. H. G. Doggart

A. C. D. Ingleby-
   Mackenzie
C. J. M. Kenny
P. E. Richardson
R. V. C. Robins

D. R. W. Silk
M. J. K. Smith
J. J. Warr
W. R. Watkins

S. C. Griffith   (Player/Manager)

1963–64

M. J. K. Smith*
W. Watson
T. W. Cartwright
R. N. S. Hobbs

L. Johnson
I. J. Jones
R. J. Langridge
J. D. F. Larter

C. Milburn
J. B. Mortimore
P. H. Parfitt
M. J. Stewart

W. Watson (Player/Manager)

New Zealand
1960–61

D. R. W. Silk*
W. Watson†
D. A. Allen
R. W. Barber
M. J. Bear

J. D. F. Larter
J. T. Murray
D. E. V. Padgett
J. M. Parks
R. M. Prideaux

W. E. Russell
D. M. Sayer
D. R. Smith
W. J. Stewart
D. Wilson

J. H. Phillipps   (Manager)
F. R. Malden   (Baggage Master)

Pakistan
1955–56

"A" Team
D. B. Carr*
W. H. H. Sutcliffe†
K. F. Barrington
D. B. Close

M. J. Cowan
G. A. R. Lock
A. E. Moss
J. M. Parks
P. J. Sainsbury

H. W. Stephenson
R. Swetman
F. J. Titmus
M. Tompkin
A. Watkins

C. G. Howard   (Manager)

1966-67

Under 25

J. M. Brearley*	M. Bissex	A. Knott
D. J. Brown†	M. A. Buss	J. A. Ormrod
R. N. Abberley	K. W. R. Fletcher	P. I. Pocock
D. L. Amiss	R. N. S. Hobbs	D. L. Underwood
G. Arnold	R. A. Hutton	A. R. Windows

L. E. G. Ames   (Manager)

South Africa

M.C.C. Schoolboys 1965-66

D. R. Walsh*	P. J. Cattrall	A. M. Jorden
C. A. Richardson†	N. J. Cosh	A. B. Palfreman
D. L. Acfield	J. R. A. Cragg	D. W. Sharp
D. R. Aers	J. Denman	P. W. Watt
C. E. P. Carter	J. M. M. Hooper	

M. R. Ricketts   (Manager)

South America

1958-59

G. H. G. Doggart*	M. H. Bushby	D. M. Sayer
D. B. Carr†	C. B. Howland	D. R. W. Silk
J. A. Bailey	A. C. D. Ingleby-	M. J. K. Smith
M. J. Bear	Mackenzie	O. S. Wheatley
P. I. Bedford	R. V. C. Robins	

1964-65

A. C. Smith*	M. G. Griffith	D. J. Mordaunt
P. I. Bedford†	R. A. Hutton	J. D. Martin
A. R. Duff	R. I. Jefferson	R. C. White
R. A. Gale	R. C. Kerslake	
C. Gibson	A. R. Lewis	

Index

Index

ABERDARE, third Baron, 134 f.

A.C.C.C.: Committee *re* resumption of cricket (1943–44), 11; *re* amateur status, 171 f., 174 f., 186; *re* Clark Committee, 220–227; *re* county cricket, state of, 73 f.; approves Cricket Enquiry, 36; *re* K.O. competition, 12, 174; *re* laws and playing conditions, 17, 21, 96, 141, 153, 173 f., 182–184, 213; *re* overseas players, 262; *re* tours, 36, 109 f.

Adam, General Sir Ronald, 14

Adcock, N. A. T., 114 f., 162 f.

Aird, R., Assistant Secretary, 12, 61; Secretary, 63, 81, 101, 106 f., 161, 177; speeches, 94, 110 f., 141; President, 279–282

Alexander, Field-Marshal, first Earl, 110, 111, 208, 269

Alim-ud-Din, 103

Allen, G. O., as player, 12, 21, 47, 49, 99, 165, 188, 259; and Y.C.A., 36, 317; Chairman of Selectors, 111, 141, 176; Chairman of Cricket Sub-committee, 121, 152; as President, 181, 194 f., 203; Chairman of LBW Sub-committee, 183 f.; as Treasurer, 196, 263, 270, 282; Vice-Chairman of Throwing Sub-committee, 211; *re* Structure of County Cricket, 220, 225

Allinson, Adrian, 319

Allom, M. J. C., 233, 269

Almond, C., 160

Altham, H. S., on state of English cricket, 19 f.; Enquiry Committee (1949–56), 37, 42; Treasurer, 41 f., 159, 185; at A.C.C.C., 73, 96, 172, 174; Chairman of Selectors, 100, 111; Committee *re* Welfare of Cricket, 120–123; Y.C.A., 126, 317; Arts and Library Sub-committee, 126; President, 142 f.; at I.C.C., 153; as speaker, 185, 195; death, 208 f., 218; memorial fund, 209, 317

Amateur status, 40 f., 76, 119 f., 171–173, 174 f., 186; Standing Committee, 172 f.

Ames, L. E. G., as player, 112; Selector, 111, 277; Manager, 246, 287

Amiss, D. L., 254

Angus, T., 112

Apartheid, 159 f., 275–285

Appleyard, R., 144

Archer, R. G., 128

Argentine, M.C.C. in (1958–59) 140, (1964–65) 201

Arlott, John, 57

Armstrong, W. W., 31, 260

Ashe, A., 284

Ashes, urn, 11; England win, 78–80, 91, 94, 99 f., 108, 288

Ashley-Cooper, F. S., 318

Ashton, Sir Hubert, 154, 174

Asif Iqbal, 258

Association of Municipal Associations, 60

Atkinson, B. G. W., 256

Attlee, Mr and Mrs C. R., 81

Australia: standard of cricket, 301; at I.C.C. (*re* illegal bowling), 96, 113, 154, 212 f.; (lbw), 266; (priority *re* tours), 35, 244; in U.K. (1948) 13, 22 f., 44 f., 298, (1953) 78–80, 88–91, (1956) 111, 128 f., 299, (1961) 141, 157 f., 166–168, (1964) 196, 202–204, (1968) 261 f., 272 f.; (women's tour, 1963), 183; in West Indies (1964–65), 207; M.C.C. in (1932–33) 293, (1946–47) 15 f., (1950–51) 56 f., 69, (1954–55) 100 f., (1958–59) 139 f., (1962–63) 176, 178 f., (1965–66) 230, 234, 239 f., (1970–71) 288;

796.358
K41e

BETHEL COLLEGE LIBRARY